Preludes to the Icelandic Financial Crisis

*Also by Robert Z. Aliber*

THE MULTINATIONAL PARADIGM

MANIAS, PANICS AND CRASHES (*co-author*)

THE NEW INTERNATIONAL MONEY GAME

YOUR MONEY AND YOUR LIFE

*Also by Gylfi Zoega*

LABOUR MARKET ADJUSTMENTS IN EUROPE (*co-editor*)

# Preludes to the Icelandic Financial Crisis

Edited by

Robert Z. Aliber

and

Gylfi Zoega

palgrave
macmillan

First published 2011 by
PALGRAVE MACMILLAN

Palgrave Macmillan in the UK is an imprint of Macmillan Publishers Limited, registered in England, company number 785998, of Houndmills, Basingstoke, Hampshire RG21 6XS.

Palgrave Macmillan in the US is a division of St Martin's Press LLC, 175 Fifth Avenue, New York, NY 10010.

Palgrave Macmillan is the global academic imprint of the above companies and has companies and representatives throughout the world.

Palgrave® and Macmillan® are registered trademarks in the United States, the United Kingdom, Europe and other countries.

ISBN 978–0–230–27692–5 hardback

This book is printed on paper suitable for recycling and made from fully managed and sustained forest sources. Logging, pulping and manufacturing processes are expected to conform to the environmental regulations of the country of origin.

A catalogue record for this book is available from the British Library.

A catalog record for this book is available from the Library of Congress.

10 9 8 7 6 5 4 3 2 1
20 19 18 17 16 15 14 13 12 11

Printed and bound in Great Britain by
CPI Antony Rowe, Chippenham and Eastbourne

# Contents

# List of Figures

# List of Tables

# Notes on the Contributors

**Robert Z. Aliber**, Professor of International Economics and Finance, Booth Graduate School of Business, University of Chicago, emeritus.

**Friðrik M. Baldursson**, Professor, School of Business, Reykjavik University.

**Willem H. Buiter**, Chief Economist, Citigroup.

**Lars Christiansen**, Senior Analyst, Danske Bank.

**Daniel Gros**, Director, Centre for European Policy Studies, Brussels.

**Thorvaldur Gylfason**, Professor of Economics, University of Iceland.

**Tryggvi T. Herbertsson**, Member of Icelandic Parliament and a former Professor of Economics at the University of Iceland.

**Frederic S. Mishkin**, Alfred Lerner Professor of Banking and Financial Institutions, Graduate School of Business, Columbia University.

**Richard Portes**, Professor of Economics, London Business School.

**Anne C. Sibert**, Professor of Economics, Department of Economics, Mathematics and Statistics, Birkbeck College, University of London.

**Throstur Olaf Sigurjonsson**, Assistant Professor, School of Business, Reykjavik University.

**Carsten Valgreen**, Chief Economist, Danske Bank.

**Gylfi Zoega**, Professor of Economics, Department of Economics, University of Iceland.

# 1
# Introduction

*Robert Z. Aliber*

## Introduction

Iceland was one of the first countries to experience the collapse of its banks in the fourth wave of financial crises since the early 1980s. Each of these waves has involved the failure of a large number of banks in a country at about the same time. Each of these waves has followed a wave of credit bubbles, when the indebtedness of a group of borrowers, usually the buyers of real estate, increased at an annual rate of 20–30 per cent a year for two, three, or more years. Most of these credit bubbles have followed an increase in the flow of money to a country that led to an increase in the value of its currency, to an increase in its current account deficit and to increases in asset prices. (The principal exception is that the credit bubble in Japan in the second half of the 1980s occurred when its current account surplus was declining, however at the same time that the Japanese yen appreciated. The other exceptions are that the credit bubbles in Ireland and Spain occurred when they were members of the European Monetary Union.)

Iceland is the smallest country with its own currency. Between 2002 and 2007 real estate prices increased sharply while prices of stocks of Icelandic firms increased by a factor of seven, one of the most rapid increases ever in any country. During this period real estate prices in the United States, Britain, Ireland, Spain, South Africa, Australia, and New Zealand increased rapidly.

Iceland gained its independence from Denmark in 1944, and its financial history is relatively short. While the quality of the human capital is extremely high, the managerial structure in the public and private sectors is thin because of the small population.

In the late 1990s Iceland participated in the global moves toward the privatization of government-owned firms. The privatization of the three Icelandic banks began in 1998, and was completed in 2002. The banks were acquired by industrial conglomerates – family firms that owned several different businesses.

My initial encounter with Iceland – and the event that led to this book – was in April 2006; a friend invited me to participate in the first class of the term at London Business School. One of the other participants was a young banker from Iceland who had recently graduated from LBS; he described the increases in stock prices in his country. Listening to his presentation was eerie because it seemed as if I could complete – figuratively – most of his sentences; his description of changes in stock prices complemented a model that I had been developing of the impact of an increase in money flows to a country on the value of its currency and on the prices of its assets. At the time I made a mental note, 'Visit Iceland on the first possible occasion.' The intuition was that the processes that lead to asset price bubbles would be more readily apparent in a small open economy than in a Mexico or a Britain or a Japan.

In the previous years I had been chasing bubbles in several different countries. There were numerous visits to Mexico in the early 1990s in the effort to understand the impact of privatization, liberalization, and macrostabilization on the nominal and real values of the peso. A newspaper headline about property prices in Hong Kong in February 1997 prompted a visit to several of the countries in South East Asia, where there had been dramatic increases in the prices of stocks and of real estate. A visit to South Korea in December 1997 occurred during a presidential election and a sharp depreciation of the won that was associated with the failure of many banks. The surge in nominal and real interest rates in Moscow in the spring of 1998 prompted a visit in the early summer in the effort to learn the source of the returns that enabled the lenders to pay such high rates. While there had been several visits to Japan in the late 1980s, it was only after the property prices had begun to decline that I began to use the term 'bubble' to describe the surge in property prices and stock prices. A few years later a taxonomy of bubbles was developed – 'credit bubbles' were distinguished from 'asset bubbles' – most but not all asset price bubbles follow from credit bubbles, and most but not all credit bubbles lead to asset price bubbles. The increase in the bank loans to the governments and government-owned firms in Mexico and ten other developing countries in the 1970s was a credit bubble; the indebtedness was increasing at a rate that was too high to be sustainable. The increase in US stock prices in the late 1990s was an asset price bubble but not a credit bubble.

In 2002 I 'inherited' *Manias, Panics, and Crashes* from Charles Kindleberger, who had brought out the first four editions. Kindleberger had developed a stylized view of the five stages of a bubble and examined these stages across many bubbles across several centuries. I prepared the fifth edition in 2003 and 2004; one of the innovations was a new chapter that focused on the three 'waves' of credit bubbles since the mid-1970s. The first centred on Mexico and about ten other developing countries in the 1970s.

One of the chapters in *Manias* centred on the supply of fraud and corruption, which seem to increase exponentially when a country experienced a bubble. Several chapters highlighted the range of responses of governments when a bubble was under way and after it imploded – should the government intervene to stabilize asset prices or should the government instead allow asset prices to decline?

My first visit to Iceland was in June 2007, in response to an invitation for a presentation at one of the workshops of the Ronald Coase Institute. Iceland seemed 'very expensive'; the prices of non-tradable goods – restaurant meals, hotel rooms, and taxis – seemed high. Ballpark estimates of purchasing power suggested that the Icelandic krona was overvalued by 30–40 per cent. There were 10 or 12 visits with economists in the Central Bank of Iceland, in the commercial banks, and at the University of Iceland. These conversations reinforced the impression that Iceland was sitting on top of a massive asset price bubble. My presentation at the Coase Institute was on the three earlier waves of global credit bubbles since the 1970s and only tangentially on the asset bubble that was then under way in the country – although several students asked about my impressions of the recent economic developments in Iceland.

One of the surprises during the visit was several sets of comments that Iceland was becoming an 'international financial centre'. These comments reflected the surge in the foreign assets and the foreign liabilities of the Icelandic banks relative to the country's GDP. The hallmark of a financial centre is that investors accept lower rates of interest because of some other pecuniary or non-pecuniary advantages, including a low inflation rate, relatively low tax rates, financial stability, and secrecy. The uniqueness of Iceland's role as an international financial intermediary is that the counterpart of the increase in its indebtedness was an increase in equity investments in other countries by Icelandic firms and banks.

In December 2007 I was invited to present a public lecture at the University of Iceland, which occurred in May 2008. The preparation involved a review of the Icelandic economic and financial data available in *International Financial Statistics* and of several of the IMF country consultation reports. The lecture was based on an essay titled 'Monetary Turbulence and the Icelandic Economy' that is Chapter 15 in this book.

The imbalances in the Icelandic economy were staggering. The current account deficit was more than 20 per cent of the country's GDP, much higher than that of any other country. While foreign firms had financed a massive enclave investment in a hydroelectric generating plant and an aluminium smelter, the inflow of real resources associated with this joint project accounted for 3–4 per cent of the country's GDP – about 20 per cent of its current account deficit. Most of the Iceland's current account deficit reflected a household consumption boom, including imports of automobiles and other durables.

A second imbalance was that the market value of the stocks of the 15 or so Icelandic firms was exceedingly high relative to Iceland's GDP. Between 2002 and 2007 the US dollar value of Iceland's GDP had increased by 80 per cent, during the same period the market value of Icelandic stocks had increased by 700 per cent. One of the idiosyncratic features of the Iceland experience is that the increase in stock prices was much larger in percentage terms than the increase in real estate prices, at least after 2003; in most other countries the percentage increases in the prices of real estate and stocks have been in the same ballpark.

A third imbalance was that in 2007 the total assets of the three Icelandic banks were seven or eight times Iceland's GDP, whereas in 2002 these assets had approximated the country's GDP. Hence bank assets had increased by more than 50 per cent a year during this period. By the end of 2007 the foreign assets of the banks were three times larger than their domestic assets.

The logic was that the rapid increase in the assets of the banks could have occurred only if there had been a comparable increase in the capital of the banks. The intuition was that the likelihood that the increase in capital of the banks could have been obtained from interest rate spreads or fees was trivially small; instead the increase in bank capital must have occurred as a result of capital gains on stocks and real estate owned by the banks, much as in Japan in the 1980s.

Another intuition was that the massive imbalances in Iceland must be systematically related; the question is whether the sharp increase in stock prices induced the money inflow or whether instead the money inflow led to the increase in stock prices. Again the intuition was the increase in stock prices could not have been spontaneous. Instead the inflow of money had led to both a sharp increase in the value of the Icelandic krona and a large increase in imports relative to exports. The balance of payments accounting identity is that if Iceland experienced an increase in its capital account surplus, adjustments must have occurred to ensure there was a corresponding increase in its current account deficit.

The increase in the flow of foreign money to Iceland led to the appreciation of the Icelandic krona and contributed to the increase in imports relative to exports. Moreover the increase in net imports resulted from the surge in household wealth. The foreign money that went to Iceland 'had to go someplace'; the only possible place that it might have gone was to one of the asset markets – the stock market, the real estate market, and the market for government debt. The debt of the Icelandic government was small, and hence the foreign money did not go to this market. The money went into the markets for stocks and real estate and the dramatic increase in household wealth led to a consumption boom and a sharp increase in the demand for foreign goods.

The extraordinary increase in the price of stocks would have led to a sharp increase in the capital of the banks if the ratio of the market value of bank-owned stocks to their total assets was in the same ballpark as the capital requirement of the banks as a share of their total assets. Because the rate of return to owners of stocks was so high, it was plausible that many of the loans made by banks were to those who bought stocks. During the Japanese bubble of the late 1980s, many industrial corporations used the money obtained from bank loans to buy stocks and real estate because the anticipated rates of return on these assets were so much higher than on the investments in plants to produce steel and autos and electronic products. Moreover it was also plausible that the surge in the value of Icelandic stocks owned by investors would lead some of them to increase their purchases of foreign assets to maintain diversified portfolios.

It was also obvious that Iceland would experience a crash like the ones observed in Mexico and Thailand, since a 'limit theorem' applies to the external indebtedness of a country, which cannot increase relative to its GDP for an extended period. Inevitably the increase in the external indebtedness of Iceland would slow and its current account deficit would decline and the krona would depreciate, perhaps suddenly and sharply because the prospect of this change would immediately deter further money inflows.

No country with a current account deficit larger than 10 per cent of GDP has ever made the transition to a sustainable current account balance without a severe financial crisis. Many countries with current account deficits of 4 or 5 per cent of their GDPs have encountered crises during similar adjustments.

This book contains most of the relevant documents about financial developments in Iceland that appeared between 2002 and 2008. Some of these documents have been reproduced in the form in which they were initially published; however, the IMF article IV consultation reports, the country studies from the Organization for Economic Cooperation and Development, and the reports of the Central Bank for Iceland have been truncated to reduce repetition. One innovation in the book is the chapter by Professor Olaf Sigurjonsson that is a timeline summary of events between the date the banks were privatized and the dates they were again brought into the orbit of the government because they had failed. The concluding chapter by Professor Anne Sibert was prepared for this book.

The next section of this introduction reviews the 'transfer problem process' when currencies are not pegged, and the impacts of an autonomous increase in the foreign demand for securities available in a country on the price of its currency and on asset prices within the country.

## The transfer problem process when currencies are floating

The impacts of changes in cross-border flows of money on an economy can be analysed using a model that is inspired by the 'transfer problem process' initiated by John Maynard Keynes in his discussion of post-First World War reparations. His analysis centred on the conditions that would have to be satisfied if the tax that the victorious Allies had imposed on Germany in the Treaty of Versailles would ever be paid. (This model evolved into the 'absorption approach' to the balance of payments.) If the intended transfer were to be successful, the German government would need to raise taxes relative to expenditures to produce a large fiscal surplus and Germany would need to develop a large trade surplus. The German government would use the money from the fiscal surplus to buy French francs from German exporters, which would be transferred to the French government. Moreover the transfer of real resources could be effected only if France developed a trade deficit.

When currencies are pegged, the immediate impact of the transfer of money from one country to another is that the international reserve assets owned by the country making the payment declines and the international reserve assets owned by the transferee increase – which usually would lead to increase in its money supply. The transfer of real goods would depend on an increase in spending that would occur either because interest rates have declined or because the entity that borrowed abroad increased its spending. There is no requirement that the increase in net imports corresponds with the increase in the capital account surplus; the payments balance may change.

The transfer problem operates in a different mode when currencies are not pegged. The increase in the flow of money to a country leads to an increase in its capital account surplus. The balance of payments accounting identity means that there must be a counterpart increase in the country's current account deficit. The money inflow leads immediately to an appreciation of the country's currency, with the result that its net imports increase. If the money inflow is a result of an autonomous increase in the foreign demand for securities available in the country, the prices of these assets will increase as part of the adjustment process to ensure that the increase in the country's net imports matches the increase in the money inflows. (The only time that the increase in money inflows will not lead to an increase in asset prices is when the inflows are a response to an increase in foreign borrowing by domestic agents, and in this case the statement about an autonomous increase in money inflows is not valid.) The increase in asset prices leads to an increase in household wealth, which in turn leads to an increase in consumption spending. Domestic saving declines in response to what in effect is an increase in the available supply of foreign saving; in effect foreign saving displaces domestic saving.

The increase in household wealth that is induced by the increase in the foreign demand for its securities is an integral part of the adjustment process to ensure that the country's current account deficit increases in response to the increase in the money inflow. The domestic residents that sell securities to the foreign investors must decide what to do with the cash receipts; their only choices are to buy securities from other domestic residents and to buy consumption goods. The likelihood is high that most of the money is used to buy securities. The sellers of these securities then have the same problem; the money is like the proverbial 'hot potato' transferred from the buyers of the securities to the sellers. The prices of securities increase and consumption spending also increases (and the domestic savings rate declines) until more and more households have satisfied their savings objectives.

The invisible hand ensures that asset prices and household wealth continue to increase until the expansion of imports and in the trade deficit corresponds with the increase in the money inflow.

The increase in the foreign demand for securities denominated in a currency triggers an asset price bubble, which – by definition – involves a non-sustainable increase in the price of a particular type of asset or security. Some of the buyers are motivated by recent increases in the price of these assets; their anticipations of the prices in the near future are based on the projection of the increases in the prices of these assets in the recent past. Various names have been given to these investors, including 'momentum traders' ('the trend is your friend'), 'extrapolators' and 'tape-watchers'. The bubble is an inevitable consequence of the initial increase and subsequent decrease in the foreign demand for securities in the country; as this demand declines, the currency depreciates and asset prices decline.

As the bubble expands, the anticipated rates of return on some securities increase from projected increases in their prices, which induces an increase in the money inflow that corresponds with the increase in the country's current account deficit.

Hence there is a two-stage process in the development of the asset price bubble. The feature of the first stage is an autonomous increase in the foreign demand for securities available in a country. The feature of the second stage is that the increase in the anticipated rates of return on assets available in the country induces an increase in the inflow of money. The country's currency appreciates to ensure its capital account surplus and its current account deficit remain equal to each other.

One of the two standard arithmetic observations is that while a bubble is expanding, the rate of growth of the borrowers' indebtedness is much higher than both the interest rate and the rate of growth of their incomes or their GDPs. During this period, the cash available to the borrowers from new loans is significantly larger than the money needed to pay the interest, so there is no real debt servicing burden – in effect the borrowers have a 'free lunch'. The implication of the limit theorem is the rate of growth of the indebtedness cannot exceed the rate of growth of the borrowers' GDP, and hence the rate of growth of indebtedness must decline.

When the inevitable decline in the flow of money to a country begins, its currency immediately depreciates. The depreciation can be quite rapid because the country may have developed a large current account deficit, which now must shrink; the depreciation is needed to stimulate exports and discourage imports to rapidly reduce the current account deficit.

At some stage, the cash available to the borrowers from new loans declines below the amount needed to pay interest to the lenders – the borrowers' free lunch is over, and now they must generate a domestic surplus that they can use to pay the interest. They may seek to increase their domestic borrowing.

The credit market tightens suddenly, and asset prices decline, often sharply. Suddenly those who had borrowed in a foreign currency to reduce their interest payments have large and accelerating revaluation losses because of the sharp increase in the domestic equivalent of their debt servicing commitments in a foreign currency.

When the increase in the autonomous foreign demand for securities available in a country initially is significantly higher than the rate of growth of its GDP, it is inevitable that the country will experience a bubble in the price of its currency and a bubble in its asset market. The bubble in the price of the currency reflects that eventually the foreign demand for securities available in the country will decline, and the country's currency will then depreciate. Similarly the decline in the foreign demand for securities available in the country will lead to a decline in the rate of increase in the price of these securities.

One of the traditional questions is whether countries that have large payments imbalances are likely to experience a 'soft landing' or a 'hard landing' as the imbalances decline. A soft landing would occur without a sharp reduction in employment, and without a sharp increase in the inflation rate and without a sharp increase in failures of banks and financial institutions. A hard landing in contrast would involve significant number of failures of financial institutions as well as an increase in unemployment and an increase in the inflation rate.

Hard landings make newspaper headlines, soft landings do not. The more extended the imbalances, the greater the likelihood that the adjustment to a sustainable payments position will involve a hard landing. That in turn leads to the identification of the date after which the probability of a hard landing becomes 80 or 90 or 95 per cent. That date in Iceland might have been in 2004 or 2005 – soon after the current account deficit reached 15 per cent of its GDP. Once the pace of money inflows declined, it was inevitable that the Icelandic krona would depreciate, and a modest initial depreciation would be like the proverbial snowball, and gather momentum.

## Reflections on the Iceland experience

The analysis of the increases in the value of the krona and of increases in the prices of real estate and stocks in Iceland is consistent with the transfer problem model of the adjustment process in response to an autonomous increase in the foreign demand for Icelandic securities. The increase in the asset prices in Iceland was necessary to induce an increase in net imports so that the increase in the country's current account deficit corresponded with the increase in its capital account surplus. Asset prices in Iceland continued to increase as long as the money flow to the country increased.

The implication of the limit theorem was that at some stage, the pace of money inflows would slow, and then the krona would depreciate and asset prices would decline.

The first wave of credit bubbles differed from the Iceland experience in that the autonomous shock was an increase in the demand for securities from governments and government-owned firms in Mexico and Brazil and ten other developing countries. The increase in bank loans to these countries at the rate of 30 per cent a year for nearly a decade led to a real appreciation of their currencies, but there was no significant increase in the asset prices. There was a bubble in the values of the currencies of these countries; when the limit theorem hit and the foreign demand for these loans declined, the currencies depreciated sharply.

The second wave of credit bubbles had two distinct aspects. The monetary aggregates in Tokyo increased sharply because the financial authorities were seeking to dampen the appreciation of the yen, at the same time that regulations that limited credit for real estate and foreign loans were relaxed. About the same time, the financial authorities in Finland, Norway, and Sweden relaxed the regulations that limited the borrowings by their banks in the offshore money markets. The increase in the loans from the offshore banks to the banks in these Nordic countries was like an autonomous increase in the foreign demand for Nordic securities, and asset prices in these countries increased sharply – much as in Iceland although not to the same extent – so the increases in the current account deficits in these countries would match the increase in their capital account surpluses.

The motivations for the money flows to various emerging market countries that preceded the Asian financial crisis differed. Some countries experienced an autonomous increase in the foreign demand for their securities; the investment banks had discovered 'emerging market equities' as a new asset class, and all the global equity index investors adjusted their portfolios. At the same time, some of the banks in these countries sourced for money in the offshore markets to reduce their funding costs. The increase in domestic asset prices was induced as part of the adjustment process, so that the increase in their currency account deficits would match the increase in their capital account surpluses.

In each of these country experiences, the rate of increase in indebtedness was much greater than the interest rate. At some stage, the limit theorem would bind, and the inevitable decline in the rate of increase in indebtedness would lead to a depreciation of the currency and to a decline in asset prices.

The idiosyncratic factor in the asset price bubble in Iceland was that the increase in stock prices led to a sharp increase in the capital of the banks, which enabled them to grow their loans at an exceedingly rapid rate. Some of the borrowers from the banks used the money to buy more stocks, and the country appeared to have a perpetual motion machine – one imported from the Japan of the 1980s juiced by local steroids.

In retrospect, however, there was one 'clue' that I wished I had followed up on after the 2007 visit. At the time, the statements that Iceland was becoming an international financial centre seemed bizarre. In 2002 and 2003, foreign investors took the initiative and acquired debt denominated in the Icelandic krona; the initial increase in the flow of money to Iceland was the counterpart of the increase in the flow to the United States, Britain, Spain, Ireland, South Africa, and Australia. Subsequently, probably in 2004 or 2005, borrowers in Iceland took the initiative in selling their IOUs to yield-hungry foreign investors. Some of these lenders were the traditional Belgian and Italian dentists, some were large financial institutions. The Icelandic borrowers then used a large part of that money to buy equity-type assets in Britain and other European countries.

Many in Iceland took parental pride in the 'Geyser Tigers'. The Icelandic authorities should have asked whether the local entrepreneurs had the experience and the skills to warrant the high prices that they paid when they acquired these foreign assets. Following that lead might have led to much more attention to the relationships between the banks and the corporate entrepreneurs.

When banks are privatized, who is likely to acquire ownership? The necessary condition is that the buyers are those with the money. The sufficient condition is that those who are willing to, pay a higher price than the other possible buyers. Those who are willing to pay the highest price for the control of a bank are those who want access to credit from the bank. And that might have led attention to the question of whether there was an 'arm's length' relationship between the owners of the banks and the large borrowers, or whether the owners of the banks were involved in self-dealing.

The intuition is that the relationships between the banks and the large borrowers should be much more evident in a small country. The financial authorities, especially those concerned with stability and regulation, should have been aware of these relationships. The question they should have been asking – the question that always should be asked – when indebtedness is increasing much more rapidly than income or GDP – is 'What is the "endgame"?' How will the economy adjust from a rate of growth of indebtedness that is much too high relative to the growth of GDP to one that is sustainable? The authorities in Iceland may not have had enough experience to think about the question. The executive directors, the senior managers, and the staff of the International Monetary Fund had extensive experience with credit bubbles in the developing countries in the 1980s, in Finland, Norway, and Sweden in the early 1990s, and with Thailand and other Asian countries as well as Russia, Brazil, and Argentina in the late 1980s. The failure to recognize the endgame question by the IMF is a major knock on its institutional memory and competence.

(The stylized fact is that the countries that experience inflows of money have had economic booms, even though the appreciation of their currencies meant that rate of growth of GDP should have declined as imports increased. The positive impact of the increase in wealth on household spending on domestic goods dominates the negative impact of the increase in spending on imports that has resulted from the appreciation of the currency.)

# 2
# The Chapters in this Volume

*Gylfi Zoega*

The collapse of Iceland's banking system in the autumn of 2008 became a symbol of the global credit crunch. This volume contains essays and reports that were written before the collapse. The chapters provide insights into how economists saw Iceland's economy. Did they see the crash coming? Did they choose to ignore it? Clearly, economists do not work in a vacuum. The application of subjective judgement in the presence of social incentives can lead economists astray. Iceland's close-knit society values loyalty and is not conducive to dissent. Economists from other countries may have to be recruited. This book is a case study of the economics profession prior to a collapse of a financial system.

The chapters document how economists spotted many of the danger signs, but sometimes hesitated to lay them all out, fearing that might trigger a run on the banks or out of misplaced loyalty to the country. They also failed to spot some of the danger signs, in particular the fragility of the banking system, and did not realize the dangers of having an oversized banking system until too late.

Following an overview of the chronology of the privatization of the banking system in Iceland by Throstur Olaf Sigurjonsson (Chapter 3), the rest of this volume is divided into three parts. The first part has excerpts of reports written by economists in international institutions that monitored the economy of Iceland and also the Central Bank of Iceland (CBI). The second part has chapters by various authors that appear in chronological order. A final chapter in Part III draws conclusions from the Iceland experience for other countries.

## I. International organizations and the Central Bank of Iceland

The chapters in this section contain excerpts from reports by the International Monetary Fund (IMF), the Organization of Economic Cooperation and Development (OECD), and the CBI published in the period 2005–8.

Chapter 4 contains the Concluding Statements from the IMF staff visits in 2006 and 2008. These reports focus on monetary and fiscal policies, perhaps guided by an economic model of aggregate demand and aggregate supply rather than a view of financial turbulence and bubbles. The authors warn that Iceland 'is the most overheated in the OECD areas', and that there 'has been a stunning expansion of debt, leverage and risk-taking that is almost without precedents anywhere in the world' (summary page). The IMF had already in its 2004 report mentioned how imbalances had started to emerge in inflation, the current account and external debt and predicted that containing these imbalances would be a challenge. That report drew attention to the rapid expansion of credit, financed by short-term foreign borrowing, a boom in the stock market and growing current account deficits. In 2005 there was explicit warning about financial stability (Public Information Notice, Article IV Consultation, 2005, p. 3):

> Directors pointed to the risks of financial instability of the ongoing credit boom and emphasized that close monitoring of the financial sector is critical. Despite the strong balance sheets of financial institutions, risks reside in accelerating asset prices, highly leveraged corporations, and rapidly expanding credit, a portion of which is financed by borrowing in foreign currency.

The subsequent reports, which are published in this volume, continue to warn of mounting imbalances and recommend that interest rates should be increased and taxes raised to restrict demand. The first report was written in August 2006, after the significant turmoil in financial markets that occurred in February. The report says that Iceland is going through an economic boom that is generating large imbalances, an overheated economy and high inflation. Interestingly, the IMF did not interpret the events of 2006 as a sign that leverage should be reduced and the banking system downsized. Instead, while stressing the need to reduce vulnerabilities in the financial sector, it welcomes steps that banks have taken to make risks more manageable and the strengthening of the supervisory frameworks. The subsequent report in the August 2007 report was surprisingly optimistic; financial markets had recovered from the 2006 shock, the economy was booming again and the high prices of stocks of the Icelandic banks indicated that credit quality and confidence in the banks remain high.

The second report included in this volume was written in September 2008 and is more explicit about the dangers than previous reports but not alarmist. It starts by saying that the rapid expansion of 2003–7 left a legacy of large macroeconomic imbalances, overstretched private sector balance sheets, and high dependence on foreign financing. The steps taken by the authorities to bolster confidence are listed: higher interest rates, enhanced liquidity provision to reduce pressures in financial markets and currency swap agreements with the Nordic central banks. It describes how the banks have slowed the growth in their lending. In a sentence that may go down as the understatement of the year (Public Information Notice, Article IV Consultation, 2008, p. 3), 'Directors observed that the authorities face the challenge of facilitating an orderly rebalancing process, while mitigating risks.'

Economists from the OECD also visited Iceland annually. They appear to have been less focused on financial markets than their IMF counterparts. In the *Economic Survey of Iceland* published in February 2006, the emphasis is on the housing market and funding for innovative start-ups. The tone is quite positive when it comes to financial markets (Contents, p. 1):

> Financial markets are thriving and access to capital has greatly improved. A significant part of the responsibility for this development lies with government policy. Controls over the operation of financial markets have been lifted, commercial banks have been privatized and the sector has been opened up to international capital markets. This liberalization programme has succeeded admirably and should be continued.

In 2008 there is also a positive tone:

> The Icelandic economy is prosperous and flexible. With its per capita income growing at double the OECD rate since the mid 1990s, it is now the fifth-highest among member countries and more than a quarter above the OECD average. This impressive performance is attributable to extensive structural reforms that deregulated and opened up the economy thereby unleashing entrepreneurial dynamism,

> as evidenced by an aggressive expansion of Icelandic companies abroad.

The OECD reports do point out mounting imbalances, the ineffective monetary policy, the distorted mortgage market and the passive fiscal policy, as did the IMF, in addition to discussing improvements in the systems of education and health care. But there are no signs that the OECD realized the mounting dangers of an expanding and oversized banking system.

The CBI published its first *Financial Stability* report as a separate publication in 2005, which is, surprisingly, more explicit on the dangers as the boom gathered pace in 2005 and 2006 than when the economy started to roll off the edge in 2007 and 2008. Already in 2005 the CBI realized the dangers posed by mounting macroeconomic imbalances. The 2005 report describes all the warning signs (p. 1, Introduction to 2005 report):

> Growing macroeconomic imbalances have emerged over the past year and have been reflected in rapidly growing domestic demand, increasing inflation, high asset prices and a widening current account deficit which will peak this year. These conditions increase the probability of eventual strain on the financial system.

The report describes how access to international capital markets has enabled banks to borrow to fund investment at home and abroad, and notes that the level of external debt is one of the weakest links in the economy (p. 2): 'A large and prolonged depreciation of the krona could cause difficulties in their debt positions of businesses with no hedges against such a development.' They state that (p. 3):

> Total large exposures have increased and the Financial Supervisory Authority (FME) has pointed out that individual borrowers or groups of connected clients can pose a large credit risk on the books of more than one financial company. Potentially, the authorized maximum amount of a single exposure could put up to one-quarter of the banking system's own funds at stake. The importance of this consideration for the solvency of individual financial companies and financial stability goes without saying.

The report then points out that considerable lending has been made against share collateral and that this form of financing contributed to the surge in equity prices in 2004–5 compared with those in other countries. Finally, the report warns that the banks' rapid expansion imposes a strain on their management and that the private interests of each of the banks do not always coincide with the interests of society. The report thus provides a frank assessment of the dangers that face the financial system and the overall economy.

The later reports, published in this volume, place increasing emphasis on the strengths of the banking system and the national economy. The report published in May 2008 describes the adverse developments in the global financial markets and how they have affected the Icelandic banks which are said to be resilient. The claim is that the stress tests confirm that the capital position, profitability and liquidity of the banks are sound. The report also says that the banks are (p. 2, Introduction to 2008 report):

> European banks no less than Icelandic, and they comply with the regulatory framework governing banks in Europe. Their income is diverse and well distributed geographically. Together, the three largest banks now generate more than half of their income from operations outside Iceland.

And the report continues (p. 2, Introduction to 2008 report): 'Iceland's banks were well prepared to face the liquidity crisis that emerged in 2007 and its impact on their regions of operation.' And later: 'The results of the analysis indicate that the banks are well prepared to withstand increased delinquency and loan losses, which have been extremely low to date.' The report then repeats previous years' description of exchange rate risks for firms and households and declining asset prices. The report lists the banks' responses to the financial crises, including slowing down lending growth and strengthening their deposit business – this is the opening of Internet accounts in Britain and the Netherlands. The strengths of the economy are also listed; a business-friendly tax environment, efficient public administration and flexible labour markets, in addition to a strengthened Financial Supervisory Authority. The report counters the claim of critics that the banking system has grown too large and reiterates that the financial system is broadly sound.

The reports of the two international institutions and the CBI all fail to spot the dangers of an oversized banking system. The authors do not point out the dangers of having either single banks that are large in comparison to the national economy or of having a large banking system. Macroeconomists working in this area appear to have downplayed or not understood that a stable banking system could not be left to the markets alone and that a lack of a credible lender of last resort was a fatal weakness, not just for the banks themselves but for the monetary economy. As discussed by Robert Skidesky in his recent book on Keynes,[1] this reflects the prevailing belief in the efficiency of markets, the efficient market hypothesis and the notion of rational expectations. Even when faced with a bubble of the size that emerged in Iceland's economy, the markets were given the benefit of the doubt.

## II. Academic reports and papers

In the autumn of 2005 I collaborated with a colleague at the University of Iceland, Dr Tryggvi Herbertsson, on a report for the Prime Minister's office on Iceland's future monetary arrangements, which was published in Icelandic in January 2006.[2] Chapter 3 was devoted to financial stability issues where the risks of increased leverage, inflated asset prices and a current account deficit were highlighted and the sequence of events that could lead to a financial crisis was described. Analogies were made with the Mexican and the Nordic financial crises in the early 1990s. In essence we updated the text from a similar report written during the Internet bubble in the autumn of 2000. However, although one chapter described the sequence of events that could lead to a financial crisis, financial instability results were underplayed in the summary.

Three renowned economists were present when the report was introduced in January 2006: Frederic Mishkin and Robert Mundell of Columbia University and Pentti Kouri, formerly at New York University. Mishkin had first visited Iceland in the spring of 1999. A few weeks later Mishkin was recruited by the Chamber of Commerce to write a paper with Herbertsson on the Icelandic economy, apparently to counter a report by the Fitch rating agency that had shook the markets.

The Fitch report, published on 22 February 2006, is reproduced in Chapter 7. It revises the rating on Iceland's long-term sovereign rating from stable to negative. Fitch describes the macroeconomic imbalances; rapid credit growth, rising asset prices, current account deficits and escalating external indebtedness, and observes that these indicators have been deteriorating rapidly. Hence 'the risks of a hard landing have increased, raising concerns about how well the broader financial system would cope in such a scenario and the likely implications for the sovereign' (p. 1). Moreover, Fitch points out that the economy is significantly indebted, yet Icelandic banks and corporations continue to expand abroad. They criticize the conduct of monetary policy which has only managed to induce an appreciation of the krona without curbing domestic demand. They also criticize fiscal policy for assuming that the imbalances will self-correct because they emanate in the private sector, since an important lesson to come out of the Asian crisis was that countries with seemingly sound public finances ignore private sector imbalances at their peril. Moreover, the report notes that Iceland's net external debt is higher than virtually any other Fitch-rated sovereign, while its external liquidity ratio is among the lowest.

Surprisingly, a report by Fitch several days later affirmed the ratings of four Icelandic banks, saying that the banks' large capital bases and significant geographic diversification of their loan portfolios offset the effect of the macro-prudential risks. It is surprising that Fitch points out the macro-prudential risks but finds the banks are stable since the macroeconomic imbalances were to a large extent generated by the expansion of the banks' balance sheets.

A report published in March 2006 by Merrill Lynch[3] – not included in this volume – is more pessimistic about the banks. The report describes the banks' debt distribution as front-loaded, making them vulnerable to shifts in market confidence; how they have enjoyed large gains on their equity investments, which could easily reverse making their revenue generation look less robust. Moreover, this report notes the pattern of cross-ownerships in Iceland's banks and businesses, the interconnectedness of the different owners and the fact that the banks co-invest alongside shareholders and customers, which are sometimes the same parties. Finally, the banks often finance these transactions.

The Fitch report was followed by another critical report from the Danske Bank, written by Lars Christiansen and Carsten Valgreen, which appeared in March 2006 entitled 'The Geyser Crisis'. This is Chapter 8 of this volume. The authors are quite explicit in their warnings about the dangers facing Iceland, which 'is the most overheated in the OECD areas', and that there 'has been a stunning expansion of debt, leverage and risk-taking that is almost without precedents anywhere in the world' (summary page). Moreover, the report says that looking at early warning indicators for financial crises 'Iceland looks worse on almost all measures than Thailand did before its crisis in 1997' and points out that the cost of capital is rising for the Icelandic banks at the same time that much of their foreign-denominated debt will mature.

The reports by Fitch and Danske Bank appeared to cause turbulence in both the stock market and the currency market or at least coincided with such turbulence. Soon, Iceland's Chamber of Commerce recruited Herbertsson and Frederic Mishkin to write a paper. Chapter 9 reproduces the report by Herbertsson and Mishkin published in May 2006 entitled *Financial Stability in Iceland*. The authors presented their report in New York in early May, then in London and Copenhagen and claimed that much of the recent criticism of Iceland's economy was not justified. The Herbertsson–Mishkin report describes the strengths of the Icelandic economy; the 'strong fiscal position', 'excellent institutions', the economy's 'ability to rewind current account deficits' and 'high quality financial regulation and supervision'. The authors claim that a financial crisis is not likely because of the strong regulation and supervision, fiscal balances and prudent monetary policy. The authors conclude that (p. 108) 'the sources of financial instability that triggered financial crises in emerging market countries in recent years are just not present in Iceland, so that comparisons of Iceland with emerging market countries are misguided'. However, the authors find that multiple equilibria cannot be excluded – concerns about a financial crisis triggering sales of Icelandic securities which would then cause a crisis – but the authors consider this unlikely to happen because of the strong fundamentals.

Mishkin and Herbertsson recommended policies to lower the likelihood of a self-fulfilling financial crisis; supervision should be consolidated inside the CBI, that banks should disclose more information about their activities, that house prices should be made to affect the CPI less and that the government should adopt a formal fiscal rule to dampen the business cycle.

In the autumn of 2007 when market conditions started to worsen again, the Icelandic Chamber of Commerce commissioned a paper by Professor Fridrik Mar Baldursson of Reykjavik University and Richard Portes of the London Business School, which is Chapter 10 of this volume. This report provides criticism of economic policy but is also defensive of the banking system. They point out the weaknesses of monetary policy; interest rate changes have a very limited effect on the real economy due to widespread indexation accompanied by fixed long-term interest rates. Moreover, they describe how high interest rates have created the carry trade that is further fuelled because the central bank links its interest rate decisions to developments in the currency market.[4] Portes and Baldursson also discuss the problems created by the size of the banking sector in relation to the national economy and the capacity of the central bank to serve as a lender of last resort but conclude that it would be feasible for the central bank to provide funds to cover the amount of foreign currency market funding maturing in a typical quarter.

Baldursson and Portes describe how the banks responded to the criticism raised in the spring of 2006. In this their report reflects and may be influenced by the optimism of the reports of the IMF and the Central Bank in 2007. They say that (executive summary)

> the 'mini-crisis' of 2006 was an informational crisis, arising from external criticism of the banks' reliance on market funding with short maturities, questions of earnings quality, cross-ownership, and lack of transparency, as well as perceived macroeconomic imbalances in the Icelandic economy.

They then move on to describe how the financial sector has responded quickly and decisively by expanding its deposit base; extended and broadened the maturities and geographical scope of their market funding; eliminated cross-holdings; and put great effort into increasing transparency and information dissemination about their activities. They find that in terms of deposit ratios and the characteristics of market funding, Icelandic banks come out well in comparison with their Nordic peers and that the banks enjoy a competitive advantage which is 'their entrepreneurial management, flat management structures, and unusual and strong business models'.

While Baldurson and Portes were completing their report, the Landsbanki approached Professor Willem Buiter of the LSE and Professor Anne Sibert of Birkbeck College in London. Chapter 11 contains their report. It concludes that the Iceland's banking system is unstable because of a lack of a credible lender of last resort because of the large volume of foreign liabilities of the Icelandic banks. They also recommend that Iceland join the European Union and the eurozone to get a credible lender of last resort and suggest some ways to acquire foreign reserves to solve their problems in the short term. However, they did not consider asset quality since they had no information on the banks' loans, which was also the case with the Mishkin–Herbertsson and Baldursson–Portes reports.

The authors sent the report to the bank toward the end of April 2008. They later wrote that 'our Icelandic interlocutors considered the paper to be too market-sensitive to be put in the public domain and we agreed to keep the paper confidential'.[5] However, they presented their report in early July 2008 to a selected group of government and bank economists. My impression was that the bank wanted to use the report to warn the authorities about the danger of having inadequate foreign reserves.

The main conclusion of Buiter and Sibert is that Iceland's banking system was not viable because even if the banks were solvent, the configuration of a very small country having its own currency and an internationally active and internationally exposed financial sector, which is very large relative to its GDP and the fiscal capacity of the state, makes it unlikely that the central bank can act as a lender of last resort.

> The Icelandic banks need a foreign-currency lender of last resort. Unfortunately, the Central Bank of Iceland cannot print foreign currency, so its undoubted competence and good intentions are not enough to cope with the crisis. The short-term solution is to seek funding abroad: from other central banks, the market and the IMF. The best medium-term solution is for Iceland to join the EU and to adopt the euro as soon as possible. The only alternative is to move its foreign-currency banking activities to the euro area. (p. 272)[6]

Chapter 12 is a CEPS (Centre for European Policy Studies) policy brief prepared by Daniel Gros entitled 'Iceland on the Brink? Options for a Small, Financially Active Economy in the Current Financial Crisis Environment' that appeared in April 2008. The thrust of the report is critical of the large increase in the foreign assets and liabilities of the Icelandic banks. Gros argues that the rapid expansion of the banking system has effectively transformed the country into a hedge fund, which is highly exposed to the current world economic crisis. He argues that the central bank as a lender of last resort would not be able to save even one of the large domestic banks. He argues that the asset price inflation and ensuing construction boom exposed the country to the classical combination of a currency cum banking crisis coupled with a real estate bust.

Chapters 13 and 14 of the volume contain two short reports published in April 2008 by Icelandic economists in *VoxEU* by Thorvaldur Gylfason and Gylfi Zoega. Gylfason had been an ardent critic of the way the banks were privatized and operated.[7] Along with Vilhjalmur Bjarnason of the University of Iceland, Gylfason was among the most vocal critics of the rapidly expanding financial sector. His report gives a historical perspective of the evolution of the Icelandic economy and the privatization of the banks, which provides a more political interpretation of the process of the privatization of the banks and complements Chapter 3 of this volume written by Sigurjonsson. He also describes the banks' business model – using an implicit state guarantee to borrow huge amounts of capital in international capital markets to lend domestically at higher rates of interest. My chapter summarizes the problems created by the macroeconomic imbalances and the oversized banking system and points out that the main danger facing the economy is a lack of a credible lender of last resort due to the oversized banking system.

At the beginning of 2008, six months before the publication of the Buiter/Sibert report, I contacted Professor Robert Aliber of the University of Chicago Business School and asked if he could undertake a study of the current state of the Icelandic economy. I thought there was an urgent need for someone who had extensive experience in studying financial crises. I first met Aliber in June 2007 when he came to my office. He is a good friend of my thesis advisor Ned Phelps at Columbia University. Some people come to Iceland to observe the geysers, but he came because a few casual anecdotes led him to believe there was a bubble. In June 2007 he said 'I give you nine months!' Chapter 15 contains the report that he presented at the University of Iceland on 5 May 2008.

Aliber's report describes how the asset price bubble, generated by a rapid expansion of credit financed in international credit markets, enabled the Icelandic banks to grow their balance sheets from being equal to the country's GDP to coming close to ten times that over a period of five years. He concluded that because the banks owned stocks, their capital grew with the asset bubble. The inflow of capital caused by borrowing by the country's banks in international wholesale markets generated an asset price bubble which raised their capital base which then enabled them to borrow even more. Hence the economy of Iceland resembled a giant Ponzi scheme. It followed that the collapse of asset prices, caused by the banks being shut out from the international wholesale markets, would quickly trigger runs on the banks and cause them to become insolvent.[8] He focused attention on the banks' solvency issues that turned out to be just as serious as the lack of a lender of last resort discussed by Buiter, Sibert and Gros and, to a lesser extent, Portes and Baldursson.

## III. Lessons for other countries

In the volume's final chapter, Professor Anne Sibert summarizes the lessons of Iceland's experience of having a large banking sector in a very small country with its own currency. She describes how the lack of a credible lender of last resort can coordinate market participants' beliefs in a bad outcome and trigger a modern bank run by wholesale creditors who fail to roll over their loans or to extend new loans because they believe that other creditors are going to fail to roll over their loans and that as a result the bank will fail. She concludes that Iceland's banking sector was inherently unstable and that the country should not have allowed its banks to expand without joining the EU and adopting the euro which would have given the country the ECB as a credible lender of last resort. Sibert lists some countries that also are 'overbanked' – defined as having too large a ratio of bank assets to GDP. These include Switzerland, the UK, Denmark, Belgium and the Netherlands. She also discusses some policies that can be used to constrain the growth of a banking system.

## IV. Concluding thoughts

The chapters in this volume describe how the economics profession identified some of the critical problems that made Iceland vulnerable to the international financial crisis. They describe the flaws of monetary policy, the absence of an effective fiscal policy, the importance of macroeconomic imbalances and, starting in 2006, the dangers of a serious financial crisis. The passivity of the government in using fiscal policy to rein in the expansion and reform the system of mortgage finance to make monetary policy more effective cannot be justified by a lack of warnings. Also, the failure of the government and the Central Bank to organize an emergency plan that could be applied if one or more banks were to collapse is inexcusable. The crisis in October 2008 was made worse by the unorganized and haphazard response of the authorities.

One shortcoming of the economic analysis and advice during this period is an underappreciation of the risks posed by the rapidly expanding banking system. The economists appear not to have spotted the clear and present danger faced by a banking system that lacks a credible lender of last resort until it was too late. Banks operating predominantly in foreign currencies need a lender of last resort in an international currency which the Icelancic krona was not.

Another shortcoming was not to link the rapid growth of asset prices sufficiently strongly to the danger of bank insolvency. The imminent dangers posed by solvency issues were only first highlighted by Aliber in May 2008. While economists had realized that the bursting of an asset price bubble would damage banks' balance sheets, they did not realize that the asset price bubble and the expansion of the banking system were two sides of the same coin. Economists did not to see how the unsustainable inflow of foreign capital had allowed the banks to raise their capital through asset price inflation and hence allowed them to keep on growing. A sudden stop to the inflow of capital would then make the banks insolvent and cause a modern bank run.

## Notes

1. Robert Skidelsky (2009), *Keynes: the Return of the Master*, BBS Public Affairs, New York.
2. Gylfi Zoega and Tryggvi Herbertsson (2006), *Fyrirkomulag gengismála á Íslandi: Horft til Framtíðar*, Institute of Economic Studies, University of Iceland.
3. Merrill Lynch, *Icelandic Banks: Not What You Are Thinking*, 7 March 2006.
4. Professor Ragnar Arnason had earlier criticized monetary policy by arguing that it mainly affected the exchange rate while the interest rate channel was not operational. See Ragnar Arnason (2006), Peningastefna Seðlabankans: Svarar hún kostnaði?,' *Rannsóknir í Félagsvísindum VII*, 269–80. Professor Thorolfur Matthiasson, in a number of newspaper articles, criticized the Central Bank's use of policy rates to curb the credit expansion and recommended that reserve requirements be raised in addition to drawing attention to the lack of policy coordination between fiscal and monetary policy. For a critical account of monetary policy, see also Gylfi Zoega (2007), 'Breytt viðhorf til peningamála: Sjálfstæði peningamálastefnu, fjármálastöðugleiki og fákeppni', in *Ný staða Íslands í Utanríkismálum*, Alþjóðamálastofnun, University of Iceland.
5. See introduction to the October version of their paper.
6. They also point out that even within the euro area the state would have to address any solvency problems which made it unlikely that the fiscal authorities would be able to come up with the necessary capital to restore the solvency of the banking sector.
7. He expresses his views in a weekly column in one of Iceland's newspapers and has published seven books containing essays on economic issues concerning Iceland.
8. A report by Merrill Lynch in March 2006 also describes how falling asset prices may affect the banks (Merrill Lynch, *Icelandic Banks: Not What You Are Thinking*, 7 March 2006, p. 12). The report says that:

   > We cannot recall a single other instance in Europe of where banks hold such substantial stakes in the local market (not to mention significant holdings of their own shares, for whatever reason) or where they have to justify such an unusual state of affairs. Our point is merely that if the stock market were to decline rapidly, it would certainly impact the equities that the banks are apparently holding as hedges (such as they are), as well as the client portfolios, wherever they are.

# 3
# Privatization and Deregulation: a Chronology of Events

*Throstur Olaf Sigurjonsson*
*Reykjavik University*

## Introduction

The saga of Iceland's largest banks begins with deregulation and privatization. Although it is incorrect to blame these two factors entirely for the subsequent collapse, the liberalization process of financial markets and capital market integration in the 1990s (which followed Iceland's membership of the EEA (European Economic Area)), created an environment where the Icelandic financial service industry could thrive and enjoy the fruits of its risk-taking and an adventurous business culture.

Deregulation and privatization in Iceland were interwoven. The consensus view of privatization is that deregulation will improve company performance and social welfare (Vickers and Yarrow, 1988, 1991; Martin and Parker, 1997; Boycko and Vishny, 1996; Bishop and Thompson, 1992; Villalonga, 2000). As many others had done before, the Icelandic government attempted, through privatization, to encourage efficiency and entrepreneurship (The Icelandic National Audit Office, 2003). However, entrepreneurship involves risk taking, and this appeared to have been a largely neglected factor in the privatization process by the government at the time. Hence, privatization was treated as a discrete act, rather than a progressive process, without necessary regulation.

In October 2008, the Icelandic government put the three major banks, Landsbanki, Kaupthing, and Glitnir, into receivership. This marked the end of a seven-year period of unprecedented growth in which the banks had grown from small local banks, serving mostly Icelandic clients, to joining the major players of banking in northern Europe. This chapter gives a chronological account of these events.

## Deregulation and privatization

The Icelandic government launched the privatization process in 1992, and by 2005, it had privatized 33 firms. Among the last of the public institutions to be privatized were the two public banks, Landsbanki and Bunadarbanki. The privatization of these two banks was completed in 2003.

Market liberalization and deregulation preceded the privatization process, throughout the late 1980s and the early 1990s. Their driver was the need to adapt the Icelandic legislative and regulatory structures to that of the European Union (EU). This was a necessary requirement as a condition of Iceland's membership in the EEA when they joined in 1994. A new political agenda with different ideology also contributed as a major driver for change. Prior to this, Iceland had joined the European Free Trade Association (EFTA) in 1970, and concluded a Free Trade Agreement with the European Economic Community in 1972.

A centre-right coalition government was in power during the 16-year period of the privatization process, with the Independence Party (Iceland's conservative party) at the helm for the whole period. The most influential political leader during this era was David Oddsson, the chair of the Independence Party, who served as Prime Minister from 1991 to 2006. Thereafter Oddsson became the governor of the Central Bank of Iceland. The government went to great lengths to promote the advantages of privatization, both to the public and to the business community. Various incentives were implemented, such as tax rebates for share purchases in the privatized firms. Policy measures were clarified, as well as the purpose and the process of the privatization programme.

Iceland's financial markets had long been plagued by both political interference and regulations, which created economic difficulties. Inflation was in double digits, resulting in high negative real interest rates that led to reduced savings, essentially halving the banking system due to dwindling deposits. Subsequently, important legislative reforms were implemented and the financial sector was opened up to the free flow of capital (see dates in Table 3.1). Interest rates were liberalized and for the first time determined by markets and, furthermore, innovation was both encouraged and rewarded. Taxes were lowered considerably along with a complete overhaul of the taxation system. A requirement for closer international cooperation and competition was to bring the tax system into line with that of other European countries. Personal income tax rates were decreased from 49 per cent to about 35 per cent.

More drastically, corporate income tax was lowered from 51 per cent to 15 per cent, making it among the lowest rates in Europe. Property and inheritance taxes were abolished. In order to speed up the privatization and in order to stimulate the stock market, the public was offered a tax discount of up to 100 per cent of the price of stocks purchased, but purchases were capped at a certain amount. A flat 10 per cent tax was imposed on all forms of capital income, i.e. dividends, capital gains, interest, and rent (Portes and Baldursson, 2007). The fiscal balance did not suffer because of the tax reforms, in fact, tax revenues actually went up (Ministry of Finance, 2007) because of the ensuing economic boom.

The restructuring of the Icelandic pension system is another contributor to the rapid development of the financial system in Iceland. The system was changed into a fully funded 'pay as you go' structure with respect to future obligations. The reforms started in 1969, but asset growth in the pension funds really began in the early 1980s, when indexation was introduced and interest rates were liberalized. In 2007, the total assets of the pension funds were over 130 per cent of GDP, up from 50 per cent of GDP in 1994 (Olafur Sigurdsson, CEO of Stafir Pension Fund, interview on March 10, 2007). This occurred concurrently with economic growth of 4.03 per cent p.a. over this period (Statistics Iceland, 2009). The liberalization of the financial markets that was taking place provided new investment opportunities for the pension funds. Through the accumulation of huge deposits, the pension funds now acted as significant investors in the Icelandic market – the pension funds had about 1255 billion ISK worth of Icelandic securities in September 2008, which was close to the country's GDP (Central Bank of Iceland, 2009).

## Bank privatization

Landsbanki and Bunadarbanki were privatized in the period between 1999 and 2003 (Bunadarbanki merged with the private investment bank Kaupthing in 2003). FBA Investment Bank (Fjarfestingarbanki atvinnulifsins), originally a public investment credit fund, was privatized in 1998 and merged with the private commercial bank Glitnir (then Islandsbanki). A wave of consolidation followed closely on the heels of privatization (Icelandic Chamber of Commerce, 2007), supplying the banks with necessary instruments and scale for both domestic and international growth. It is fair to say that the privatization of the public banks stimulated strong growth in the Icelandic financial system.

The Icelandic banking privatization was somewhat different from the process of privatization in other countries. While most countries had privatized their institutions with at least some foreign ownership, the Icelandic government initially decided to encourage foreign ownership, then backed away from that decision. Instead, single identities gained a controlling interest in the banks. The investment group Samson acquired a 48.5 per cent share in Landsbanki, which was the largest bank in Iceland at the time. The Samson group consisted of three people, Bjorgolfur Gudmundsson, his son Bjorgolfur Thor Bjorgolfsson and their business partner Magnus Thorsteinsson. The media discussed the close relationship between Bjorgolfur Gudmundsson and the Independence Party, particularly the fact that Gudmundsson had previously been the president of the largest faction of the Independence Party, Vordur (Gunnarsson, 2003). Not selling Landsbanki to smaller institutional investors and individuals met resistance within the privatization committee and one of its members resigned as a result. The Icelandic Financial Supervisory Authority (FME) made representations against the deal, particularly the decision not to avoid the controlling ownership of one group. This aspect was also widely criticized by other interest groups. After several months of negotiations, the FME approved the privatization. However, the same circumstance arose when Bunadarbanki was privatized. A small group of investors, called the S-Group, gained controlling ownership of the bank, which was a 45.8 per cent stake (The Icelandic National Audit Office, 2003). The S-Group consisted of a few companies and individuals closely related to the other ruling party in the Icelandic Parliament, the Progressive Party (Framsóknarflokkur). The German bank, Hauck & Aufhauser, joined the consortium because one of the conditions for the privatization was to have, at least partially, an international owner. The S-Group consisted of an insurance company (VIS), a pension fund (Samvinnutryggingar), a shipping company (Samskip) and an investment house (Egla). The people behind these companies were (among others) Finnur Ingolfsson, the former Minister of Commerce for the Progressive Party and the former Governor of the Central Bank, and Olafur Olafsson, the CEO and majority owner of the firms Egla and Samskip. One of the consultants to the government regarding the privatization process, HSBC, expressed their concern regarding the extensive cross-ownership between the investors behind the purchase of Bunadarbanki. Hauck & Aufhauser sold its shares to Egla roughly a year after privatization, so it took little or no part in the privatized operations. The two groups of investors in Bunadarbanki and Landsbanki had absolutely no prior experience in commercial banking. The new owners financed their deals at each other's banks, debts that were still not fully paid at their collapse.

## Growing abroad

The future growth of the newly privatized Icelandic banks could only come from abroad. Hence, the banks began seeking consolidation and growth opportunities by implementing a strategy of foreign acquisitions. That strategy was closely related to the foreign expansion of their owners' interests. The diversification of risk was a significant concern. The banks needed to start a process of variation in their income statements (Halldor Jonsson, CEO of Landsbanki, interview on 13 April 2007). Meanwhile, internationally, an ideal platform for fast growth was emerging. Historically low global interest rates and decreased credit spreads brought into existence lucrative opportunities. At the same time (2002–5), capital appreciation was strong in Iceland, especially in equity and real estate. In 1984, the establishment of an individual transferable fishing quota system created new equity of 350 billion ISK (36 per cent of GDP). The privatization yielded some 370 billion ISK (38 per cent of GDP) until 2005. The fast-growing pension funds also controlled considerable equity (130 per cent of GDP) and searched for investment opportunities (Sigurmundsson, 2009). The domestic economy could never provide an adequate investment platform for this capital and therefore international exposure was necessary to generate acceptable returns (Portes and Baldursson, 2007).

The authorities apparently did not appreciate fully the macro- and micro-prudential risks of the process of privatization, deregulation, and the subsequent expansion of the banking system. Rapid growth and cross-border expansion do not come about without risk and the Icelandic banks encountered what has been called the *Informational Crisis* in early 2006. Among other things, the lack of information about the banks and their activities was raised as a serious issue by Fitch Ratings in February 2006 and Danske Bank in March the same year (Fitch Ratings, 2006; Danske Bank, 2006). The criticism centred on the banks' dependence on the wholesale market for financing and borrowing short term but lending long term, leading the banks to become very sensitive to financial turmoil in international markets. In addition, doubts about earning quality, cross-ownership, and the overall lack of transparency drew criticism.

The Icelandic stock market fell by some 25 per cent as a result. Simultaneously, the ISK fell on a comparable scale. In financing their rapid growth, the banks had relied heavily on wholesale funding and at the time of the criticism, the maturities of the securities were relatively front-loaded. The banks had to alter their strategy and limit their reliance on the wholesale markets and, considering the banks already had a dominant market share in the domestic market, raise retail deposits. Through their subsidiaries and branches abroad, they managed to raise further customer deposits. In 2006, the market conditions were still such that there was a huge spread between foreign interest rates and domestic interest rates, which were among the highest in the world (around 15 per cent). The Icelandic banks continued to borrow heavily abroad in order to take advantage of this situation, according to the banks' annual reports. Within a short period Iceland became one of the highest leveraged countries in the world. In 2000 the banks' assets were less than Iceland's GDP. At the point of their collapse their balance sheets had grown to become 11 times Iceland's GDP (Central Bank of Iceland, 2009; Jännäri, 2009). With such a vast inflow of capital, observers began to question the quality of the asset side of the banks' balance sheets as well as the continuing lack of transparency, and feared the complicated cross-ownership in the Icelandic business community.

Corporate governance issues arose when cross-ownership was examined and the lack of transparency became evident. The root of this is traced to when the banks began their growth period after privatization. In the small and fast-growing economy, ownership seemed to be more entwined than in the larger economies. The most significant cases involved Kaupthing and Landsbanki. When the investment company Exista was established, Kaupthing had acquired a stake in the firm (which went up to about 21 per cent of ownership). Then, over a short period, Exista became the largest shareholder in Kaupthing, owning more than 25 per cent (Nasdaq OMX Nordic, 2009). Within a few years, Exista had grown to be the largest investment firm in Iceland with huge stakes in various Nordic financial firms. This cross-ownership was widely criticized. Kaupthing solved the cross-ownership issue by distributing its shares in Exista to shareholders of the bank itself (Nasdaq OMX Nordic, 2009). In the other case, Landsbanki owned a substantial share in one of the largest investment banks, Straumur. Landsbanki aimed to solve the cross-ownership dilemma by selling its shares in Straumur to Grettir Investments (Fjárfestingarfélagið Grettir hf) in May 2006. The major stakeholder in Landsbanki and chair of the board, Björgólfur Gudmundsson, owned 28.52 per cent in Grettir through his company Hansa. His son, Björgólfur Thor Bjorgolfsson, owned 20.66 per cent in Grettir through his company Opera Investments (Opera fjárfestingar ehf).

Björgólfur Thor was the chair of the board at Straumur. After this transaction, firms under the control of Björgólfur Gudmundsson and his son Björgólfur Thor managed 37 per cent of Straumur (Nasdaq OMX Nordic, 2009). Corporate governance issues in the private sector in Iceland thus remained convoluted and opaque (Vaiman et al., 2010).

## The descent

A broader income base and dispersed risk were intended to soften any setbacks that the Icelandic economy might suffer. On the other hand, large shifts in the values of the foreign assets and liabilities of the banks created problems of how to insulate the domestic real economy from the financial turbulence. Over a period of a few years (2003–8), the Icelandic banks leveraged their capital base to buy up banking assets worth several times the country's GDP. If the value of these assets (mostly bought in the years of the banking and credit boom between 2003 and 2006) were to be revalued at much lower prices, the financial institutions would become insolvent. Moreover, they lent money to private businesses that made investments locally and abroad, and collapsing asset prices were likely to make them insolvent, hence affecting the banks' loan books adversely. Neither the Central Bank of Iceland nor the National Treasury had the necessary reserves to serve as a lender of last resort for the larger individual banks (Sigurjonsson, 2010). The cost of support was way beyond their capacity.

The months of September and October in 2008 were decisive for the Icelandic banks. After the fall of the investment bank Lehman Brothers in September 2008, money markets and interbank lending froze completely. The Central Bank of Iceland was unable to act as an effective lender of last resort to the Icelandic banks as it simply did not hold enough foreign currency to do this and Glitnir was the first bank affected. With its short-run credit lines closed, Glitnir had to request a short-term loan from the Central Bank of Iceland, which refused. The government put Glitnir into receivership on 6 October 2008, which was the first step towards a formal bankruptcy. The bank was not nationalized, as the state would have become responsible for the bank's huge liabilities. The consequence was a debt downgrade and a sharp fall in the already depreciated ISK.

After this, short-run funding evaporated and margin calls came from the European Central Bank. Landsbanki also found itself unable to meet its commitments and on 7 October was put into receivership.

However, for the moment, Kaupthing appeared viable. To add to the crisis, Landsbanki operated the Icesave 1200 billion ISK deposit account out of Iceland as a branch (not as a subsidiary) in the United Kingdom (UK) and the Netherlands, passing the ultimate liability onto the Icelandic Depositors' and Investors' Guarantee Fund. The Icelandic Central Bank made some remarks that were construed to mean that Iceland would not meet these obligations to British depositors. The reaction of the British government was to seize the UK assets of all the Icelandic banks by instigating anti-terrorist laws (HM Treasury, 2008). Subsequently, Kaupthing was ruined by the confiscation of its UK subsidiary, Singer and Friedlander, as covenants on loan agreements were activated. Kaupthing was then put into receivership on 9 October. The state took over the Icelandic operations of the three banks through an emergency law enacted on 7 October 2008, leaving the foreign operations in the old banks (Figure 3.1 shows the evolution of the banks' share prices from privatization to the collapse). Three new state banks were erected from the ruins of the old; NBI hf (New Bank of Iceland/Landsbanki), Nyi Kaupthing Banki hf (the New Kaupthing Bank, which changed its name to Arion bank in November 2009) and Nyi Glitnir (the New Glitnir, which changed its name as well, to Islandsbanki at end of March 2009). Table 3.1 gives a chronology of these events.

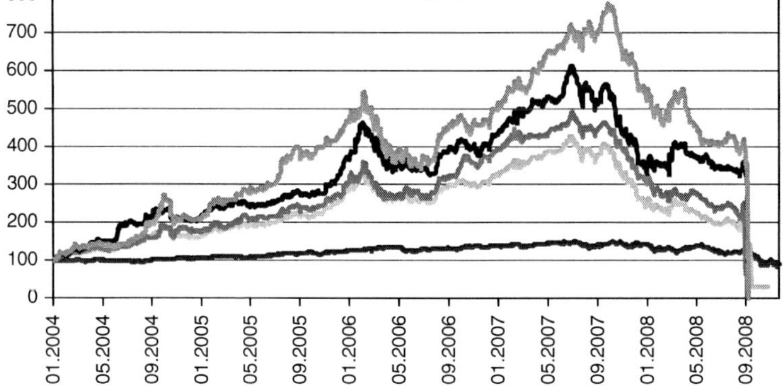


*Figure 3.1* Evolution of the banks' share prices

*Table 3.1* A chronology of events

| Year | Event |
|---|---|
| 1984–86 | Liberalization of domestic bank rates. |
| 1985 | Iceland Stock Exchange established. |
| 1987 | Interest Rate Act: Interest rates fully liberalized. |
| 1990 | Stepwise liberalization of capital movements begins. |
| 1993 | Interbank market for foreign exchange established. |
| 1994 | Iceland becomes a founding member of EEA (European Economic Area). |
| | Long-term capital movements fully liberalized. |
| 1995 | Short-term capital movements fully liberalized. |
| | Foreign direct investment liberalized in accordance with EEA agreement. |
| 1998 | |
| Autumn | The privatization process of the Icelandic banks begins, by sale of shares in Landsbanki and Bunadarbanki. |
| 1999 | |
| January 1 | The merger of the Bank Inspectorate and the Association of Insurance Supervisors establishes the Financial Supervisory Authority. |
| February | The Central Bank of Iceland (CBI) implements provisions for liquid resources to the Icelandic banks, endeavouring to decrease domestic demand, strengthen the foreign currency reserve, decrease lending, and decrease risk in the banks' own financing. |
| 2000 | |
| January 1 | The CBI implements new provisions for liquid resources. |
| May 15 | Islandsbanki and the FBA Investment Bank merge (name later changed into Glitnir). |
| October 5 | Heritable Bank in the UK becomes a subsidiary of Landsbanki. |
| October | Current account reserve of the CBI is 35.1 billion ISK. |
| 2001 | |
| March 27 | Confidence limits on the exchange rate of the ISK are abolished and the currency is floated. Official inflation target implemented, the goal being to keep inflation close to 2.5%. |
| May 23 | New laws regarding the CBI come into effect. |
| 2002 | |
| March | The foreign currency reserve of the CBI is 36 billion ISK. |
| May 29 | The CBI enforces rules on balance of foreign currency accounts for financial institutions, with permissible balance between exchange-rate-adjusted assets and liabilities 15% of equity. |
| Sept 3 | The Minister of Trade grants permission for the Karahnjukar hydropower project. |
| October 21 | Samson ehf buys 45.8% of the state shares in Landsbanki for 12.3 billion ISK. State ownership after this becomes minimal. The privatization of Landsbanki is completed. |

(*continued*)

*Table 3.1* Continued

| Year | Event |
|---|---|
| 2003 | |
| January 16 | The Icelandic state sells 45.8% in Bunadarbanki. The buyer is the 'S-group' and the German bank Hauck & Aufhauser. After this, the state owns 9% in Bunadarbanki. |
| March 22 | What is left of the state ownership in Bunadarbanki (9%) is sold and the privatization of Bunadarbanki is completed. The reserve requirement at the CBI is lowered. Some 8 billion ISK is released to the Icelandic banks this way. |
| April 12 | Bunadarbanki and Kaupthing merge to form KB Bank (later renamed Kaupthing). |
| June | Islandsbanki opens a subsidiary in Luxembourg. |
| December 7 | The reserve requirement lowered further. Some 15 billion ISK is released. After that 2% reserve requirement on deposits and securities from the banks is due in the next 2 years or less, to bring the business environment of the banks in line with European standards. |
| 2004 | |
| June | The current account reserve of the CBI is 68.5 billion ISK. |
| August | Kaupthing is the first of the Icelandic banks to announce it will compete with the public Housing Financing Fund and offer housing credits. |
| September 29 | Kaupthing buys the Danish investment bank FIH for 85 billion ISK. |
| November 5 | Islandsbanki announces it offers 100% loan on housing credit. |
| November 8 | Landsbanki and Kaupthing begin 100% lending on housing credit. |
| December | The Housing Financing Fund (state owned) begins providing house loans for 90% of the market value. Glitnir (the new name for Islandsbanki) buys BN bank in Norway for 33 billion ISK. |
| December 28 | Landsbanki stops providing 100% housing credit. The argument is to stimulate more risk-adverse behaviour in households. |
| 2005 | |
| February 1 | Landsbanki buys the UK Teather & Greenwood. |
| April | Kaupthing buys the UK Singer & Friedlander for 52 billion ISK. The Danish newspaper *Berlingske Tidende* reports that the Icelandic economy is overheating (20 April 2005). Jyske Bank in Denmark worries that both Icelandic households and companies have increased their debts considerably and the ISK will drop in coming months (20 April 2005). |
| July | Iceland Telecom is privatized. The state now has privatized 33 companies and very few privatization opportunities are left. |

*(continued)*

*Table 3.1* Continued

| ***Year*** | ***Event*** |
|---|---|
| September 5 | Landsbanki buys Kepler Equities. |
| November 15 | Landsbanki buys the Irish securities firm Merrion Capital. |
| December 16 | The Danish radio reports that 'the Icelandic wonder' rests on a bubble that will burst. |
| 2006 | |
| January 1 | Personal income tax decreased, property tax and high income tax discontinued.<br>Glitnir stops offering 100% housing credit. |
| February 21 | Fitch Ratings revise the outlook on Iceland from stable to negative. |
| March | Glitnir buys the Norwegian real estate firm Union Group.<br>Danske Bank issues on the 22nd 'Iceland: Geyser Crisis', a report that is perceived to be very negative towards Iceland. The chief economists of the Icelandic banks reply fiercely; the chief economist at Kaupthing: 'Danske Bank report is full of misinterpretation and wild fantasy' (*Vidskiptabladid*, 22 March 2006). Chief economist at Landsbanki: 'Danske Bank analysts fully misunderstand the Icelandic economy' (*Vidskiptabladid*, 22 March 2006). Economist at Glitnir: 'That Iceland will experience financial crisis, devaluation of the ISK, drop in consumption, all at same time, is highly unlikely' (*Vidskiptabladid*, 22 March 2006). The CBI Governor, David Oddsson, comments: 'Danske Bank report is being characterized by ignorance, haste and mean will' (*Frettabladid*, 23 March 2006). Prime Minister of Iceland, Mr Asgrimsson, on the issue: 'Criticism from many of the foreign banks is simply an act of competitors who want to crush the Icelandic competition' (*Morgunbladid*, 26 March 2006). Trade Minister of Iceland, Mrs Sverrisdottir, on the Danske Bank report: 'It must be kept in mind that Danske Bank triggered the economic burst in the Faroe Islands' (*Vidskiptabladid*, 24 March 2006).<br>Merrill Lynch issues on the 31st 'Resolving Iceland's Banking Crisis', criticizing the Icelandic banks, stating they are not as reliable as previously perceived, gaining huge media attention in Iceland and causing the falling-out of both politicians and bankers. |
| May 1 | The CBI eases the rules on banks' foreign currency reserves. Permissible imbalance between exchange-rate-adjusted assets and liabilities increased to 30% of equity.<br>Mishkin and Herbertsson publish their report 'Financial Stability in Iceland'. |
| June 7 | Standard & Poor downgrade the Icelandic state, from stable to negative. |

(*continued*)

*Table 3.1* Continued

| *Year* | *Event* |
|---|---|
| June 17 | An interview with Prof Mishkin: '... comparing Iceland with emerging economies is very ill-judged ... there is nearly no risk of financial crisis in Iceland' (*Morgunbladid*). |
| June 24 | Glitnir buys the Swedish securities firm Fisher Partners. |
| September | The foreign currency reserve of the CBI is 100 billion ISK. |
| September 25 | Landsbanki buys Cheshire Guernsey Ltd. |
| October 3 | Operations to increase the aluminium smelter Nordural up to 220,000 tons are started. |
| October | Landsbanki begins operating the Icesave deposit account in the UK. |
| 2007 | |
| February | Moody's upgrades the Icelandic banks to AAA from A1 and A2. Glitnir buys the Finnish FIM Group. |
| May | Professor Gregory Miller from Harvard Business School, interviewed by *Morgunbladid*, criticizes Danske Bank for wrong reporting and lack of knowledge about the Icelandic circumstances. |
| July 2007 | CDS-spread on the Icelandic banks is 50 points. |
| August | Danske Bank publishes (3 August 2007) a report where it states that Iceland is the first country to rest its economy on leveraged buyout.<br>Kaupthing announces its intention to acquire the Dutch investment bank NIBC. |
| November 29 | Portes and Baldursson publish their report 'The Internationalization of Iceland's Financial Sector'.<br>Operations to increase the aluminium smelter Nordural up to 260,000 t are started. |
| November 30 | The aluminium smelter Karahnjukar begins operation. |
| Year end 2007 | Icesave deposit accounts in the UK reach 590 billion ISK. Landsbanki wins marketing award for the project. |
| 2008 | |
| January | CDS-spread of the Icelandic banks reaches 400 points. |
| January 30 | Kaupthing exits negotiations regarding buying the Dutch NIBC, a takeover that would have cost the bank 286 billion ISK. |
| Jan/Feb | Kaupthing begins operating the deposit account Edge, in the UK, Belgium, Finland, Norway, and Sweden. |
| February | In a memorandum by the Central Bank, after its meetings with some major banks, creditors of the Icelandic banks and Moody's, it is stated that these foreign stakeholders have serious concerns about the solvency of the Icelandic banks (12 February 2008).<br>Nordea Bank in Denmark, analyst Henrik Drusebjerg: 'We have no belief in the Icelandic economy.' |

(*continued*)

*Table 3.1* Continued

| *Year* | *Event* |
|---|---|
| | In a memo from the CBI, which had a meeting in London (12 February 2008) with ratings firms and major banks, the foreign agents express great worries regarding the Icelandic banks, claiming that the banks may have put themselves in insoluble difficulties.<br>The Prime Minister M. Haarde states that the Icelandic bankers know what they are doing and their investments abroad will make good returns and can be sold if needed.<br>The *Financial Times* calls Iceland 'One big hedge fund'. |
| March | The British Financial Supervisory Authority warns British depositors that the Icelandic banks are not safe.<br>Foreign Minister, Mrs Gisladottir, states that 'The question on the Icelandic banks' solvency is only theoretical.' |
| March 25 | The CBI increases interest rates from 13.75 to 15%.<br>The CBI abolishes its reserve requirements on foreign liabilities for Icelandic subsidiaries abroad. |
| April | The Prime Minister of Iceland meets with the British Prime Minister to discuss swap agreements to bolster the foreign exchange reserves. |
| May | Landsbanki opens Icesave deposit accounts in the Netherlands. |
| May 16 | Currency swap agreements with the Nordic countries are reached. |
| June 4 | The Central Bank tightens foreign currency balance of the banks. The permitted balance on currency indexed assets becomes 10% of equity. |
| August 14 | The Icelandic banks withstand the stress test of the Financial Supervisory Advisory (FME). |
| September | The CBI's foreign account reserve is 500 billion ISK. The Central Bank of USA denies Iceland a currency swap, arguing that the banking system in Iceland is too big in relation to its GDP.<br>Lehman Brothers file for bankruptcy (15 September 2008).<br>Glitnir requests an emergency loan of €600m from the CBI (25 September 2008).<br>The Icelandic government makes a statement that it intends to take Glitnir over (29 September 2008). Iceland's credit ratings fall. Credit lines to Icelandic banks close. |
| October | The British FSA demands additional £200m cash liquidity reserves for Landsbanki Icesave accounts (3 October 2008).<br>The CBI and the government refuse to lend the money to Landsbanki.<br>Kaupthing, fighting liquidity difficulties, receives a €500m loan from the CBI, pledging the FIH Danish subsidiary as collateral. |

(*continued*)

*Table 3.1* Continued

| **Year** | **Event** |
|---|---|
| | The parliament passes a bill that enables the FME to take the banks over (6 October 2009).<br>FME takes over Glitnir and Landsbanki (7 October 2008).<br>UK authorities, using the powers under the Anti-Terrorism, Crime and Security Act, 2001, freeze assets relating to Landsbanki in Britain. The FSA in UK closes Kaupthing's Singer & Friedlander operations (8 October 2008).<br>The FME takes over Kaupthing (9 October 2008).<br>The Icelandic financial system collapses and emergency laws are enforced. Glitnir, Landsbanki and Kaupthing are taken into receivership (9 October 2008). |

## References


Bishop, M. and Thompson, D. (1992), 'Privatization in the UK Internal Organization and Productive Efficiency', *Annals of Public and Cooperative Economics*, 63(2), 171–88.

Boycko, A. S. and Vishny, R. (1996), 'A Theory of Privatization', *Economic Journal*, 106, 309–19.

Central Bank of Iceland (2009), *Financial Stability 2009*, retrieved 15 November 2009 from: http://sedlabanki.is/lisalib/getfile.aspx?itemid=7357.

Danske Bank (2006), *Iceland: Geyser Crisis*, retrieved 25 March 2006 from: http://danskeresearch.danskebank.com/link/FokusAndreIceland21032006/$file/GeyserCrises.pdf.

Fitch Ratings (2006), *Fitch Revises Iceland's Outlook to Negative on Widening Macro Imbalances*, retrieved 26 March 2006 from: http://www.fitchratings.com/corporate/index.cfm.

Gunnarsson, I. (2003), *Ísland í aldanna rás 1900–2000*, Forlagið, Reykjavík.

HM Treasury (2008), *The Landsbanki Freezing (Amendment) Order 2008*, retrieved 22 June 2009 from: http://www.hm-treasury.gov.uk/d/landsbanki_freezing_amendment08.pdf.

Icelandic Chamber of Commerce. (2007), *Iceland's Advance, Foreign Investments 2001–2006*, retrieved 25 September 2009 from: http://www.vi.is/files/1519398707VIDSKIP%20COMPLETE.pdf.

Jännäri, K. (2009), *Report on Banking Regulation and Supervision in Iceland: Past, Present and Future*, retrieved 15 July 2009, from: http://eng.forsaetisraduneyti.is/media/frettir/KaarloJannari__2009.pdf

Martin, S. and Parker, D. (1997), *The Impact of Privatization. Ownership and Corporate Performance in the UK*, Routledge, London.

Ministry of Finance (2007), *Chronicle of Economic Events 2007*, retrieved 29 November 2009 from: http://www.ministryoffinance.is/Publications/Chronicleofeconomicevents/nr/7608.

Nasdaq OMX Nordic (2009). Retrieved 1 November 2009 from: http://www.nasdaqomxnordic.com/Frettir/.

Portes, R. and Baldursson, F. M. (2007), *The Internationalisation of Iceland's Financial Sector, Iceland Chamber of Commerce,* retrieved 20 August 2009 from: http://www.vi.is/files/15921776Vid4WEB.pdf.

Sigurjonsson, T. O. (2010), 'The Icelandic Bank Collapse: Challenges to Governance and Risk Management', *Corporate Governance: the International Journal of Business in Society,* January 2010.

Sigurmundsson, A. (2009), 'Ræða Arnars Sigurmundssonar formanns stjórnar Landssamtaka lífeyrissjóða á aðalfundi 14. maí 2009' (Written speech), retrieved from Icelandic Pension Funds Association (IPFA) website: http://ll.is/files/bcecdihcbi/Avarp_Arnars_a_adalfundi_LL_15._mai_2009.pdf.

Statistics Iceland (2009), *Overview of Gross Domestic Product and Gross National Product 1945–2008,* retrieved 2 December 2009 from: http://www.statice.is/Statistics/National-accounts-and-public-fin/National-accounts-overview.

The Icelandic National Audit Office (2003), *Einkavæðing helstu ríkisfyrirtækja árin 1998–2003,* retrieved 5 October 2009 from: http://www.rikisend.is/files/skyrslur_2003/einkavaeding.pdf.

Vaiman, V., Davidsson, P. and Sigurjonsson, T. O. (2010), 'Revising a Concept of Corruption as a Result of the Global Economic Crisis – the Case of Iceland.' In Stachowicz Stanusch (ed.), *Organizational Immunity to Corruption. Building Theoretical and Research Foundations*. Polish Academy of Science Commission Regional Department, Katowice, Poland.

Vickers, J. and Yarrow, G. (1988), 'Privatization: an Economic Analysis', World Bank Policy Research Working Paper Series, Washington, DC.

Vickers, J. and Yarrow, G. (1991), 'Economic Perspectives on Privatization', *Journal of Economic Perspectives,* 5, 111–32.

Villalonga, B. (2000), 'Privatization and Efficiency: Differentiating Ownership Effects from Political, Organizational and Dynamics Effects', *Journal of Economic Behavior and Organization,* 42, 43–74.

# Part I
# International Organizations and the Central Bank of Iceland

# 4
# International Monetary Fund, Article IV Consultations 2006 and 2008

## IMF Executive Board concludes 2006 Article IV consultation with Iceland

On 4 August 2006, the Executive Board of the International Monetary Fund (IMF) concluded the Article IV consultation with Iceland.[1]

### Background

Driven by an expansion of the aluminium sector, Iceland is going through an economic boom that is generating large imbalances. Strong domestic demand, reflecting rapidly growing investment and private consumption, is overheating the economy and leading to high inflation and record current account deficits. As global monetary policy tightened early in the year, volatility in Icelandic financial markets increased as international investors became concerned about the risks associated with macroeconomic imbalances and potential vulnerabilities in the financial sector.

Following a recession in 2002, economic growth accelerated sharply reaching 8.2 per cent in 2004, slowing only modestly to 5.5 per cent in 2005. Pre-announced income tax cuts, an appreciated exchange rate, and an easing in household credit constraints stimulated private consumption. With investment also growing rapidly due to the aluminium sector projects, domestic demand posted growth of 10.5 per cent in 2004 and 15.1 per cent in 2005. As domestic demand gathered speed, the trade deficit more than doubled, reaching 12.8 per cent of GDP in 2005 and the current account deficit hit 16.5 per cent of GDP. Meanwhile inflation rose to 8.4 per cent year-on-year in June 2006, well above the 4 per cent upper bound of Central Bank's tolerance range.

Monetary authorities responded to growing demand pressures by raising interest rates to 13 per cent in July 2006 from 5.3 per cent in May 2004. However, until recently, the monetary tightening impacted the economy primarily through an appreciated exchange rate because the increased competition between the state-owned Housing Finance Fund (HFF) and commercial banks lowered long-term mortgage rates and increased the availability of household credit. The fiscal stance also tightened, with the general government balance moving to a surplus of 3.2 per cent of GDP in 2005 from a deficit of 2.0 per cent of GDP in 2003.

In the first half of 2006, a series of negative reports by analysts and rating agents increased international investors' concerns about the consequences of Iceland's macroeconomic imbalances. As global monetary conditions tightened, investor concerns led to an unwinding of carry-trade positions, putting downward pressure on the exchange rate and equity prices, as well as widening credit spreads for Icelandic banks whose balance sheets had been expanding rapidly.

GDP is forecast to grow by 4.0 per cent in 2006, reflecting completion of the investment projects and continued strong private consumption. However, as investment returns to normal levels and consumption weakens due to currency depreciation and tighter credit conditions, growth is projected to fall to 1.0 per cent in 2007. Inflationary pressures are expected to persist and further tightening of monetary policy is likely. The fiscal surplus is projected to decline slightly, although steps, undertaken mid year, to postpone additional public investment projects should improve the fiscal balance relative to that previously expected as well as help ease demand pressures. The current account deficit is forecast to remain high in 2006 (12.5 per cent of GDP) and then improve sharply in 2007 (4.4 per cent of GDP) as growth rebalances toward the export sector reflecting, in part, increased aluminium-sector capacity and a more competitive exchange rate.

### Executive Board assessment

The Executive Directors noted that, while medium-term prospects are favourable, large and growing imbalances, evidenced by current account and inflation developments, pose risks to real growth and financial stability in the short term. Thus, Directors welcomed measures taken to curb demand pressures, including those recently announced, but they called for further decisive policy actions to stabilize confidence, help ensure an orderly adjustment, and maintain financial stability.

Directors emphasized that, despite low and declining public debt, further fiscal restraint, beyond current plans, is essential to reducing imbalances and averting their associated risks. The required fiscal tightening could be achieved by some combination of postponing additional public investment projects and reducing growth in public consumption expenditure. Looking ahead, Directors stressed that there is a strong case for considering further restraint in the budget for 2007 if domestic demand pressures do not abate as required.

Directors called for a further strengthening of the medium-term fiscal framework to help reduce volatility in the Icelandic economy. They observed that the introduction of multi-year budgeting was the first step along the path to a rules-based multi-year framework. Adding more structure to the budgeting and implementation processes will ensure a consistently countercyclical fiscal stance that would reinforce monetary policy and thereby increase economic stability.

Directors agreed that further increases in the monetary policy rate would likely be required to anchor expectations and return inflation to target. With additional inflationary pressures expected from currency depreciation, and tight goods and labour markets, real interest rates needed to rise. In this context. Directors viewed the recent rate increases as appropriate and welcomed the early signs that monetary policy is starting to have more of an impact on credit conditions faced by households and firms. The recent consensus reached by the social partners to maintain the current wage agreement should also help reduce uncertainty. This notwithstanding, given the high output cost of returning inflation to target should inflationary expectations become entrenched, Directors concurred that monetary policy should be biased toward a tight stance.

Directors noted that the flexible exchange rate regime in the context of the inflation-targeting monetary policy framework has served Iceland well. Although the year-to-date depreciation of the krona occurred sooner and faster than expected. Directors generally viewed the depreciation in the currency as an appropriate adjustment toward its equilibrium value.

Directors stressed the importance of actions directed at reducing vulnerabilities in the financial sector. Despite the strong balance sheets of financial institutions, the banks' rapid expansion has increased their risk profile. Directors welcomed the steps banks have taken so far to make these risks more manageable. Nevertheless, they stressed that the process needs to continue, with the encouragement and close monitoring of the supervisory authorities.

Directors welcomed the strengthening of the supervisory and financial stability frameworks. They commended the Financial Supervisory

Authority (FME) for quickly implementing broader and more stringent stress tests, which should provide positive assurance to the markets.

Directors recommended an immediate reform of the Housing Finance Fund. They noted that the increased competition in the mortgage market between the banks and the state-owned Housing Finance Fund had undermined the effectiveness of monetary policy, exacerbated excess demand, and increased the risks to financial stability. Following international experiences, Directors encouraged the authorities to consider a new privately held wholesale funding institution that would retain the positive features of the current system as well as allow for healthy competition in the mortgage market.

## IMF Executive Board concludes 2008 Article IV consultation with Iceland

On 10 September 2008, the Executive Board of the International Monetary Fund (IMF) concluded the Article IV consultation with Iceland.[1]

### Background

The economy experienced an extraordinary foreign-funded boom in recent years, with output rising by over 25 per cent during 2003–7. This rapid expansion, however, left a legacy of large macroeconomic imbalances, overstretched private sector balance sheets, and high dependence on foreign financing. The financial sector assets expanded to over 1000 per cent of GDP, while gross external indebtedness reached 550 per cent of GDP at end 2007, largely on account of the banking sector.

The global turbulence has taken a significant toll on domestic financial markets since end 2007. The credit default swap (CDS) spreads of the three largest domestic banks have risen sharply, approaching 1000 basis points, and the freely floating Icelandic krona has depreciated by over 40 per cent.

Despite minimum public sector debt the sovereign is facing a significantly increased risk premium.

In response to the turmoil, the authorities have taken steps to shore up confidence. The Central Bank of Iceland (CBI) tightened the policy rate, enhanced liquidity provision to reduce pressures in foreign exchange and domestic markets, and improved its foreign exchange liquidity access by entering into currency swap agreements with other Nordic central banks. The government indicated its willingness to boost the CBI's international reserves and pledged to pursue fiscal prudence and to reform the fiscal framework and the Housing Financing Fund (HFF).

At the same time, banks have sought to strengthen their balance sheets and enhance liquidity buffers. The three largest banks have slowed lending growth, consolidated funding needs, withdrawn from marginal markets, mobilized retail deposits abroad, and reduced costs, although their ability to deleverage has been limited by global risk aversion.

With foreign financing constraints binding, the economy is cooling. Output growth slowed in the first half of 2008, pulled by a significant retrenchment in domestic expenditure. Consumer confidence plunged in the first half of 2008, retail sale turnover decelerated sharply and domestic investment, especially in the construction sector, came to a halt.

The sharp depreciation of the Icelandic krona contributed to a jump in domestic prices. Annual inflation shot up from 5.9 per cent at end 2007 to 14.5 per cent in August 2008. With inflationary pressures mounting, the CBI raised its target interest rate by 1 per cent in March–May 2008 and kept it unchanged at 15.5 per cent since then. Inflation is expected to remain persistently above target in the near term, with significant risks on the upside.

The fiscal position is set to deteriorate and spending pressures to rise. The 2008 budget implies a loosening of the fiscal stance, and the government's commitment to cutting taxes further and boosting spending in early 2008 will contribute to an expansionary policy in 2009 and beyond. Given these policies, staff forecast the fiscal deficit to reach 5 per cent of GDP in 2010.

Against this background, economic activity is projected to come to a standstill in 2008 and contract in 2009–10. Tighter lending conditions, significantly lower real estate prices, weaker private balance sheets, and declining purchasing power point to a sharp retrenchment in private consumption. Investment is also expected to decline in 2009–10 while net exports should remain supportive, on the back of strong aluminium exports and a contraction in imports. The risks to the outlook are on the downside, dominated by external considerations.

### Executive Board assessment

Executive Directors observed that the Icelandic economy is at a difficult turning point. The long economic expansion, initiated by aluminium sector investments, sustained by a boom in private consumption, and fuelled by ready access to external financing, contributed to a build-up of macroeconomic imbalances and financial vulnerabilities. With external liquidity constraints binding, economic growth is expected to decline rapidly from unsustainably high levels and inflation to remain well above the central bank's target although the current account deficit is likely to narrow. Directors considered that there are large uncertainties surrounding the near-term outlook, with significant downside risks. At the same time, they noted that the long-term prospects for the economy remain promising – even enviable – given Iceland's sound governance and stable institutions, open and flexible markets, large and well-managed renewable natural resource base, and the authorities' long track record of resilience and adaptability to changing circumstances.

Directors observed that the authorities face the challenge of facilitating an orderly rebalancing process, while mitigating risks. They welcomed the authorities' efforts to bolster confidence, including by entering into currency swap arrangements with other Nordic central banks, and by committing to maintain tight macroeconomic policies and boost international reserves. Effective coordination between monetary policy and fiscal policies, and actions to reduce financial sector vulnerabilities, will be key to achieving orderly adjustment.

Directors recommended that monetary policy maintain its tight stance in order to return inflation to target and bolster confidence in the krona. They noted the staff's assessment that the real exchange rate of the krona is somewhat below its equilibrium level. A further krona depreciation could fuel inflationary pressures, erode households' purchasing power, and, against the background of the high level of private sector external debt and the current global financial market turbulence, squeeze private sector balance sheets and exert pressure on the capital account. Directors therefore saw little or no scope for monetary easing until inflation is placed firmly on a downward path. They also called on the authorities to manage carefully the provision of domestic liquidity.

Directors encouraged the authorities to act promptly on their pledge to reform the publicly owned Housing Finance Fund (HFF), which will be important to increase the effectiveness of monetary policy. They recommended redefining the HFF's role in the financial market by separating the social component, which provides targeted support, from the market-based component, which should not benefit from state aid.

Most Directors considered that a less expansionary fiscal policy would help support the central bank's efforts to combat inflation and maintain confidence, and called on the authorities to resist mounting pressures to boost spending further. A few Directors, however, laying greater emphasis on the threat of recession, saw scope for an active countercyclical fiscal policy to smooth the downturn. Directors welcomed the authorities' commitment to strengthen the fiscal framework.

Directors encouraged the authorities to pursue vigorously policy actions to mitigate banking sector risks. Measures to enlarge capital cushions and boost liquidity buffers could help restrain the growth of banks' balance sheets. Directors recommended strengthening overall transparency, including through better enforcement of disclosure requirements for all corporations.

Directors welcomed the progress made in strengthening the crisis prevention and resolution framework. They recommended that all existing elements of contingency planning be integrated into a single framework, that the bank resolution framework be enhanced, and that the authorities' commitment to boost the central bank's foreign exchange reserves be made effective when conditions permit.

## Note

1. Under Article IV of the IMF's Articles of Agreement, the IMF holds bilateral discussions with members, usually every year. A staff team visits the country, collects economic and financial information, and discusses with officials the country's economic developments and policies. On return to headquarters, the staff prepares a report, which forms the basis for discussion by the Executive Board. At the conclusion of the discussion, the Managing Director, as Chairman of the Board, summarizes the views of Executive Directors, and this summary is transmitted to the country's authorities.

# 5
# OECD *Economic Survey of Iceland*, 2006 and 2008

## *Economic Survey of Iceland 2006*: Executive Summary

The following is the Executive Summary of the OECD assessment and recommendations, taken from the *Economic Survey of Iceland 2006* published on 9 August 2006.

Iceland's economy and per capita income have grown at an impressive pace since the mid-1990s, making the country one of the most prosperous in the OECD. However, growth has been volatile and accompanied by recurrent large external and internal economic imbalances that reflect in part major investments in the energy and aluminium smelting sectors but also buoyant credit-funded household demand. In the recent period, concerns about these developments have led to a decline in investor confidence and sharp exchange rate correction, boosting inflation. While exchange rate depreciation was widely anticipated, the major challenge for macroeconomic policy is to swiftly restore economic balance and to strengthen the policy framework in a way that would avoid the recurrence of recent problems. Another challenge is to ensure that the financial sector continues to contribute to good economic performance both by minimizing the risk to stability and by completing reforms. Finally, human capital development is the key to sustaining the rise in prosperity achieved over the last decade.

### Promote economic stability by swiftly restoring balance and strengthening the policy framework

The implementation of monetary policy needs to be improved, so as to strengthen the credibility of the inflation target. In the near term, this implies that the monetary stance has to be tightened further until expected inflation is brought into line with the official target. Clearer communication could enhance the effectiveness of policy, likely leading to higher longer-term interest rates. The expansionary effect of tax cuts needs to be offset by additional expenditure restraint until domestic demand pressures abate. Budgetary control and enforcement mechanisms need to be strengthened to meet spending targets more effectively and the fiscal framework should become progressively more outcome-based. New major investment projects should not go ahead before economic imbalances have unwound and a comprehensive assessment has been made of their net benefits to the economy (taking account of resource use and environmental aspects). Greater transparency in the electricity sector would be helpful.

### Continue financial sector liberalization so as to foster growth and stability

Although the financial system is believed to be broadly sound, it is advisable to continue efforts aimed at assessing its robustness and to take supervisory steps, if needed, to address possible shortcomings. The successful liberalization of the financial sector could be completed in various ways. First, distortions in the housing market need to be removed. One way is to charge the Housing Financing Fund a fee reflecting the cost of the government guarantee and the required return to capital. Home ownership should instead be promoted through a means-tested grant for first home owners, rather than cross-subsidization of mortgage rates. Second, remaining restrictions on indexation in financial markets should be repealed. Finally, to improve the financing of innovative start-ups, consideration should be given to whether government-sponsored investment funds should be run along private-sector lines.

### Adapt the education system to a rapidly changing economic environment

It is important that children from rural areas, who perform poorly in literacy tests, leave school with a set of basic competences. At the compulsory level, the focus should be on teacher quality and not quantity. Moreover, effective teaching time will need to be increased when some of the subject matter currently taught in upper-secondary schools is moved to the compulsory level in the context of a shortening of upper-secondary education. It needs to be ensured that this shortening does not undermine educational outcomes. Increased teaching time and a rapid and coherent adjustment of curricula can deliver this. Potential drop-outs should be encouraged to select vocational programmes. At the tertiary level, new legislation aimed at ensuring educational quality should be expedited, tuition fees should be introduced in public institutions, and instead of trying to offer a full range of programmes, studies abroad should be encouraged.

## *Economic Survey of Iceland 2008*: Executive Summary

The following is the Executive Summary of the OECD assessment and recommendations, taken from the *Economic Survey of Iceland*, published on 28 February 2008.

Following significant structural reforms and foreign direct investment projects, the Icelandic economy enjoyed several years of rapid expansion, which entailed major internal and external imbalances. While growth has slowed and imbalances have diminished, the adjustment process has been uneven, with wage developments, improving financial conditions and government measures rekindling demand and inflation pressures during the course of 2007. The economy is quite flexible and resilient but remains vulnerable to changes in foreign-investor sentiment, as evidenced by the recent volatility in the exchange rate and share prices. Thus, the key challenge for policy in the near term is to restore macroeconomic stability by ensuring that steady progress is made in unwinding imbalances. Additionally, steps need to be taken to strengthen the ability of both monetary and fiscal policy to moderate economic volatility and prevent the re-emergence of major imbalances with a view to sustaining Iceland's favourable growth performance. In a longer-term perspective, there will be many spending pressures and a key challenge for policymakers will be health-care reform. Although the overall fiscal position is favourable, health care (which is largely government-financed) is a major source of public spending pressures. Health outcomes are very good, but the system is costly, suggesting that there is room for enhancing cost-effectiveness. The major issues addressed in this survey are as follows.

### Swiftly restoring economic balance

- Make it perfectly clear that the Central Bank would not hesitate to tighten the monetary stance further if this is necessary to anchor inflation expectations at the official target. In order to support the credibility and the effectiveness of monetary policy, it would be helpful if members of government respected the independence of Central Bank policymaking.
- As long as excess demand and inflation pressures persist, avoid expansionary fiscal measures. Likewise, to the extent possible, phase in gradually new major energy-intensive investments, which, in any

case, must not proceed without prior evaluation within a transparent, broad cost–benefit framework (including environmental impacts).

**Strengthening the macroeconomic policy framework**

- After inflation has stabilized, further strengthen the 'frame budgeting approach' by adopting binding nominal multi-year spending ceilings consistent with the inflation target. Introduce similar fiscal rules for local governments, including spending limits. This would increase the contribution of fiscal policy to macroeconomic stabilization and enhance public ownership of the inflation target.
- Once inflation has been durably brought down to the target, refinements to the inflation targeting framework could be considered (such as adjustments to the target variable).
- Reform the publicly owned Housing Financing Fund (HFF), which not only distorts resource allocation but also undermines the effectiveness of monetary policy and contributes to economic imbalances. At a minimum, charge the HFF a fee reflecting the benefit of its government guarantee. Morever, it is recommended that its social functions and wholesale market operations be split up, with targeted transfers addressing the social objectives.

**Improving cost-effectiveness in the health-care sector**

- Facilitate private provision, which accounts for only one-quarter of publicly financed health services, and open up the sector to competition, thereby enhancing efficiency and broadening patient choice. Consider more reliance on co-payments so as to avoid a situation in which competition among providers in a context of no, or very low, cost sharing leads to overconsumption of medical services. These measures would also relieve pressure on public finances.
- Strengthen the government's role as a buyer of health services, establishing ceilings on public spending, speeding up cost-efficiency analysis of major services and introducing activity-based funding arrangements.
- Further reduce the reliance on, and increase the efficiency of, costly hospital care and take measures to reduce the high cost of pharmaceuticals by promoting the use of generic drugs.

# 6
# Central Bank of Iceland *Financial Stability* Reports 2006–8

## Introduction – 2006

### A challenging course to navigate ahead

The finding of the Central Bank's previous *Financial Stability* report, in 2005, was that in spite of rapid expansion and the macroeconomic imbalances that needed to be tackled in the coming years, the Icelandic financial system was broadly sound. In the present report this overall finding is unchanged, but more challenging waters clearly lie ahead. The adjustment to changed conditions has already begun. It is important to keep a firm course and exercise caution in all respects.

The Central Bank of Iceland's report on *Financial Stability* assesses the financial sector's capability for withstanding a conceivable shock. It examines the position of financial companies, and their operating conditions and regulatory and supervision framework. Likewise, it discusses the position of households and businesses and the risks that they may face from such factors as a decrease in income, a fall in real estate prices or exchange rate volatility. Risk is always present, especially in times of great change, but measures are needed to minimize the likelihood of disruptions to the operations of major financial companies which could impair productive capacity.

Two main changes have occurred since the *Financial Stability* analysis was published in 2005. One has been intensified macroeconomic imbalances. The Central Bank has responded to inflationary pressures caused by surging demand with significant rises in its policy interest rate. The other turnaround was in the commercial banks' funding in international markets. There are many indications that the recent easy access to capital and favourable terms for it will deteriorate. Icelandic banks in particular face a changed situation. Over the past year they have expanded rapidly and raised large amounts of capital in international markets. Changed conditions now require financial companies to slow down the pace of this growth.

External conditions are favourable and on the whole stable. However, growing imbalances in the global economy could alter international financial conditions. The economic outlook in the main market regions for Icelandic businesses is nonetheless bright, with stable demand and high prices for major export products.

Macroeconomic imbalances can undermine stability. Exchange rate volatility in the wake of a wide current account deficit and falling asset prices could have a considerable impact on heavily indebted households and businesses, and on the operating conditions of financial companies. Although the Central Bank had expected the krona to weaken, the depreciation has come both sooner and faster than had been hoped. In the long run, this will prove healthy for the Icelandic economy, since the krona was valued significantly above a rate compatible with macroeconomic balance. Equity prices have also slipped considerably from their peak, after surges in recent years.

Total debt of Icelandic households is now equivalent to twice their annual disposable income, after a record rate of growth in 2005. Nonetheless, the household debt service burden has not increased, because of longer loan maturities and lower interest rates. Only a minor share of household debt is denominated in foreign currency. Household assets grew in net terms last year, i.e. gross assets grew faster than their debt. However, housing prices are very high, especially relative to construction cost and rent. A fall in real estate prices could squeeze the most heavily mortgaged borrowers, especially if disposable income declines temporarily and the employment outlook takes a turn for the worse.

In general, the profitability and position of businesses look sound. Admittedly, corporate debt grew at a record rate in 2005, but much of the increase has been deployed on foreign investment. Higher interest rates and borrower risk premia, and a weaker krona and equity prices, could have an adverse effect on many businesses, particularly the most leveraged ones. Exporters will benefit from the depreciation of the krona, and so will most listed companies. However, conditions of various companies in the domestic market, such as in the construction sector, will deteriorate. On the whole, households and businesses should be able to meet their debt service, but their position will tighten.

The Central Bank has firmly recommended a change in mortgage loan arrangements with less direct participation by the public sector.

Competition is desirable in this market and the commercial banks and savings banks can consolidate their position in the long term by providing housing mortgages. The Central Bank opposed the easing of lending rules at the Housing Financing Fund (HFF) in 2004, largely on account of the timing of this move. Feeling encroached upon, the commercial banks and savings banks responded with higher loan-to-value ratios and longer maturities. The resulting credit boom drove up household debt, real estate prices, consumption and imports, with an accompanying widening of the current account deficit. Interest rate formation in the housing mortgage market has been abnormal and the commercial banks and savings banks have not adequately matched their own borrowing and lending terms. The present situation is unacceptable and a reform is called for.

The position of the three large commercial banks is crucial for the financial markets. They have recorded outstanding profitability and strong capital adequacy. An important part of the exceptionally high bank profitability in 2005 and the first months of 2006 stems from trading gains, but even if these items are excluded, their operating profit would still be very healthy. The same applies to the savings banks, but the declining share of net interest income in their operations is some cause for concern.

Two-thirds of outstanding total lending by the commercial bank groups at the end of 2005 was to borrowers outside Iceland, the lion's share of which was to customers in the Nordic countries. Virtually all lending to non-residents is confined to regions with sound and stable economies. However, growth in domestic lending is far in excess of a level compatible with stability. Although this lending meets credit quality criteria, growth on such a scale heightens the risk of later impairment. Lending growth has remained buoyant so far in 2006 and clear signs of an improvement have yet to be seen.

Leveraged share purchases and forward contracts for shares in Icelandic companies entail a special risk, in particular because of the small size of the market. Although these transactions conform to international practice, the banks need to show caution about scope and maturity profiles. The banks' equity portfolios at own risk grew in 2005, after adjustment for forward contracts. Large exposures also increased in nominal terms, but decreased as a ratio of the banks' equity capital.

Dynamic operations by Icelandic banks and the upgrading of credit ratings for them and the Republic of Iceland have ensured easy access for Icelandic financial companies to international capital markets in recent years. This access has been used liberally and the banks have become more dependent on market financing. Macroeconomic imbalances, rapid banking sector growth and recent negative press prompted foreign investors to raise Iceland's risk profile. Higher required yields in the secondary market for bank bonds and for credit default swaps indicate that their financing costs will rise. While there is nothing unusual about such a development, what is surprising is how much wider spreads have been required relative to the terms offered to banks with comparable credit ratings. Revised market risk profiles for banks signal that, sooner or later, their customers' financing costs will go up.

A pronounced economic contraction could diminish financial stability. A fall in asset prices coinciding with a depreciation of the krona and higher international interest rates would exacerbate the adjustment. Simulations using the Central Bank's macroeconomic model support this finding. However, a stress test applied by the Financial Supervisory Authority (FME), and the Central Bank's assessment of possible loan losses, indicate firmly that the commercial banks' capital position is strong enough to withstand a significant economic crisis entailing several large shocks in tandem.

Work is continuing on technological and regulatory development of domestic financial markets. Apart from the bond market, turnover has increased, but markets are still limited by their small size, which increases the probability that fluctuations will be exaggerated. A takeover panel has been set up for the equity market and has published a few opinions, but has yet to leave a lasting mark. Largely because of the abnormal state of the housing mortgage market, the bond market has not evolved satisfactorily. The HFF has less need to issue bonds because borrowers are prepaying its older loans, and in the current climate the commercial banks and savings banks have not deemed it advisable to issue comparable bond series for their own funding.

In the recent past the Central Bank has focused on action to reduce operating risks in payment and settlement systems. Experience of system operation is positive and there is little likelihood of serious disruptions. However, the division of tasks among system participants needs to be clarified and their organization and contingency plans strengthened. Forthcoming tasks include activating automatic locks in the netting setting for smaller payments, tailoring fees in the real-time gross settlement (RTGS) system to actual costs, and more contingency exercises.

Over the past few years, the government authorities have built up a sound legal, regulatory and supervisory framework in line with international best practice. This achievement has been noted in the IMF's Financial Sector Assessment Programmes, reports by international credit rating agencies, and elsewhere. Under normal conditions, there is little probability of operating difficulties among banks which are sound and apply effective liquidity and risk management. Through their foreign investments, the Icelandic banks have changed their focus and spread their risks. They can now be defined as cross-border banks, but headquartered in Iceland where their liquidity and risks are managed. Their owners bear responsibility for resolving any difficulties that may be encountered – those who benefit from the profits on operations should also meet such setbacks as may occur. However, financial shocks can have more sweeping consequences. For this reason, government authorities in most countries including Iceland draw up contingency plans to deal with events in the financial markets and present frank, public accounts of their viewpoints.

Major advances in recent years have created much economic value for Iceland, and the long-term income outlook is bright. The economy is market-driven with a regulatory framework on a par with the best in Europe. Iceland's fiscal position is very strong and the economy is both highly flexible and resilient. Rapid advances tend to be accompanied by growing pains. A slower pace of growth is long overdue, in order to attain better balance in the financial position of households and businesses, including financial companies. If conditions are borne in mind and signals about the need to reduce risk are heeded, the outcome should only be favourable.

## The Central Bank's assessment – 2007

### The commercial banks are more resilient

In its analysis published in *Financial Stability* at the beginning of May 2006, the Central Bank of Iceland's finding was that the financial system was broadly sound, but more challenging waters lay ahead. Two main causes of concern were identified: macroeconomic imbalances and uncertainty about the commercial banks' refinancing of their foreign borrowing. Refinancing was successfully completed. However, macroeconomic imbalances increased. A year ago the focus was on short-term risks on the liabilities side of the financial companies' balance sheets, but now it has shifted more to long-term asset quality.

*Macroeconomic imbalances remain a cause for concern . . .*

The most pressing economic policy task is to restore stability. The conclusion of large investments in the aluminium and power sectors will automatically reduce imbalances, but other adjustment has been slower than expected. Increased foreign debt service has delayed the unwinding of the current account deficit, which will hardly be brought down to a sustainable level without a substantial contraction in demand. The latest forecast in *Monetary Bulletin* in March 2007 indicates that such a contraction lies ahead, as growth of investment and private consumption slows down. As discussed in this report, a depreciation of the krona coinciding with a fall in asset prices – possibly originating in tighter global financial conditions – could amplify the forecast contraction.

The necessary reduction of pressures in the economy will squeeze businesses and households, many of which are vulnerable due to heavy debt. They could withstand a short-lived reversal, but a lasting contraction would be difficult to weather.

*. . . but the banks' financing is in better order*

In late autumn 2005, after a surge in borrowing by Icelandic banks in international bond markets, investors revised their risk assessments of the banks. CDS spreads and secondary market yields on their issues increased. The banks deferred further borrowing in the European bond markets, which had been their main source of funding. Foreign analysts and agencies published negative reports about the banks and the state of the Icelandic economy. The climate turned most adverse at the end of February 2006 after Fitch Ratings changed Iceland's sovereign outlook from stable to negative, claiming *inter alia* that the banks' tight financing could have implications for the Treasury.

This situation and its aftermath squeezed the banks for a while, forcing them to respond firmly to the uncomfortable position that had arisen. The Icelandic banks made efforts to explain their structure and organization. They adjusted certain aspects of their operations and cross-ownership in response to relevant criticisms, and refuted what was less relevant with both communication and successful business performance. Temporarily they needed to look beyond their traditional markets for funding, with issuance in the US and Japan. The problem that loomed around this time a year ago is a thing of the past and terms in the secondary market are more favourable again.

The Central Bank underlines that global market conditions can take a sudden turn for the worse and it is important to be on the alert and prepared for such a contingency.

*When liquidity risk declines . . .*

The current episode of ample liquidity and lower interest rates which has been ideal for risk-seeking investors may change unexpectedly.

Short-term interest rates have been rising in most markets recently and capital costs are no longer so favourable. The Icelandic banks are better equipped for such a reversal than a year ago, because experience has taught them to extend and disperse their borrowing, and build up substantial liquid reserves in foreign currency. In 2006 the spotlight was on the banks' liquidity risk. Now that this risk has ebbed, the focus has shifted to credit risk and the potential impact of higher interest rates and a depreciation of the krona.

*. . . the spotlight moves onto credit risk, . . .*

Amidst the turbulence of 2006, the banks slowed down their credit growth and expansion of their balance sheets. No major foreign financial companies were acquired and equity exposures were reduced. Nonetheless, it is natural to consider their credit risk and vulnerability towards a fall in asset prices.

Icelandic households' debts with credit institutions have soared in recent years, especially average-income and young households. Debt service has not risen by the same proportion, due to rising incomes and easier credit terms, and arrears are at a low. However, some borrowers have stretched their capacity to the limit and the most indebted group has seen its debt grow substantially as a proportion of income and assets in recent years. Conditions will not need to change much to cause them serious difficulties. The bulk of household debt is in the form of CPI-indexed mortgage loans, making low inflation critical. Household debt in foreign currency was very low, but has been increasing. High levels of foreign currency-denominated debt could prove questionable for households with no income in foreign currency. Since house prices are currently buoyant, they are likely to rise by less than general inflation or even fall in nominal terms. Household equity could shrink under such conditions.

Business profitability appears to have been strong in 2006, in spite of a massive increase in financial expenses from exchange rate losses on foreign borrowing, higher interest expenses and a substantial increase in interest-bearing debt. Debt of listed companies grew as a ratio of equity and the same is probably true of other businesses. Higher debt levels leave them more vulnerable to a contraction in the economy.

Equity prices have soared in Iceland in recent years, One explanation for the increase may be that Icelandic companies were undervalued by the markets, for example by international comparison, and another that bold investment ventures have driven up their value. But risk and high yield often go hand in hand and it must be assumed that equity prices can fall just as easily as rise.

The Central Bank has assessed the banks' credit portfolio quality on the basis of geographical and sectoral distribution. It is no longer enough to focus solely on activities in Iceland, because three-quarters of the banks' total lending on a consolidated basis was to non-residents, especially in the other Nordic countries and the UK. The assessment indicates that the banks' loss provisioning is more than adequate to meet expected losses. However, this view must be tempered by hefty credit growth in recent years and the large increase in leveraged buyouts and forward contracts connected with them. House prices are at a historical peak in real terms and may unwind. Equity prices reflect expectations of ongoing rapid output growth, but such sentiment can quickly reverse, as recent experience has shown. Arrears and impairment are minimal, but both may be expected to increase in the coming years.

*. . . interest rates . . .*

One major vulnerability of the Icelandic economy at present is the risk of a rapid and unforeseen rise in international interest rates and premia. Short-term rates have already risen widely and may go up further. Long-term rates have not changed much but could begin to climb. Premia are prone to change at short notice due to shifts in investors' risk assessments or risk-seeking.

*. . . and the exchange rate*

The Icelandic economy has never been so sensitive to changes in global markets, which could significantly affect it. It is critical to achieve some redress of imbalances before external conditions tighten.

Strange as it may sound, the banks' efforts to hedge against the effect of a conceivable depreciation of the krona on their equity ratios has increased the market risk on their foreign exchange exposures. Credit institutions fulfil the Central Bank's rules on foreign exchange balance, but have been permitted to maintain separate additional currency balances. Thus the banks' capital positions are well hedged against a conceivable depreciation of the krona, but a short-term appreciation cannot be ruled out. The banks' customers, on the other hand, are less protected against shocks from a depreciation, although data from the banks show that borrowers of the bulk of foreign currency-denominated loans also have substantial currency earnings and thereby a natural hedge against exchange rate movements.

*The worst-case scenario*

*Financial Stability* 2006 reported on a Central Bank stress test of the impact of a serious shock involving a simultaneous large rise in global interest rates, depreciation of the krona and fall in asset prices. This simulation has now been repeated using new data and assuming an even larger depreciation and decrease in house prices. Were all these shocks to coincide, estimates show that the contraction in national expenditure could prove considerably greater than in the Central Bank's most recent macroeconomic forecast in *Monetary Bulletin* in March 2007. The pressure on the financial sector will be determined to some extent by the pace of the adjustment and the banks' own responses to it. Although the adjustment would ultimately be greater if it occurred slowly, a very rapid contraction would deliver such a jolt to the finances of many households and businesses that loan losses would result.

*Risks are present . . .*

It is likely that a range of risks will have to be faced, but efforts must be made to minimize the probability of a financial crisis that could harm potential output and living standards. In the final analysis, the critical factor is how strong and well equipped the financial system is to withstand shocks, i.e. its resilience.

*. . . but resilience has grown*

The crucial factor behind the Central Bank's assessment that the financial system is now more resilient to shocks is the banks' stronger liquidity and equity positions than a year ago. The major commercial banks have a diversified income base that extends to many countries. Another advantage is the somewhat different business models they have used in their expansion. Their diversified assets give less reason to fear the consequences of an unexpected strain on the financial system.

Iceland's strong fiscal position underpins the banks' international credit ratings. Other important factors have been the strengthening of Iceland's foreign reserves and the Central Bank's capital. Both measures represent natural responses to changes caused in the Central Bank's operating environment by the very rapid expansion of the commercial banks, especially abroad.

Although the main function of a financial stability report is to highlight risks, factors conducive to strengthening the long-term economic outlook should also be duly noted. Iceland's economy is advanced, transparent and dynamic. The population is relatively young, well educated and quick to adapt to technological and scientific innovations. A strong fully funded pension system has been built up and, unlike other countries, there is no reason to fear for its sustainability. GDP per capita ranks with the highest in the world, and the economic and social infrastructure is solid. The openness of the economy results in a smaller effect from a contraction in domestic demand on employment than might be expected.

*Institutional framework and supervision are also important*

The authorities shape the framework in which businesses and the financial system operate. Through its membership of the European Economic Area, Iceland enjoys similar operating conditions to those within the European Union. Nonetheless, it retains various features that influence economic advancement, such as a rather business-friendly tax environment, efficient public administration and flexible labour market. Extensive and rapid transformation of the financial sector puts supervisory agencies under pressure. The Financial Supervisory Authority (FME) has been granted an increasingly wide remit in recent years and its activities have been strengthened. One task is to monitor the banks' transactions with major shareholders and executives.

Payment and settlement systems are a key component of an efficient and sound financial system. Steps have recently been completed towards bringing their regulatory framework into line with international best practice. Although such work tends to go relatively unnoticed, it is crucial for enhancing security of settlements and reducing technical risks.

*The financial system is broadly sound*

The main financial sector vulnerabilities are presented in Table 6.1. The first three relate to macroeconomic imbalances that could cause a further widening of the current account deficit, higher external debt and a depreciation of the krona. Vulnerability on these counts is no less than a year ago, and higher global interest rates and premia could have widespread repercussions. On the other hand, much of the uncertainty about the banks' access to financing has been dispelled and they have built up ample liquid reserves. Under such conditions, the focus shifts to asset quality. Table 6.2 highlights factors that contribute to financial system resilience. The most noteworthy development is the banks' stronger position in the form of ample liquidity and capital adequacy ratios which are very comfortable and historically high.

*Table 6.1* Main vulnerabilities

| ***Risk*** | ***Explanation*** |
|---|---|
| Exchange rate development | Macroeconomic imbalances are pronounced. The current account deficit poses the risk of a depreciation of the krona. Shifts in carry trades and other exposures could catalyse a sudden turnaround. The FX market relies on three market makers and is still relatively thin. Some borrowers from the commercial banks have little or no hedge against exchange rate movements |
| Global interest rates and premia | In recent years, interest rates and premia have been at a historical low. Interest rates have begun to climb and sooner or later premia will rise again, increasing corporate financing costs |
| Terms of trade | Export prices could drop and oil prices rise. Unfavourable developments could widen the current account deficit and erode national income. The Central Bank's macroeconomic forecast assumes a deterioration in the terms of trade |
| International market funding | High dependence on market funding and deposits on call makes credit ratings and global market conditions crucial for the commercial banks. Experience shows that credit assessment can shift suddenly |
| Asset quality of commercial banks | Rapid credit growth often eventually leads to poorer loan quality, Loans with equities as collateral are substantial. Prices of equities and real estate are buoyant. Although arrears and impairment are at a low, they are unlikely to remain so over the next few years |

On the whole, the Central Bank's finding is that the financial system is broadly sound. It is equipped to withstand shocks to the economy and financial markets, to mediate credit and payments, and to redistribute risks appropriately. In other words, it is capable of performing its function in an orderly and efficient way. Iceland's banking system meets the demands made of it and performs well on stress tests conducted by the Central Bank and FME.

*Table 6.2* Resilience

| ***Resilience*** | ***Explanation*** |
|---|---|
| Economy | The economy is flexible and in the past has shown itself capable of tackling cyclical swings through adjustment of imports. Investment and output growth have been robust. The long-term economic outlook is favourable |
| Strength of the commercial banks | The commercial banks' liquidity and capital ratios have never been higher. They have built up liquidity in foreign currency and secured refinancing into 2008. Profitability is strong from the banks' diverse operations and assets are diversified |
| Institutional and supervisory framework | Iceland's framework is the EEA Agreement and its guidelines are international best practice and transparency. Economic and social infrastructure is sound. Financial supervision has been boosted and extensive cross-border cooperation is in place |
| Payment and settlement systems | Payment system infrastructure is largely electronic and efficient. Steps have been taken to enhance security and contingency plans. Systems meet international standards |
| Fiscal position | The Treasury's position is strong with consecutive fiscal surpluses. Net external Treasury debt, including foreign reserves, is virtually zero. No pension gap is foreseeable |

## The Central Bank's assessment – 2008

### Current conditions test the banks' resilience

In the analysis published in *Financial Stability* 2007, the Central Bank of Iceland concluded that the financial system was broadly sound. That has not changed.

The chain of events that began in mid-2007 and its effect on the global financial markets were quite unexpected. Risk appetite yielded to risk aversion, and there is no end in sight to the uncertainty that surfaced as a liquidity squeeze and broad-based concerns about the economic outlook. The Central Bank did not expect the heavy weather to turn into the tempest that ensued; however, in *Financial Stability* 2007 the Bank warned that challenging waters lay ahead. The report states as follows:

> The Central Bank underlines that global market conditions can take a sudden turn for the worse and it is important to be on the alert and prepared for such a contingency. The current episode of ample liquidity and lower interest rates which has been ideal for risk-seeking investors may change unexpectedly.

It goes on to state: 'One major vulnerability of the Icelandic economy at present is the risk of a rapid and unforeseen rise in international interest rates and premia.'

These projections have now materialized. The present report attempts to evaluate the strength of the financial system under the currently reigning conditions.

*Tighter global credit markets . . .*

The changes in the global credit market can be traced to the United States, but the roots of the problem are deeper and extend to a broader area. Over the past several years, a segment of the housing loan market had developed in the US, focusing on borrowers with extremely limited capacity to pay: the so-called sub-prime market. Financial institutions used the majority of sub-prime loans to create structured securities, adding to them loans with a much higher credit rating – including bond issues from the Icelandic banks – and overall, the structures received good credit ratings. When delinquency began to rise on housing loans in the US and real estate prices to drop, these structures began selling at discounts. As a result, rating agencies lowered the credit ratings on many of them. When investors attempted to reduce their positions in structured instruments, the secondary market dried up. Icelandic banks invested very little in these securities but have nonetheless been indirectly affected by their fate.

Losses on these and other risky investments have been a heavy burden for a number of banks in the US and Europe. Uncertainty concerning the extent to which banks had invested in them pressed interbank interest rates sharply upwards. The supply of short-term credit contracted markedly because banks squirreled away liquid assets and mistrusted one another as counterparties. A number of banks have been forced to write off enormous losses, which has undermined their capital position. Many of them have had to obtain new capital as well, and it is likely that other banks will follow suit.

As a result of the liquidity crisis in the global inter-bank market during the autumn of 2007, central banks in the United States, Europe and the United Kingdom adopted a variety of measures in order to provide their banks with short-term credit. In addition, governments on both sides of the Atlantic have directly or indirectly lent support to individual financial institutions and guaranteed their deposits over and above the protection provided by guarantee funds.

*. . . puts the banks' resilience to the test*

The 2007 annual accounts of Iceland's financial companies, particularly the three largest banks, show that they remain robust. Their capital position, profitability and liquidity are sound, as is confirmed by the stress tests conducted by the Financial Supervisory Authority (FME) and the Central Bank. Their interim accounts for the first quarter of 2008 bear out this assessment. Because they owned ample foreign currency, they did not suffer losses because of the depreciation of the Icelandic krona in the early months of the year; in fact, they gained on it.

Roughly half of the banking groups' combined assets are in foreign subsidiaries, and a large proportion of the parent banks' lending is to non-residents. It is considered advantageous that the banks' portfolios and funding be well diversified. The largest banks in Iceland have greatly expanded their overseas activities in the past few years. They are European banks no less than Icelandic, and they comply with the regulatory framework governing banks in Europe. Their income is diverse and well distributed geographically. Together, the three largest banks now generate more than half of their income from operations outside Iceland. It is also to their advantage that they have used different business models in their expansion. Their portfolios and funding derive largely from Western Europe and North America.

In many ways, Iceland's banks were well prepared to face the liquidity crisis that emerged in 2007 and its impact on their regions of operation. To some extent, this preparedness can be attributed to their response to the headwinds they faced early in 2006, though that problem was not an international one. Now they must deal with reduced asset prices, increased cost of capital, and limited access to foreign credit markets.

This report discusses in depth the position, risk, funding, and resilience of the Icelandic banks. Also included is an analysis of the banks' loan portfolio quality based on the banking groups' lending activity;

that is, a risk classification of resident and non-resident borrowers, an estimate of expected and unexpected loss. The results of the analysis indicate that the banks are well prepared to withstand increased delinquency and loan losses, which have been extremely low to date. It is necessary, however, to point out risk factors that could prove challenging under the conditions that may be in the offing. In 2007 the banks' large exposures increased as a proportion of capital, as did the proportion of holding companies among borrowers. There is good reason to monitor this development. A considerable number of loans are still secured by equities, and the value of that collateral has dropped in the recent term. There have been few forced sales due to margin calls, however, and the banks' margining levels are ample, according to data from the FME.

*Economic adjustment proves burdensome for household and business balance sheets . . .*

The conditions in the banks' principal market areas are satisfactory, but uncertainty has mounted. Lending to Icelandic residents constitutes a smaller part of financial institutions' loan portfolios than it did several years ago but remains an important part of lending activity. Economic developments and changes in asset values will affect the quality of these portfolios. The economic imbalances that have been discussed in *Financial Stability* in recent years have now led to a sharp depreciation of the krona, among other developments. This weakens the balance sheets of those households and businesses which have stepped up their borrowing in recent years and taken on foreign exchange risk as well. High inflation makes it more problematic than otherwise to battle the economic contraction that inevitably accompanies a strong downturn in asset markets. This is why it is critical that the Central Bank attain the inflation target as soon as may be, so as to build confidence in the krona.

Increased foreign exchange risk among households and businesses without foreign-currency income is food for thought, as is the growing share of loans to indebted holding companies. Nonetheless, foreign-denominated household debt constitutes only a small proportion of total household debt, and the bulk of foreign-currency loans have been granted to borrowers with sizeable foreign-currency income. These borrowers will be less hard hit by the drop in the exchange rate, but those not protected by foreign-currency income will be more vulnerable, and the problem is compounded by a simultaneous decline in the market value of the assets used to secure collateralized loans. It is very important, however, that the loan-to-value ratios for banks' housing loans dropped year-on-year and are acceptable from the standpoint of financial stability.

Despite the accumulation of debt, households' net position has improved in recent years. On the whole, the debt burden is quite manageable if disposable income does not fall too sharply. However, many households will be faced with an uphill climb over the next few years. Among the most indebted households, the level of debt has increased far in excess of the average, and these households could find themselves in financial difficulties as a result. Many indicators suggest that house prices are far above long-term equilibrium; therefore, the price of residential and commercial housing can be expected to fall in real terms over the next few years as the cost of capital increases. Turnover in the housing market has contracted rapidly in the recent term, and real prices have begun to fall.

Businesses now feel the effects of increased cost of capital, which weakens their position and forces them to adapt their activities to the banks' increased restraint in granting credit. To some extent, the financial institutions' higher cost of capital has already begun to affect businesses and households adversely. Although financial institutions can thereby recover a portion of their expense and reduce their operating costs, this inevitably undermines their competitive position, especially in foreign markets.

*. . . the banks respond . . .*

Under normal conditions, a bank with a satisfactory capital position should not have difficulty funding its activities. Because of uncertainty and risk aversion, however, access to capital has become more limited and credit ratings have suffered. These conditions affect the Icelandic banks more than they might otherwise because foreign market funding constitutes a relatively large share of their debt. Extensive foreign funding requires an excellent credit rating and a sound reputation. Since the autumn of 2007, the banks have avoided public issues on foreign credit markets and sought other avenues for funding.

They have responded to the tight credit market by slowing their lending growth, engaging in private issues, strengthening their deposit business, and reducing costs. For example, plans to acquire foreign financial institutions have been abandoned, and asset financing and mortgage lending operations abroad have been divested so as to free up capital for other uses. In general, the banks have been successful at increasing deposits, and at year-end 2007 more than two-thirds of the three main commercial banks' deposits were from non-residents. Various market areas have seen moderate fluctuations in deposits. The banks' CDS spreads dropped significantly in April, after rising sharply toward the end of 2007 and early in 2008.

For the short term, the banks' most critical task is to gain better access to foreign credit and reduce their borrowing requirement. The confidence of investors and depositors is also vital to their success. It is unlikely that conditions in the international markets will improve to any dramatic extent in the near future, and when they do, investors will undoubtedly demonstrate more caution and conservatism than they did previously.

*. . . and public authorities strengthen their preparedness*

In the past several years, public authorities in Iceland – that is, the Government, the Financial Supervisory Authority, and the Central Bank – have strengthened their collaboration in contingency affairs. They also engage in broader international cooperation, including participation in a Nordic-Baltic contingency exercise held in September 2007 and participation in EU financial stability committees.[1]

European authorities have sharpened their focus on preparation for the situations that could arise in financial undertakings with cross-border operations. An example of this is the newly concluded agreement among the ministries of finance, financial supervisory authorities, and central banks of the EU nations. Such cooperative work is extremely important, especially for smaller countries where large banks have their headquarters.

Through its membership to the EEA, Iceland enjoys operating conditions similar to those within the EU. Nonetheless, it retains various features that influence economic advancement, such as a rather business-friendly tax environment, efficient public administration, and a flexible labour market. Surveillance and monitoring are of considerable importance, and the Financial Supervisory Authority has been strengthened. Iceland's payment and settlement systems have been bolstered as well, so that the risk of shocks of technical origin is at a minimum, and counterparty risk has been eliminated.

The strong position of the Treasury is of paramount importance. There have been budgetary surpluses in recent years, and the Treasury's deposits in the Central Bank are sizeable. Net external Treasury debt, including foreign reserves, is non-existent. The foreign reserves were doubled in 2006 and the Central Bank's capital position was strengthened, which is quite fortunate in the current circumstances, and the government has expressed its willingness to strengthen them still further. However, it is critical not to create a moral hazard in the process.

Critics have asserted that the Icelandic banks have grown too large. This might be true if a major financial crisis were imminent and the Icelandic government were forced to resolve a critical situation affecting banking operations both in Iceland and abroad. In other respects, however, it should not cause difficulty if companies choose the operational arena that suits them and where they enjoy comparative advantage – for example, Iceland's fishing and aluminium industries, whose domestic operations far outstrip the needs of the country. Iceland is a full participant in the internal market of the EU, including the internal market for financial services. Ever since 1992, when the policy was formulated concerning the internal market for products, services, capital and labour, the objective has been to ensure that it functions as a single unit. There has been encouragement to engage in cross-border trade and enhance cross-border operations. Nowhere has it been suggested that the banking systems of individual countries should be subjected to size limitations, and protests have been made against preventing foreign investors from acquiring domestic banks. There are examples of countries whose banks are largely headquartered abroad – for instance, the Baltic nations – and of the reverse, countries whose domestic banks are active in other markets – such as Iceland, Luxembourg, Holland, Great Britain, Denmark and Ireland.

*The financial system is sound, but contingency plans are necessary*

The main financial system vulnerabilities are presented in Table 6.3. They centre on a sensitive foreign exchange market and limited access to capital, which implies short-term risk. For the longer term, vulnerabilities centre rather on the effects of higher cost of capital and the risk of diminished asset quality.

In the final analysis, the critical factor is how strong and well equipped the financial system is to withstand shocks, i.e. its resilience. Table 6.4 highlights factors that contribute to financial system resilience. These are a positive long-term economic outlook, a satisfactory position among the banks, a sound institutional and supervisory framework, and secure payment and settlement systems, as well as a financially strong Treasury. These same factors were specified in the last issue of *Financial Stability*, but the banks' position has weakened since then, especially because of the contraction in global credit supply.

Many of the factors that were considered cause for concern in that report have materialized, such as a depreciation of the krona, falling

*Table 6.3* Main vulnerabilities

| ***Risk*** | ***Explanation*** |
|---|---|
| Foreign exchange market | The current account deficit, and possible changes in carry trade, entail the risk of volatility. and depreciation beyond that already experienced. The FX market is both a spot market and a swap market. It relies on three market makers and is relatively thin. The banks themselves are well protected against depreciation of the krona, but some of their borrowers have little or no protection against exchange rate fluctuation |
| Access to capital | High dependence on market funding and deposits on call makes credit ratings and global market conditions crucial for the commercial banks. The banks have responded to changed conditions and must continue to do so. Access to capital is more limited than before, and credit ratings have been lowered |
| Cost of capital | Significant increase in risk premia reduces output growth and widens the current account deficit. Businesses' higher cost of capital undermines their competitive position and increases customers' debt service burden |
| Asset quality of commercial banks | Prices of equities and real estate have fallen Increasing write-offs of loans and other assets can be expected. Default and impairment were at a minimum at year-end 2007 but will inevitably increase in the near future |

stock prices, a cooling real estate market, rising interest rate premia, and others. It is likely that a range of risks will have to be faced, but efforts must be made to minimize the probability of a financial crisis that could harm potential output and erode living standards, The experience of other countries shows how important this is.

On the whole, the Central Bank's finding is still that the financial system is broadly sound. Iceland's banking system meets the demands made of it, and it performs well on stress tests conducted by the Central Bank and FME.

*Table 6.4* Resilience

| ***Resilience*** | ***Explanation*** |
|---|---|
| Economy | The economy is flexible and, in the past, has shown itself capable of tackling cyclical swings through prompt adjustment of imports and private consumption. Investment and output growth have been robust, and the long-term economic outlook is favourable |
| Strength of the commercial banks | The banks' capital ratios are satisfactory, profitability is strong from broad-based operations, and assets are diversified. Their liquidity has been ample but will be put to the test in 2008 |
| Institutional and supervisory framework and payment systems | Iceland's framework is the EEA Agreement, and its guidelines are international best practice and transparency, Financial supervision has been boosted, and extensive cross-border cooperation is in place. Payment systems meet internationally recognized standards |
| Fiscal position | The Treasury's position is strong, with consecutive fiscal surpluses. Net external Treasury debt, including foreign reserves, is non-existent |

## Note

1. Among the documents on the Central Bank of Iceland website are the Memorandum of Understanding among the Icelandic public authorities, the Memorandum of Understanding among the Nordic central banks (as well as a joint press release from the banks), and an Appendix on cooperation by government authorities, which appeared in *Financial Stability* 2006.

# Part II
# Other Reports

# 7

# Iceland – Macro Imbalances Trigger Negative Outlook

*Fitch Ratings*

Fitch has revised the outlooks on Iceland's long-term sovereign ratings to negative from stable. This rating action reflects the agency's view that there has been a material deterioration in Iceland's macro-prudential risk indicators, accompanied by a greater than expected deterioration in the current account balance and soaring net external indebtedness.

Fitch acknowledges that the growing globalization of Icelandic banks and corporates is a natural development for a small developed economy. But the agency is concerned that the associated rise in net external indebtedness has reached unprecedented proportions and has occurred in the context of clear signs of domestic credit and asset price bubbles.

Given the magnitude of Iceland's macro imbalances, the risks of a 'hard landing' have increased in Fitch's view, raising concerns about how well the broader financial system would cope in such a scenario and the likely fall-out for the sovereign. Public debt is low, but other sectors of the economy are heavily indebted and vulnerable to shifts in asset prices and the exchange rate, while Icelandic banks fund themselves primarily in investor-sensitive international capital and inter-bank markets.

Iceland's experience with a floating exchange rate and inflation targeting is still a fairly short one, while systematic coordination of monetary and fiscal policies has tended to be weak, heightening the risk of a hard landing once the current imbalances start to unwind. To date, the authorities have been content to let monetary policy take the strain – notwithstanding some increasingly apparent limitations – while fiscal policy has imparted a more benign message.

Iceland's public debt ratios are in line with 'AA' medians and net public external debt has come down to less than half its 2002 peak of 70 per cent of current external receipts. Nonetheless, Fitch says that one of the most important lessons to come out of the Asia crisis was that countries with seemingly sound public finances ignore private sector imbalances at their peril. Iceland's largely bank-related net external debt is close to being the highest of any Fitch rated sovereign, while its external liquidity position is among the weakest.

While noting that other comparably rated countries like Australia and New Zealand display similar, albeit less extreme, external imbalances to Iceland, Fitch argues that the structure and hedging characteristics of these countries' external indebtedness are much better documented than in Iceland. Moreover, whereas the Australian and New Zealand economies have been successfully stress tested over a long period of time, Iceland has yet to establish a similar track record in more indebted circumstances.

## Rationale

Fitch has revised the outlooks on Iceland's long-term sovereign ratings from stable to negative. This negative rating action reflects the agency's view that there has been a material deterioration in Iceland's macro-prudential risk indicators,[1] accompanied by a greater than expected deterioration in the current account deficit and a seemingly relentless rise in net external indebtedness. As such, Fitch believes that the risks of a hard landing have increased, raising concerns about how well the broader financial system would cope in such a scenario and the likely fall-out for the sovereign.

The long-term local and foreign currency ratings are affirmed at 'AAA' and 'AA−' (AA minus) respectively in recognition of the fact that Iceland's economy is much more flexible than it was – thanks to more than a decade of structural reforms – while Iceland's robust public finances are in line with 'AA' medians. Fitch acknowledges that the growing globalization of Icelandic banks and corporates is a natural development for a small developed economy. However, the agency worries that the attendant rise in net external indebtedness has been unprecedented and has occurred in the context of clear signs of domestic credit and asset price bubbles.

## Macroeconomic imbalances

Iceland's economy is in the midst of a supply-side-driven expansion entailing huge investment in the aluminium and associated energy sectors. Over the long term, these projects should broaden the export base, boost foreign exchange earnings and enhance external debt sustainability. In the short term, they pose a considerable challenge to macroeconomic stability, which has been exacerbated by the unexpected shock delivered to the financial markets by the liberalization of the mortgage market in 2004.

As a small, very open economy with a narrow export base, Iceland is not unaccustomed to output volatility, economic overheating and the sharp corrective policy actions that often follow. A similar investment boom in the late 1990s engendered rapid growth and outsize current account deficits, followed by a sharp recession in 2002. While all the signs of overheating – rising inflation, soaring asset prices, a steep current account deficit and escalating external debt – were evident at the time of our last review in August 2005, the rate at which some of the imbalances have deteriorated has gone beyond our expectations as Table 7.1 indicates. Consequently, in Fitch's view, the risk of a sharp and potentially disorderly correction manifesting itself as a 'hard landing' has increased.

Iceland's economy is undoubtedly more resilient to external shocks now than before due to a wave of structural reforms since the 1990s and the adoption of a floating exchange rate in 2001. These changes are cited as a reason why the economy recovered so rapidly from the 2002 recession, although the role of the latest investment boom can hardly be ignored. Moreover, the public finances continue to go from strength to strength with general government debt forecast to decline to 25 per cent of GDP in 2006, compared to a peak of 60 per cent in 1995. However, because of the nature and the magnitude of the current imbalances, there is a question mark over how well the rest of the economy would fare in the event of a hard landing.

Apart from the public sector, all sectors of the economy are significantly indebted, while the growth of lending continues unabated, aided and abetted by corporate expansion abroad and the liberalization of the

*Table 7.1* Iceland: forecasts and outcomes

| | *2005f* | *2005e* | *2006f* |
|---|---|---|---|
| Real GDP growth (% change) | 6.4 | 6.0 | 5.3 |
| Inflation (avg. % change) | 3.8 | 4.4 | 4.8 |
| Current account balance (% of GDP) | –11.8 | –15.0 | –13.6 |
| Net external debt (% CXR) | 367.5 | 442.6 | 455.8 |

*Source*: Fitch.

residential mortgage market in 2004. Among the main areas of concern are:

- Private sector credit increased by an estimated 45 per cent of GDP in 2005 and now stands at over 200 per cent of GDP, a twofold increase in three years;
- Domestic asset prices – property and the stock market – are running far above trend;
- Household indebtedness – mostly housing related and indexed to inflation – exceeds 100 per cent of GDP and 180 per cent of disposable income;
- Corporate debt exceeds 160 per cent of GDP;
- Net external debt, mostly owed by banks, has risen from 243 per cent of current external receipts in 2002 to around 443 per cent in 2005;
- The real effective exchange rate now stands at its highest level since the 1980s, while a record current account deficit heralds sizeable future inflationary pressures;
- With unemployment at near record lows, there are clear signs of growing wage pressures.

## Systemic financial concerns

Some of these factors – above-trend growth rates of lending, asset prices and the real effective exchange rate – feed directly into the macro-prudential indicators (Table 7.2) that Fitch monitors when gauging countries' vulnerability to financial stress. Many of these trends currently flatter Icelandic banks' financial performance and their balance sheets have rarely looked stronger.

By the same token, however, a sudden turn for the worse in the credit cycle, accompanied by a sharp fall in property and equity prices and a rise in unemployment, could have an adverse impact on banks' financial performance. Were such a turn of the credit cycle to be accompanied by

*Table 7.2* Iceland: macro-prudential indicators

| **(% change)** | ***2003*** | ***2004*** | ***2005e*** |
|---|---|---|---|
| Private credit (% GDP) | 135.3 | 173.0 | 218.1 |
| Real exchange rate | 5.5 | 2.6 | 12.7 |
| Real equity prices | 56.2 | 54.6 | 32.1 |
| Real property prices | 9.5 | 9.7 | 34.2 |

*Source*: Fitch.

a sharp fall in the exchange rate and/or a loss of international investor confidence, Fitch fears that Icelandic banks could come under multiple pressures.

A large share of household and corporate debt is price-indexed or exchange rate linked. Residential property lending still only accounts for 10–20 per cent of banks' portfolios, but the banks have relatively large exposures to the small and volatile stock market through a combination of direct equity holdings and collateralized exposure to Icelandic corporates. In addition, over half of banks' lending is denominated in foreign currency, more than 70 per cent of which has been lent to residents, chiefly corporates for onward purchase of overseas assets.

Iceland's narrow deposit base means that banks fund themselves mostly in the international capital markets, chiefly through securities issuance. At the end of 2004, more than 90 per cent of deposit money banks' securities issues was denominated in foreign currency. The short-term component of banks' external liabilities is still relatively low and the average maturity is about three years. Nonetheless, the near-term roll-over risk remains substantial (see Figure 7.1) and a sudden bout of investor unease in the international credit markets could rapidly manifest itself in a sharp rise in the cost of funding.

Both the banks themselves and the Financial Supervisory Authority have conducted stress tests on their balance sheets for interest rate, market and exchange rate risk and appear comfortable with these risks. Banks also point to their growing international diversification as an important line of defence: foreign assets have more than doubled in

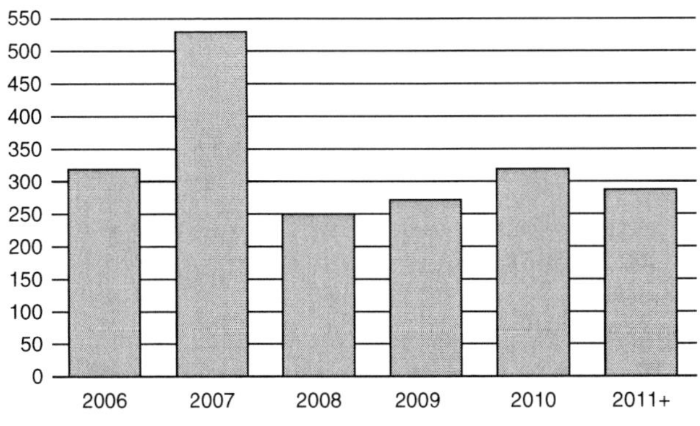


*Figure 7.1* Major banks' refinancing risk: redemption schedule for EMTN issuance (ISKbn)
*Source*: Central Bank of Iceland.

the past year, reflecting overseas acquisitions and higher foreign currency lending, and an increasing proportion of their income is derived from abroad. While these factors provide some comfort, Fitch remains concerned about the magnitude of the exchange rate induced credit risk associated with foreign currency loans to residents, should they turn sour in the face of severe currency volatility.

To be fair, some banks have started to provide details on this aspect of their lending. However, in contrast to Australia and New Zealand – similarly rated sovereigns with high levels of private sector external debt – the Icelandic authorities have yet to compile a detailed macro picture of the foreign currency hedging strategies of private sector borrowers. These comparable rating peers have lived with a floating exchange rate for much longer than Iceland and private sector borrowers within their jurisdiction have become more accustomed to coping with currency volatility. Fitch looks forward to the forthcoming publication of the Central Bank's Financial Stability Report in May to shed further light on its concerns.

## Mixed policy response

Iceland's experience with a floating exchange rate and inflation targeting is still a fairly short one, while systematic coordination of monetary and fiscal policies has tended to be weak, heightening the risk of a hard landing once the current imbalances start to unwind.

Looking at the policy framework in the context of the current economic cycle, the overriding impression is that monetary policy has been left to take the strain, while fiscal policy has delivered a more benign message. The Central Bank of Iceland (CBI) has raised its policy rate 12 times since May 2004, lifting the rate from 5.3 to 10.75 per cent at present. Even so, inflation has remained above the upper bound of the CBI's target range (4 per cent), not least because housing costs form a weighty component of the consumer price index. Moreover, in the current climate of easy access to long-term housing credit at low interest rates, the impact of higher policy rates has been confined almost exclusively to the short end of the yield curve, mainly affecting the money markets and the exchange rate.

While the CBI has effectively been reduced to relying upon a stronger exchange rate to deliver monetary tightening and lower inflation, it can hardly remain indifferent to the fact that the current account deficit has widened to a record 15–16 per cent of GDP in 2005. Some of this deterioration was to be expected on the back of the investment boom.

However, a combination of robust lending, wage drift, tax cuts and the highest real exchange rate since the 1980s have fed domestic demand to the point where the CBI now believes that excessive consumption may account for up to half the current account deficit.

This development is potentially alarming on a number of counts. First, it suggests that the current account deficit will not be self-correcting once the investment boom starts to unwind. Second, with the strong real exchange rate feeding imports and constraining exports, the smooth transition which the authorities envisage from falling domestic demand to more robust net exports seems less likely to materialize, accentuating the risk of a hard landing and a steep fall in the currency. Yet the CBI has few other tools in its armoury beyond higher interest rates, while modest international reserves limit its ability to support the currency.

The government's more benign stance rests on its view that the current imbalances are private sector driven and will be self-correcting over time. As such, it continues to budget for small surpluses over the course of the economic cycle and remains committed to its campaign promise of tax cuts through 2006–7. Such adjustments as the authorities have been prepared to make have fallen on public investment but with municipal elections this year and a general election in 2007, some relaxation of expenditure would not be unexpected.

This is not to say that there has been no fiscal tightening – the general government balance has swung from a deficit of 2.1 per cent of GDP in 2003 to a surplus of 3.3 per cent in 2005, aided by the automatic stabilizers – but the overall policy message has been less austere than the current situation would seem to warrant. Thus, IMF estimates suggest that the original policy settings for 2005 implied a small cyclically adjusted deficit, while the expected headline general government surplus for 2006 is budgeted to come in much lower at 1.1 per cent of GDP.

## Rating implications

In pure public finance terms it is not hard to make the case for Iceland's long-term ratings of 'AAA' (local currency) and 'AA–' (AA minus) (foreign currency). Fiscal consolidation has set general government debt on a declining trend since the mid-1990s and it is set to fall to 25 per cent of GDP, further aided by one-off revenues from the sale of Iceland Telecom. As Figure 7.2 shows, this ratio is close to the 'AA' median. Externally, the government has been prepaying debt and net public external debt is forecast to fall to 29 per cent of current external receipts

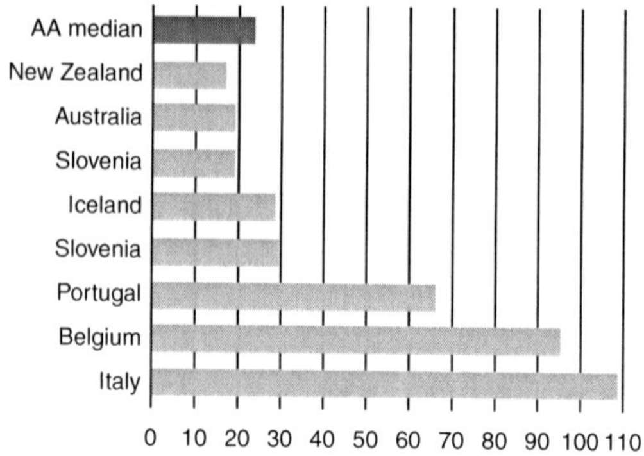


*Figure 7.2* General government debt (% of GPD, 2005e)
*Source*: Fitch.

in 2006 compared to 70 per cent in 2002. In short, the public sector's solvency is not in doubt and it is well placed to ride out an economic hard landing.

That said, one of the most important lessons to come out of the Asia crisis was that countries with seemingly sound public finances ignore private sector imbalances at their peril. Thus, Korea, a similarly rated sovereign to Iceland on the eve of the crisis, rapidly discovered that it was not immune to broader external liquidity and solvency concerns rooted in the financial system and the corporate sector. In other words, country risk matters and contingent liabilities invariably come home to roost on the public sector's balance sheet.

The speed with which the current account balance adjusted in 2001–2 – moving from a deficit of 4.5 per cent to a surplus of 1.4 per cent of GDP – highlighted that the economy has become more flexible. However, the imbalances are much greater now. Moreover, with bank credit to the private sector running at more than 200 per cent of GDP, the externalities of an Icelandic bank failure, however remote, would be severe and it is hard to see how the authorities could avoid becoming involved.

Iceland is a much wealthier and more open economy than Korea, the financial system is much stronger and transparency is infinitely greater. Nonetheless, as a rating agency it is impossible for us to ignore the seemingly relentless rise in Iceland's external debt ratios and its comparatively weak external liquidity position. Moreover, as aforementioned, the debt ratios have deteriorated faster than we anticipated in our 2005 review. At over 400 per cent of current external receipts, Iceland's net

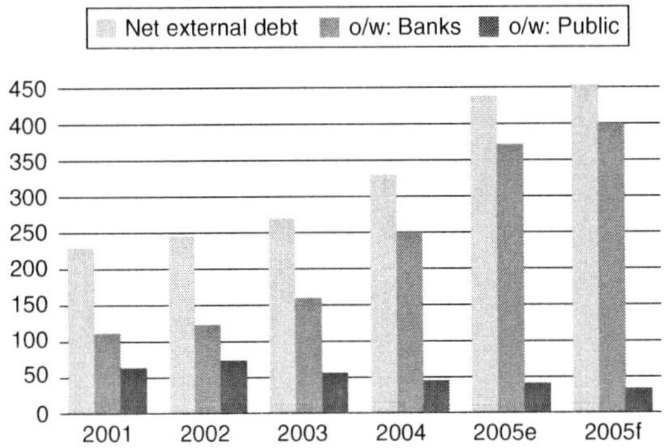


*Figure 7.3* Iceland: net external debt (% of CXR)
*Source*: Fitch.

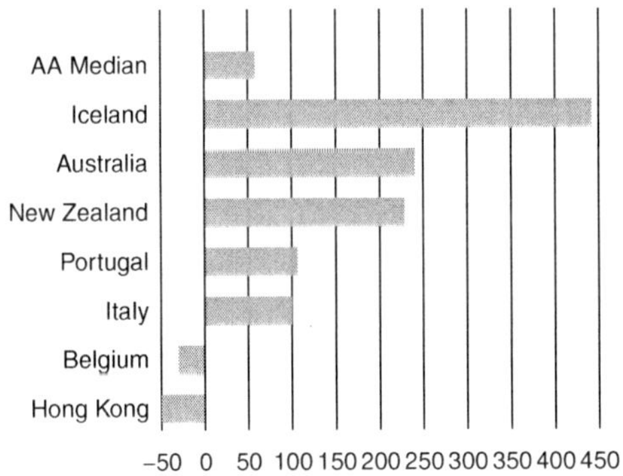


*Figure 7.4* Net external debt (% of current external receipts, 2005e)
*Source*: Fitch.

external debt is higher than virtually any other Fitch rated sovereign and essentially in uncharted territory (Figure 7.3).

Admittedly, there are other outliers in the 'AA' rating category, notably Australia and New Zealand, but Iceland's net external debt ratio now goes far beyond these (see Figure 7.4), and a somewhat higher external liquidity ratio hardly compensates for this differential. A common phenomenon in all three cases has been the role of the banks in elevating external indebtedness. However, in the case of Iceland the increase in banks' external exposure has been staggering, with gross external indebtedness doubling in every year since 2003. Moreover, whereas the Australian and New Zealand economies have been successfully stress

*Table 7.3* Balance of payments (USDm)

| | *2000* | *2001* | *2002* | *2003* | *2004* | *2005e* | *2006f* | *2007f* |
|---|---|---|---|---|---|---|---|---|
| **Current account balance** | **–881** | **–346** | **117** | **–526** | **–1053** | **–2421** | **–2433** | **–1371** |
| % of GDP % of CXR | *–10.4* | *–4.5* | *1.4* | *–5.0* | *–8.4* | *–15.0* | *–13.6* | *–7.6* |
| | *28.7* | *–10.6* | *3.2* | *–12.7* | *–20.6* | *–42.3* | *–37.0* | *–19.7* |
| **Trade balance** | **–477** | **–61** | **154** | **–207** | **–521** | **–1 293** | **–1 215** | **–549** |
| Exports, FOB (annual % change) | 1 899 | 2 018 | 2 229 | 2 380 | 2 883 | 3 045 | 3 376 | 3 595 |
| | 5.2 | 6.3 | 10.5 | 6.8 | 21.1 | 5.6 | 10.9 | 6.5 |
| Imports, FOB (annual % change) | 2 375 | 2 079 | 2 075 | 2 587 | 3 404 | 4 337 | 4 591 | 4 144 |
| | 2.7 | –12.5 | –0.2 | 24.7 | 31.6 | 27.4 | 5.8 | –9.7 |
| **Services, net** | **–148** | **–16** | **–4** | **–121** | **–208** | **–619** | **–569** | **–206** |
| Services, credit | 1 021 | 1 055 | 1 108 | 1 376 | 1 620 | 1 711 | 1 897 | 2 020 |
| Services, debit | 1 169 | 1 071 | 1 112 | 1 497 | 1 828 | 2 330 | 2 466 | 2 226 |
| **Income,** Net Income, Credit | **–247** | **–260** | **–45** | **–183** | **–308** | **–489** | **–629** | **–595** |
| Income, Debit o/w: Interest | 148 | 174 | 296 | 370 | 587 | 952 | 1 280 | 1 333 |
| Payments | 394 | 433 | 342 | 553 | 894 | 1 441 | 1 909 | 1 928 |
| | 364 | 424 | 374 | 409 | 502 | 809 | 1 071 | 1 082 |
| **Current transfers, net** | **–10** | **–10** | **13** | **–15** | **–17** | **–21** | **–21** | **–21** |
| **Capital and financial account, net** | **–3** | **4** | **–1** | **–5** | **–3** | **–6** | **–6** | **–6** |
| **Non-debt creating flows, net** | **–912** | **–135** | **–525** | **–677** | **–3 056** | **–4 950** | **–3 960** | **–2 889** |
| Direct investment, net portfolio equity | –217 | –114 | –293 | –74 | –2 314 | –4 000 | –3 000 | –2 000 |
| Investment, net | –695 | –21 | –232 | –603 | –742 | –950 | –960 | –889 |
| **External borrowing, net** | **1833** | **840** | **895** | **3 324** | **8 740** | **13 750** | **9 350** | **6 000** |
| **Net lending abroad** | **–44** | **–476** | **–320** | **–2 135** | **–3 525** | **–6 000** | **–3 000** | **–1 500** |
| **Net errors and omissions** | **–67** | **65** | **–105** | **325** | **–900** | **–400** | **0** | **0** |
| **Overall balance = change in reserves** | **–74** | **–49** | **62** | **305** | **203** | **–27** | **–50** | **234** |
| **Memo** | 2 737 | 2 078 | 2 226 | 4 929 | 10 531 | 15 782 | 12 498 | 9 656 |
| Gross borrowing (incl. short-term) gross | 1 786 | 1 585 | 1 214 | 2 131 | 2 844 | 4 452 | 5 581 | 5 027 |
| External financing requirement as % of official | 361.0 | 391.3 | 341.5 | 461.7 | 347.3 | 414.5 | 530.6 | 501.3 |
| Reserves stock of international reserves, excl. gold | 389 | 338 | 440 | 792 | 1 046 | 1 019 | 969 | 1 203 |

*Source*: Central Bank of Iceland, Fitch estimates and forecasts.

*Table 7.4* External debt and liquidity (USDm)

| | *2000* | *2001* | *2002* | *2003* | *2004* | *2005e* | *2006f* | *2007f* |
|---|---|---|---|---|---|---|---|---|
| **Gross external debt** | **8 544** | **9 099** | **11 135** | **16 265** | **26 645** | **41 281** | **47 955** | **51 178** |
| % of GDP % of CXR | 101.5 | 118.2 | 130.5 | 153.8 | 211.3 | 255.7 | 267.7 | 283.9 |
| | 281.3 | 279.6 | 303.5 | 393.0 | 522.1 | 721.4 | 730.0 | 734.8 |
| **By maturity** | 7 253 | 7 555 | 8 760 | 12 790 | 21 782 | 33 019 | 38 085 | 40 510 |
| Medium- and long-term | 1 391 | 1 544 | 2 375 | 3 475 | 4 863 | 8 263 | 9 870 | 10 668 |
| Short-term % total debt | 16.1 | 17.0 | 21.3 | 21.4 | 18.3 | 20.0 | 20.6 | 20.8 |
| **By debtor** | 2 168 | 2 475 | 3 025 | 3 012 | 3 373 | 3 350 | 3 171 | 3 008 |
| Public sector non-bank | 2 309 | 2 534 | 2 485 | 3 060 | 3 283 | 3 265 | 3 125 | 3 022 |
| Private sector banks | 4 167 | 4 090 | 5 625 | 10 193 | 19 989 | 34 666 | 41 659 | 45 148 |
| **Gross external assets** | 405 | 355 | 462 | 819 | 1 074 | 1 052 | 1 003 | 1 236 |
| International reserves, incl. gold deposit money | 266 | 324 | 1 491 | 1 593 | 2 857 | 6 000 | 6 500 | 7 500 |
| Banks' foreign assets non-bank private sector's foreign assets | 453 | 779 | 608 | 666 | 1 346 | 1 812 | 2 046 | 2 162 |
| **Net external debt** | **7 519** | **7 504** | **8 930** | **11 223** | **16 985** | **25 327** | **29 941** | **32 325** |
| % of GDP % of CXR | 88.3 | 97.5 | 104.6 | 106.1 | 134.7 | 156.9 | 167.1 | 179.3 |
| | 244.7 | 230.6 | 243.4 | 271.2 | 332.8 | 442.6 | 455.8 | 464.1 |
| **Debt service (principal and interest)** debt | **1 269** | **1 663** | **1 705** | **2 014** | **2 292** | **2 840** | **4 219** | **4 738** |
| Service (% of CXR) interest service (% of CXR) | 41.3 | 51.1 | 46.5 | 48.7 | 44.9 | 49.6 | 64.2 | 68.0 |
| | 11.9 | 13.0 | 10.2 | 9.9 | 9.8 | 14.1 | 16.3 | 15.5 |
| **Liquidity ratio (%)** | **28.4** | **21.7** | **20.6** | **43.2** | **40.6** | **49.5** | **55.3** | **50.5** |
| Excl. banks' foreign assets | 19.7 | 13.1 | 10.8 | 10.2 | 13.8 | 13.5 | 8.3 | 6.8 |
| **Memo** | | 2 102 | 2 415 | 2 487 | 2 752 | 2 733 | 2 587 | 2 454 |
| Public foreign currency & FC indexed debt | 1 805 | | | | | | | |

*Source*: Central Bank of Iceland, Fitch estimates and forecasts.

tested over a long period, Iceland has yet to establish a similar track record in more indebted circumstances.

The fact that Iceland's net international investment position – net holdings of equity and debt combined – has deteriorated less rapidly than the net debt position[2] underlines the point that the private sector is borrowing to invest in real and financial assets abroad. But, in the final analysis, debt brings with it fixed contractual obligations whereas equity does not. Fitch estimates that external debt service may have climbed to an estimated 50 per cent of current external receipts in 2005, while the gross external financing requirement could exceed 500 per cent of international reserves in 2006 (see Tables 7.3 and 7.4).

In our last sovereign review of Iceland we noted that the continued evolution of macroeconomic imbalances, the speed at which they could unwind and the likely fall-out for the economy as a whole would be important pointers for the rating. Clearly there are mitigating factors in the shape of the financial strength of the public sector, a more flexible economy (including a floating exchange rate) and much enhanced financial supervision. However, as this report has highlighted, other factors loom large, most notably:

- rising macro-prudential risks;
- unsustainable external finances;
- uncertainties about banks' exposure to currency related and asset price volatility;
- and an inappropriate policy mix.

As such, the balance of risk has shifted against Iceland and the outlooks on the sovereign ratings are revised to negative from stable.

## Notes

1. These concerns were flagged up in Fitch's Bank Systemic Risk Report published on 14 February 2006.
2. At the end of 2004 Iceland's net international investment position indicated that liabilities exceeded assets by the equivalent of 90 per cent of GDP. This compared to a net external debt position of 135 per cent of GDP.

# 8
# Iceland: Geyser Crisis

*Lars Christiansen*

- On most measures, the small Icelandic economy is the most overheated in the OECD area. Unemployment stands at 1 per cent, wage growth is above 7 per cent and inflation is running above 4 per cent despite a strong ISK. The current account deficit is closing in on 20 per cent of GDP. The Icelandic Central Bank has been hiking rates substantially in order to cool the economy, and rates are now above 10 per cent. Based on the macro data alone, we think the economy is heading for a recession in 2006–7. GDP could probably dip 5–10 per cent in the next two years, and inflation is likely to spike above 10 per cent as the ISK depreciates markedly.
- However, on top of the macro boom, there has been a stunning expansion of debt, leverage and risk-taking that is almost without precedent anywhere in the world. External debt is now nearly 300 per cent of GDP, while short-term external debt is just short of 55 per cent of GDP. This is 133 per cent of annual Icelandic export revenues.
- We look at early warning indicators for financial crises and conclude that Iceland looks worse on almost all measures than Thailand did before its crisis in 1997, and only moderately more healthy than Turkey before its 2001 crisis.
- Looking at currency exposure, the banking system is broadly hedged in a direct sense, as foreign currency lending and borrowing are broadly matched. However, as household mortgage debt is primarily inflation indexed, a weakening ISK will indirectly weaken household balance sheets through rising inflation. Inflation-linked mortgage debt stood at 165 per cent of disposable income at end-2004.

- The cost of tapping into the global capital market is rising for the Icelandic banking sector. As they have substantial foreign-denominated debt falling due over the next 18 months, Icelandic banks are facing financial headwinds.
- To be sure, there are some areas where the Icelandic situation is better than the ones Turkey and Thailand faced. The extension of credit has to a large degree (but not entirely) been used to fund foreign equity acquisitions. These assets are probably yielding a positive cash flow that might help fund corporations and, in turn, banks going forward.
- Against this background, we see a substantial risk of a financial crisis developing as an integral part of an Icelandic recession in 2006–7. The banks' funding squeeze will probably force them to reduce lending to domestic players and could force a sell-off of external assets.

## Assessing Iceland: a storm building in the North Atlantic

Iceland is not a core part of our research universe. We cover the currency, but we do not publish fixed-frequency forecasts on the economy.

Even so, we have now chosen to make this special report on the economy. There are two reasons. Firstly, we have seen a great surge in interest in Iceland as the boom in the economy has attracted attention. Secondly, recent market jitters suggest that a material change of dynamics is in the air.

We have long been sceptical about the sustainability of the Icelandic boom. And we have not been alone. Reports from the IMF and the OECD, as well as the Financial Stability report from the Sedlabanki (the Icelandic Central Bank), prepared in 2004 and 2005, all seemed wary of the situation. The imbalances have only grown worse since then.

Many of the conclusions in this report could have been reached six months ago. However, as always, it is hard to time the turning point from boom to bust in a period of financial exuberance. Recent jitters, the sell-off in the ISK and increasing scepticism about Icelandic risks in global credit markets have convinced us that the time is 'now'.

This being the case we felt a need to issue a report laying out the facts about the Icelandic boom as we see them.

To be sure, Iceland has good long-term fundamentals. This is an economy with an innovative and well-educated workforce. The economy is quite flexible, entrepreneurial spirit abounds and the political situation is stable. This implies that the economy will weather this storm and emerge rich and well functioning on the other side. However, the recession is coming and it will be tough – as Icelandic recessions usually are.

## Living on the edge: hot smelters, hot springs ... hot economy

During recent years, the Icelandic economy has steamed ahead. At the moment this small economy is the most overheated in the OECD area, measured in almost all ways.

Since 2003 the Icelandic upswing has been driven by exceptionally strong domestic demand, spurred on by both consumer spending and investments (see Figure 8.1).

Much of the investment boom has been driven by large-scale energy investments and heavy foreign investments in aluminium production. Indirect export of thermal energy through aluminium production is the second most important component of Icelandic exports – next to marine products. It accounts for approximately 20 per cent of total exports. However, even if one subtracts the effect of aluminium investments, growth in fixed investments is running at around 20 per cent y/y (Figure 8.2).

The expansion has a flip side, however. Strong domestic demand has caused a severe deterioration of net exports. While some of this deterioration may be explained by the – temporary – effects of energy and aluminium investments, this is far from the whole story.

The trade deficit is currently running above 10 per cent of GDP.

Moreover, the income balance has been deteriorating dramatically as well due to increasing expenditure on interest and dividend payments as foreign debt and investment inflows have increased during recent

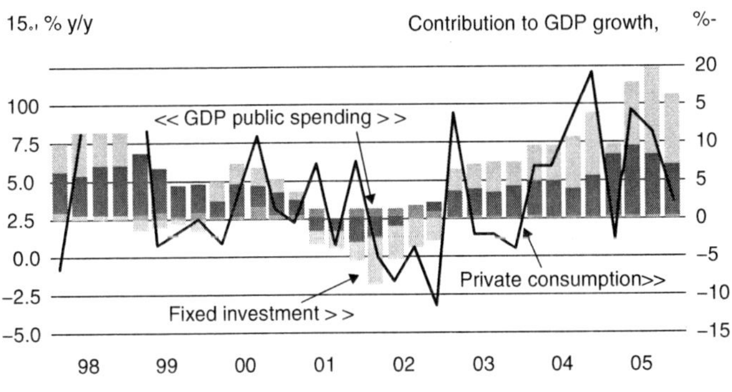


*Figure 8.1* Upswing driven by strong domestic demand

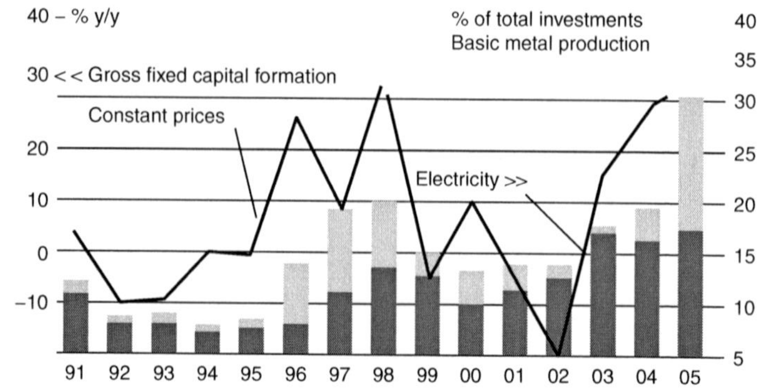


*Figure 8.2* Energy and metal sectors are driving investments

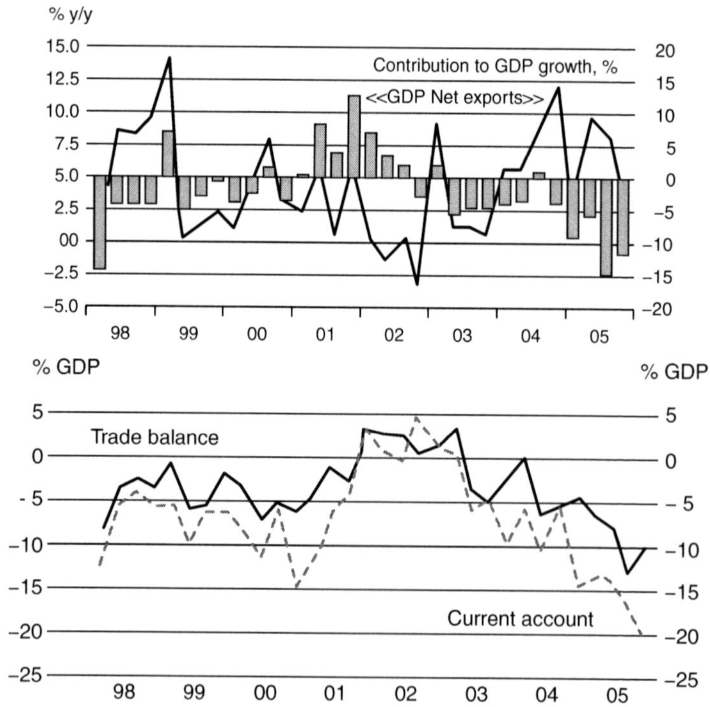


*Figure 8.3* Net exports have deteriorated …
… and external imbalances are widening

years. This is reflected in the current account deficit, which currently stands at 20 per cent of GDP (Figure 8.3).

It has often been argued that the large Icelandic current account deficit is primarily due to heavy foreign investment in the aluminium sector.

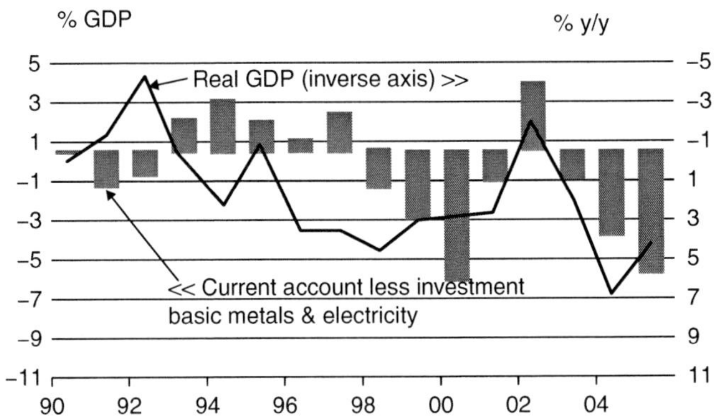


*Figure 8.4* Large imbalances even disregarding aluminium

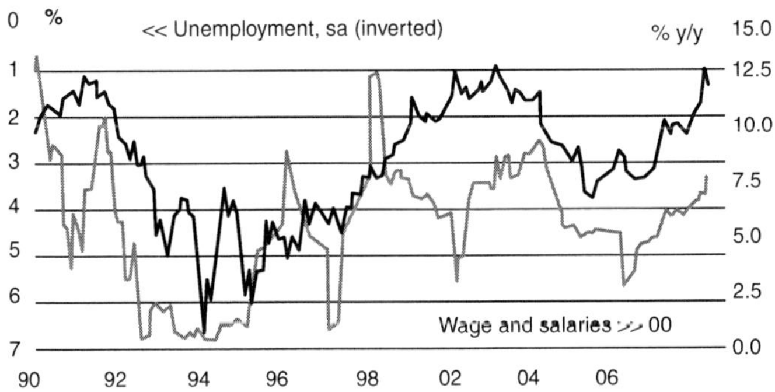


*Figure 8.5* Tight labour market is driving up wages

But this is not entirely correct, as Figure 8.4 illustrates. In the graph we have deducted total investment in the energy and metal sectors from the current account balance. This shows that, even with this correction, the current account deficit is substantial and among the largest in the world.

The strong pace of growth has created an extremely tight labour market. The unemployment rate is currently running at around 1 per cent, touching the extreme lows of previous Icelandic cycles. When unemployment reached 1 per cent in 1991 and 2000, deep recessions followed in 1992 and 2001.[1]

The strained labour market has fuelled wage and price growth during recent years. This drove inflation above the Icelandic Central Bank, Sedlabanki's, upper inflation band of 4 per cent during 2005 – pretty impressive going (Figure 8.5).

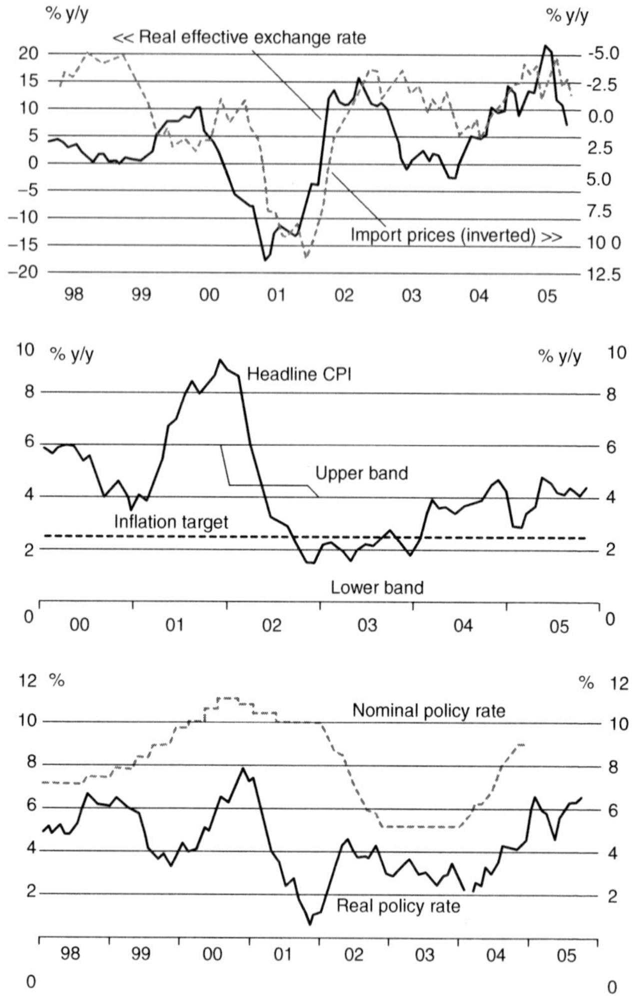


*Figure 8.6* Even through the ISK is extremely strong
... inflation is rising above target
... which has forced Sedlabanki to hit the brakes

Note that the ISK has strengthened by more than 20 per cent in real terms since 2004 and that this small economy has an imports-to-GDP ratio of more than 45 per cent. This being the case, the currency's strengthening has actually *dampened* inflation significantly (Figure 8.6).

To contain inflationary pressures, the Sedlabanki has been forced to hike its policy rate from 5.3 per cent in mid-2004 to the current

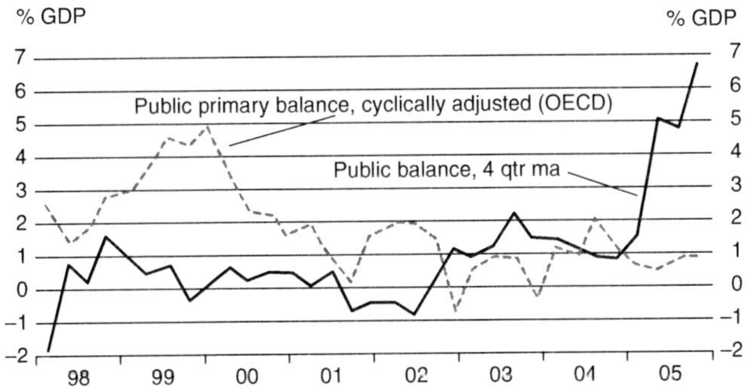


*Figure 8.7* Public finances have not been tightened enough

10.75 per cent. With headline inflation running at 4.5 per cent, this implies that the real rate now exceeds 6 per cent – a rather high level.

In previous periods – in 1998 and 2001 – when the real rate moved above 6 per cent for longer periods of time, the following years saw significant slumps in GDP growth.

Even though public finances are looking strong, with the budget surplus currently running above 5 per cent of GDP, this is not the full picture. Public revenues have been boosted by the strong growth in the economy and the strength of the labour market. Adjusting for these cyclical factors shows that public finances have not been tightened during recent years – in spite of the urgent need for tightening (Figure 8.7).

The economy is clearly overheating, since the labour market is extremely tight, wage pressures are unsustainable, the inflation rate is among the highest in the OECD area despite an overvalued currency, and the Central Bank is stamping on the brakes.

Based on these facts alone our judgement would be that the economy is heading for a significant slowdown in 2006/7.

But this is not the full story.

## Debt and leverage

### Extreme ratios

External debt, foreign currency debt and leverage come on top of the classic macro worries outlined earlier. In the credit system, signs of overheating are abundant. Growth in credit (from deposit money banks) to the private sector has virtually exploded and is currently running at more than 60 per cent y/y (Figure 8.8).

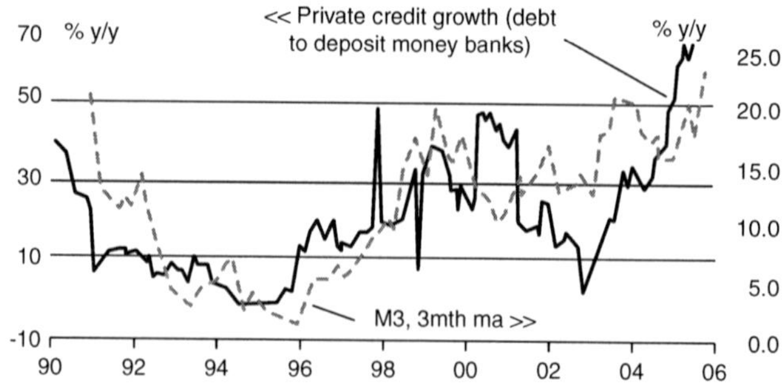


*Figure 8.8* Credit and money growth is spiking

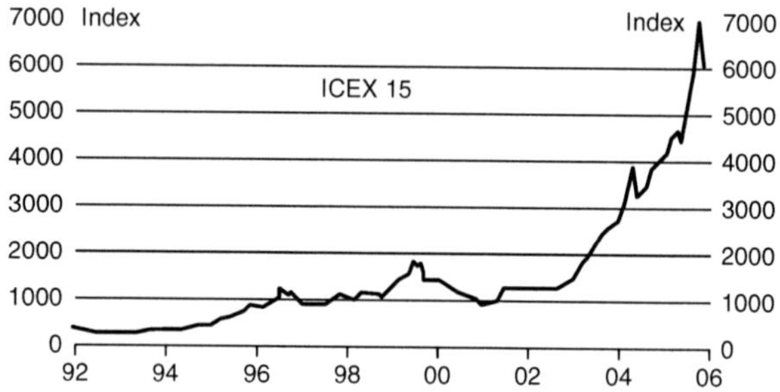


*Figure 8.9* Easy liquidity is inflating asset markets

Looking at a broader measure of liquidity, the M3 money stock, confirms this picture. M3 growth has been surging as well during the past couple of years and is up more than 22 per cent y/y. Moreover, M3 has been growing by more than 10 per cent y/y every year since 1998. Evidently non-bank agents have been leveraging extremely fast.

Liquidity has also fed into asset markets, which have been booming. Since early 2004, the Icelandic stock market has gained almost 300 per cent (Figure 8.9).

High credit growth is mirrored in debt ratios. Since 1990 total debt as a percentage of annual GDP has more than doubled to 350 per cent. This development has primarily been driven by the corporate and household sectors, which have tripled and doubled debt as a percentage of GDP, respectively (Figure 8.10).

This is also reflected in funding of the debt increase. External debt has risen to nearly 300 per cent of GDP (Figure 8.11).

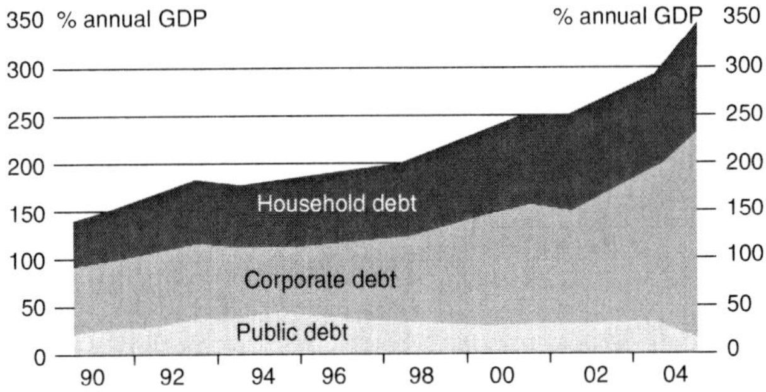


*Figure 8.10* Corporate and household debt is surging

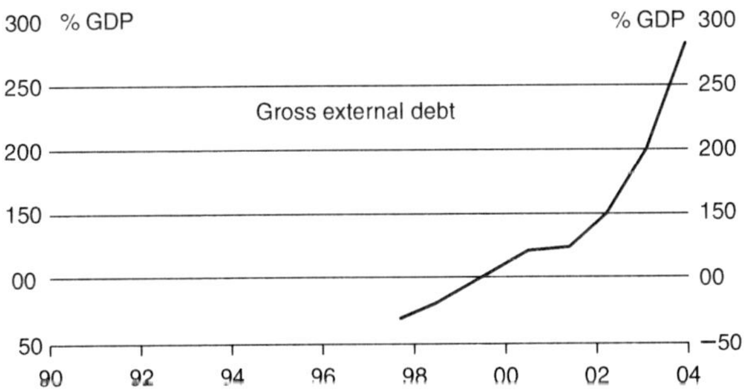


*Figure 8.11* External borrowing has exploded

External debt now accounts for more than 80 per cent of total debt. It is probably safe to assume that this debt is almost entirely denominated in foreign currency. The recent boom in corporate debt reflects the aggressive acquisitive expansion of many Icelandic firms in northern Europe. As a consequence, net equity capital holdings have increased substantially. However, as Figure 8.12 indicates, the net external debt position has, nevertheless, deteriorated.

Consequently, the Icelandic economy has become increasingly dependent on foreign capital and international terms of lending. Iceland seems not only to be overheating, but also looks very dependent on the willingness-to-lend of global financial markets. This raises the question of whether the economy is facing not just a recession – but also a severe financial crisis.

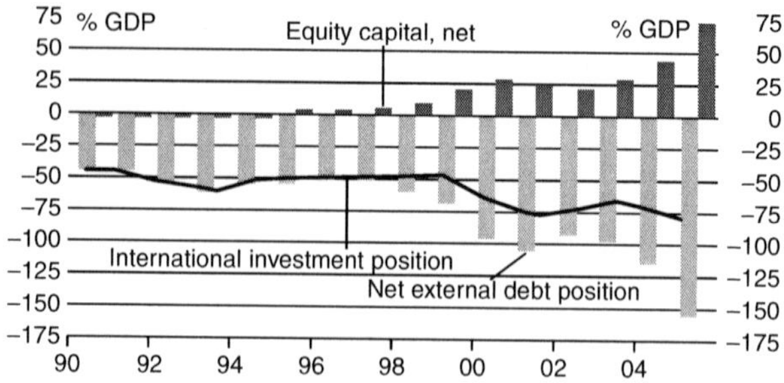


*Figure 8.12* International investment position has deteriorated

## A textbook financial crisis? How Iceland compares

A quick look at the fundamentals of the Icelandic economy clearly shows that the economy is dominated by large imbalances (Table 8.1). The natural question is then whether these imbalances are large enough to trigger a financial crisis. To get a more qualified view on this we have looked at a number of indicators which are normally used in the academic literature to study currency and banking crises.[2]

We have looked at the following indicators:

- Credit growth
- Current account (per cent of GDP)
- Public finance surplus (per cent of GDP)
- Inflation
- M3 growth
- Foreign reserves as a per cent of total imports

By way of comparison we focus on the Thai crisis in 1997 and the Turkish crisis of 2001. These two cases closely resemble the situation in Iceland today. Measured by the key indicators above, the imbalances are even larger than in Thailand in 1997, but not quite as large as in Turkey in 2001, as the spider web diagram in Figure 8.13 illustrates.

In fact the only indicator that looks healthier now in Iceland relative to Thailand in 1997 is public finances. However, it should be noted that the apparently strong fiscal position in Iceland can largely be explained by the strong growth and the boom in asset prices (cf. the discussion above).

That being said, the comparison between Iceland, Thailand and Turkey is primarily meant as an illustration of the magnitude of the

*Table 8.1* Table of imbalances

| | *2005* | *2004* | *2003* | *2002* | *2001* | *2000* |
|---|---|---|---|---|---|---|
| Current account, % of GDP, Q4 figures | –20.8 | –14.8 | –9.5 | 1.4 | 3.1 | –14.7 |
| Total debt, % of GDP, end of period | 346.2 | 289.2 | 267.6 | 247.9 | 251.0 | 237.6 |
| Gross external debt, % of GDP, end of period | 299.9 | 205.3 | 148.3 | 124.6 | 121.8 | 104.2 |
| Short-term foreign debt, % of FX reserves, end of period | 692.0 | 480.1 | 462.4 | 546.1 | 470.9 | 389.9 |
| Public balance surplus (last four quarters), % of GDP, end of period | 4.8 | 0.9 | 2.3 | 0.4 | –0.6 | 0.5 |
| M3 growth (3 mth moving average), % y/y, end of period | 23.4 | 16.6 | 19.4 | 14.3 | 14.8 | 10.5 |
| Private credit growth, % y/y , end of period | 64.5 | 39.6 | 27.7 | 11.2 | 16.4 | 43.9 |

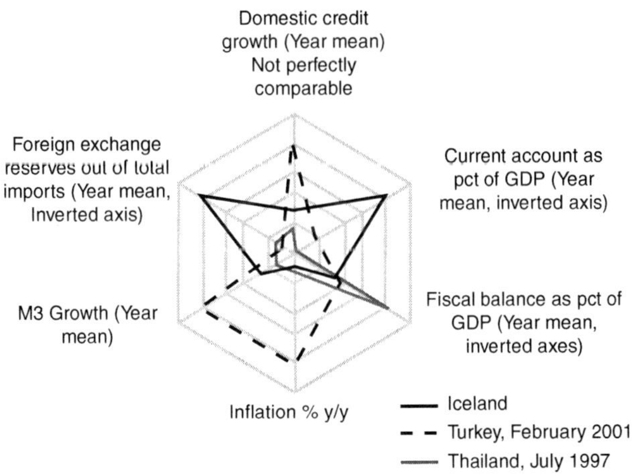


*Figure 8.13* Crisis indicators – worse than Thailand, 1997

imbalances in the Icelandic economy. There are obviously differences between the cases.

First of all, the Icelandic krónur is a free-floating currency, unlike the Thai baht (1997) and the Turkish lira (in 2001), which naturally reduces the likelihood of an abrupt correction in the currency – though it should be stressed that the krónur has been overvalued.

Secondly, a large part of the credit expansion has been used by the corporate sector to purchase foreign assets, as noted earlier. This should cushion the economy to a greater degree than was the case in Thailand in 1997 and Turkey in 2001. These assets are likely to continue to be (partly) liquid, and foreign asset markets are not likely to be stressed during a possible Icelandic financial crisis.

However, putting these differences aside for a moment, we think that a possible Icelandic crisis could follow much the same lines as in Thailand and Turkey.

## A scenario for a hard landing

The discussion above clearly illustrates that the present state of the Icelandic economy necessitates a major correction in not only the Icelandic financial markets, but also in the macro economy. It is hard to imagine that such a correction could be a 'soft landing' given the size of the imbalances in the economy.

However, the complexity and extent of the problems in the Icelandic economy make it very difficult to predict the extent and timing of the correction. We have therefore chosen not to make a forecast for the Icelandic economy, but rather to look at one possible – and not unlikely – scenario for how such an economic and financial correction could play out. However, it should be stressed that the correction could be less painful if Icelandic policymakers take the appropriate action to facilitate the correction.

In our scenario we look, in all, at four phases in the correction, based on the experience from the crises mentioned above:

1. Building an unbalanced economy
2. Getting worried
3. Cutting off the oxygen supply
4. A hard landing

### *Phase 1: Building an unbalanced economy*

We have already passed this phase in the sense that the imbalances have built up as described above. In terms of the correction, it is enough to note that the imbalances are so large now that a correction in the markets and the economy seems unavoidable.

*Phase 2: Getting worried*

Phase 2 has already started. This phase was initiated when the rating agency, Fitch, revised its outlook for Iceland's sovereign debt to negative on 21 February and sparked frantic selling in the Icelandic FX, fixed income and equity markets. Fitch's rating action undoubtedly helped open the market's eyes to the large imbalances in the Icelandic economy (Figure 8.14).

The revised outlook undoubtedly led many creditors to further restrict access to credit for Icelandic borrowers. This has been visible in spreads on Icelandic euro bonds, which have widened significantly.

We do not think this phase has come to an end yet. The banks will not be able to tap the global capital market again until the smoke clears on the economy.

The liquidity strains concern, in particular, debt denominated in foreign currency. The magnitude of the liquidity strains facing the Icelandic economy is illustrated by the fact that short-term debt amounts to six times the total Icelandic foreign exchange reserve and 133 per cent of yearly exports. As a comparison, the short-term debt/reserve ratio for South Korea prior to the Asian crisis in 1997 was around 2 per cent.

The fact that most of the Icelandic debt is held in foreign currency raises concerns about a possible liquidity and funding crisis. The Icelandic Central Bank's possibility of functioning as a *lender-of last-resort* is basically limited by the size of the FX reserve (Figure 8.15). Therefore, the Central Bank's scope for easing the pains of a possible external lending crisis is rather limited.

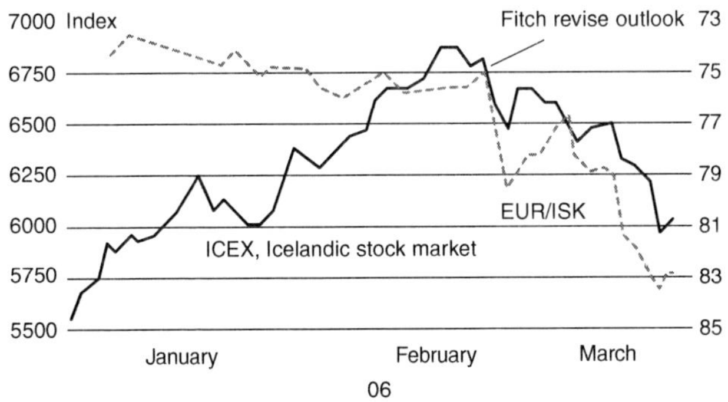


*Figure 8.14* Fitch sparks market correction

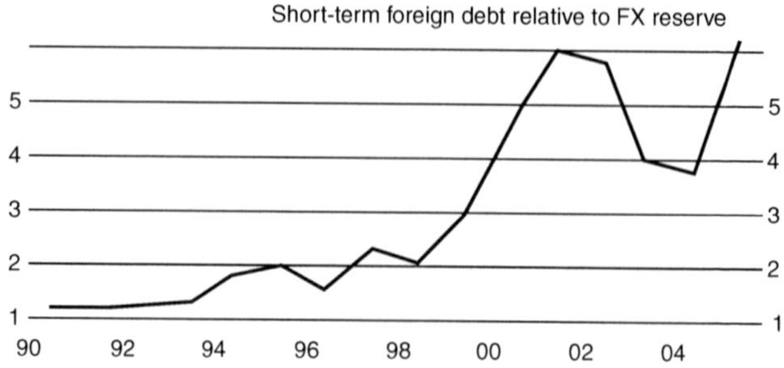


*Figure 8.15* Heading for a funding crisis?

*Phase 3: Cutting off the oxygen supply*

As liquidity conditions in the Icelandic economy are expected to get tighter, it is likely that the situation will turn from one of financial jitters into a full-scale financial crisis. Banks will have to reduce their lending to Icelandic companies and households significantly. Hence, a liquidity crisis could spread rapidly from the banking sector to the rest of the economy.

A significant funding and liquidity crisis in the Icelandic banking sector would most likely spark rating downgrades of the major Icelandic banks by the international rating agencies. Initially, this would only increase the wariness of global markets, and Icelandic banks and private entities would face strongly increasing funding costs. This would force the Icelandic banks to tighten lending conditions until cash flows are matched. For the economy this implies a fast and dramatic current account adjustment through domestic demand.

However, one special feature of the Icelandic expansion is that borrowing has been used to such a large extent to fund corporate acquisitions abroad. These assets yield a cash flow and can be sold if necessary. In this respect Iceland is in a better position than Thailand in 1997 and Turkey in 2001.

The question remains, however, of whether the cash flow of these external assets can match the negative cash flow on the external liabilities and instalments going forward. If the net cash flow of foreign assets cannot be made to match the interest and debt falling due, the argument that 'expansion has been abroad' does not really help. To assess this aspect of the situation, we looked at net interest payments and equity payments on the Icelandic income account. This serves as a crude measure of net Icelandic external position cash flow, including acquisitions abroad. The running income deficit on this position is 3–4 per cent of GDP (Figure 8.16).

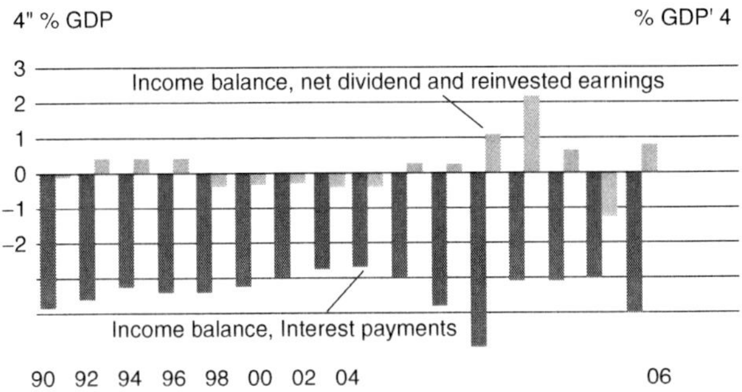


*Figure 8.16* Big gap between debt costs and equity income

Judging by these data, foreign assets are far from generating a cash flow that can fund debt costs going forward – especially as 55 per cent of GDP in short-term external debt will fall due in the next year.

If Icelandic banks continue to face strongly rising funding costs, the result is likely to be a sale of foreign assets by Icelandic banks and Icelandic corporations.

Previous similar crises in other countries have sparked very large market reactions. In Thailand (1997) and Turkey (2001) the currencies weakened by 50–60 per cent. This might seem like an extreme reaction but, as we have noted above, the imbalances in the Icelandic economy are of a similar size. Hence, we would not rule out the possibility that the Icelandic krónur could weaken by a similar degree (note though that the krónur has already weakened by around 20 per cent since the start of the market correction).

Such a depreciation of the krónur would increase inflationary pressures. Inflation would likely spike well above 10 per cent y/y within a relatively short span of time. This would force the Icelandic Central Bank to tighten monetary policy in order to bring inflation under control again.

The Icelandic banks are generally well hedged against currency moves, as their funding and lending in foreign currency are broadly matched.

That said, the banks may have implicit currency risks that have not been hedged. One special feature of the Icelandic financial system is that the bulk of household borrowing is in inflation-linked mortgages. These mortgages correspond to 165 per cent of disposable income. Hence, households are paying the real rate in ISK on their mortgages. This partly explains why the rather high nominal interest rates have so far done little to halt growth (Figure 8.17).

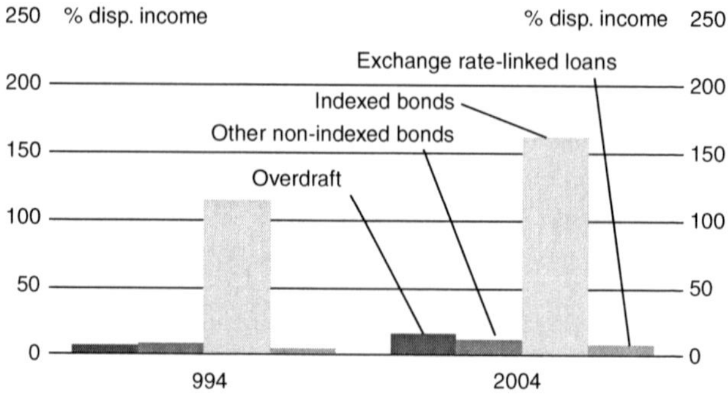


*Figure 8.17* Household debt: inflation linked

On the other hand, the link to the CPI implies that households are indirectly exposed to movements in the ISK, as the ISK is crucial for inflation in such a tiny and very open economy. Should the ISK depreciate substantially as the economy dips into recession, households could find themselves in a serious bind, given that inflation could spike above 10 per cent while wage growth would slow. In this – rather important – sense, the credit quality of households is indirectly linked to the ISK.

### *Phase 4: a hard landing*

The ramifications of a liquidity crisis are obvious – both the expected significant tightening of monetary policy and the negative wealth effects from the drop in the currency would hit investment and consumption. It is, of course, impossible to predict the size of such a negative correction. However, in Thailand in 1997 and in Turkey 2001, investments plummeted to the tune of 30–40 per cent. Such a fall in investment seems very possible in Iceland as well – especially taking into account the size of the imbalances in the Icelandic economy and the fact that the Icelandic economy has historically been the most volatile economy in the OCED area by far. Furthermore, note that investment dropped by more than 25 per cent in 2002 during the latest Icelandic recession – when imbalances and the leverage of the economy were somewhat less than today.

Private consumption would also suffer. This declined by 10–15 per cent in Thailand in 1997 and in Turkey in 2001. Private consumption weakened by around 5 per cent during the Icelandic recession of 2002. Given the scale of foreign-denominated debt (and the indexation of mortgage debt to inflation), a slide in the currency of, say, 20–30 per cent (and a strong spike in inflation) would erode the net wealth of Icelandic private households – hence, a drop in private consumption of 5–10 per cent is easily imaginable.

Falls in investment and private consumption of these magnitudes mean GDP could drop 5–10 per cent.

Such a drop in GDP would obviously lead to a significant deterioration of public finances in Iceland, and the budget surplus would most likely turn very quickly into a deficit. The direct effect would come through a drop in revenues and higher expenditure (mostly social transfers) as a result of negative growth. However, if the crisis developed into a wider banking sector crisis, it would probably force the government to assume some of the increased debt burden from the banks – as was the case in, for example, the Turkish crisis of 2001 and the Swedish banking crisis of 1992–93.

## No major contagion

### Little effect from a bust in the Icelandic economy

How much will a bust in the Icelandic economy affect the Scandinavian countries? Our view is that the impact will generally be very limited, from both the macroeconomic and financial perspectives.

As the share of exports from the Scandinavian economies going to Iceland is very small, the ramifications of a bust in the Icelandic economy on trading patterns should be rather limited (Figure 8.18).

However, the financial sector could feel some impact through the Icelandic ownership of Scandinavian assets. If the Icelandic banking and corporate sectors are forced to realize their foreign assets to meet some of their short-term foreign debt obligations, some spillover could occur in the Scandinavian financial markets. But the impact would be limited to specific assets with Icelandic ownership and is not likely to have any aggregate market impact.

### Limited impact on emerging markets ... but focus on quality versus imbalances

The recent sell-off in the Icelandic financial markets has to some extent impacted negatively on, especially, other high-yield markets. However, it should be stressed that the size of foreign investment positions in Icelandic markets is very small compared to the general positions in other high-yield markets. We would therefore not expect any strong spillover effects on other high-yield markets. Continuing turmoil in the

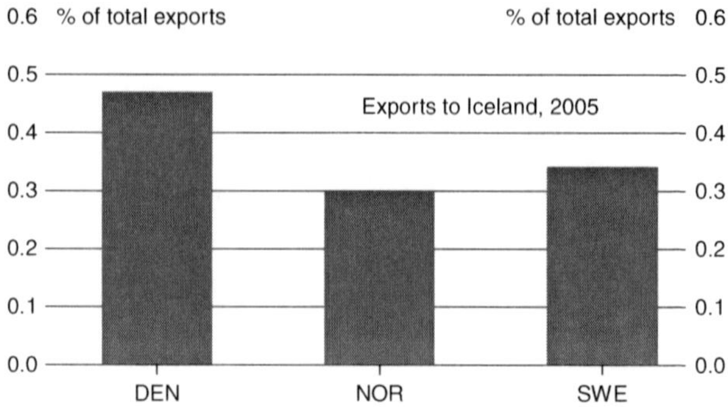


*Figure 8.18* Very little impact through trade patterns

Icelandic markets should, though, act as a further reminder to focus on the quality of high-yield assets.

Therefore, we would expect some spillover from the Icelandic situation to other markets with similar problems, i.e. especially to countries with large and unsustainable current account deficits. Hungary, in particular, looks like a possible target, and a large negative correction in Iceland could easily trigger further corrections in the already fragile Hungarian markets. Likewise, the New Zealand markets could come under some pressure given the country's large current deficit.

In conclusion, we find it unlikely that a further correction in the Icelandic markets could trigger a broader emerging markets crisis, but it could trigger a self-off in markets with unsustainably large current account deficits.

## Notes

1. The first version of this report said the latest recession took off in 2001 and not in 2002. This typo has now been corrected.
2. For a standard reference in the literature see, for example, Graciela L. Kaminsky, 1999, 'Currency and Banking Crises: the Early Warnings of Distress', IMF Working Paper 99/178.

# 9
# Financial Stability in Iceland

*Frederic S. Mishkin and Tryggvi T. Herbertsson*

## Executive summary

There has been good and bad news for the Icelandic economy. The good news is that it is receiving a lot of attention. The bad news is that it is receiving a lot of attention. Recent volatility in Iceland's asset markets have raised concerns about the fragility of Iceland's economy. In this respect many have looked to the country's large current account deficit. This study provides a framework for evaluating financial fragility by examining the fundamentals of Iceland's economy to see whether they suggest that the country could go down the traditional routes to financial instability.

Iceland is unique in that it is the smallest economy in the world to have its own currency and a flexible exchange rate. It has experienced high current account deficits before, but rapid adjustment has taken place in the past without significantly stressing the Icelandic financial system. Iceland is also an advanced country with excellent institutions (low corruption, rule of law, high education, and freedom of the press). In addition, its financial regulation and supervision are considered to be of high quality. Iceland also has a strong fiscal position that is far superior to what is seen in the United States, Japan and Europe. Iceland's financial sector has undergone a substantial liberalization, which was complete over a decade ago, and its banking sector has been transformed from one focused mainly on domestic markets to one providing financial intermediation services to the rest of the world, particularly Scandinavia and the UK.

There are three traditional routes to financial instability that have manifested themselves in recent financial crises: (1) financial liberalization with weak prudential regulation and supervision, (2) severe fiscal imbalances, and (3) imprudent monetary policy. None of these routes describe the current situation in Iceland. The economy has already adjusted to financial liberalization, which was already completed a long time ago, while prudential regulation and supervision are generally quite strong. Fiscal imbalances are not a problem in Iceland: quite the opposite, with Iceland having an excellent fiscal position with low government net debt (less than 10 per cent of GDP) and a fully funded pension system (with assets amounting to more than 120 per cent of GDP). Monetary policy has also been successful in keeping inflation low and near the inflation target, particularly when housing prices are excluded from the inflation measure, as is the case in the United States and the eurozone. It is true, however, that Iceland is running very large current account deficits, but current account deficits by themselves do not lead to financial instability. Our analysis indicates that the sources of financial instability that triggered financial crises in emerging market countries in recent years are just not present in Iceland, so that comparisons of Iceland with emerging market countries are misguided.

The fact that Iceland is not going down traditional routes to financial instability does not mean that there are no other potential problems looming. There are concerns that the banks could experience refinancing problems. Although the banks' reliance on external financing poses the biggest risk to the financial system right now, the probability of a credit event occurring is low. The rapid credit growth in the banking system and the banks' transformation from concentrating on domestic lending to becoming international financial intermediaries, also presents some risk because the banks may not have been able to develop organizational capital fast enough to run their new business safely. These concerns have led to criticism of Iceland's banks for lack of transparency. However, the Financial Supervisory Authority's awareness of these risks and the fact that Iceland has high-quality governmental institutions make it unlikely that there are serious problems with safety and soundness in the banking system.

Iceland's small size and openness make it more vulnerable because small changes in financial flows as a percentage of overall flows in international flows in financial markets can have a huge impact on Iceland's asset prices and particularly the exchange rate. Self-fulfilling prophecies, otherwise known as multiple equilibria, in which concerns about an Icelandic financial meltdown could lead to massive withdrawals out of Icelandic assets, which would then lead to a financial meltdown, even if fundamentals do not warrant it, cannot be ruled out. However, research on multiple equilibria suggests that self-fulfilling prophecies are unlikely to occur when fundamentals are strong, as they are in Iceland.

The analysis in our study suggests that although Iceland's economy does have some imbalances that will eventually be reversed, financial fragility is currently not a problem, and the likelihood of a financial meltdown is low. However, the possibility that multiple equilibria might occur suggests that policy measures to bolster confidence in the Icelandic economy and financial system would be beneficial. We suggest four such measures: (1) financial supervision might be more effective if it were consolidated inside the Central Bank; (2) Iceland's commercial banks should be encouraged, and should also see that it is in their own interest, to disclose more information about their activities; (3) the inflation measure used for the inflation target should minimize the influence of housing price fluctuations, and (4) the government should implement a formal fiscal rule to dampen the Icelandic business cycle. These measures are by no means exhaustive but could help improve the future stability of the Icelandic economy.

## Introduction

For such a small country, Iceland has been receiving an enormous amount of attention in the financial media. After Fitch Ratings downgraded the outlook for long-term Icelandic Treasury securities from stable to negative on 21 February this year, financial markets in Iceland have been in turmoil. With several other negative reports by bank analysts, the Icelandic krona (ISK) fell by more than 15 per cent in the course of the next month, while the Iceland stock market (ICEX-15 equity price index) fell by a similar amount (but by about 4 per cent since the beginning of this year). With this increased volatility and concern about the huge current account deficit of over 16 per cent of GDP, some analysts have raised the possibility that Iceland might undergo a financial meltdown, similar to ones that we have seen in recent years in emerging market countries. Do these fears have any validity?

To assess whether Iceland's economy is fragile, it is important to understand the unique features of Iceland's economy and then use deeper analysis of why financial fragility occurs to evaluate the potential for serious disruptions to Iceland's financial system. We begin our study with an overview of the Icelandic economy and then turn to a general analysis of why financial instability occurs. We can then use this analysis to ask whether Iceland is going down the traditional path to financial instability. We find that the answer is no. However, Iceland's unique situation raises some potential concerns about other possible sources of financial instability, and we examine them in order to provide a fuller assessment of the risks to the Icelandic economy. Although we conclude that Iceland's economy and financial system are on a sound footing, we believe that adoption of certain policy measures might help more rapidly restore confidence in Iceland's economy and restore the country's financial markets to normalcy more quickly.

## 9.1 Overview of the Icelandic economy

There are four features of the Icelandic economy that are particularly relevant to evaluating financial fragility: (1) its unique size, (2) its excellent institutional framework, (3) its strong fiscal position, and (4) its unique financial system.

### 9.1.1 Unique in size

Iceland is the smallest sovereign state in the world that has an independent monetary policy, with only 300,000 inhabitants. Since 2001 its policy has been based on inflation targeting and a floating exchange rate.

*Flexibility and the current account*

In recent years a large and growing current account deficit (Figures 9.1 and 9.2) has been a topic of debate as well as a source of criticism of economic policy management in Iceland as in many countries. Although Iceland has a generally favourable economic situation – with large private investments, rapid economic growth and low unemployment – the spiralling external deficit has raised concerns in the international financial community.

By definition, the current account is the difference between domestic investment and savings. As such it measures the change in the nation's net foreign assets, the difference between foreign assets and the external debt. When domestic investment exceeds domestic savings, the net asset position deteriorates and imports in excess of exports are paid for by borrowing or by the sale of domestically owned assets.

Depending on why it is occurring, a current account deficit could result from optimal behaviour on the part of households, firms and government. Current account deficits thus do not necessarily constitute a macroeconomic problem, and a strictly balanced current account should not belong to the list of key policy goals. A current account deficit – that is, foreign savings – can be used to finance increased domestic investment as well as consumption.

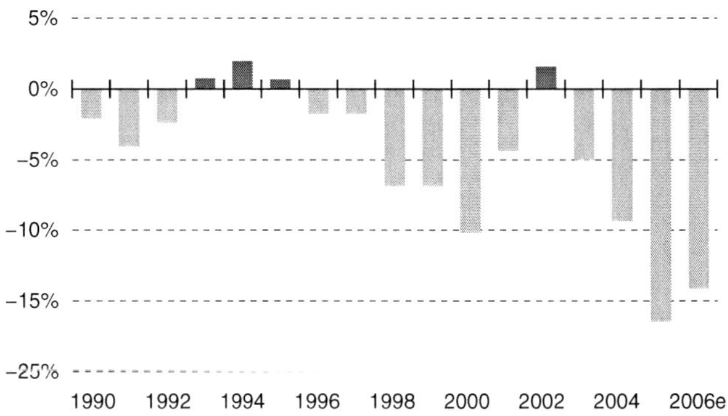


*Figure 9.1* Current account GDP ratio
*Source*: Central Bank of Iceland.

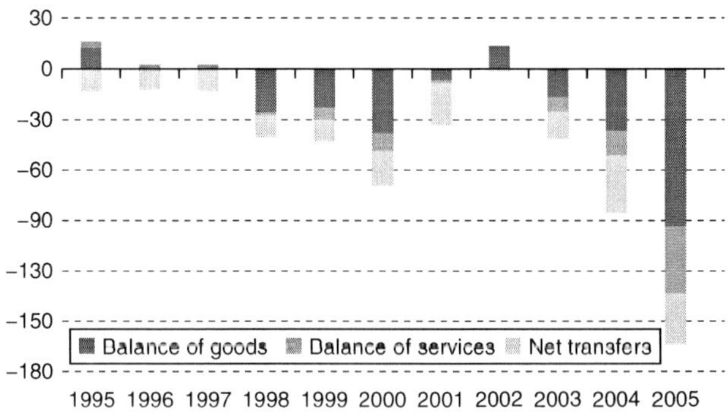


*Figure 9.2* Current account breakdown (bISK)
*Source*: Central Bank of Iceland.

Increased investment results in higher output in the future as well as higher interest payments on foreign debt. If the investment is sufficiently profitable (i.e. has a positive net present value), future generations will then benefit. Research also shows that demographic effects may be of paramount importance in causing either persistent surpluses or deficits. Nations largely at work should have current account surpluses, while those with proportionately more young and old people should have deficits.[1] The former are saving for retirement, while the latter are running down past and future savings. Iceland has a young population.

If a current account deficit coincides with low investment, there is a concern that the current account deficit might result from too much consumption (not enough saving). But even here, a current account deficit can be misleading. If domestic output falls transitorily, or the exchange rate is for some reason unusually favourable for imports, it is optimal behaviour for households to smooth consumption over time by borrowing to finance consumption of imported goods (or invest in imported consumer durables). The situation in Iceland in recent years may then well be a mixture of the two. Investment in the metal and energy sector and in residential housing has increased demand in the country, which has in fact forced the Central Bank to increase its policy rate, which has strengthened the ISK and increased imports, and the current account has deteriorated.

Another problem for small countries is the lumpiness nature of investment. As it turns out, firms in an industry that is dependent on the world market usually invest when world prices are high for their products (uncertainty is low). If investments are lumpy, the current account in small countries will be much more volatile than in big, diversified economies. To test the hypothesis we ran statistical tests to investigate the partial relationship between the standard deviation of the current account GDP ratio and the logarithm of population in 175 countries over the period 1980–2004.[2] Our preliminary results show that the Spearman rank correlation (which is a non-parametric correlation test) between the two variables is −0.54, which is high by any standard. To further investigate the relationship, we ran cross-sectional regressions on the variables (see Figure 9.3).[3]

In short our hypothesis is supported by the data: small countries have more volatile current accounts than big countries, and one must

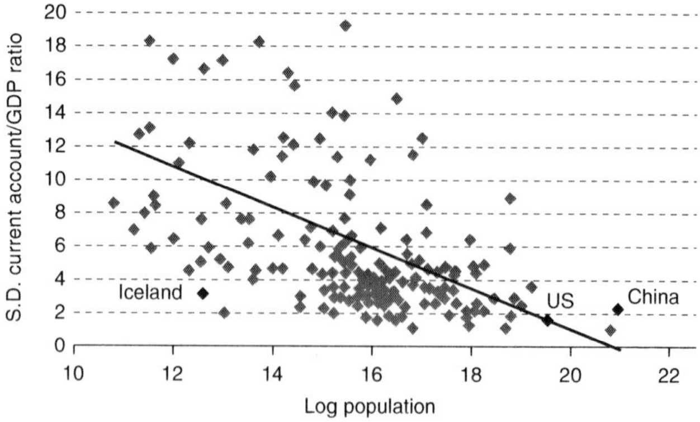


*Figure 9.3* The partial relationship between volatility of the current account GDP ratio and size of countries
*Source*: World Bank and author calculations.

therefore be cautious in concluding similarities between countries on the basis of current account deficits. However, the puzzling fact that the current account in Iceland is only marginally more volatile than in the US and China remains to be explained.

As history shows, another characteristic of the Icelandic economy is a highly volatile exchange rate and rapid adjustment of the current account via the exchange rate (see Figure 9.4). After years of stagnation the Icelandic economy finally took off in 1995, and economic growth was around 4–5 per cent for six consecutive years until 2002 (see Figure 9.5). At the same time the current account deficit started to grow, and in 2000 it amounted to more than 10 per cent of GDP (see Figures 9.1 and 9.2). With inflationary pressures building up in 2000 the Central Bank raised its policy rates (Figure 9.6 and 9.7). Finally, in 2000 the ISK started to depreciate, inflation picked up, and demand contracted, leading to a decline of GDP of around 1 per cent in 2002. From 2000 to 2002, the current account underwent a dramatic swing, improving by over ten percentage points, ending up with a current account surplus of 1.6 per cent of GDP.

In 2003 inflation was close to the inflation target, of 2.5 per cent, demand picked up, and the economy grew at the rate of 3 per cent. The evolution of the Icelandic economy over this period illustrates how flexible the Icelandic economy is to external shocks. The flexibility arises from the fact that Iceland has modern and efficient institutions that are able to smooth the adjustment process.

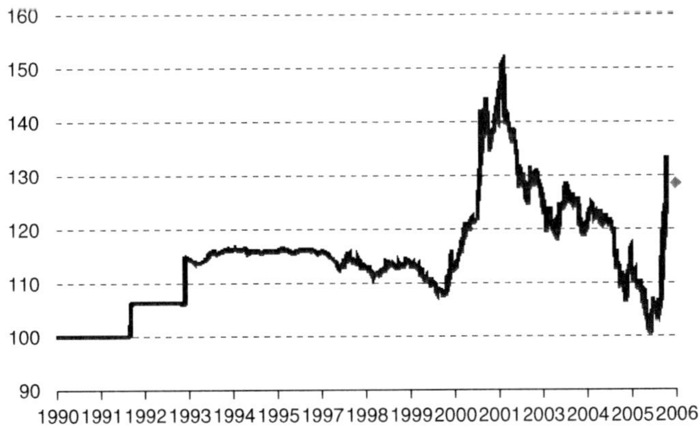


*Figure 9.4* The ISK index
*Source*: Central Bank of Iceland.

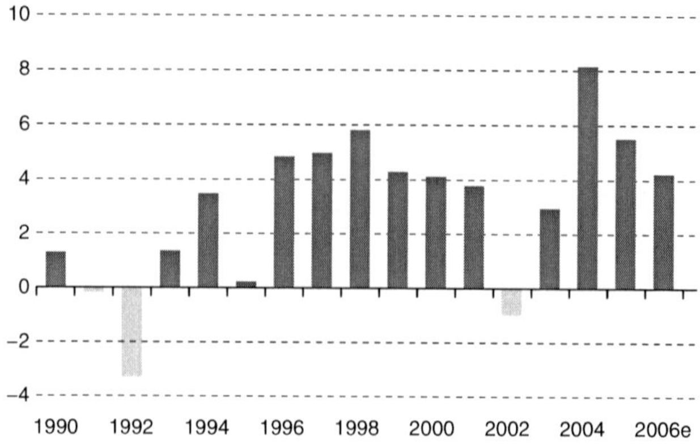


*Figure 9.5* Annual growth of GDP (%)
*Source*: Statistics Iceland.

*Figure 9.6* The policy rate of the Central Bank of Iceland
*Source*: Central Bank of Iceland.

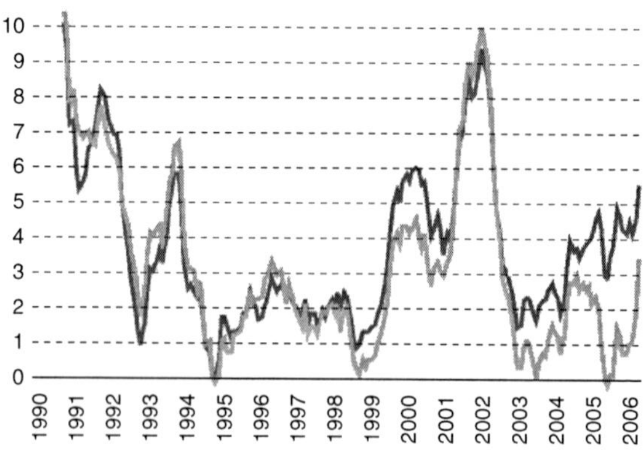


*Figure 9.7* Inflation, with housing (—) and without housing (—) (%)
*Source*: Statistics Iceland.

### 9.1.2 Advanced country with excellent institutions

Iceland is an advanced country with high-quality institutions. GDP per capita (adjusted for PPP) ranks fifth highest in the world; longevity is the highest for females and second highest for males; unemployment is almost non-existent and way below the natural rate; net government debt is almost nil, labour force participation among older workers the highest in the world, and of women the highest in the OECD (almost 80 per cent, compared with 56 per cent on average in the OECD) (see Table 9.1). Noteworthy among Iceland's country rankings for quality of institutions is that Iceland ranks fifth in economic freedom, first in terms of the lowest corruption, seventh in terms of competitiveness, first in the percentage of population connected to the Internet (ADSL or ISDN), and the first in terms of freedom of the press, compared with number 113 for Turkey and 59 for Thailand.[4] These rankings are of course sometimes arbitrary, but they clearly illustrate that Iceland is a well-run, advanced Nordic country that has little in common with emerging market countries, a fact important to recognize when we start discussing financial stability in the next section.

*Table 9.1* Overview statistics for the Icelandic economy

| | |
|---|---|
| GDP per papita (US$, PPP) (1) | 35 749 |
| GDP per capita, current exchange rate (US$) (1) | 53 555 |
| GDP growth 2005 (%) (1) | 5.5 |
| Unemployment (%) (1) | 2.4 |
| Life expectancy at birth (years) (9) | 80.7 |
| Annual stock market change 2005 (%) (2) | 65 |
| Corruption perception index (rank) (3) | 1 |
| Worldwide competitiveness (rank) (4) | 4 |
| Growth competitiveness index (rank) (5) | 7 |
| Political rights and civil liberties (rank) (6) | 1 |
| Economic freedom (rank) (7) | 5 |
| Balance of trade (% of GDP) (1) | −9.3 |
| Current account balance 2005 (% of GDP) (8) | −16.5 |
| Central government revenue (% of GDP) (1) | 37.0 |
| Central government expenditure (% of GDP) (1) | 33.2 |
| General government financial balance 2005 (% of GDP) (1) | 3.0 |
| Net savings (% of GDP) (1) | 0.23 |
| Gross savings (% of GDP) (1) | 12 |
| Gross domestic investment (% of GDP) (8) | 28.7 |
| Central government, gross debt 2005 (% of GDP) (8) | 20.2 |
| Central government, net debt 2005 (% of GDP) (8) | 7.7 |

*Data sources*: (1) Statistics Iceland, (2) Iceland Stock Exchange, (3) Transparency International, (4) IMD World Competitiveness Report, (5) The World Economic Forum, (6) Freedom House, (7) *The Wall Street Journal* and The Heritage Foundation, (8) Ministry of Finance, (9) OECD.

The country was an early member of the UN and a founding member of the OEEC (now the OECD), the Bretton Woods Agreement and consequently the World Bank and the International Monetary Fund (IMF). The country has a seat on the board of the IMF for two years every 10 years and at the World Bank for three years every 15 years. Iceland is a candidate for the UN Security Council in 2009. Iceland has not drawn on the IMF since 1982 and has not borrowed from the World Bank since the 1960s except for an emergency loan in 1974 because of a volcanic eruption in Vestmanna Islands. The Central Bank of Iceland is independent from politics and has based its monetary policy on inflation targeting since the spring of 2001.

The Financial Supervisory Authority (FSA) is independent from the Central Bank, which, however, monitors overall financial stability in the country. The FSA is entrusted with considerable enforcing powers. It monitors the credit market, the pension system, the insurance market, and the securities market. The FSA has access to all information from parties subject to supervision and relevant information from qualified shareholders and others closely linked to the parties. The FSA insists on corrective action if activities are not consistent with rules and regulations or sound and proper business practices, and it has the authority to call and chair board meetings. The FSA can publicly issue its interpretations of rules and regulations or guidelines for sound and proper business practices; it can conduct a house search and confiscate any material, relying on a court order; it can impose financial sanctions and withdraws licences.

The monitoring and inspection activities are both off- and on-site. The off-site approach is based on regular information gathering and analysis. Key reports on the credit system are on capital adequacy, large exposures, connected lending, defaults, liquidity, major interests in non-financial companies, lending collaterized on shares, etc. The analysis is based on general data inspection, stress testing and CAMELS, which is a risk assessment tool focusing on six key variables (capital, asset quality, management, earnings, liquidity, and sensitivity to market risk). The stress testing is discussed in detail in Section 9.3. Iceland implemented the Basel II standard as a part of its fulfilment of the EEA Agreement in 2004.

The on-site inspections are based on benchmark meetings with the management of the banks, where financial results and goals and risks are discussed. The risk categories emphasized are credit, liquidity, market and operational risks. Furthermore, the FSA monitors how well the bank measures and controls its risk. After the on-site inspections, remarks and requests for corrective actions are sent to the board and management of the banks.

### 9.1.3 Strong fiscal position

The fiscal position of the central government has been strong over the last 10 years. There has been a government budget surplus in most years (see Figure 9.8). However, there have been some concerns that this favourable position is due to the current business cycle boom rather than fiscal policies.

There is some truth to these concerns because structural fiscal balances (which are adjusted to reflect the state of the business cycle) have not been as favourable.[5] However, the differences are relatively small and do not suggest that fiscal policy is irresponsible. Favourable public finances as well as privatization of state-owned enterprises, such as the banks, have made it possible to repay almost all government debt (see Figure 9.9). It has been estimated that the net debt of the central government will amount to 1.3 per cent of GDP in 2006, a situation that other European countries would be thrilled to have.

Is it enough when discussing countries' fiscal policies to point only to surpluses and explicit debt? The answer is no. Even if the explicit debt is favourable, there could be a ticking time bomb from growing implicit debt due to, for example, unfunded pension obligations. There are numerous examples of this from around the world, and even from Iceland's neighbours in northern Europe.

Unlike many other countries Iceland is not threatened by a looming pension crisis. A reform of the pension system, which began in 1969,

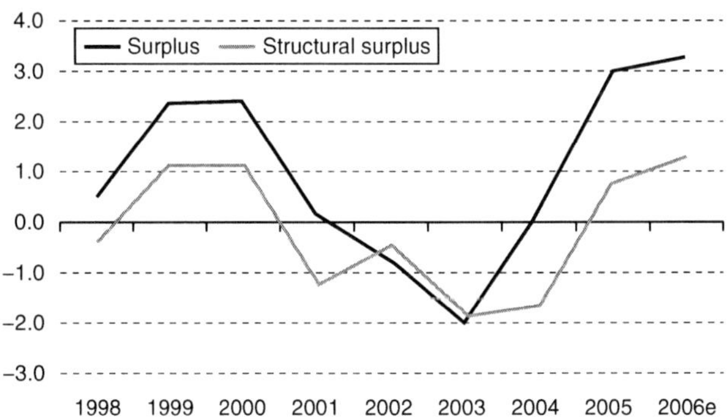


*Figure 9.8* General government surplus GDP ratio (%)
*Source*: Central Bank of Iceland.

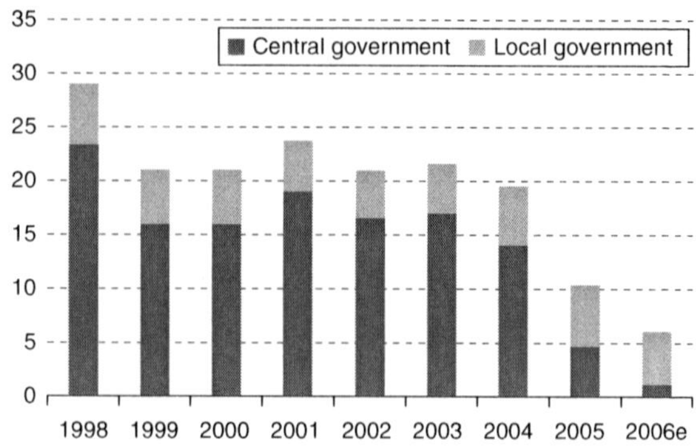


*Figure 9.9* Net government debt GDP ratio (%)
*Source*: Central Bank of Iceland.

is not only responsible for the stable outlook for future pensions but has also been an important stimulus to the rapid expansion of the country's banking system since 1996.

The pension system in Iceland is chiefly characterized by the operation of occupational pension funds. These funds became general in 1969 and mandatory by law in 1974. Under the agreement, every wage earner working in the private sector is obliged to contribute a minimum of 11 per cent of his wages to an occupational fund of his choice or, in most cases, a fund predetermined by his trade union. However, more than half of the burden is carried by the respective employer, who currently contributes a minimum of 7 per cent of the total contribution. A similar arrangement exists in the public sector.[6]

Before 1979, at the time of financial repression the assets of the pension funds were dissipated. But asset growth took off during 1979–86 when financial indexation and market-determined interest rates were introduced. Assets now amount to more than 120 per cent of the country's GDP (see Figure 9.10). Prior to the liberalization of the financial system, the pension funds had very few choices for properly investing their funds. However, the almost simultaneous emergence of the new pension system and the liberalization of financial markets had powerful interactive effects. Strong demand by the pension funds for financial instruments, combined with new opportunities for supplying securities and bonds, was the catalyst that in the 1990s rapidly triggered a vibrant market for financial securities in Iceland.

The pension fund system also served an indirect educational function by training investment managers and providing challenging opportunities

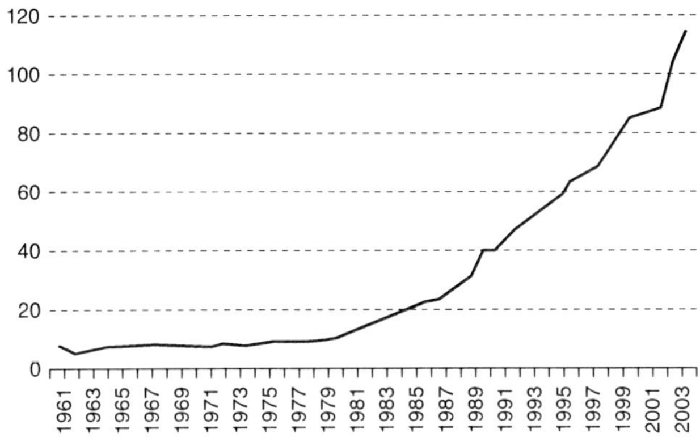


*Figure 9.10* Pension fund assets GDP ratio (%)
*Source*: The Icelandic Financial Supervisory Authority.

for young experts often educated abroad at major business schools. The opportunity to manage the assets of the pension system as well as the constant need for new financial products provided opportunities for a new generation of financial managers, who were also helped by a stable and favourable economic climate during the 1990s. The outcome has been a dynamic financial system that has outgrown the Icelandic market.

To investigate further whether Iceland has hidden implicit liabilities we use generational accounts; such accounts have been calculated for Iceland since 1994.[7] The accounts show long-term sustainability of public finances. A generational account is the net present value of expected current and future taxes paid and transfers received over the life by a representative individual of a given age. The sum of generational accounts, for all current and future individuals, forms part of the government intertemporal budget constraint, together with the net present value of other government expenditures and government debt. If there is balance between revenues, expenditure and debt, the current tax structure may be sustained for the future. If the debt is too large, as in countries with looming pension crises, future generations will have to pay for higher intertemporal debt through rising taxes or lower transfers. Implicit public liabilities measure the imbalance proportional to GDP (see Table 9.2).[8]

If Table 9.2 is compared with the GDP growth numbers in Figure 9.5, one observes that the state of implicit debt depends on the business cycle. The table shows that intertemporal public liabilities are in a relatively good state with debt amounting to a little more than 50 per cent of

*Table 9.2* Generational accounts (% of GDP)

| | *Gross external debt* | *Implicit debt* | *Intertemporal public liabilities* |
|---|---|---|---|
| 1994 | 42 | 78 | 120 |
| 1995 | 44 | 28 | 72 |
| 1996 | 43 | −5 | 38 |
| 1997 | 40 | −40 | 0 |
| 1998 | 39 | −55 | −16 |
| 1999 | 33 | −89 | −56 |
| 2000 | 36 | −79 | −43 |
| 2001 | 37 | −28 | 9 |
| 2002 | 36 | 30 | 66 |
| 2003e | 33 | 42 | 74 |
| 2004e | 28 | 25 | 53 |

*Table 9.3* Generational accounts in selected countries (% of GDP in 1995)

| | *Intertemporal public liabilities* |
|---|---|
| Norway | 10 |
| United States | 87 |
| Italy | 107 |
| Germany | 136 |
| Spain | 152 |
| United Kingdom | 185 |
| Austria | 193 |
| Finland | 253 |

GDP, which is low by international standards, as we can see in Table 9.3. Unfortunately the latest comparable figures we could find were from 1995.[9]

The age structure of the population is young by European standards. It is comparable to that of the US. This is due to longevity and unusually high fertility rates for an industrialized country. Life expectancy at birth is the highest in the world for females (82.8 years) and the second highest after Japan for males (78.9 years). Morbidity rates are also low in Iceland, indicating that costs arising from disability are low in the country. Early retirement is almost unheard of. People normally do not retire until the age of 70 although they could retire at the age of 65 and collect benefits from their pension fund. The official retirement age entitling people to collect social security benefits from the state is 67 years. As a result, Iceland has the highest labour force participation rate of older workers in the world. Total costs from retirement pension benefits amount to approximately 6 per cent of GDP, about half of which is borne by the state. The comparable figure for neighbouring

Sweden at the beginning of this century was around 11 per cent of GDP, fully financed out of taxes.[10]

Although public finances are in good order, the gross external debt of the country has grown dramatically the last few years. Since 2000 debt (excluding equity and FDI) has grown from a little more than 100 per cent of GDP to almost 294 per cent of GDP at year-end 2005 (see Figure 9.11).

Although the majority of the increased foreign debt of Icelanders is due to the banking system's becoming international, the net international investment position has deteriorated in recent years, from 65 per cent of GDP in 2000 to 86 per cent in 2005, where the increase occurred mostly in 2004 and 2005 (compared with 91 per cent in New Zealand) (see Figure 9.12).

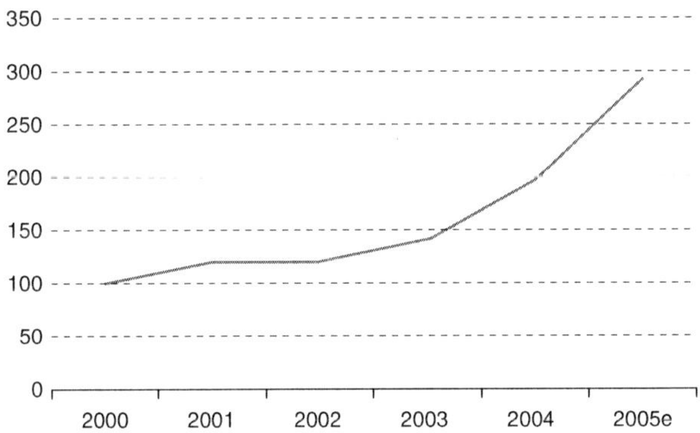


*Figure 9.11* External debt GDP ratio (%)
*Source*: Central Bank of Iceland.

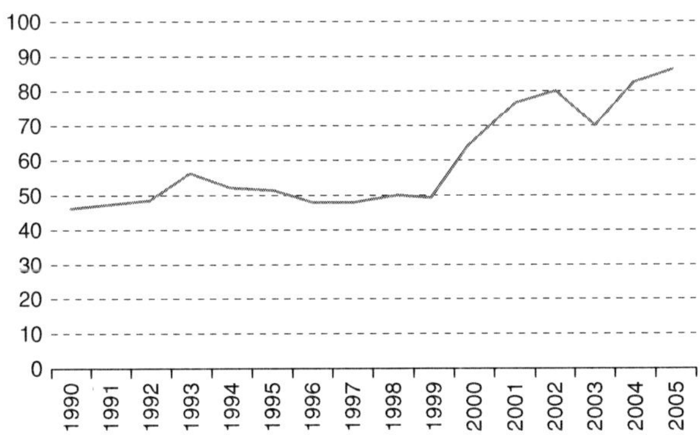


*Figure 9.12* Net international investment position GDP ratio (%)
*Source*: Central Bank of Iceland.

This increase of 21 percentage points of GDP was mostly due to increases in housing prices and the financing of investments in the energy sector, with the debt of the biggest energy company, Landsvirkjun, amounting to 12 per cent of year-end GDP in 2005.

### 9.1.4 Uniqueness of the financial sector

In the last 120 years Iceland has experienced four types of financial institutions: barter, an immature liberal system, a repressed financial market, and a full-fledged liberal market since 1979. Since the turn of the century the Icelandic banking system has moved into international financial intermediation.[11]

In the first period, which ended in 1886, commercial banks did not exist, and there was primary reliance on barter, while public funds provided limited amounts of credit after 1850. The lack of adequate financial arrangements slowed down nascent modernization of the economy. The second period, 1886–1930, saw the emergence of rural savings banks in the last quarter of the nineteenth century and the establishment of the first two commercial banks in 1886 and 1904.

Independence from Denmark in 1918 gradually introduced mistrust of foreign investors and a belief in hands-on government management of financial markets. Private foreign investment was not permitted; access to foreign currency was strictly regulated; typically real interest rates were negative; management of financial institutions was openly divided between the political parties, and political managers rationed credit to favoured industries and borrowers. By the 1960s and 1970s the financial system more closely resembled arrangements in the Third World than those in north-western Europe. The mutual self-interest of leading political actors and pressure groups preserved the system.

The third phase came to an end in 1979 when the system practically self-destructed. A rapidly rising rate of inflation created double-digit negative real interest rates that reduced the demand for real deposits, slicing the banking system in half (measured by deposits). The political managers reacted by protecting their favourite customers, partly by substantially increasing foreign borrowing, but it soon became clear that the old system was untenable.

Repressed financial systems were a common phenomenon in the twentieth century, especially among countries in the Third World. According to the Frasier Economic Freedom Index in 1980, toward the end of Iceland's period of financial repression, the country's credit market ranked number 62 of 102 markets in terms of liberalization.

Iceland has now moved up dramatically, ranking 14 of 123 in terms of liberalization in 2002, with the most liberal being Hong Kong, and Myanmar the most regulated.[12]

The first step in the modern reform process was taken in 1979 when the authorities, while still controlling nominal interest rates, introduced general indexation of financial obligations, including bank deposits and bank loans. Financial indexation proved highly successful in gradually restoring the stock of financial saving.

The next major step was taken in 1984–86 when government control of interest rates was abolished, which along with other forms of deregulation stimulated rapid development of markets for various types of securities. The Central Bank gradually reduced the reserve requirement ratios of the commercial banks from 28 per cent in 1979 to 5 per cent in 1992 (and to 2 per cent in 2003). In the old system the Treasury met its financial needs through overdrafts with the Central Bank but a new policy in 1992 ended that practice.[13]

Privatization of the three commercial banks at the turn of this century marks the final important stage in the development of the Icelandic financial system. In this respect the timing is interesting. The process took place when long-term interest rates were historically low in the world (due to high savings in Asia and the oil-producing countries, and decreasing tax rates in the industrialized countries), which in fact made transformation of the business sector in Iceland relatively easy and consequently created many new business opportunities for the banks.

The most unusual aspect of the reform process in Iceland is the extraordinary expansion of the banking system that has occurred since the reform process was completed (see Table 9.4). In the period from 1995 to 2004 the ratio of deposits to GNP had increased from 37 to 68 per cent, and the bank lending/GNP ratio increased from 55 to 254 per cent. The *Banker*, in a survey of the performance of the world's 1000 largest banks in 2004, reported that the three Icelandic commercial banks are among the fastest-growing banks in the world.

Total assets of the Icelandic banking system have grown from a little less than 60 per cent of GDP in 1990 to more than 396 per cent in 2005, which is high by any standard, but not out of line with small countries that have become international financial centres, such as Hong Kong, the Netherlands and Switzerland (Table 9.4).

To sum up, Iceland's path from repression to a modern market economy can be explained by general liberalization of the economy, privatization, globalization (the European Economic Area agreement), and well-educated young people who are often educated abroad and trained

*Table 9.4* Total bank assets GDP ratio

| | *1980*[a] | *1985* | *1990*[b] | *1995*[c] | *2000* | *2003* | *2004* |
|---|---|---|---|---|---|---|---|
| Australia | na | na | na | 1.29 | 1.57 | 1.62 | 1.78 |
| Belgium | na | na | na | na | 3.14 | 3.33 | na |
| Canada | 0.98 | 0.93 | 0.91 | 1.14 | 1.46 | 1.47 | 1.47 |
| Chile | na | na | 0.92 | 0.84 | 0.98 | 0.94 | 1.02 |
| Czech Republic | na | na | na | 1.33 | 1.34 | 1.02 | 0.96 |
| Finland | na | na | na | na | na | 1.11 | 1.23 |
| France | na | na | na | 2.22 | 2.43 | 2.54 | na |
| Germany | na | na | na | na | 3.03 | 3.04 | 3.02 |
| Hong Kong | na | 5.70 | 8.91 | 7.15 | 5.17 | 5.32 | 5.53 |
| Hungary | na | na | na | 0.69 | 0.64 | 0.73 | 0.77 |
| Iceland | 0.37 | 0.50 | 0.57 | 0.55 | 1.18 | 1.80 | 2.54 |
| Italy | na | na | na | na | 1.53 | 1.73 | 1.76 |
| Japan | na | 1.66 | 2.11 | 1.72 | 1.62 | na | na |
| Malaysia | na | na | na | 2.03 | 1.92 | 2.07 | 1.94 |
| Netherlands | na | na | na | na | 4.03 | 4.26 | 4.44 |
| Norway | na | na | 0.85 | 0.76 | 0.91 | 1.10 | 1.07 |
| Saudi Arabia | na | na | na | 0.64 | 0.64 | 0.68 | 0.70 |
| South Africa | na | na | 0.77 | 0.73 | 0.92 | 1.14 | na |
| Spain | na | na | na | na | 1.84 | 2.02 | 2.05 |
| Sweden | na | na | na | na | 2.13 | 2.14 | 2.35 |
| Switzerland | 2.63 | 3.18 | 3.30 | 3.56 | 5.11 | 5.19 | 5.60 |
| Thailand | na | na | na | na | 1.27 | 1.15 | 1.11 |
| UK | 0.47 | 0.68 | 1.09 | 1.05 | 1.54 | 1.72 | 1.81 |
| USA | 0.57 | 0.58 | 0.57 | 0.57 | 0.62 | 0.67 | 0.68 |

*Source*: BIS, unofficial statistics.
[a]1981 for Canada and Iceland.
[b]1991 for South Africa.
[c]1996 for Malaysia, and 2001 for Sweden.

in a financial market that is disproportionate to the size of the country due to the extent of its pension wealth. The result has been a movement toward Iceland's becoming an international banking centre (although on a small scale because the country is, after all, a microstate), where its banks perform financial intermediation, mostly outside of the country.

It is fairly obvious that the internalization of Icelandic financial institutions has changed the way they are financed (see Table 9.5). The total assets of the system were about 80 per cent of GDP in 2000 but were more than four times GDP in 2006. A banking system that is only serving the local market can finance itself domestically. In early 2000 less than one-third of the financing came from abroad, while in 2006 almost two-thirds came from the international financial market.

Almost half of the financing came out of domestic deposits in 2000 but only about 15 per cent in 2006. At the same time, deposits grew

*Table 9.5* Financing of the banking system

| | ***Feb 2006*** | | ***Feb 2005*** | | ***Feb 2004*** | | ***Feb 2003*** | | ***Feb 2002*** | | ***Feb 2001*** | | ***Feb 2000*** | |
|---|---|---|---|---|---|---|---|---|---|---|---|---|---|---|
| **Domestic liabilities** | **922 084** | **21%** | **708 727** | **30%** | **592 916** | **39%** | **499 577** | **47%** | **446 283** | **46%** | **360 057** | **46%** | **335 328** | **62%** |
| Deposits | 654 152 | 15% | 541 152 | 23% | 468 258 | 31% | 386 337 | 37% | 343 896 | 36% | 290 149 | 37% | 260 827 | 48% |
| Bond issues | 133 574 | 3% | 98 950 | 4% | 74 290 | 5% | 80 541 | 8% | 68 886 | 7% | 51 004 | 7% | 58 729 | 11% |
| Other borrowing | 134 358 | 3% | 68 625 | 3% | 50 368 | 3% | 32 699 | 3% | 33 501 | 3% | 18 904 | 2% | 15 772 | 3% |
| **Foreign liabilities** | **2 589 534** | **60%** | **1 213 549** | **52%** | **709 588** | **47%** | **454 145** | **43%** | **427 609** | **44%** | **357 988** | **46%** | **156 069** | **29%** |
| Deposits | 135 375 | 3% | 11 685 | 0% | 6 155 | 0% | 0 | 0% | 0 | 0% | 0 | 0% | 0 | 0% |
| Bond issues | 1 954 724 | 45% | 956 506 | 41% | 529 148 | 35% | 214 839 | 20% | 201 534 | 21% | 124 096 | 16% | 156 069 | 0% |
| Direct lending | 499 436 | 12% | 245 358 | 10% | 174 285 | 12% | 239 306 | 23% | 226 075 | 24% | 233 892 | 30% | 52 573 | 29% |
| **Capital and subordinated debt** | **670 104** | **16%** | **395 700** | **17%** | **170 749** | **11%** | **127 446** | **12%** | **111 341** | **12%** | **76 869** | **10%** | **52 573** | **10%** |
| **Other items** | **114 763** | **3%** | **21 923** | **1%** | **39 260** | **3%** | **−27 104** | **−3%** | **−23 749** | **−2%** | **−19 249** | **−2%** | **−3 643** | **−1%** |
| **Total** | **4 296 485** | **100%** | **2 339 899** | **100%** | **1 512 513** | **100%** | **1 054 064** | **100%** | **961 484** | **100%** | **775 665** | **100%** | **540 327** | **100%** |

*Source*: Central Bank of Iceland.

from 38 per cent of GDP in 2000 to 65 per cent in 2006. This illustrates that the Icelandic banking system has changed from a system of local depositary institutions to an international financial intermediator in only five years.

In 2000 the external debt of the banks was a little more than 50 per cent of GDP but almost 240 per cent in 2005 (see Figure 9.13). Until recently the banks operated almost solely in the small domestic Icelandic market. As global liquidity has increased, and Icelandic entrepreneurs have started to make use of historically low interest rates to acquire businesses outside Iceland, the banks have followed. Assets of the banking system abroad have consequently increased (see Figure 9.14).

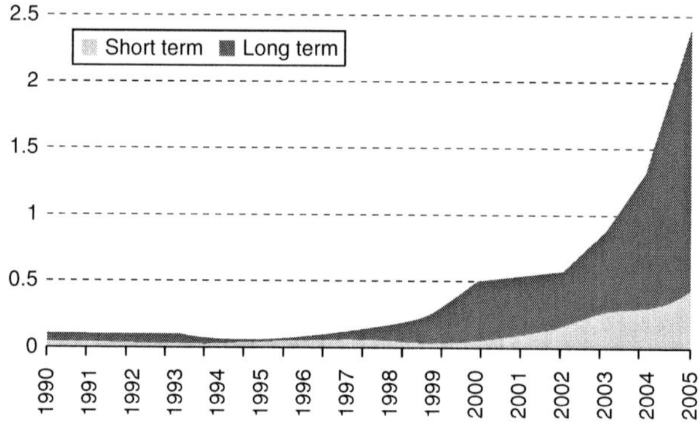


*Figure 9.13* External debt of the banking system GDP ratio
*Source*: Central Bank of Iceland.

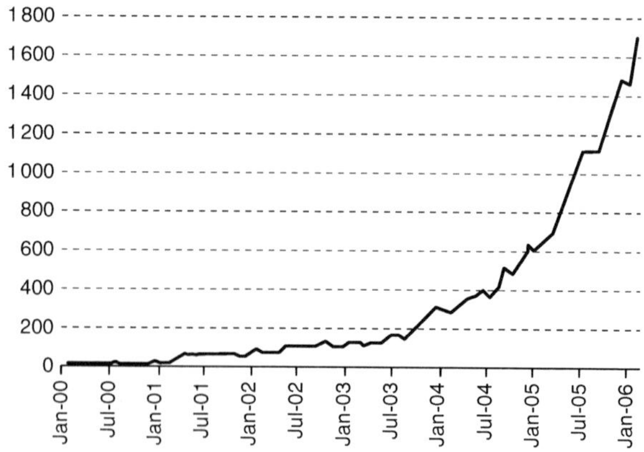


*Figure 9.14* Foreign assests of the banking system (bISK)
*Source*: Central Bank of Iceland.

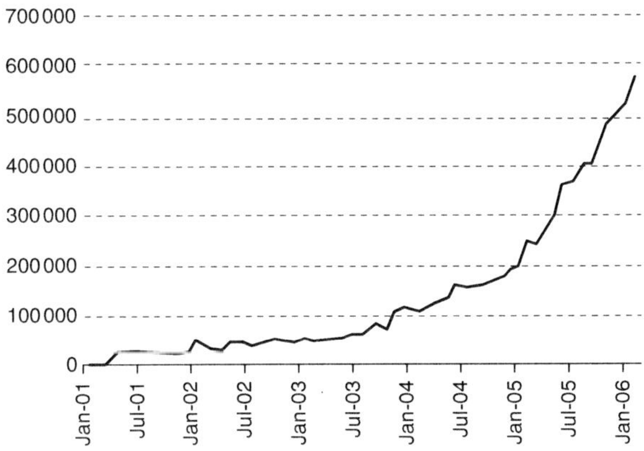


*Figure 9.15* Foreign lending (bISK)
*Source*: Central Bank of Iceland.

The growth in assets abroad February 2005 to February 2006, is 160 per cent from 661 bISK to 1719 bISK, almost double the country's GDP. Foreign lending has also increased considerably (see Figure 9.15).

## 9.2 Understanding financial instability

Recent reports by research departments of international banks on the Icelandic economy have raised the spectre of a possible financial meltdown, and they see possible parallels between Iceland's economic situation and that of emerging market countries, such as Thailand, which experienced financial crises in the late 1990s.[14] In order to evaluate whether Iceland's economy is financially fragile, we need to step back a bit and examine what economic analysis tells us about the sources of financial instability. Then we can ask whether the conditions that led to financial instability elsewhere are also present in Iceland.

### 9.2.1 What is financial instability?

A financial system performs the essential function of channelling funds to those individuals or firms with productive investment opportunities. To do this well, participants in financial markets must be able to make accurate judgements about which investment opportunities are more or less creditworthy. Thus, a financial system must confront problems of asymmetric information, in which one party to a financial contract has much less accurate information than the other party. For example, borrowers who take out loans usually have better information about the potential returns and risk associated with the investment projects they plan to undertake than lenders do. Asymmetric information leads to two basic problems in the financial system (and elsewhere): adverse selection and moral hazard.

Adverse selection occurs before the financial transaction takes place, when potential bad credit risks are the ones most actively seeking loans. For example, those wanting to take on big risks are likely to be the most eager to take out a loan, even at a high rate of interest, because they are less concerned with paying the loan back. Thus, the lender must be concerned that the parties most likely to produce an undesirable or adverse outcome are also most likely to be selected as borrowers. Lenders will try to tackle the problem posed by asymmetric information by screening out bad from good credit risks. But this process is inevitably imperfect, and fear of adverse selection, particularly if it is harder to get information about potential borrowers, will lead lenders to reduce the quantity of loans they might otherwise make.

Moral hazard occurs after the transaction takes place. It occurs because a borrower has incentives to engage in risky activities that are undesirable from the lender's point of view because they decrease the likelihood that the loan will be paid back. Higher-risk activities, if they pay off, produce high returns for the borrower, but if they fail, the lender bears most of the loss. Lenders often impose restrictions (restrictive covenants) on borrowers so that borrowers do not engage in behaviour making it less likely that they can pay back the loan. However, such restrictions are costly to enforce and monitor, particularly when information is harder to collect, again leading lenders to reduce the amount of lending they might otherwise make.

The asymmetric information problems described above provide a definition of what financial instability is:[15]

> Financial instability occurs when there is a disruption to financial markets in which asymmetric information and hence adverse selection and moral hazard problems become much worse, so that financial markets are unable to channel funds eficiently to those with the most productive investment opportunities.

Financial instability thus results in the inability of financial markets to function efficiently, which can lead to a sharp contraction in economic activity.

### 9.2.2 What causes financial instability to occur?

Although there can be general increases in uncertainty making it harder to collect information in financial markets and thus leading to increases in adverse selection and moral hazard problems, the main source of financial instability is deterioration in balance sheets, both in the financial and the non-financial sectors.

*Deterioration in bank balance sheets*

The literature on asymmetric information and financial structure explains why financial intermediaries (commercial banks, thrift institutions, finance companies, insurance companies, mutual funds and pension funds), play such an important role in the financial system.[16] They have both the ability and the economic incentive to address asymmetric information problems. For example, banks have an obvious ability to collect information at the time they consider making a loan, and this ability is only increased when banks engage in long-term customer relationships and a line of credit arrangements. In addition, their ability to scrutinize the checking account balances of their borrowers provides banks with an additional advantage in monitoring the borrowers' behaviour. Banks also have advantages in reducing moral hazard;[17] they can engage in lower-cost monitoring than individuals, and they have advantages in preventing risk taking by borrowers since they can use the threat of cutting off lending in the future to improve a borrower's behaviour.[18] Banks' natural advantages in collecting information and reducing moral hazard explain why banks have such an important role in financial markets throughout the world.

The special importance of banks and other financial intermediaries in the financial system implies that if their ability to lend is impaired, overall lending will decline and the economy will contract. If banks (and other financial intermediaries making loans) suffer deterioration in their balance sheets, and so have substantial contraction in their capital, they have two choices: they can either cut back on their lending or try to raise new capital. However, when these institutions experience deterioration in their balance sheets, it is very hard for them to raise new capital at a reasonable cost. Thus, the typical response of financial institutions to weakened balance sheets is a contraction in their lending, which slows economic activity.

If the deterioration in bank balance sheets is severe enough, it can even lead to bank panics, in which there are multiple, simultaneous failures of banking institutions. Indeed, in the absence of a government safety net, there is some risk that contagion can spread from one bank failure to another, causing even healthy banks to fail. The source of the contagion is again asymmetric information. In a panic, depositors, fearing the safety of their deposits and not knowing the quality of the banks' loan portfolios, withdraw their deposits from the banking system, causing a contraction in loans and a multiple contraction in deposits, which then causes other banks to fail. In turn, the failure of a bank means the loss of the information relationships in which that bank participated, and thus a direct loss in the amount of financial intermediation that can be done by the banking sector. The outcome is an even sharper decline in lending to facilitate productive investments, with an additional resulting contraction in economic activity.

*Deterioration of non-financial balance sheets*

If there is a widespread deterioration of balance sheets among non-financial borrowers, it worsens both adverse selection and moral hazard problems in financial markets, thus promoting financial instability. This problem can arise in a variety of ways.

For example, lenders often use collateral as an important way of addressing asymmetric information problems. Collateral reduces the consequences of adverse selection or moral hazard because it reduces the lender's losses in the case of a default. If a borrower defaults on a loan, the lender can sell the collateral to make up for at least some of the losses on the loan. But if asset prices in an economy fall, and the value of collateral falls as well, then the problems of asymmetric information suddenly increase.

Net worth can perform a similar role to collateral. If a firm has high net worth, then even if it defaults on its debt payments, the lender can take title to the firm's net worth, sell it off, and use the proceeds to recoup some of the losses from the loan. High net worth also directly decreases the incentives for borrowers to commit moral hazard because borrowers now have more at stake, and thus more to lose, if they default on their loans. The importance of net worth explains why stock market crashes can cause financial instability. A sharp decline in the stock market reduces the market valuation of a firm's net worth, and thus can increase adverse selection and moral hazard problems in financial markets.[19] Since the stock market decline reducing net worth increases incentives for borrowers to engage in moral hazard, and since lenders are now less protected against the consequences of adverse selection because the value of net assets is worth less, lending decreases and economic activity declines.

*The role of currency crises in balance sheet deterioration*

A prominent feature of recent episodes of financial crises is that they have been triggered by a collapse of the domestic currency. But not all currency crises lead to financial instability. For example, the successful attack on the British pound in the ERM currency crisis of September 1992 did not lead to financial instability in the United Kingdom. Indeed, the resulting currency depreciation ended up stimulating the UK economy because it made British goods cheaper internationally, which increased the demand for British goods and services and promoted an expansion in the British economy. This was also the case in Iceland in 2001. Although the ISK depreciated dramatically, the health of the financial system remained strong. On the other hand, currency crises in emerging market countries have been accompanied by full-scale financial crises, a phenomenon that is referred to as 'twin crises'.[20] Currency crises in these countries result in financial instability because they produce a sharp deterioration in balance sheets.

A key characteristic distinguishing emerging market economies from advanced economies like Iceland's is the structure of their debt markets. In advanced economies inflation has tended to be moderate, and so debt contracts are typically of fairly long duration, with fixed nominal interest rates. In contrast, emerging market countries have experienced very high and variable inflation rates in the past, with accompanying wide swings in the value of the domestic currency. One result of their experience is that debt contracts are of very short duration in order to minimize the inflation risk. In many emerging market countries, for example, almost all bank lending is very short term, with variable rate contracts that are adjusted on a monthly, or sometimes daily, basis. In addition, because of the likelihood that their currency's value will change for the worse, many non-financial firms, banks and governments in emerging market countries find it much easier to issue debt denominated in foreign currencies, often US dollars.[21] This phenomenon is called liability dollarization, although other foreign currencies besides dollars are used to denominate debt. In comparison, less than 5 per cent of household debt in Iceland is foreign currency denominated and more than 85 per cent of the debt stock is long term (duration of the stock more than 30 years). Also, more than 70 per cent of loans to companies are with natural or derivative hedges as we will see in the next section.

When debt contracts are denominated in foreign currency, and there is an unanticipated depreciation or devaluation of the domestic currency, the debt burden of domestic firms increases in terms of domestic currency because it takes more domestic currency to pay back the dollarized debt. If the goods and services produced by most firms are priced in the domestic currency, the firms' assets do not rise in value in terms of domestic currency, while the debt does. The depreciation of the domestic currency then increases the value of debt relative to assets, and the firm's net worth declines. The decline in net worth then increases adverse selection and moral hazard problems described earlier, which lead, in turn, to a decline in investment and economic activity.

For firms exporting most of their output (generally priced in foreign currency), the impact of depreciation on the balance sheet is, however, far less severe when they have foreign-denominated debt because it is in effect hedged. The depreciation leads to a rise in the prices of the goods and services the exporter produces, thereby raising the value of its assets in terms of the domestic currency. The increase in asset values helps to offset the rise in the value of the exporter's debt. This outcome suggests that when the export sector in an emerging market economy is large, the consequences of a currency collapse on balance sheets and the overall economy will be less severe, and this is what empirical evidence finds.[22]

Although depreciation in an emerging market country under a floating exchange rate regime can lead to financial fragility, it is less likely than a pegged exchange rate regime to cause a full-fledged financial crisis in which financial markets seize up and stop performing their role of moving funds to those with productive investment opportunities. First, a floating exchange rate regime makes currency risk clearer so that firms, both financial and non-financial, are more likely to hedge against this currency risk. Second, in contrast to a floating exchange rate regime, when a successful speculative attack occurs against a pegged exchange rate regime, the decline in the value of the domestic currency is usually much larger, more rapid and more unanticipated than when depreciation occurs under a floating exchange rate regime.[23] For example, during the East Asian crisis in 1997, currencies fell by 50 per cent, with the worst-hit country Indonesia seeing its currency decline by 75 per cent in a very short period.

In addition, a pegged exchange rate regime encourages unhedged liability dollarization which makes the financial system more vulnerable when depreciation occurs: domestic firms whose output is denominated in the local currency are more likely to borrow in foreign currency because the government's commitment to preventing a decline in the value of the domestic currency reduces their risk. With a guarantee that the local currency will remain fixed in terms of foreign currency, the domestic firm does not have to worry that the local currency will depreciate, which would require the firm to pony up more of its local currency to pay back foreign-currency debt.[24]

The dangers of a pegged exchange rate regime prompted Stanley Fischer, the first deputy managing director of the IMF, to state:[25]

> Each of the major international capital market-related crises since 1994 – Mexico in 1994, Thailand, Indonesia and Korea in 1997, Russia and Brazil in 1998, and Argentina and Turkey in 2000 – has in some way involved a fixed or pegged exchange rate regime. At the same time, countries that did not have pegged rates – among them South Africa, Israel in 1998, Mexico in 1998 – avoided crises of the type that aflicted emerging market countries with pegged rates.

Fischer even went so far as to declare that adoption of a flexible exchange rate system is the most important preventitive measure an emerging market can take against crises.

### 9.2.3 Routes to financial instability

Now that we understand what causes financial instability, we can examine the routes through which it occurs so that we can see if what is happening in Iceland currently suggests that financial instability is a potential problem. There are three basic routes to financial instability: (1) financial liberalization with inadequate prudential regulation and supervision; (2) severe fiscal imbalances, and (3) imprudent monetary policy. We examine each of these in turn.[26]

*Financial liberalization with weak prudential regulation and supervision*

The seeds of financial instability are often sown when countries liberalize their financial systems, usually several years before the crisis hits. Eighteen of 26 crises in the last 20 years occurred after the financial sector had been liberalized, both internally and externally, in the preceding five years.[27]

With internal restrictions lifted, banks go on a lending spree and expand their lending by 15–30 per cent per year, which is more than double the typical lending growth rate.[28] The lending boom can be exacerbated by capital inflows, which adds fuel to the fire. Not only do banks increase their lending, they give out more loans to firms in industries about which they have little knowledge. Because the managers of the banking institutions in emerging market countries typically do not have the required expertise to manage risk appropriately in these new lines of business and are unable to cope with the rapid growth of lending typically following financial liberalization, problems are bound to arise. Even if the required managerial expertise is available initially, the rapid lending growth would likely outstrip the information resources available to banking institutions. Increased lending to industries about which banks know little results in excessive risk taking on the banks' part.

Because of this lack of expertise in screening and monitoring borrowers, losses on the loans begin to mount, driving down the net worth (capital) of the bank. With less capital, banks become riskier, and so depositors and other potential lenders to the banks are less willing to supply them with funds. Fewer funds then mean fewer loans and lending. The lending boom will turn into a lending crash.

The lending boom is also exacerbated by the presence of a government safety net for the banking system which is present in some form in all countries. If depositors and other providers of funds to banks are protected from losses, they will keep on supplying banks with funds so banks can continue to lend and will not fail. This is the good news. The bad news is that the government safety net weakens market discipline for the bank because with a safety net, depositors know that they will not lose anything if a bank fails, and so the bank can still acquire funds even if it takes on excessive risk. The government safety net increases the moral hazard incentive for banks to take on greater risk than they otherwise would, because if their risky, but high-interest, loans pay off, the banks make a lot of money; if they do not and the bank fails, taxpayers pay most of the bill for the safety net protecting the banks' depositors. In other words, banks can play the game of 'heads, I win: tails, the taxpayer loses'.

The moral hazard incentives to take on excessive risk arising from the government safety net are most likely to be a source of bad loans than bank managers' lack of expertise. Even in countries with well-developed banking sectors, financial liberalization has often led to lending booms and banking crises, as the experience in the 1980s and 1990s in Japan, the United States and Scandinavia suggests. A government safety net has the unintended consequence of making it more likely that a lending boom will occur, followed by an economic bust, and this is exactly what happened in East Asia.[29]

A solution preventing a lending boom and bust is prudential regulation and supervision of the banking system to prevent banks from taking on excessive risk.[30] However, financial liberalization is often undertaken with completely inadequate prudential regulation and supervision. This is not an accident. In countries with weak institutional frameworks (endemic corruption and a weak free press that has little incentive to keep politicians honest), powerful business interests that own banks are able to prevent the bank supervisors from doing their job properly. They are often able to persuade politicians to weaken regulations restricting their banks from engaging in high-risk/high-payoff strategies. After all, if bank owners can go for growth and expand bank lending rapidly, they stand to make a fortune. But, if the bank gets in trouble, the government is likely to bail it out, and the taxpayer foots the bill. In addition, these business interests can also make sure that the supervisory agencies are starved of resources, so that even in the presence of tough regulations, the supervisory agency does not have the capability to effectively monitor banking institutions or to close them down.

The deterioration in bank balance sheets triggers currency crises because when banks and other financial institutions are in trouble, it is not as easy for governments to defend their currencies by raising interest rates and thus encourage capital inflows. If the government raises interest rates, banks must pay more to obtain funds. This increase in costs decreases bank profitability, which may lead them to insolvency. Thus, when the banking system is in trouble, the government and Central Bank are now between a rock and a hard place: if they raise interest rates too much, they will destroy their already weakened banks, and if they do not they cannot maintain the value of their currency.

Once speculators in the market for foreign currency recognize the troubles in a country's financial sector and realize that the government's ability to defend the currency is limited, they know that they are presented with an almost sure-thing bet because the currency has only one way to go, downward in value. Speculators engage in a feeding frenzy and sell the currency in anticipation of its decline, which will provide them with huge profits. These sales rapidly use up the country's holdings of reserves of foreign currency because it has to sell its reserves to buy the domestic currency and keep it from falling in value. Once the country's Central Bank has exhausted its holdings of foreign currency reserves, the jig is up. It no longer has the resources to intervene in the foreign exchange market and must let the value of the domestic currency fall: that is, the government must allow a devaluation.

Now depreciation of the currency tips the economy over into a full-fledged financial crisis because it increases the value of debt relative to assets, with the result that firms' balance sheets deteriorate sharply, leading to increased adverse selection and moral hazard problems, which lead, in turn, to a decline in investment and economic activity. To see how the currency crisis destroys balance sheets and provokes a financial crisis, we can look at what happened in Indonesia after its 1997 currency crisis during which the rupiah's value fell by 75 per cent and dollar-denominated debt became four times as expensive in terms of rupiah. In this situation, almost every Indonesian firm with a substantial amount of dollar debt became insolvent. The moral hazard and adverse selection problems of lending to an insolvent firm were so severe that even if an Indonesian firm in this situation initially had a strong balance sheet, was run well, and had superb investment opportunities, no one would lend to it. Investment and spending collapsed as did the entire economy: output declined by over 10 per cent in 1998 (larger than the decline the United States experienced in the first year of the Great Depression), and the percentage of the population living in poverty doubled.

*Severe fiscal imbalances*

The second route through which countries end up experiencing a financial crisis is through government fiscal imbalances entailing substantial budget deficits that need to be financed. The recent financial crisis in Argentina in 2001–2 is of this type, but other recent crises, for example in Russia in 1998, Ecuador in 1999 and Turkey in 2001, also have some elements of this type of crisis.[31]

In contrast to Mexico and the East Asian crisis countries, Argentina had a well-supervised banking system, and a lending boom did not occur before the crisis. Thus, the banks were in surprisingly good shape before the crisis, even though a severe recession had begun in 1998. This recession led to declining tax revenue and a widening gap between expenditures and taxes. The subsequent severe fiscal imbalances (budget deficits) were so large that the government had trouble getting both domestic residents and foreigners to buy enough of its bonds. It then had to look for other sources to finance its deficits.

When governments face large fiscal imbalances and cannot finance their debt, they often cajole or force banks to purchase government debt. This is exactly what the Argentine government did in the run-up to its financial crisis in 2001. When investors lose confidence in the ability of the government to repay this debt, they unload government bonds, which causes their prices to plummet. Now the banks that are holding this debt have a big hole on the asset side of their balance sheets, with a huge decline in their net worth. The deterioration in bank balance sheets then causes a decline in bank lending and can even lead to a bank panic, and this is exactly what happened in Argentina. Severe fiscal imbalances spill over into and weaken the banking system, which leads to a worsening of adverse selection and moral hazard problems, which, in turn, cause an economic contraction.

We have seen that severe fiscal imbalances, as in Argentina, can lead to a deterioration in bank balance sheets, and so can help produce a currency crisis and financial crisis along the lines described above. Fiscal imbalances can also directly trigger a currency/financial crisis. When government budget deficits spin out of control, foreign and domestic investors begin to suspect that the country may not be able to pay back its government debt and so will start pulling money out of the country and selling the domestic currency. Recognition that the fiscal situation is out of control thus results in a speculative attack against the currency, which eventually results in its collapse, as occurred in Argentina on 6 January 2002. Then the depreciation of the currency destroys balance sheets, particularly if there is extensive liability dollarization, as there was in Argentina, triggering a financial crisis and a great depression.

*Imprudent monetary policy*

Monetary policy which produces episodes of high inflation can also promote financial instability. When countries have a past history of high inflation, debt contracts are often denominated in foreign currencies, and this liability dollarization makes the financial system more fragile because currency depreciation is then likely to trigger a financial crisis.[32]

Furthermore, a weakening of the credibility of the monetary authorities to keep inflation under control can lead to depreciation of the currency which leads to a destruction of balance sheets and financial instability. Indeed, we saw this scenario played out in Argentina when Domingo Cavallo, who was appointed as the economy minister in March 2001, used his special powers to revise the charter of the Banco Central de Republica Argentina to remove limits on the ability of the Central Bank to inject liquidity into the economy. This allowed the Central Bank, which was effectively controlled by the government after its respected president Pedro Pou was forced to resign, to pursue discretionary expansionary policy, which it eventually did. These actions compromised the independence of the Banco Central de Republica Argentina, weakened its credibility and opened the door for expansionary monetary policy that would help bring the currency board down.

## 9.3 Is Iceland going down traditonal routes to financial instability?

Armed with an economic analysis of financial instability from the last section and the overview of the Icelandic economy in the first, we can ask if the current situation in Iceland suggests that it might be headed for the type of instability experienced by other countries in recent years.

### 9.3.1 Financial liberalization with weak prudential regulation and supervision?

Financial instability often follows financial liberalization, but financial instability almost always manifests itself within five or so years of the financial liberalization. As our overview of the Icelandic economy indicates, financial liberalization began in earnest in the 1980s and was mostly complete by 1995. Banks have therefore had more than sufficient time to develop the expertise to manage risk appropriately in the new lines of business that are opened up by financial liberalization. Having stated this, one has to be cautious and discuss the possible dangers from the credit boom in Iceland in recent years, as we will do later in this section.

Financial instability also results from inadequate regulation and supervision of the financial system, often resulting from a weak institutional framework, making it unlikely that bank supervisors will be able to impose the appropriate oversight of the financial system so that it avoids taking on excessive risk. Iceland, however, has excellent institutions: indeed, as we have seen, the quality of its bureaucracy and low levels of corruption rank it among the best-run countries in the world as we saw in the overview section. In contrast to the inadequate prudential supervision in countries that have experienced financial instability, Iceland's prudential supervisors are seen as honest and competent. Their statements that the banking system in Iceland is safe and sound should be taken at face value. In the last annual report of the Financial Supervisory Authority (FSA), it is recognized that the credit expansion is a source of risk, and that the internationalization of the Icelandic banks will create challenges for the authority.[33] The rapid growth in foreign operations means new risks and calls for more complex and more robust risk management than before. At the same time, the FSA has noted the strong capital position of the banks, and that they are well equipped to meet potential challenges.

Another factor that can lead to financial instability is a large amount of unhedged liability dollarization: in other words, a large amount of foreign-denominated debt that is lent to businesses whose cash flow, and hence assets, are priced in local currency. It is certainly true that Iceland's banks have an enormous amount of liabilities denominated in foreign currency relative to the size of Iceland's economy, close to 250 per cent of GDP (Figure 9.13).

As the Icelandic banking system has become more international, new risks have surfaced. One key issue is how vulnerable the banks are to large swings in the domestic currency. The direct exposure of the banks to risk associated with depreciation of the currency is minimal as foreign assets and liability must more or less match by law. The foreign currency assets of the banks (spot, forwards, and options) at the end of March 2006 were approximately 5103 bISK, but liabilities were 5005 bISK, leaving a positive net position in foreign currency of approximately 100 bISK, or 19.2 per cent of the banks' total net assets. The liabilities are thus hedged fully for currency risks and a considerable chunk of net assets of the banks.

A natural question to ask now is how vulnerable the credit stock is for currency depreciations. How common is it for firms and households to have foreign currency dominated debt but income in ISK, leaving them vulnerable to sudden drops in the ISK?

*Households*

The total debt of households to the credit system, year-end 2005, was 1082 bISK, just over 100 per cent of GDP (Figure 9.16). Of this a little more than 540 bISK was owed to the banks, while the remainder was owed to the Housing Finance Fund (HFF), the Student Loan Fund, the pension funds, etc. The loans from the funds are all long term and indexed; in fact most household debt is indexed with fixed interest rates (over 85 per cent). The inflation component of the interest rates is spread over the entire maturity of the loan, and thus it insulates households from fluctuations in nominal interest rates. This is positive

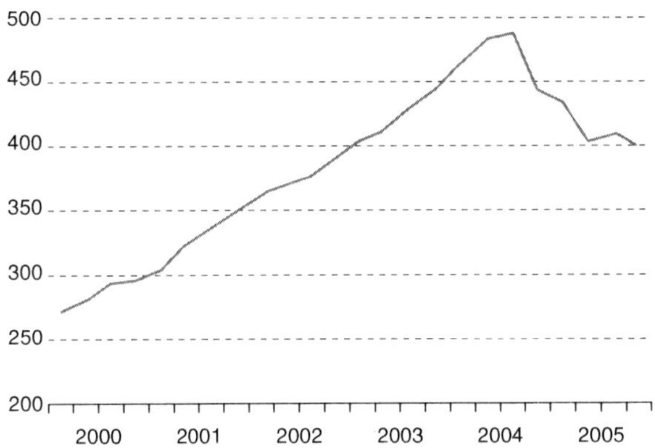


*Figure 9.16* Lending of the Housing Finance Fund (bISK)
*Source*: Central Bank of Iceland.

from a financial stability perspective but negative from a price stability (monetary policy) perspective.

Figure 9.16 shows that the majority of households' debt (around 75 per cent) was to other parts of the credit system rather than the banks until the third quarter of 2004. In August 2004 banks went into the mortgage market, offering fixed-rate indexed loans of up to 40 years with rates about 100 basis points lower (4.15 per cent real) than the state-run HFF was offering. Moreover, the banks had no maximum on the loans, while the HFF had been limiting the maximum to 65 per cent of the market value of the residential property or up to ISK 9.2 million. Needless to say, many borrowers used the opportunity, refinanced their mortgages and moved their business from the HFF to the banks (see Figure 9.16). As Figure 9.17 shows, household debt to the credit system moved to the banks from other parts of the system, most notably from the HFF. In only 15 months banks' financing of total debt of households changed from being about 25 per cent of the total stock to 50 per cent, and the debt increased by almost 250 bISK, most of it mortgages.

Despite a rise in total household debt in recent years, debt service as a percentage of disposable income has not risen since 2000. This is due to disposable income rising dramatically and the duration of the total outstanding loan stock increasing by about four years since June 2004. Furthermore, average interest rates have fallen by about 150 basis points on fixed-rate indexed mortgages and most of the high-interest-bearing, short-term debt has been refinanced since the banks started actively in the mortgages market in autumn 2004. Households are thus basically at

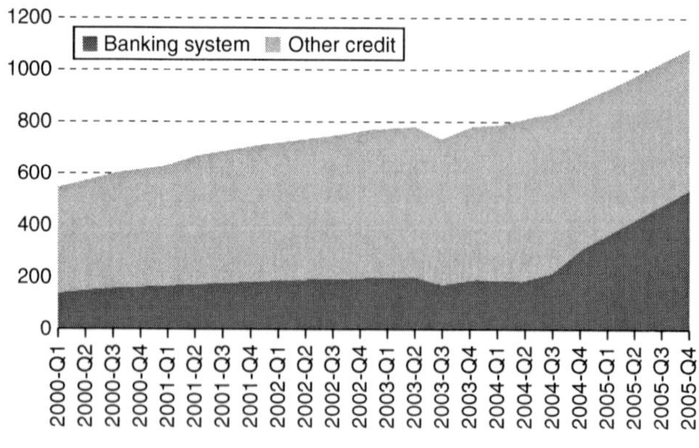


*Figure 9.17* Household borrowing from the credit system (bISK)
*Source*: Central Bank of Iceland.

the same starting point as in 2000 in terms of debt service ratio. A fall in the ISK would of course result in inflation hikes, but that would not lead to an excessive debt service burden as loans are indexed and bear fixed real rates. A rule of thumb is that a 10 per cent lasting depreciation increases inflation by 3.5 per cent and debt service approximately in the same proportion. Loan-to-value ratio for new bank mortgages has been 70 per cent on average, but due to increases in real estate prices the current loan-to-value ratio is estimated at 61 per cent. The mortgage collateral coverage of credit institutions is thus high, which should enable them to withstand substantial price changes.[34] Furthermore, only about 4 per cent of households have foreign currency dominated loans amounting to less than 5 per cent of the total household debt stock in 2004. In conclusion, a fall in the ISK is likely to increase household credit risks for the banking system, but only marginally. There is actually an upside for the banks from a fall in the ISK. As most of the debt is indexed, but liabilities only to a smaller extent, an inflation spike would thus benefit the banks.

*Firms*

Industries' debt to the credit system stood at 2172 bISK at the end of 2005, an increase of 49 per cent year-on-year. Most of the increase occurred in the banking system. Around 52 per cent of the banking system's corporate lendings is foreign currency dominated, down from 58 per cent in 2000 (see Figure 9.18). About 77 per cent of the income of the

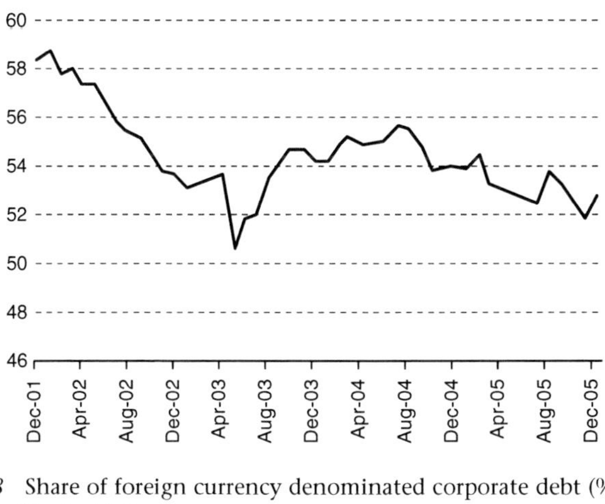


*Figure 9.18* Share of foreign currency denominated corporate debt (%)
*Source*: Central Bank of Iceland.

15 companies making up the ICEX-15 stock index is generated abroad. About 33 per cent of their income is in British pounds, 24 per cent in euros, 23 per cent in ISK, 11 per cent in US dollars and 9 per cent in other currencies. It is interesting that as the currency depreciates, the value of companies on the Iceland Stock Exchange in ISK increases as most of their income is in foreign currency. Almost 100 per cent of the fish and fish processing firms have their income in foreign currency, almost 100 per cent of the tourist industry, and 100 per cent of the metal industry. Landsbanki has estimated that 73 per cent of banks' foreign currency lending is to foreign companies and domestic companies with natural or derivative hedges. It thus appears that risks for the banking system from depreciation effects of the ISK are moderate.

Balance sheets of both firms and households in Iceland appear to be quite well insulated from exchange rate shocks. The floating exchange rate regime in Iceland also means that the risks from currency movements are well recognized by both the banks and bank supervisors. Indeed, the supervisors have put the top three Icelandic banks through stress tests to see if they can withstand major shocks.

The stress test is such that the banks must be in a position to face setbacks that may simultaneously lead to 20 per cent reduction in value of non-performing loans and appropriated assets, a 25 per cent reduction in value of foreign shares of the bank, a 35 per cent reduction in the value of domestic shares of the bank, a 7 per cent reduction in value of bonds owned by the bank, and a 20 per cent weakening of the ISK. If a bank fails to meet the criteria, the FSA may request a minimum capital adequacy ratio above 8 per cent for the undertaking in question. Prior to taking such a decision, the supervisor is required to initiate talks with the board and management of the institution in question on its risk measurement methods and capital position and the action intended on behalf of the management in order to meet the statutory minimum requirements. A recent stress test by the FSA shows a need to increase the minimum capital adequacy ratio to approximately 10–11.5 per cent in a worst-case scenario. This is below the current capital adequacy ratio of the Icelandic banks, which is 15.7 per cent for Landsbanki, 14.6 per cent for Glitnir and 11.8 per cent for Kaupthing Bank. The test is done on a regular basis, and risks measured on this scale seem to have been fairly constant in recent years. Furthermore, the capital adequacy ratios of the banks have recently increased substantially (see Table 9.4).

### 9.3.2 Severe fiscal imbalances?

Fiscal imbalances are not a problem in Iceland. Indeed, the case is quite the opposite. As discussed in Section 9.1.3, the fiscal situation in Iceland is one of the strongest in the world. Not only is net government debt, relative to GDP, less than 10 per cent, but in contrast to many other countries, Iceland has a fully funded pension system. The United States, Japan and the countries in the European Union would all love to be in Iceland's shoes.

### 9.3.3 Imprudent monetary policy?

Monetary policy has also been quite good in Iceland in recent years. Since 2001 Iceland has been operating under an inflation-targeting regime that has been quite successful. The Central Bank aims for an annual rate of inflation, measured as the annual 12-month increase in the CPI, which in general will be as close as possible to 2½ per cent. If inflation deviates by more than ±1½ per cent from the target, the Central Bank shall be obliged to submit a report to the government, explaining the reason for the deviation, how it intends to respond, and when it expects the inflation target to be reached once again. The report is also made public. The Central Bank publishes inflation forecasts, projecting inflation at least two years ahead. Forecasts are published in the Bank's *Monetary Bulletin*. The report also contains the Bank's assessment of the main uncertainties pertaining to the inflation forecast, its assessment of the current economic situation and outlook. Since monetary policy aims at maintaining price stability, it will not be applied in order to achieve other economic targets by law except as consistent with the Bank's inflation target. The Bank implements its monetary policy by affecting money market interest rates, primarily through interest rate decisions for its repurchase agreements with credit institutions. Yields in the money market have a strong impact on currency flows and thereby on the exchange rate, and in the long run on domestic demand. Repurchase agreements with the banks are the Bank's main instrument. Auctions of seven-day agreements are held every week. Credit institutions need to put up securities that qualify as collateral. Auctions so far have been based on fixed prices.

Once the high inflation of the 2001–2 period was overcome, the inflation rate has been moderate. It is true that over the last two years, CPI inflation has climbed above the 4 per cent level, but this reflects the substantial increase in housing prices (see Figure 9.7).[35]

Economic theory suggests that an inflation target should use price measures that are mostly comprised of sticky prices, and so exclude asset prices such as housing, but which can take account of the imputed rents from these assets.[36] Then, targeting on inflation helps stabilize output fluctuations as well as inflation. Indeed, this is an important reason why the inflation indices used for monetary policy in the United

States, United Kingdom and the eurozone exclude housing prices. The recent climb in Iceland's CPI measure of inflation is an artefact of the recent surge in housing prices. An inflation measure that excludes housing prices, similar to the eurozone's HICP measure, has Icelandic inflation closer to the 2.5 per cent target. In general, we can conclude that monetary policy in Iceland is cutting-edge, and it seems to have coped well with keeping inflation in check when increases in housing prices are excluded from the index.

### 9.3.4 But what about the current account deficit?

Financial market participants have expressed major concern about the extremely large current account deficit in Iceland, which currently exceeds 15 per cent of GDP. Clearly such a deficit is not sustainable, and the fact that many of the countries that have experienced currency and financial crises had high current account deficits makes analysts wonder whether Iceland could suffer a financial meltdown. Importantly, the theory in Sections 9.2.2 and 9.2.3 does not list a high current account deficit as a primary factor promoting financial instability. Rather, it is deeper fundamentals that drive financial instability.[37] The consensus from many empirical studies is that current account measures have little predictive power in forecasting currency or financial crises.[38] On the other hand, deeper fundamentals such as botched financial liberalization or problems in the banking sector, do help predict these crises, and these problems seem not to exist in Iceland.[39]

It is true, however, that large current account deficits, which are the counterpart to large capital inflows, can help precipitate financial instability if the capital inflows lead to a lending boom and excessive risk taking on the part of banks. On the other hand, as pointed out in our overview of the Icelandic economy, large current account deficits of above 10 per cent of GDP are not unprecedented in Iceland's history, which is not surprising given the small size of the economy. Furthermore, reversals of current account imbalances have not been associated with problems in the financial sector. This is not surprising in an economy like Iceland's with its strong fundamentals. Indeed, there is generally a better case for Iceland's current account imbalances being a reflection of optimal policies than is true for many other countries.

### 9.3.5 Iceland is not an emerging market economy

The academic literature on financial instability and the facts of the state of the Icelandic economy indicate that comparisons of Iceland with emerging market countries, such as Thailand or Turkey, are not only facile, but completely misguided. Our analysis indicates that the sources of financial fragility in emerging market countries that eventually experienced currency and financial crises in recent years are just not present in Iceland. However, there are some other concerns about potential financial instability in Iceland. We turn to these in the next section and then conclude with some policy recommendations as to how to ensure financial stability in Iceland.

## 9.4 Are there other financial stability concerns?

In the last section we asked the question whether Iceland was going down traditional routes to financial crisis. The answer is definitely no. But having said that, are there other potential problems looming?

### 9.4.1 Could bank refinancing be a problem?

As we saw in Table 9.5, almost two-thirds of the financing of the banking system comes from abroad. This is natural since the Icelandic banks are engaged in international financial intermediation. Until recently the banks have had access to cheap capital in the international financial market, which they have lent domestically but to a greater extent internationally, especially in the UK and Scandinavia.

However, since last autumn and especially the last two months, it has become more difficult for the banks to finance themselves externally, and this is despite the fact that the international rating agencies have not changed their ratings of the banks or the country.[40] In light of this, it is natural to ask if the banks could be facing liquidity problems in the coming months.

A starting point is to look for evidence of increased risk perception of the Icelandic banks in the market. To do this we can look at what has been happening to spreads on credit default swaps (CDS), which measure the cost of insuring buyers of the Icelandic banks' bonds from credit default of the banks (see Figure 9.19).

It is apparent from the figure that the risk perception of the market started to deteriorate last November. During this time investors started to sell short Icelandic bank bonds, mainly in Kaupthing Bank but also in Landsbanki, and that is thought to have triggered the increase in the spreads. On 21 February Fitch Ratings published a change in its outlook for Iceland from stable to negative, and the spreads climbed sharply. In the following weeks, a number of negative reports from research departments of major international banks and news agencies were published on both the banks and the country. At the same time,

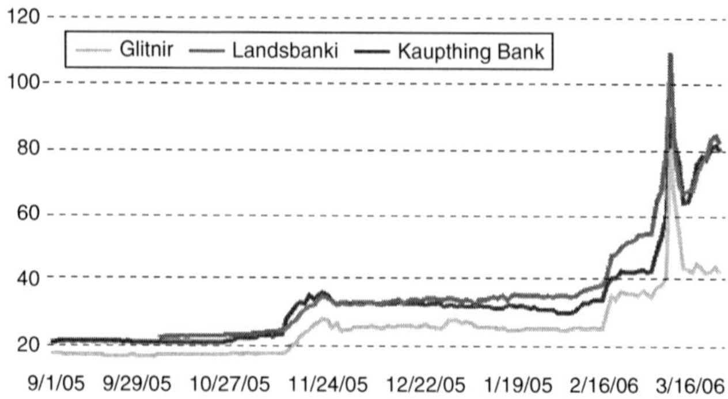


*Figure 9.19* Development of CDS spreads of the Icelandic banks, 5 year senior, basis points
*Source*: Central Bank of Iceland and Bloomberg.

the rating agencies Moody's and Fitch affirmed their previous ratings of the banks and S&P started to rate Glitnir with an initial rating of A−. During all this the carry traders, traders that borrowed at a low interest rate in the world markets and invested in high interest rates in the Icelandic money market, became nervous and closed their positions in Iceland (and in many emerging market countries), some at a great loss. This of course triggered depreciation of the currency and attracted the attention of the financial community.

It is obvious that the carry traders were hurt and labelled the event as a 'financial meltdown'. But as we have seen, this labelling is not at all warranted – the cause of the events is simply adjustment of an economy with macroeconomic imbalances. The CDS spreads, however, do contain information about the market's perception of how risky Iceland is.

The relationship between the spreads and the probability of a crisis can be derived, based on assumptions about what spread constitutes a bad state (financial crisis). In line with the analysis by Barclays Capital, we assume that a financial crisis has occurred if the spread reaches 500 basis points. Using this definition and a statistical formula with additional assumptions, the implied probability of a financial crisis in Iceland is 7 per cent (see Figure 9.20).[41]

Figure 9.20 shows all possible pairs of CDS spreads and probabilities of a financial crisis. As one can see from the figure, a 500-point spread implies a 100 per cent certainty of a financial crisis by assumption. If, for example, the spread were 125 basis points the implied probability of a crisis would be 20 per cent. A 50/50 chance of a crisis constitutes a 266-basis-point spread.

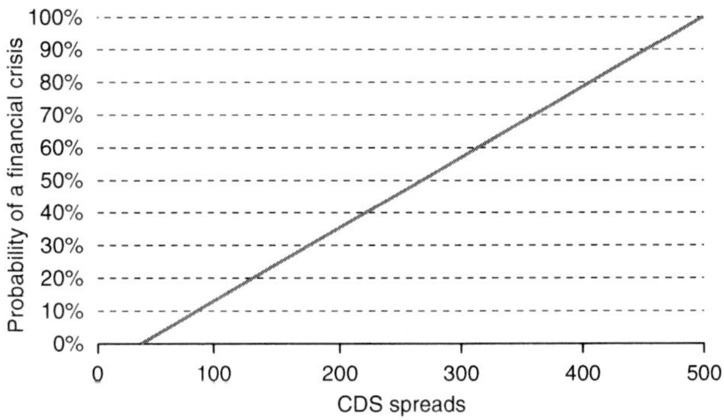


*Figure 9.20* Probability of a financial crisis based on CDS spreads
*Source*: Authors' calculations.

Sudden-stop theories suggest that as creditors lose faith in a country, they stop financing it, which in itself leads to a financial meltdown.[42] The standard way to address how well a country is equipped to meet a dry-up of liquidity is to look at how large the reserves of a country's Central Bank are and compare the amount with its short-term loans (often defined as loans and repayments that are due within the next 12 months). But this is somewhat misleading for developed countries like Iceland. For example, the Central Bank of Iceland and the Treasury have committed credit lines internationally amounting to about one-tenth of the country's GDP and uncommitted lines possibly many times that (remember, net government debt is only 1.3 per cent in 2006, so adding to that debt should not pose any problems).

The Central Bank also has arrangements with the other Nordic countries (Denmark, Finland, Norway and Sweden) to jointly preserve financial stability in the countries. The agreement does not list specific measures but states that it includes securing liquidity to the banking system in the countries in times of distress.

The liquidity of the banks is monitored by the Central Bank and regulated. The banks also have precautionary rules to meet sudden stops of credit from abroad. For example, the largest bank, Kaupthing Bank, has an in-house liquidity policy consisting of three steps that can be viewed as an indicator of the bank's liquidity. The first requirement is to have enough secured liquidity to be able to service and repay all maturing debts and wholesale deposits for at least 180 days without any access to capital markets (secured assets are: deposits, repo-able bonds and unused revolvers).

The second key liquidity requirement stipulates that a minimum of 360 days of sufficient unsecured liquidity is needed to cover liabilities within that time frame (unsecured liquidity is defined as secured liquidity in addition to unused euro commercial paper room and unused money market lines). The third requirement is to cover short-term liabilities for 390 days with unsecured liquidity when including listed and liquid securities.

Although we believe that the banks' reliance on external financing poses the biggest risk to the system at the moment, we firmly believe that Iceland will not be the next credit event.

### 9.4.2 Could rapid credit growth of banks be a problem?

A natural question to ask is whether the banks have been growing too fast, and whether they have consequently become more risky. If banks grow too fast, credit risk can increase because they may not have been able to develop the organizational capital fast enough to run the business prudently, as we discussed in Section 9.3. As a result, the quality of the debt stock can deteriorate if the growth of a financial institution is too rapid. But how well does this apply to the Icelandic scenario?

Growth of the Icelandic banks has mainly been through two channels: increased mortgages and acquisitions of financial companies in other countries. As discussed earlier, increased mortgages have probably increased the quality of the debt stock. Foreign subsidiaries were already in full operation with their own client base and credit screening, and there is little reason to believe that adverse selection and moral hazard problems have increased there.

Because a situation in which a country's banks have gone from being almost entirely domestic lenders to major international financial intermediaries in a five-year period is unprecedented, there are legitimate concerns whether the banks have been managing this successfully. These concerns have rightfully led to criticism of Iceland's banks for lack of transparency due to off-balance-sheet items (forwards), cross-ownership, etc. The increased investment banking activities of the banks have also led to decreased transparency. The risk of loans to Icelandic entrepreneurs abroad is, for example, unknown. The banks are beginning to deal with this criticism by selling (or planning to sell) shares in companies where cross-ownership seems to be a potential problem.

### 9.4.3 Is the financial supervisory authority monitoring risk sufficiently?

Although as the overview of the Icelandic economy suggests, the Financial Supervisory Authority appears to be pursuing best practice in its prudential supervisory activities in evaluating the riskiness of Iceland's banks, there are still questions as to whether it is able to sufficiently monitor the risks that might arise from the uniqueness of the transition of the Icelandic banking system. The FSA is well aware of the problems, however. In discussing the generally favourable developments in the banking industry, it states in its recently published annual report:[43] 'On the other hand, the rapid growth in their foreign operations, especially in acquiring existing financial enterprises, means new risks and calls for more complex and more robust risk management than before.' Although concerns about the risks from rapid growth in new business areas for the banks are not unwarranted, the FSA's awareness of the potential risks and the fact that Iceland has high-quality governmental institutions provide some comfort about the safety and soundness of Iceland's banks.

### 9.4.4 Could there be multiple equilibria?

There has been good news and bad news for the Icelandic economy. The good news is that it is receiving a lot of attention. The bad news is that it is receiving a lot of attention. Because Iceland's economy is so small, marginal changes in financial flows as a percentage of the overall flows in international financial markets can have a huge impact on Icelandic asset prices, and particularly the exchange rate. If a significant fraction of traders in international financial markets think that Iceland will be undergoing a financial meltdown, even if fundamentals do not warrant it, they could create a self-fulfilling prophecy by massively pulling out of Icelandic assets. Economists refer to such an outcome as multiple equilibria.

However, research on multiple equilibria suggests that they are unlikely to occur when the underlying fundamentals of a country are strong. Our assessment of Iceland's economy is that the fundamentals are, in general, quite strong.[44] Although we therefore see the probability of multiple equilibria to be small, the small size of Iceland's financial markets, relative to the rest of the world, means that this possibility cannot be ruled out, as with any risk.

## 9.5 Conclusions and policy recommendations

The analysis in this study suggests that although Iceland's economy does have imbalances that will eventually be reversed, financial fragility is not high and the likelihood of a financial meltdown is very low. However, the possibility that multiple equilibria could occur in which self-fufilling prophecies could do serious damage to Iceland's economy suggests that policies to bolster confidence in the Icelandic economy and financial system would be very beneficial in the current economic environment.

We have recommendations on microeconomic policies as well as macroeconomic policies that we think would benefit the Icelandic economy.

### 9.5.1 Microeconomic policies

*Recommendation 1: Financial supervision might be more effective if it was consolidated inside the Central Bank of Iceland*

There is an active debate in policymaking circles whether prudential supervision of the financial system should be housed inside central banks. Because central banks can create liquidity effectively out of thin air, they can play an enormously important role in preventing financial crises by being a lender of last resort when systemic shocks to the financial system might trigger a financial crisis. This is why central banks have as their mandate not only the pursuit of price stability but also the pursuit of financial stability. This is also why central banks not only issue so-called inflation reports, which describe how monetary policy will be conducted to promote price stability, but also financial stability reports, which examine whether the financial system is vulnerable to systemic risks. The Central Bank of Iceland puts much of its capacity into doing this as it publishes an inflation report four times a year and a financial stability report annually, both online and in print and in Icelandic and English.

In order to perform the role of a lender of last resort effectively, central banks must have timely information about whether a lender of last resort operation is necessary, and to do this, they need information about the safety and soundness of major financial institutions. Although central banks might be able to get this information from financial supervisory authorities that are independent of the Central Bank, an independent supervisory authority might lead to barriers to the Central Bank's timely acquisition of this information. This provides a strong argument for the Central Bank having an important role in the supervisory process, as it does in some countries like the United States.

For Iceland, however, there is an additional argument for consolidating supervision of the financial system inside the Central Bank. As we mention repeatedly, Iceland is unique in its small size. Its tiny population means that getting enough individuals with the expertise to effectively supervise complex financial institutions, which Iceland has recently been developing, will not be easy. Splitting up the expertise between two organizations may thus be very costly because it can lead to both being spread too thin. By necessity the Central Bank must monitor systemic risks to the financial system; putting all financial supervision under the Central Bank has a lot to recommend it.

*Recommendation 2: Iceland's commercial banks should be encouraged and should also see that it is in their best interest to disclose more information about their activities*

The possibility of multiple equilibria in which, despite strong fundamentals, Iceland's banks could face refinancing problems which could bring on severe financial distress, suggests that Iceland's banks would benefit by providing more information to the markets. Bad equilibria occur when market participants think that there are problems in the banks' balance sheets and then pull out funding from the banks, which can then lead to asset price collapses and funding problems for banks that produce losses that destroy the banks' balance sheets even if they were initially strong. These bad equilibria can be avoided if Iceland's banks demonstrate that their fundamentals are indeed strong by releasing sufficient information so that market participants have the objective information to come to a more favourable assessment of the banks' health. It is therefore in the banks' best interest to disclose more information to rule out bad equilibria, but they can also be encouraged to do so by the Financial Supervisory Authority.

### 9.5.2 Macroeconomic policies

*Recommendation 3: The Central Bank of Iceland should change the measure that it uses for its inflation target to minimize the influence of housing price fluctuations*

As was mentioned earlier, monetary theory suggests that central banks should not target inflation measures in which fluctuations in housing prices have a large impact on the inflation measure. (Note, however, that this does not mean that housing prices should be ignored in conducting monetary policy: housing prices can have an important impact on spending and aggregate demand and can thus have an important impact on future inflation.) The high weight of housing prices in the CPI measure of inflation that the Central Bank of Iceland targets has been a particular problem lately because it suggests that the Central Bank is overshooting the target by a wide margin, even though an inflation measure excluding housing prices indicates that inflation is well within the $\pm 1\frac{1}{2}$ per cent band around the target. The inappropriateness of Iceland's currently constructed CPI measure for evaluating monetary policy in Iceland has possibly damaged the credibility of the Central Bank's seriousness about inflation control and has created doubts about the quality of monetary policy in Iceland. The loss of Central Bank credibility can lead to currency crises, and use of the CPI measure as the inflation target may have in part contributed to some of the recent decline in the ISK.

The problem created by housing prices in the targeted measure of inflation can be fixed in either of two ways. One approach is the one used in the United States which involves having the statistical agency redefine the CPI measure to deal more appropriately with housing prices. The CPI inflation measure in the United States was revised in 1983 to remove the direct impact of housing prices, which led to a substantial overstatement of inflation in the late 1970s when there was a sharp appreciation of housing prices. Since 1983, the US CPI uses a rental equivalence measure to calculate housing costs, and this measure has far less volatility than housing prices. The alternative approach is for the Central Bank to target an inflation measure that removes the impact of fluctuations in housing prices, as occurs in the eurozone, because the European Central Bank evaluates monetary policy on the basis of the HICP (Harmonized Index of Consumer Prices) inflation measure, which excludes housing prices. Given the volatility of housing prices in Iceland, there are strong reasons for Iceland to adopt a measure of inflation that is less influenced by housing price fluctuations in evaluating monetary policy. If, however, Iceland were to exclude housing prices from their target measure, it is important to do so during more tranquil times when both measures are relatively close to the target.

*Recommendation 4: The government should implement a formal fiscal policy rule in order to dampen the Icelandic business cycle to support monetary policy better*

Although fiscal policy in Iceland has been quite good in recent years by international standards it could be even more countercyclical in order to deal with terms of trade shocks and business cycle fluctuations. As we have already discussed, investment is lumpy, and in small countries like Iceland this can be the source of internal and external imbalances. In order to mitigate these shocks and better support monetary policy we propose a simple fiscal rule. The government should increase its expenditure budget annually by no more and no less than the long-term productivity growth (proxied by growth of GDP) in the Icelandic economy. By doing this, the government would run even greater surpluses than currently in good years but also greater deficits in bad years, while retaining its share of the economy. This rule would dampen the business cycle and current account deficits, be automatic, and does not require too much information to implement. However, mechanisms to make the rule credible have to be designed. Discretionary fiscal policies should be avoided altogether as they can lead to time-inconsistency problems and can create cycles of their own.

### 9.5.3 Conclusion

We believe that by following our four recommendations, which are by no means exhaustive, stability of the Icelandic economy would increase, credibility of monetary policy would be strengthened, and the probability of multiple equilibria incidences lowered. If this could be achieved, we believe that confidence of the international financial community in the Icelandic economy will be strengthened.

## Selected links: The Icelandic economy and its institutions

| | |
|---|---|
| Central Bank of Iceland | www.sedlabanki.is |
| Chamber of Commerce | www.chamber.is |
| Confederation of Icelandic Employers | www.sa.is |
| Financial Supervisory Authority | www.fme.is |
| Glitnir Bank | www.glitnir.is |
| Housing Financing Fund | www.ils.is |
| Iceland Export Directory | www.icelandexport.is |
| Iceland Stock Exchange | www.icex.is |
| Icelandic Banks Data Centre | www.rb.is |
| Icelandic Bonds | www.bonds.is |
| Icelandic Pension Funds Association | www.ll.is |
| Icelandic Securities Depository | www.vbsi.is |
| Institute of Economic Studies | www.ioes.hi.is |
| Invest in Iceland Agency | www.invest.is |
| Kaupthing Bank | www.kaupthing.net |
| Landsbanki | www.landsbanki.is |
| Ministry of Commerce | www.vidskiptaraduneyti.is |
| Ministry of Finance | www.ministryoffinance.is |
| Ministry for Foreign Affairs | www.mfa.is |
| National Debt Management Agency | www.lanasysla.is |
| Statistics Iceland | www.statice.is |
| Straumur – Burdaras Investment Bank | www.straumur.net |
| Trade Council of Iceland | www.icetrade.is |

## Notes

1. Tryggvi Thor Herbertsson and Gylfi Zoega (1999) 'Trade Surpluses and Life-Cycle Saving Behaviour', *Economics Letters* 65, No. 2, November, pp. 227–37.
2. The data are compiled from the World Data Bank, an online database maintained by the World Bank.
3. The estimated equation is: $CA = 22.5 - 1.11POP + 27.59D$ (where White heteroskedasticity-consistent standard errors are: 0.29, 0.14 and 7.29, respectively), CA is the average current account–GDP ratio 1980–2004, POP the natural logarithm of the population 1980, and $D$ is a dummy variable for outliers (outliers are defined here as observations that lie outside two standard deviations of the mean of the sample). The regressors capture about 60 per cent of the variation in the dependent variable (i.e. R2 (adjusted for degrees of freedom) is 0.60).
4. Worldwide Press Freedom Index (www.rsf.org).
5. The balance is calculated such that income and expenditures are corrected for the increase/decrease that occurs because of the business cycle. For example, expenditures increase in recessions due to increased unemployment benefits, and income increases as the tax base gets bigger during booms. The GDP used in the calculation is not the usual one, but potential output.
6. Tryggvi Thor Herbertsson (2006) 'Collective Pension Arrangements: the Case of Iceland', paper prepared for the OECD.
7. Source: Institute of Economic Studies at the University of Iceland.
8. Carl E. Gjersem (2002) 'Generational Accounting in the Nordic Countries', *Nordic Journal of Political Economy* 28, pp. 3–11.
9. See Jagadeesh Gokhale and Bernt Rafelhüsen (1999) 'Population Aging and Fiscal Policy in Europe and the US', mimeo.
10. Tryggvi Thor Herbertsson, J. Michael Orszag and Peter Orszag (2000) *Retirement in the Nordic Countries: Prospects and Proposals for Reform*, a report to the Nordic Council of Ministers (ECOFIN), TemaNord No. 2000:548, Nordic Council of Ministers, Copenhagen.
11. See Thráinn Eggertsson and Tryggvi Thor Herbertsson (2005) 'Evolution of Financial Institutions: Iceland's Path from Repression to Eruption', IoES Working Paper No. W05:10, University of Iceland (downloadable at www.ioes.hi.is).
12. James Gwartney and Robert Lawson (2005) *Economic Freedom of the World*: 2005 Annual Report, Frasier Institute.
13. Although this was done twice in the following years and finally became explicitly banned in the new Central Bank legislation in 2001.
14. See e.g. *Den Danske Bank, Iceland: Geyser Crisis*, 21 March 21 2006.
15. Frederic S. Mishkin (1996) 'Understanding Financial Crises: a Developing Country Perspective', Annual World Bank Conference on Development Economics, pp. 29–62.
16. See Mark Gertler (1988) 'Financial Structure and Aggregate Economic Activity: an Overview', *Journal of Money Credit and Banking* 20, Part 2, pp. 559–88, and Ben S. Bernanke, Mark Gertler and Simon Gilchrist (1998) 'The Financial Accelerator in a Quantitative Business Cycle Framework', in John Taylor and Michael Woodford (eds) (1999) *Handbook of Macroeconomics*, Amsterdam: North Holland, for excellent surveys.

17. Douglas Diamond (1984) 'Financial Intermediation and Delegated Monitoring', *Review of Economic Studies* 51, pp. 393–414.
18. Joseph E. Stiglitz and Andrew Weiss (1983) 'Incentive Efects of Terminations: Applications to Credit and Labour Markets', *American Economic Review* 73, pp. 912–27.
19. See Ben S. Bernanke and Mark Gertler (1989) 'Agency Costs, Collateral, and Business Fluctuations', *American Economic Review* 79, pp. 14–31 and Charles W. Calomiris and R. Glenn Hubbard (1990) 'Firm Heterogeneity, Internal Finance, and Credit Rationing', *Economic Journal* 100, pp. 90–104.
20. See Graciela L. Kaminsky and Carmen M. Reinhart (1999) 'The Twin Crises: the Causes of Banking and Balance-of-Payments Problems', *American Economic Review* 89, pp. 473–500.
21. Barry Eichengreen and Ricardo Hausmann (1999) 'Exchange Rates and Financial Fragility', in *New Challenges for Monetary Policy*, Kansas City, Mo.: Federal Reserve Bank of Kansas City, pp. 329–68.
22. Guillermo A. Calvo, Alejandro Izquierdo and Ernesto Talvi (2003) 'Sudden Stops, the Real Exchange Rate, and Fiscal Sustainability: Argentina's Lessons', NBER Working Paper 9828 (July) and Jeffrey Frankel (2005) 'Contractionary Currency Crashes in Developing Countries', NBER Working Paper 11508 (July).
23. Frederic S. Mishkin (1998). 'The Dangers of Exchange Rate Pegging in Emerging-Market Countries', *International Finance* 1, No. 1 (October), pp. 81–101.
24. Eduardo Levy-Yeyati (2003) 'Financial Dollarization: Where Do We Stand?', paper presented at the IDB/World Bank Conference, Financial Dedollarization: Policy Options, 1–2 December, Washington, DC and Christian Broda and Eduardo Levy-Yeyati (2003) 'Endogenous Deposit Dollarization', Federal Reserve Bank of New York Staff Reports 60.
25. Stanley Fischer (2001) 'Exchange Rate Regimes: Is the Bipolar View Correct?' *Journal of Economic Perspectives* 15, No. 2 (Spring), pp. 3–24.
26. For a detailed discussion of how financial instability can develop, see Frederic S. Mishkin (2006) *The Next Great Globalization: How Disadvantaged Nations Can Harness Their Financial Systems to Get Rich*, Princeton, NJ: Princeton University Press.
27. Graciela L. Kaminsky and Carmen M. Reinhart (1999) 'The Twin Crises: the Causes of Banking and Balance-of-Payments Problems', *American Economic Review* 89, No. 3, pp. 473–500; Reuven Glick and Michael Hutchison (1999) 'Banking and Currency Crises: How Common as Twins', in Reuven Glick, F. Moreno and M. Spiegel (eds), *Financial Crises in Emerging Market Countries*, New York: Cambridge; Asli Demirguc-Kunt and Detragiarche Enrica (1998) 'The Determinants of Banking Crises: Evidence from Developed and Developing Countries'. IMF Staff Papers, 45(1), pp. 81–109; and John Williamson and M. Mahar (1998) *A Survey of Financial Liberalization*, Princeton Essays in International Finance 211, Princeton, NJ: Princeton University.
28. Frederic S. Mishkin (1999) 'Global Financial Instability: Framework, Events, Issues', *Journal of Economic Perspectives* Fall, 13 (4), pp. 3–20.
29. Paul Krugman (1998) 'What Happened to Asia?' MIT mimeo and Michael Dooley (2000) 'A Model of Crises in Emerging Markets', *Economic Journal* 110, No. 1, pp. 256–72.

30. In contrast to the East Asian countries that suffered crises in the late 1990s, Singapore, Hong Kong and Taiwan all had strong prudential regulatory and supervisory systems and avoided the crises that engulfed their neighbours.
31. Although Brazil underwent a fiscal and currency crisis in 1999 and another currency crisis in the run-up to the election of Lula in 2002, it did not undergo a financial crisis because its banking system was hedged against foreign exchange rate risk, in contrast to the other emerging market countries discussed here.
32. G. De Nicolo, Patrick Honohan, and Alain Ize (2003) 'Dollarization of the Banking System: Good or Bad?' IMF Working Paper 03/146 (July) and Inter-American Development Bank, *Unlocking Credit: the Quest for Deep and Stable Bank Lending*, 2005 Report, Economic and Social Progress in Latin America (Washington, DC: Inter-American Development Bank and Johns Hopkins University Press, 2005).
33. See www.fme.is
34. *Source*: Landsbanki, research department.
35. The housing component in the CPI is calculated such that an annual payment is calculated from an annuity were the principal the market value of the property. The discount rated used is the 12-month average interest rate on mortgages. The change in the housing price index is thus a function of the market rate on housing loans and housing prices. This arrangement leads to the peculiar effect that when interest rates on mortgages are increased (monetary policy tightened) inflation increases.
36. See Marvin Goodfriend and Robert G. King (1997) 'The New Neoclassical Synthesis and the Role of Monetary Policy', NBER Macro Annual 1997, and Michael Woodford (2003) *Interest and Prices: Foundations of a Theory of Monetary Policy*, Princeton University Press, Princeton, NJ. The conclusions from this research go even further and suggest that monetary policy should target on a core inflation measure rather than a headline measure.
37. Frederic S. Mishkin (1998) 'International Capital Movements, Financial Volatility and Financial Instability', NBER Working Paper No. 6390 (January), published in *Schriften des Vereins für Socialpolitik*, Band 261, zugleich Beiheft 7, *Zeitschrift fur Wirtschafts- und Sozialwissenschaften*, Jahrestagung 1997, Finanzmarkete im Spannungsfeld von Globalisierung, Regulierung und Geldpolitik, Dieter Duwendag (ed.) (Drucker & Humblot: Berlin), pp. 11–40.
38. See the excellent survey in Graciela Kaminsky, Saul Lizondo and Carmen Reinhart (1998) 'Leading Indicators of Currency Crises', IMF Staff Papers 45, No. 1 (March), pp. 1–48.
39. Graciela L. Kaminsky and Carmen M. Reinhart (1999) 'The Twin Crises: the Causes of Banking and Balance-of-Payments Problems', *American Economic Review* 89, No. 3, pp. 473–500.
40. Fitch did change its outlook for the country from stable to negative but affirmed their previous rating on the banks.
41. This is calculated by using the arbitrage condition, $P(U)U = P(D)D$, where $P(U)$ is the probability that things will revert to normal, while $P(D)$ is the probability of a full-fledged financial crisis, $D$ is how much the spreads will widen if a financial crisis occurs and $U$ is how much the spreads will fall if things will revert to normal. A financial crisis constitutes in the example a 500-basis-point spread on the credit default swaps and thus the downside spread change is $D = 433$ (500 minus the current CDS spread of the banks

(which is 67 basis points)). Before the current turmoil the CDS spread of the Icelandic banks was around 32 basis points, which means that the upside spread change is $U = 35$ (67 minus 32). In our example 32 basis points thus constitutes a 0 excess risk in lending to Icelandic banks (where excess risk means more risk in lending to Icelandic banks than similar banks in other countries). We are here using the assumption that the outcome is binary, i.e. that things will either go bad or good ($P(U) + P(D) = 1$). This analysis is partly based on research by Barclays Capital; see the report Icelandic Banks published on 11 April 2006.

42. Guillermo A. Calvo, Alejandro Izquierdo and Ernesto Talvi (2003) 'Sudden Stops, the Real Exchange Rate, and Fiscal Sustainability: Argentina's Lessons', NBER Working Paper 9828 (July).
43. The Financial Supervisory Authority, *Annual Report 2005*, p. 11, see www.fme.is.
44. Maurice Obstfeld (1996) 'Models of Currency Crises with Self-Fufilling Features', *European Economic Review*, April.

## References


Barclays Capital (2006) *Icelandic Banks*, 11 April.

Bernanke, Ben S. (2005) 'Comment', in Ben S. Bernanke and Michael Woodford (eds), *The Inflation-Targeting Debate*, Chicago: University of Chicago Press, pp. 293–8.

Bernanke, Ben S. and Mark Gertler (1989) 'Agency Costs, Collateral, and Business Fluctuations', *American Economic Review* 79, pp. 14–31.

Bernanke, Ben S., Mark Gertler and Simon Gilchrist (1998) 'The Financial Accelerator in a Quantitative Business Cycle Framework', in John Taylor and Michael Woodford (eds), *Handbook of Macroeconomics*, Amsterdam: North Holland.

Broda, Christian and Eduardo Levy-Yeyati (2003) 'Endogenous Deposit Dollarization', *Federal Reserve Bank of New York Staff Reports* 60.

Calomiris, Charles W. and R. Glenn Hubbard (1990) 'Firm Heterogeneity, Internal Finance, and Credit Rationing', *Economic Journal* 100, pp. 90–104.

Calvo, Guillermo A., Alejandro Izquierdo and Ernesto Talvi (2003) 'Sudden Stops, the Real Exchange Rate, and Fiscal Sustainability: Argentina's Lessons', NBER Working Paper 9828 (July).

Demirguc-Kunt, Asli and Enrica Detragiarche (1998) 'The Determinants of Banking Crises: Evidence from Developed and Developing Countries', *IMF Staff Papers* 45, No. 1, pp. 81–109.

Den Danske Bank (2006) Iceland: Geyser Crisis, 21 March.

De Nicolo, G., Patrick Honohan and Alain Ize (2003) 'Dollarization of the Banking System: Good or Bad?' IMF Working Paper 03/146 (July).

Diamond, Douglas (1984) 'Financial Intermediation and Delegated Monitoring', *Review of Economic Studies* 51, pp. 393–414.

Dooley, Michael (2000) 'A Model of Crises in Emerging Markets', *Economic Journal* 110, pp. 256–72.

Eggertsson, Thráinn and Tryggvi Thor Herbertsson (2005) 'Evolution of Financial Institutions: Iceland's Path from Repression to Eruption', IoES Working Paper No. W05:10, University of Iceland.

Eichengreen, Barry and Ricardo Hausmann (1999) 'Exchange Rates and Financial Fragility', in *New Challenges for Monetary Policy*, Kansas City, Mo.: Federal Reserve Bank of Kansas City, pp. 329–68.

Fischer, Stanley (2001) 'Exchange Rate Regimes: Is the Bipolar View Correct?' *Journal of Economic Perspectives* 15, No. 2, pp. 3–24.

Frankel, Jeffrey (2005) 'Contractionary Currency Crashes in Developing Countries', NBER Working Paper 11508, July.

Gertler, Mark (1988) 'Financial Structure and Aggregate Economic Activity: an Overview', *Journal of Money Credit and Banking* 20, Part 2, pp. 559–88.

Gjersem, Carl E. (2002) 'Generational Accounting in the Nordic Countries', *Nordic Journal of Political Economy* 28, pp. 3–11.

Glick, Reuven and Michael Hutchison (1999) 'Banking and Currency Crises: How Common as Twins,' in Reuven Glick, F. Moreno and M. Spiegel (eds), *Financial Crises in Emerging Market Countries*, New York: Cambridge.

Gokhale, Jagadeesh and Bernt Raffelhüsen (1999) 'Population Aging and Fiscal Policy in Europe and the US', mimeo.

Goodfriend, Marvin and Robert G. King (1988) 'Financial Deregulation, Monetary Policy and Central Banking', *Federal Reserve Bank of Richmond Economic Review*, May/June, pp. 3–22.

Goodfriend, Marvin and Robert G. King (1997) 'The New Neoclassical Synthesis and the Role of Monetary Policy', *NBER Macro Annual 1997*.

Gwartney, James and Robert Lawson (2005) *Economic Freedom of the World: 2005 Annual Report*, Frasier Institute.

Herbertsson, Tryggvi Thor (2006) 'Collective Pension Arrangements: the Case of Iceland', paper prepared for the OECD.

Herbertsson, Tryggvi Thor and Gylfi Zoega (1999) 'Trade Surpluses and Life-Cycle Saving Behaviour', *Economics Letters* 65, No. 2, November, pp. 227–37.

Herbertsson, Tryggvi Thor, J. Michael Orszag, and Peter Orszag (2000) *Retirement in the Nordic Countries: Prospects and Proposals for Reform*, a report to the Nordic Council of Ministers (ECOFIN), TemaNord No. 2000:548, Nordic Council of Ministers, Copenhagen.

Inter-American Development Bank (2005) *Unlocking Credit: the Quest for Deep and Stable Bank Lending*. 2005 Report, Economic and Social Progress in Latin America. Washington, DC: Inter-American Development Bank and Johns Hopkins University Press.

Kaminsky, Graciela L. and Carmen M. Reinhart (1999) 'The Twin Crises: the Causes of Banking and Balance-of-Payments Problems', *American Economic Review* 89, No. 3, pp. 473–500.

Kaminsky, Graciela, Saul Lizondo and Carmen Reinhart (1998) 'Leading Indicators of Currency Crises', *IMF Staff Papers*, Vol. 45, No. 1, March, pp. 1–48.

Krugman, Paul (1998) 'What Happened to Asia?', MIT mimeo.

Levy-Yeyati, Eduardo (2003) 'Financial Dollarization: Where Do We Stand?' Paper presented at the IDB/World Bank Conference, Financial Dedollarization: Policy Options, 1–2 December, Washington, DC.

Mishkin, Frederic S. (1991) 'Asymmetric Information and Financial Crises: a Historical Perspective', in R. Glenn Hubbard (ed.), *Financial Markets and Financial Crises*, University of Chicago Press: Chicago, pp. 69–108.

Mishkin, Frederic S. (1992) 'An Evaluation of the Treasury Plan for Banking Reform', *Journal of Economic Perspectives* 6, No. 1 (Winter 1992), pp. 133–53.

Mishkin, Frederic S. (1996) 'Understanding Financial Crises: a Developing Country Perspective', *Annual World Bank Conference on Development Economics*, pp. 29–62.

Mishkin, Frederic S. (1998a) 'The Dangers of Exchange Rate Pegging in Emerging-Market Countries', *International Finance* 1, No. 1 (October), pp. 81–101.

Mishkin, Frederic S. (1998b) 'International Capital Movements, Financial Volatility and Financial Instability', NBER Working Paper No. 6390 (January), published in *Schriften des Vereins fur Socialpolitik, Band 261, zugleich Beiheft 7, Zeitschrift fur Wirtschafts- und Sozialwissenschaften, Jahrestagung 1997, Finanzmarkete im Spannungsfeld von Globalisierung, Regulierung und Geldpolitik*, Dieter Duwendag (ed.), Drucker & Humblot: Berlin, pp. 11–40.

Mishkin, Frederic S. (1999) 'Global Financial Instability: Framework, Events, Issues', *Journal of Economic Perspectives* 13 (4), pp. 3–20.

Mishin, Frederic S. (2004) *The Economics of Money, Banking and Financial Markets*, 7th edn, Boston: Addison-Wesley.

Mishkin, Frederic S. (2006) *The Next Great Globalization: How Disadvantaged Nations Can Harness Their Financial Systems to Get Rich*, Princeton, NJ: Princeton University Press.

Obstfeld, Maurice (1996) 'Models of Currency Crises with Self Fufilling Features', *European Economic Review* (April).

Stiglitz, Joseph E. and Andrew Weiss (1983) 'Incentive Effects of Terminations: Applications to Credit and Labour Markets', *American Economic Review* 73, pp. 912–27.

Williamson, John and M. Mahar (1998) *A Survey of Financial Liberalization*, Princeton Essays in International Finance 211, Princeton, NJ.: Princeton University.

Woodford, Michael (2003) *Interest and Prices: Foundations of a Theory of Monetary Policy*, Princeton, NJ: Princeton University Press.

# 10
# The Internationalization of Iceland's Financial Sector

*Richard Portes*
*London Business School Centre for Economic Policy Research*

and

*Friđrik Már Baldursson*
*Reykjavik University Financial Research Institute*

in collaboration with

*Frosti Ólafsson*
*Iceland Chamber of Commerce*

## Executive summary

1. The internationalization of the Icelandic financial sector proceeded from market liberalization, European integration, and privatization, on the base of a strong, well-funded pension system and an exceptionally healthy institutional framework.
2. The growth of the banks has been spectacular: total assets of the banking sector have grown from 96 per cent of GDP at the end of 2000 to eight times GDP at the end of 2006. The majority of the banks' revenues originate outside Iceland, mainly in other northern European countries.
3. Rapid financial sector expansion and growing cross-border activities, together with macroeconomic tensions, led to market suspicion and the mini-crisis of early 2006. The exchange rate depreciated by approximately 25 per cent, the OMXI15 stock index fell by a comparable percentage, and the banks were in trouble.
4. The 'mini-crisis' of 2006 was an informational crisis, arising from external criticisms of the banks' reliance on market funding with short maturities, questions of earnings quality, cross-ownership and lack of transparency, as well as perceived macroeconomic imbalances in the Icelandic economy.

5. The Icelandic financial sector responded quickly and decisively:
   - They expanded their deposit base, and deposit ratios are now higher.
   - They extended and broadened the maturities and geographical scope of their market funding.
   - They have mainly eliminated cross-holdings.
   - They put great effort into increasing transparency and information dissemination about their structure and activities.
6. The resilience and responsiveness of the banking sector have been impressive. Yet in the current financial turmoil, is that enough? Despite their strong performance, Icelandic banks still have lower ratings than their Nordic peers, and a much higher risk premium is currently placed on their debt. We see no justification for this in their risk exposure. This suggests that either the markets are not fully aware of their situation, or that markets place a country premium on the banks.
7. Our report examines closely the current state of the Icelandic banks and financial sector, as well as the regulatory and macroeconomic environment.
8. The institutional and regulatory framework appears highly advanced and stable. Iceland fully implements the directives of the European Union's Financial Services Action Plan (unlike some EU member states). The budget of its Financial Services Authority was recently doubled.
9. We see reasons for concern, however, with macroeconomic imbalances. Although the fiscal position is enviably strong, the economy has been running at a high pressure of demand, because of major investment projects in aluminium and hydroelectricity, as well as capital inflows. The resulting current account deficit is very high, the net international investment position is highly negative and is increasing. But the current account deficit has already fallen significantly from its 2006 peak, and we believe the path will prove sustainable.
10. That is partly because the official data exaggerate the deficits. In addition to doubts about the data raised by other observers (including the IMF), our own calculations of the apparent rate of return on Iceland's foreign assets and liabilities yield implausible results. The data suggest that Iceland's investments abroad are substantially less profitable than foreigners' investments in Iceland. This is simply inconsistent with the outstanding profitability and growth of Iceland's international banks and corporations in recent years.
11. We therefore strongly recommend efforts to improve the collection of data to account more accurately for the balance of international

income and the international investment position. The CBI should also publish parallel accounts for items such as equities where the most glaring inconsistencies arise.

12. We conclude that analysis should focus less on the current account deficit and NIIP numbers and more on the resilience of the financial system – which has proven to be excellent – and the flexibility of the economy, where Iceland has a proven track record over many decades.
13. In an economy so small and so highly leveraged in international financial markets, one might expect a high volatility of financial variables: the exchange rate, equity prices and bond yields. We do not find especially high volatilities. We focus in particular on the Icelandic krona, which many see as an important risk factor for Iceland and the Icelandic banks. In fact, the krona is not much more volatile against major currencies than the currencies of New Zealand, Sweden and Australia.
14. The banks are now hedged fully against currency volatility, so their exchange rate risk is primarily associated with loan quality. Icelandic firms have a long history of borrowing in foreign currency. For many this provides a natural hedge, others are in a strong market position and can pass exchange rate effects into prices. Households have increasingly been borrowing in foreign currency. This is still only a minor share (7–8 per cent) of overall lending, but the risk there bears continued attention.
15. The krona does represent a disadvantage for listed firms, because it tends to fluctuate with equity prices. Exchange rate volatility is therefore added to stock market volatility. This makes shares in firms listed in ISK less attractive to foreign investors, so equity financing is more costly for firms. These firms are now moving to adopt the euro as their listing currency and to use the euro rather than the krona in other ways as well.
16. The euro is evidently becoming more important in Iceland. As it is outside the EU, Iceland cannot join the European Monetary Union. The possibility remains, however, of unilateral adoption of the euro – 'euroization'.
17. We do not recommend for or against unilateral euroization. This is an issue that requires extensive political as well as economic debate. We do, however, caution against the possible destabilizing consequences of a *gradual* shift to using the euro.
18. The CBI is on an inflation target of 2.5 per cent. Inflation driven by housing prices, however, has remained above the target for some

time. The policy rate of the CBI is very high, and monetary policy appears to be ineffective. First, the Housing Financing Fund is a major obstacle to the transmission of monetary policy. We agree with many other commentators (including the IMF) that the HFF's role should be changed so that it no longer competes with banks in mortgage markets. Second, price indexation of financial contracts is widespread, which tends to weaken monetary policy. Third, the CBI has undermined its own policy by linking its decisions to exchange rate developments. The high policy rate leads to distortions in the financial system, such as the large carry trade. If only for that reason, we urge the CBI to reconsider its strategy.

19. On the criteria of deposit ratios, the characteristics of market funding and others, Icelandic banks come out well in a comparison with their Nordic peers – and their overall and core profitability is higher. That is despite the high CAD and Tier 1 ratios with which they counterbalance their equity exposure. They are well hedged against volatility in the krona. Stress tests by the FSA indicate that the banks can withstand quite extreme movements in market variables specific to Iceland. The banks have negligible exposure to the US subprime market, structured finance products, and related financial vehicles.
20. Most fundamentally, the banks exploit strong competitive advantage, arising from their entrepreneurial management, flat management structures, and unusual and strong business models.
21. We conclude that the Icelandic economy and financial sector are highly resilient, as shown in their response to the mini-crisis of early 2006 and their stability in the current turmoil. With regard to both the macroeconomic situation and the characteristics and performance of the banks, we consider that the current market premium on Icelandic banks is excessive relative to their risk exposure and in comparison with their Nordic peers. If this is in fact a country risk premium, we think it is not justified by Iceland's economic situation. It is reasonable to expect the CDS spreads (for example) for Icelandic banks to return to more normal levels.
22. Overall, the internationalization of the Icelandic financial sector is a remarkable success story that the markets should better acknowledge.

## Introduction

Iceland's financial sector has grown dramatically in the past few years along with the advance of firms in other sectors into new markets.

The foreign advance of Icelandic firms has resulted from several factors. The Icelandic pension system has underpinned the financial sector as a whole, providing savings and liquidity; the individual transferable quota system in fisheries created substantial new equity that could be used for investments in other sectors; market liberalization and European integration provided a modern institutional framework for investors and entrepreneurs. Most importantly, the Icelandic banks were privatized at the same time that international interest rates were low and liquidity was ample. The banks could therefore escape the limitations set by the small size of the Icelandic economy and seek new markets. This they did with alacrity, acquiring financial firms in other countries and establishing branches. Their growth has been spectacular: total assets of the banking sector have grown from 96 per cent of GDP at the end of 2000 to eight times GDP at the end of 2006. The majority of the banks' revenues originate outside Iceland, mainly in other northern European countries.

The fast growth has generated an enormous amount of value, but there have also been growing pains. In early 2006 the banks went through a period of turmoil that for a while obstructed their access to market funding. The 'mini-crisis' of 2006 was an informational crisis in the sense that the only shocks that hit the sector were negative views of rating firms like Fitch and other analysts. There were no credit events such as loan defaults. Rather, external criticisms of certain aspects of the way the banks were run, for example reliance on market funding with short maturities and cross-ownership, as well as perceived macroeconomic imbalances in the Icelandic economy, triggered the episode.

We discuss how the banks responded to these criticisms. We find that they have improved on all fronts. Indeed they perform very well in comparison with their peers in other Nordic countries. They also proved remarkably resilient in the face of adversity and came through the crisis unscathed. In May 2006 the Icelandic Chamber of Commerce published a report, *Financial Stability in Iceland*, by Frederic Mishkin and Tryggvi Thor Herbertsson. That report focused on whether Iceland was going down the path to financial instability. The report concluded that this was not the case. Its analysis was widely accepted.

Icelandic banks are now again in a storm. The difference this time is that this is part of more general turmoil in the international financial system. We consider whether Iceland's macroeconomic situation and its external ramifications should cause concern. We also examine the Icelandic banks in some detail, with international comparisons.

There are macroeconomic imbalances, but their reflection in the external accounts is exaggerated. Despite problems with monetary policy and its effectiveness, the imbalances are being corrected, and the demonstrated, exceptional flexibility of the economy gives cause for optimism. We find that their effective response to the shock of early 2006 has made the banks much better placed now to cope with domestic macroeconomic shocks, credit events and external liquidity constraints. They are well managed, and their business models are strong.

We consider, therefore, that the current market premium on Icelandic banks is excessive relative to their risk exposure and in comparison with their Nordic peers. If this is in fact a country risk premium, we think it is not justified by Iceland's economic situation.

In extreme cases, such risk premia can be self-fulfilling, when funds become so expensive or restricted that the health of the borrower is impaired. We believe that is very unlikely in the Icelandic case, and it is reasonable to expect the CDS spreads (for example) for Icelandic banks to return to more normal levels. Overall, the internationalization of the financial sector is a remarkable success story that the markets should better acknowlege.

## 10.1 The Icelandic economy

### 10.1.1 Background

#### *10.1.1.1 Size and composition of the Icelandic economy*[1]

Iceland's population is just over 300,000, so the Icelandic economy is the smallest in the OECD, generating GDP of EUR 13 billion in 2006. But its GDP per capita of approximately USD 40,000 in 2006, measured in terms of purchasing power parity (PPP), was the sixth highest among OECD countries and somewhat above the EU average. In comparison to the Nordic countries, Iceland's per capita GDP is lower than Norway's, equals Denmark's and exceeds that of Finland and Sweden (see Table 10.1).

Iceland's abundant marine and energy resources have historically fuelled economic growth, though more recently services, particularly in the financial sector, have taken over that role. While the fishing industry is still the most important source of export revenue, its share of GDP has declined from 16 per cent in 1980 to 6 per cent in 2006. The fastest growth of recent years is in the finance, insurance and real estate sectors, whose share of GDP has risen from 17 per cent in 1998 to 26 per cent in 2006.

As in other developed economies, services form the bulk of economic activity, accounting for approximately 67 per cent of GDP in 2005. Private consumption contributed, on average, about 58 per cent of

*Table 10.1* An overview of the Icelandic economy

| | |
|---|---|
| Population size at year-end 2006 (thousands) | 307,700 |
| GDP per capita (USD, PPP) | 39,986 |
| GDP rank among OECD countries | 6 |
| GDP per capita (USD) | 54,764 |
| GDP growth 2006 | 4.20% |
| Average annual growth rate of GDP in last 10 years | 3.80% |
| Stock market change (first 9m 2007) | 22.20% |
| Current policy rate of the Central Bank | 13.75% |
| Inflation rate with housing (past 12 months) | 5.20% |
| Inflation rate without housing (past 12 months) | 1.90% |
| Current labour force participation | 84.10% |
| Current labour force participation (women) | 79.60% |
| Foreign labour (percentage of total labour force) | 9.00% |
| Unemployment rate | 2.10% |
| Balance of trade 2006 (% of GDP) | –13.50% |
| Current account balance 2006 (% of GDP) | –25.50% |
| Gross domestic investment 2006 (% of GDP) | 33.40% |
| Gross national savings 2006 (% of GDP) | 8.80% |
| International investment position at year-end 2006 (% of GDP) | –122.40% |
| Government revenue 2006 (% of GDP) | 46.70% |
| Government expenditure 2006 (% 2006) | 41.40% |
| Central government, gross debt 2006 (% of GDP) | 13.60% |
| Central government, net debt 2006 (% of GDP) | 3.90% |
| Life expectancy (males) | 79.4 |
| Life expectancy (females) | 83 |
| Infant mortality (% of 1000 live births) | 1.4 |
| Worldwide competitiveness (rank) | 7 |
| Households connected to Internet (% total) | 88% |
| Economic freedom (rank) | 11 |
| Corruption perception index (rank) | 6 |

*Source*: Statistics Iceland, Central Bank of Iceland, OECD, OMX Iceland, Iceland Directorate of Labour, Iceland Ministry of Finance, IMD *World Competitiveness Report, The Wall Street Journal* and The Heritage Foundation, Transparency International.

GDP from 2002 to 2006, and public consumption over the same period rose to 25 per cent after remaining broadly stable at about 20 per cent through most of the 1990s. Gross fixed investment of 24 per cent over the past five years represents a substantial rise in the average investment-to-GDP ratio, which fell below 1/5 in the mid-1990s.

Iceland's trade balance represents its fairly open economy, with imports and exports of goods and services averaging 42 and 34 per cent of GDP, respectively, in 2002 to 2006. External trade involves a fairly large share of primary products and commodities, but exports have been diversifying significantly in recent years.

### *10.1.1.2 Education and health*

Iceland is a modern welfare state, spending just over a quarter of GDP on health, education, social security, welfare and other social services in 2003. The state guarantees access to universal health care, education and a high degree of social security, and scores highly on all relevant indicators.

Life expectancy of 81.4 years is the fourth highest in the world, and Iceland has the second lowest infant mortality rate (1.4 per 1000 live births in 2006), testifying to the high quality of health care.

Public education is compulsory until the age of 16, and university enrolment of those completing secondary education was around 79 per cent in 2004, third highest among the OECD countries (average 53 per cent). In 2005, 30.6 per cent of the employed labour force held a university degree. Although higher education is offered at several universities in Iceland, one out of every five university degrees held by Icelanders is obtained outside of Iceland.

### *10.1.1.3 The labour market*

The Icelandic labour market is highly centralized, with 85 per cent unionization and comprehensive wage settlements. It is, however, highly flexible as well. Labour is mobile both within the country and between Iceland and other countries. Participation rates are high compared to other OECD economies and have been consistently at or above 85 per cent for the last decade. Icelanders also tend to work long hours. The participation rate, number of hours worked, inflow of labour and real wages are all positively correlated with the economic cycle, thereby dampening cyclical movements in unemployment.

Iceland's EEA membership and the free flow of labour within the Area have helped increase the flexibility of the labour market in recent years. With the rapid economic growth of the last few years the influx of foreign labour has increased substantially, helping to sustain growth and contain inflation. In 2006 approximately 7 per cent of the labour force was foreign compared with 2.3 per cent in 1998. Foreign participation has continued to rise and now stands at approximately 9 per cent.

### *10.1.1.4 Public finance*

In comparison with its neighbours, Iceland has a relatively modest public sector, which has become smaller in recent years after a rise in spending on health, social services and education from 1998 to 2003. Expenditures of around 41 per cent of GDP in 2006 represented a

4 per cent drop from 2003 and a total lower than in the Nordic countries (49 per cent) and the mainland countries of the European Union (48 per cent), though higher than for the US, Japan or South Korea.

Iceland's fiscal balance has been well above the OECD average since the mid-1990s, with a predicted surplus of 3½ per cent of GDP in 2007. Like many other OECD members, Iceland accrued a relatively large public sector deficit in the late 1980s and early 1990s, with deficits averaging 3 per cent of GDP from 1985 to 1995, but economic recovery led to surpluses in 1999 and 2000. After a brief return to deficit as the economy slowed slightly in 2002–3, budget surpluses rose to exceed 5 per cent of GDP in 2005–7.

Although structural fiscal balances (which are adjusted to reflect the state of the business cycle) have not been as favourable, the surplus in public finances, as well as the privatization of state-owned enterprises such as the banks, has made it possible to repay almost all central government debt. Net debt stood at only 3.9 per cent of GDP at the end of 2006, an enviable situation.

#### *10.1.1.5 External relations*

Iceland participates actively in the international community, primarily as part of the group of Nordic countries – Denmark, Sweden, Norway and Finland, as well as Greenland and the Faroe Islands – which has adopted wide-ranging measures for cooperation in a variety of fields, including economic affairs and international representation. It is a member of the Nordic Council and specialized institutions such as the Nordic Investment Bank.

Iceland became a member of the United Nations in 1946 and is an active participant in most of its affiliated agencies; it is a founding member of the Bretton Woods institutions that were established in 1945 – the International Monetary Fund (IMF) and the International Bank for Reconstruction and Development (World Bank); it is one of the original members of the Organization for Economic Cooperation and Development (OECD) and of the European Bank for Reconstruction and Development (EBRD); it joined the Council of Europe in 1950; and it has participated in the Organization for Security and Cooperation in Europe since it was initiated in 1975.

In 1964, Iceland became a signatory of the General Agreement on Tariffs and Trade (GATT), the predecessor to the World Trade Organization (WTO). Iceland then joined the European Free Trade Association (EFTA) in 1970 and entered into a free-trade agreement with the European Economic Community in 1972. In May 1992, the member states of EFTA and the European Union signed an agreement to establish a zone for the free movement of goods, services, capital and persons, creating the European Economic Area (EEA), of which Iceland became a part in 1994.

This development marked a major milestone in Iceland's integration into the global economy. The agreement focuses on the four fundamental pillars of the internal market, ensuring the freedom of movement of goods (although agriculture and fisheries are included only to a limited extent), persons, services and capital. Adopting the agreement gave Icelandic companies unprecedented access to European markets and played a fundamental role in facilitating future developments.

#### *10.1.1.6 A market-based economy*

Policies of market liberalization in Iceland were implemented in the late 1980s and early 1990s, when significant structural reforms targeted enhanced efficiency through fiscal consolidation and privatization of state-owned enterprises. This process was motivated by the need to align the Icelandic legislative and regulatory framework to that of the European Union in preparation for Iceland's role as one of the founding members of the EEA in 1994.

With the exception of the energy sector, which is still largely publicly owned, and agriculture, still widely supported by government subsidies, import protection and a system of production quotas, the liberalization process continued during the second half of the 1990s. Most government-owned businesses have been privatized in recent years, leading to increased competition and a restructuring of Icelandic financial markets and institutions.

### 10.1.2 The financial system

In 1979, the Icelandic financial system was in crisis after a period of political interference and severe restrictions in the financial market. Rapidly rising inflation created double-digit negative real interest rates, which significantly reduced the demand for deposits and cut the banking system by half. These circumstances prompted dramatic changes, and in the following decades the system was transformed into a fully modernized and very liberal financial system.

The first step in the reform process was taken in 1979 when the authorities, still controlling nominal interest rates, introduced general indexation of financial obligations, including bank deposits and loans. Indexation involves the adjustment of the nominal values of financial assets to reflect changes in price levels, so that real interest rates are

*Table 10.2* Recent developments in financial markets

| | |
|---|---|
| Financial indexation permitted | 1979 |
| Liberalization of domestic bank rates | 1984–86 |
| Iceland Stock Exchange established (presently OMX Nordic Exchange Iceland) | 1985 |
| Interest Rate Act – interest rates fully liberalized | 1987 |
| Stepwise liberalization of capital movement begins | 1990 |
| Treasury overdraft facility in the Central Bank closed | 1992–93 |
| Liberalization of cross-border capital movements starts | 1992 |
| Interbank market for foreign exchange established | 1993 |
| Iceland becomes a founding member of the EEA | 1994 |
| Long-term capital movements fully liberalized | 1994 |
| Short-term capital movements fully liberalized | 1995 |
| Foreign direct investment liberalized per EEA agreement | 1995 |
| Interbank money market | 1998 |
| Interbank FX swap market | 2001 |
| Instrument independence for the Central Bank | 2001 |
| Privatization of state-owned banks completed | 2003 |

*Source*: Central Bank of Iceland.

normally positive as long as nominal rates are positive. In Iceland, financial indexation (see Table 10.2 for the evolution of financial market development) proved highly successful in restoring the stock of financial savings.

The final steps in the transition toward a fully modernized financial system were taken in May 2001, when a new Act on the Central Bank of Iceland entered into force. This act gave instrument independence to the Central Bank, making Iceland the smallest state in the world with an independent monetary policy. An inflation target had been adopted two months earlier through a joint declaration of the government and the Central Bank, and the bank changed the exchange rate policy of the Icelandic krona (ISK) from a fixed rate to a floating one. Structural and legislative reforms, along with the massive expansion in financial services and activity that they have engendered, have made Iceland's financial system even more internationalized than European norms.

### *10.1.2.1 Main players*

There are currently three major commercial banks in Iceland – Glitnir, Kaupthing and Landsbanki – which all provide conventional banking and securities services. Total assets of the three bank groups amounted to over EUR 110 billion (ISK 9502 billion) at the end of 2006, a sum eight times the GDP of Iceland (see Table 10.3).

*Table 10.3* Main players in Iceland's banking sector

| | *Glitnir* | | *Kaupthing* | | *Landsbanki* | |
|---|---|---|---|---|---|---|
| | *2006* | *9m 2007* | *2006* | *9m 2007* | *2006* | *9m 2007* |
| After-tax profit (EUR billion)* | 0.45 | 0.3 | 1.01 | 0.71 | 0.47 | 0.41 |
| Total assets (EUR billion) | 26.4 | 32.5 | 47.6 | 57.4 | 25.5 | 33.4 |
| Cost/income ratio (%) | 38.0 | 49.9 | 35.9 | 41.3 | 43.0 | 48.0 |
| ROE (%) | 39.0 | 24.1 | 42.4 | 27.5 | 36.0 | 33.0 |
| CAD ratio (%) | 15.0 | 11.7 | 15.0 | 12.1 | 14.8 | 11.2 |
| Tier 1 ratio (%) | 10.8 | 8.5 | 10.5 | 9.3 | 13.0 | 9.9 |
| Moody's rating | Aa3/P1/C | | Aa3/P1/C | | Aa3/P1/C | |
| Fitch rating | A/F1 | | A/F1 | | A/F1 | |

*EUR/ISK = 85.2 (this exchange rate is used in all authors' calculations).
*Source:* Annual reports and authors' calculations.

After a decade of consolidation and reforms, by 2000 the banking system was fully privatized, leading to a period of sharp growth in the financial sector that continues. The three main commercial banks have driven this growth, and their foreign advance has been complementary with the international expansion of other Icelandic businesses, for example in retail, pharmaceuticals, food production and high-tech manufacturing. At the end of 2006, almost half of the total assets of the largest commercial bank groups were held in foreign subsidiaries, mostly in northern Europe, and in 2006 about 50 per cent of their overall income was generated abroad. The three largest commercial banks (as well as Straumur-Burðarás) are rated by international rating agencies.

At the end of 2006 there were 23 savings banks in Iceland and two commercial banks in addition to the three major ones described above. These are Icebank, which serves as a banking institution for most of the savings banks, and Straumur-Burðarás, which operates mainly as an investment bank and only recently received a licence for commercial banking. Twelve other credit institutions currently operate as well in Iceland, comprising five investment banks, two payment card companies, two investment funds and three leasing companies, plus the Housing Financing Fund, a state-owned mortgage credit fund.

There are also 12 insurance companies authorized to operate in Iceland, with total assets of around EUR 1.8 billion (ISK 171 billion) at year-end 2006. The three largest, Sjóvá, VÍS and TM, together serve over 90 per cent of the market. These are fully owned by investment companies, FL Group and Exista, which are listed on the OMX Nordic Exchange Iceland (OMX ICE).

#### *10.1.2.2 Pension funds*

Unlike many other countries, Iceland is not threatened by a looming pension crisis. The reform of the pension system, which began in 1969, has not only generated a stable outlook for future pensions, but also has contributed to the rapid expansion of the economy in the past decade. The pension system is chiefly organized around occupational pension funds. Instead of the common 'pay as you go' structure, this system is fully funded through accumulated payments.

Growth in pension funds' assets took off during the period 1979–86, when indexation was introduced and interest rates were liberalized. The emergence of a new pension system and the liberalization of financial markets had powerful interactive effects. Strong demand by the pension funds for financial instruments, combined with new opportunities for supplying securities, provided the catalyst that in the 1990s triggered a vibrant market for securities in Iceland.

The pension fund system has gradually developed into a three-pillar system: firstly, a tax-financed public plan that provides a flat-rate or means-tested basic pension. Secondly, there is a mandatory occupation- or private-funded, but publicly regulated, pension scheme. The third pillar is a voluntary pension saving scheme, which offers incentives in the form of complementary contributions from employers. All contributions are exempted from income tax until reception of pension and therefore allow employees to defer taxes.

The total assets of Icelandic pension funds have grown over the past decade to over 130 per cent relative to the country's GDP, from 50 per cent of GDP in 1994, despite impressive economic growth over the period. It is estimated that total assets may exceed the equivalent of twice GDP within a decade. Creating massive savings and liquidity, the funds serve as important investors in many of Iceland's largest companies.

### 10.1.3 Markets and infrastructure

The Iceland Stock Exchange, founded in 1985, merged in December 2006 with OMX, which owns exchanges in all the Nordic and Baltic countries except Norway. The resulting OMX Nordic Exchange Iceland (OMX ICE) is the only authorized stock exchange operating in Iceland for all public listing of securities and securities trading, and it is also licensed to operate a regulated OTC market. The Stock Exchange Act, modelled on European Union laws, regulates listing, takeover bids, disclosures and flagging in the event of the major transactions.[2]

The Icelandic bond market consists of a primary market, which usually takes the form of bond auctions, and a secondary market, which is mainly operated on OMX ICE. It has several unique features in comparison with other countries: first, indexed bonds dominate the market, with the bulk of issues with a maturity exceeding five years being linked to the CPI. Second, a large share of the bonds carries a state guarantee, including HFF bonds, the market's most liquid issues. Third, yields on the Icelandic bond market have been high by international comparison. Icelandic bond issues can be broadly divided into four categories:

1. Treasury notes and Treasury bills, which are non-indexed, zero-coupon bonds.
2. Housing Financing Fund (HFF) bonds, housing authority bonds and housing bonds which are indexed, interest-bearing bonds in an annuity format.
3. Bonds that are issued by government agencies, private firms or institutions such as banks.
4. Government bonds, issued by the Treasury, are indexed against inflation and paid up with accrued interest at maturity date. However, these bonds have not been issued for a while now and currently account for only ISK 14.5 billion (approx. EUR 170 million).

An active market-making programme ensures liquidity in the market for benchmark government bonds, HFF bonds, housing bonds and housing authority bonds. A primary dealer system is also in place for Treasury notes and bills.

A total of 25 companies are now listed on the OMX Iceland main list. Market capitalization of Icelandic equities has increased in recent years as equity prices have risen, with current total capitalization of approximately EUR 38 billion (ISK 3150 billion), almost three times the country's GDP in 2006.

The money market consists of a secondary market in Treasury bills, bank bills and other short-term bonds on the Stock Exchange, and the interbank loan market. The Central Bank of Iceland (CBI) operates the interbank market and trading involves unsecured loans between members, who must display indicative bid and ask yields on various maturities, ranging from overnight to 12-month loans. Trades must be reported to the CBI, which fixes REIBID and REIBOR rates daily.

Iceland's foreign exchange market is an interbank market run by the CBI since 1993 consisting of the three largest commercial banks and the CBI, though it has not been an active market maker for a number of years. The CBI has purchased foreign exchange in the interbank market on behalf of the Treasury and to boost its own reserves since 2003. In November 2001 an informal FX swap interbank market was launched, for which the CBI issued rules in March 2002. Other derivative instruments are used in Iceland but not in a formal market.

*10.1.3.1 Central Bank*

The Central Bank of Iceland is managed by a board of three governors. The bank is part of the portfolio of the Prime Minister who, *inter alia,* appoints the chairman of the bank board. There is also a supervisory board, elected by Parliament. The supervisory board, however, has mostly an oversight role and is not supposed to play any role in monetary policy decisions.

Iceland has employed an inflation targeting regime since March 2001. The CBI has the mandate to aim for an annual rate of inflation of 2.5 per cent as measured by the 12-month increase in the CPI. If inflation deviates by more than 1.5 per cent from the target, the CBI is obliged to submit a (public) report to the government where it explains the reason for the deviation, how it intends to respond and when it expects the inflation target to be reached again. Monetary policy is not to be used to reach other economic targets, such as to attain balance on the current account or to maintain a high level of employment, except to the extent that this is consistent with the Bank's inflation target. The Bank's main policy instrument is the interest rate it sets for 7-day collateral loan agreements with credit institutions. The Bank announces its decisions regarding the policy rate at least six times each year.

As of March 2007 the CBI bases its inflation forecasts – a forward extrapolation of two and a half years – on a policy rate path 'that its staff estimates as appropriate for attaining the inflation target' within an acceptable horizon which – based on the most recent *Monetary Bulletin* – appears to be defined as approximately two years.[3] In the *Bulletin,* the Bank publishes its inflation forecast, the policy rate path the forecast is based on and other underlying assumptions.

The CBI shows great transparency regarding monetary policy decisions. As explained above, it publishes not only an inflation forecast for two and a half years ahead but also the policy rate path on which the forecast is based, the exchange rate and the predicted output gap. It also publishes the model used for forecasting along with its database, so, in principle the forecasts can be independently replicated. The Bank does not, however, publish the minutes of the board meetings where the decisions are made.

#### *10.1.3.2 Financial Supervisory Authority*

Financial regulation in Iceland is strong. The CBI monitors overall financial stability, and the Financial Supervisory Authority (FSA) is an independent entity entrusted with considerable enforcement powers. It monitors the credit market, the pension system, the insurance market and the securities market, and has access to all information from all parties subject to supervision. The FSA has the authority to impose financial sanctions and withdraw licences. It is also entitled to conduct house searches and to confiscate relevant material, supported by a court order. It can call and chair board meetings of a bank under investigation and can publicly issue its interpretations of rules and regulations for sound and proper business practices.

Monitoring and inspection activities are both off- and on-site. The off-site approach is based on regular information gathering and analysis, producing reports on capital adequacy, large exposures, connected lending, defaults, liquidity, major interests in non-financial companies, lending collateral on shares, etc. Analysis is based on general data inspection, stress testing and CAMELS, a risk assessment tool focusing on six key variables (capital, asset quality, management, earnings, liquidity, and sensitivity to market risk). The stress testing is discussed in detail in Section 10.3. Iceland implemented the Basel II standard as a part of its fulfilment of the EEA Agreement in 2004.

On-site inspections are based on benchmark meetings with the management of the banks, where financial results, goals and risks are discussed, with an emphasis on credit, liquidity, market and operational risks. Furthermore, the FSA monitors how well the bank measures and controls its risk.

The FSA budget has recently been doubled to enable it to keep pace with the rapid growth of the financial sector and the increasing foreign expansion of the main players in the market. It also plays the major role in implementing the EU Financial Services Action Plan (which applies to the EEA countries), including the important Markets in Financial Instruments Directive (MiFID). Unlike several EU member states, Iceland was able to apply MiFID as from the starting implementation date of 1 November 2007.

### 10.1.4 Putting the size of the Icelandic economy into perspective

The Icelandic economy is very special in many ways. In absolute terms the economy is only about 0.1 per cent of the US economy, and about

5 per cent of the Danish economy, but its small size has been one reason why rapid growth has been possible. A population of only 300,000 allows much higher flexibility and adaptability than is possible in a larger economy. These special circumstances cause some features particular to the Icelandic economy. In addition, asset markets have been growing noticeably, foreign investment has been booming, unemployment is almost non-existent and economic growth has been high. Recent developments may therefore seem unconventional to people who are unaware of the unique character of the Icelandic economy.

#### *10.1.4.1 Size of companies and foreign operations*

A distinctive feature of the Icelandic economy is the relative size of the largest companies. The total market capitalization of the four largest companies listed on OMX Iceland is almost twice the country's GDP, and single investments can sometimes amount to a substantial proportion of GDP. Kaupthing recently acquired Dutch bank NIBC for close to EUR 3 billion. This is approximately a quarter of Iceland's GDP. Earlier this year Exista acquired a 20 per cent share in the Finnish financial company Sampo for close to EUR 2 billion. Those two acquisitions combined are close to half of Iceland's GDP. It should therefore not come as a surprise that economic indicators such as FDI, gross debt and balance of payments seem off the chart. When single investments are on this scale, minor errors or disequilibria can have enormous effects on aggregate indicators. In many cases these problems are related to standard accounting conventions that are not created to deal with such unorthodox situations, rather than economic imbalances as the indicators might suggest on first sight.

The financial system has undergone extraordinary expansion during the past several years. Total assets of the Icelandic credit system have grown from approximately 140 per cent of GDP in 1990 to 400 per cent in 2006, which is high, but not out of line with small countries that have become international financial centres (see Figure 10.1). This fast growth has contributed to the increasing external debt of the country.

The total number of employees working for Icelandic companies abroad is approximately the same as the total domestic labour force (see Table 10.4). In the domestic market, about 9 per cent of the labour force are foreigners. These are good indicators of the international integration of the Icelandic economy.

#### *10.1.4.2 Investments in the energy sector*

In the past few years the biggest investment project in the history of Iceland has been taking place in the eastern part of the country.

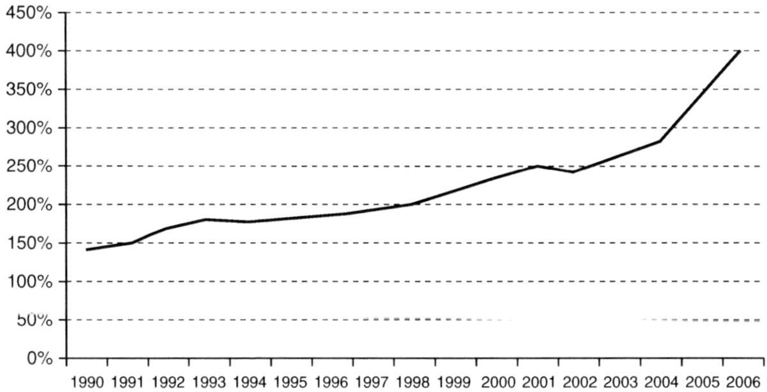


*Figure 10.1* Credit system (% of GDP)
*Source*: Central Bank of Iceland.

*Table 10.4* Foreign workforce of Icelandic companies (as of June 2007)

| | *Number of foreign employees* | *As % of domestic labour force* |
|---|---|---|
| Baugur Group | 67 000 | 38.3 |
| Bakkavör | 20 000 | 11.4 |
| Eimskip | 14 000 | 8.0 |
| Actavis | 11 000 | 6.3 |
| Nordic Partners | 7 500 | 4.3 |
| Promens | 5 400 | 3.1 |
| Icelandic Group | 4 600 | 2.6 |
| Alfesca | 3 400 | 1.9 |
| Kaupthing | 2 500 | 1.4 |
| Glitnir | 1 000 | 0.6 |

*Source*: Data gathered from companies.

A large-scale hydroelectric power plant (called Karahnjukavirkjun) is well on its way to being finished, and a new aluminium smelter will utilize the energy. Both the power plant and the aluminium smelter will be the largest of their kind in Iceland. Total investment cost of these large projects will be approximately EUR 2.5 billion, close to 20 per cent of the country's GDP. Since the Icelandic economy is approximately 0.1 per cent of the US economy, this can be compared to a single project of EUR 2.5 trillion (EUR 2,500,000,000,000) taking place in the US. It is not surprising that these investments have led to some economic imbalances in Iceland.

Due in large part to extensive investments in renewable energy and aluminium production, business investment in 2005 soared 57 per cent from 2004, and reached its peak in 2006 when it grew a further 20 per cent compared to 2005. Gross domestic investment in 2006 was 33.4 per cent of GDP. It is obvious that this project has had enormous impact on the economy and its indicators, such as inflation, interest rates, exchange rates and current account deficit. If the investment is sufficiently profitable (i.e. has a positive net present value), however, future generations will benefit from it despite these short-term imbalances.

#### *10.1.4.3 The Icelandic krona*

Iceland is the smallest sovereign state in the world that has an independent monetary policy. Since 2001 its policy has been based on inflation targeting and a floating exchange rate. While the Icelandic FX market has always been relatively thin, turnover has grown fast in recent years. The main factor at work is growing participation by non-residents in ISK trades, mostly against the euro.

The domestic market now resembles international FX markets more closely in that an ever-smaller share of trade is connected with actual merchandise trade. Foreign investors and speculators have become more active, both through position-taking and in order to manage or hedge against risks. Speculation may induce exchange rate volatility but has significantly deepened the market to create more active price formation. Nonetheless, the small size of the ISK market remains its greatest weakness. Only three market makers are active, and it is difficult to see how it could function normally if their number falls.

Comparison is useful in order to gain a perspective of how small the market for the ISK really is. Total turnover in 2006 was EUR 52.9 billion, and in the first six months of 2007 it had reached EUR 28.7 billion. The ISK market is in fact too small to figure separately in the BIS Triennial Central Bank Survey data on currency markets (it is not among the top 35 currencies in turnover). We can, however, do our own calculation. According to the Survey, in April 2007 average daily turnover of the world foreign exchange markets was approximately EUR 2.9 trillion. With close to 260 business days a year this would amount to an annual turnover of EUR 754 trillion. This means that the turnover in the ISK market should be approximately only 0.007 per cent of the total world market.

## 10.2 The Icelandic financial sector going forward

### 10.2.1 Events of February 2006

The banks relied heavily on favourable global financial market conditions in the beginning of their foreign advance. Possibly, they were not sufficiently prudent. The first sign of change was a rise in bank credit default swap (CDS) spreads and yields on their bond issues starting November 2005. Economic imbalances along with scepticism about the banks' funding position had raised concerns about the financial stability of Iceland's economy and financial system. Fitch changed its sovereign outlook for Iceland from stable to negative on 21 February 2006.[4] That immediately triggered ISK depreciation and a sequence of negative analyst reports, in particular that of Merrill Lynch on March 7.[5,6]

The rating downgrade, criticism of the banks and negative discussion about the Icelandic economy in general caused the krona to depreciate by one-quarter in the first half of 2006, and share prices on the Iceland Stock Exchange also fell by one-quarter from their peak in February until mid-year. The access of Icelandic banks to foreign credit in traditional markets was seriously curtailed. Negative coverage of the banks and Icelandic economy went hand in hand at this time, both temporarily eroding international investors' confidence.

The main criticism of the Icelandic banks concerned heavy reliance on capital market funding, exposure of the banks to market risks on the asset side, the quality of the loan portfolio (considering the rapid asset growth in recent years), foreign exchange risk on regulatory capital, cross-ownership issues, and earnings quality (outsize gains on equity). Much of this criticism was based on valid arguments, but some was due to lack of transparency and information flow from the banks.

Since February 2006 the banks have made great efforts to improve those factors in order to strengthen their credibility in international markets. A test came earlier than expected with the recent credit crunch. The global turmoil of the fixed-income markets seems to have hindered their access to wholesale funding, but on a different scale. During this period, senior five-year CDSs have widened to a record level. On this measure, the risk related to Icelandic banks seems to be estimated well above average, despite their efforts since February 2006. It is therefore important to consider what the current situation of the Icelandic banks really is.

### 10.2.2 Skating on thin ice?

#### *10.2.2.1 Financial structure*

Despite dominant market shares in their domestic market, both in retail and corporate banking, given the small size of this market, the three largest banks (Glitnir, Kaupthing and Landsbanki) have had to use substantial wholesale funding to finance rapid asset growth (both organic and external growth) over the past five years. In February 2006, the maturities of securities were relatively front-loaded for all the banks. Together with the heavy reliance on market funding, this posed a significant threat to the banks in the financial turmoil following Fitch's announcement of a negative outlook on the sovereign credit rating of Iceland. The banks went through a real-life stress test of their access to capital market funding, but within a few months, the situation normalized as they demonstrated their ability to absorb shocks.

Nevertheless, these events have changed the banks' strategies, since they have all been seeking to limit their dependence on the wholesale markets by diversifying their investor base and raising retail deposits. The February 2006 turbulence worked as an alarm bell, putting the banks in a much stronger position to come through the current liquidity squeeze unscathed.

#### *10.2.2.2 Deposit ratios and debt maturities*

With already dominant positions in their domestic markets, it is mostly through their subsidiaries that the three main commercial banks have been seeking to raise customer deposits. Landsbanki has so far been the most successful. This is mainly due to a deposit programme called Icesave, which was launched by the bank in the UK in October 2006. As Table 10.5 shows, all three banks have thus improved their deposit ratios substantially since February 2006.

Despite their continuing reliance on wholesale funding, as underlined during the previous turbulence in early 2006, a number of elements mitigate this risk. First, the Icelandic banks have made significant efforts to diversify their investor base, enabling them to raise funds in many regions. 'New' markets targeted since 2006 include, for example, the US, Japan, Canada and Australia. In addition, the average maturity of funding has been markedly lengthened, with the majority of recent bond issues maturing in 2010 or after. The maturity has moved from being relatively front-loaded to a much more even distribution. Figures 10.2–10.4 show outstanding debt at each year as a percentage of total outstanding debt, and therefore show the relative debt distribution.[7]

*Table 10.5* Deposit ratios (%)

| | *Glitnir* | *Kaupthing* | *Landsbanki* |
|---|---|---|---|
| Year-end 2005 | 25.9 | 31.5 | 33.9 |
| End of Q3 2007 | 37.6 | 42.7 | 75.5 |
| **Change** | **+12.3** | **+11.2** | **+41.4** |

*Source*: Annual Reports.

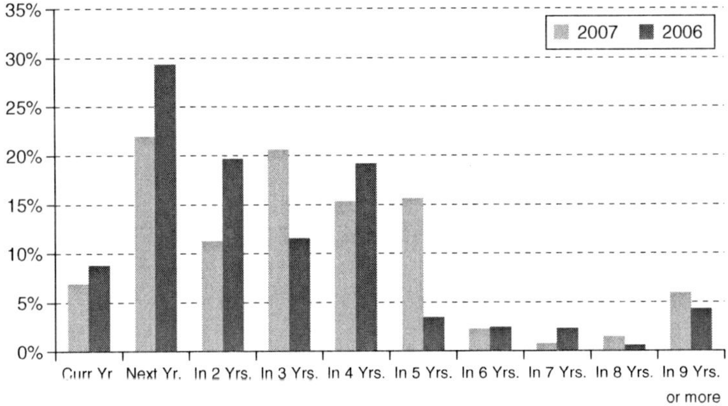


*Figure 10.2* Glitnir Bank debt distribution

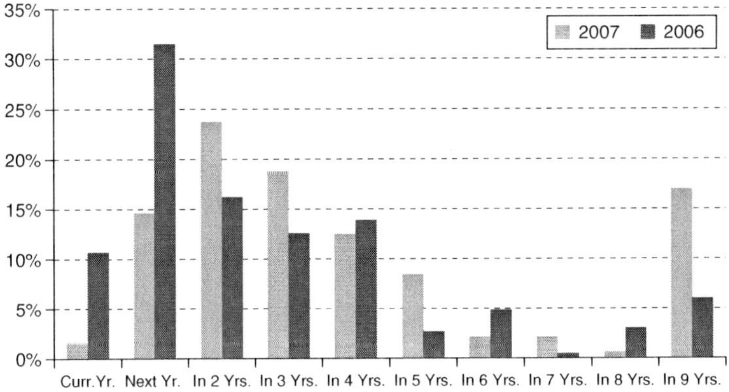


*Figure 10.3* Kaupthing Bank debt distribution

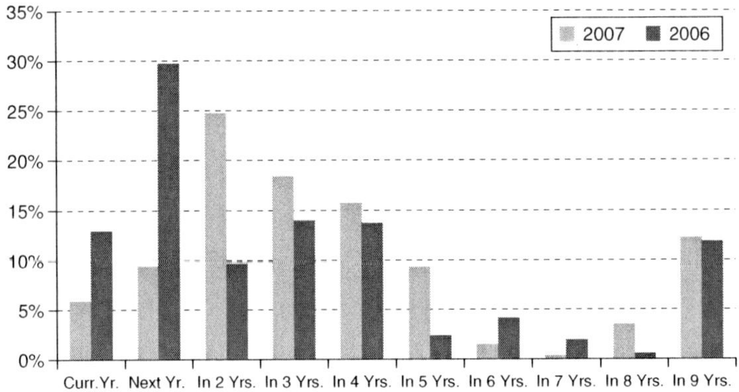


*Figure 10.4* Landsbanki debt distribution

The three major banks all have defined policies in relation to liquidity. The key criterion for all the banks is to be able to serve and repay all maturing debts for 360 days without any access to capital markets.

Despite the current market turbulence, the Icelandic banks have been able to access the wholesale markets, although at a higher price than in the past. A prolonged liquidity squeeze and deterioration in some of the markets in which the banks operate would undoubtedly affect performance. But underlying profitability should benefit from the increased diversification of the banks' revenue and exposure by geography and product, despite the potential volatility in some of the banks' activities, most notably investment banking.

### 10.2.3 Loan portfolio

Until recently, markets have been very favourable in relation to the cost of risk on the asset side with decreasing provisions to loans for most banks around the world. With banks at a favourable point in the credit cycle, the cost of holding a risky asset portfolio becomes far less transparent, making it hard to judge whether credit risk is substantial or not.

The asset growth of the Icelandic banks has been extraordinary during the past few years. It is therefore natural to observe some scepticism concerning the quality of the assets. Taking this into consideration, the asset quality of the Icelandic banks would have been far less visible had it not been for the financial turmoil in February 2006. In a period of two months the domestic equity market dropped a quarter of its value and simultaneously the Icelandic krona depreciated rapidly, by approximately 30 per cent over a three-month period.

Despite these extreme circumstances, the combined credit loss allowance (provisions) account of the largest commercial banks amounted to approximately EUR 0.5 billion at the end of 2006. Although they increased in nominal terms, credit loss allowance accounts have shrunk relative to lending growth. As a proportion of total outstanding loan stock, the largest commercial banks' credit loss allowance accounts stood at 0.8 per cent at the end of 2006, the lowest ratio ever. This is due primarily to low levels of delinquency.

There are several features that distinguish the loan portfolio of Icelandic banks from that of their peers. The most obvious is exposure to the Icelandic market, i.e. equity and real estate. In addition, domestic customers take foreign-denominated loans on a large scale, and therefore the client base currency exposure needs to be taken into consideration. The exposure to Icelandic markets varies substantially between banks. Landsbanki has the highest domestic exposure with 63 per cent of loans located in Iceland, Glitnir has 45 per cent of its loan portfolio in Iceland and Kaupthing has only 22 per cent of its loans in Iceland.

In regard to equity and fixed income exposure, it is worth noting that Icelandic banks have all acted as middle-market investment banks investing alongside their clients in leveraged transactions, Kaupthing being the most active out of the three. The market risk from equity varies between banks, with Kaupthing having market risk of approximately ISK 162 billion at year end (4 per cent of total assets), Landsbanki ISK 52 billion (2.3 per cent of total assets) and Glitnir ISK 21 billion (0.9 per cent of total assets). As a result of derivative contracts with their clients, the market risk on equity exposures is not the same as their book value. The risk of equity positions will be discussed further below in relation to market risk.

*10.2.3.1 Domestic housing market*

Until 2004, the state-owned Housing Financing Fund (HFF) dominated the mortgage market in Iceland through state-backed bond issues that were sold to private investors, so the retail banks had trouble competing with their cost advantage. However, restrictions on the types of loans the HFF could offer and the low interest rate environment allowed the banks to penetrate the residential mortgage market.

The expectation of the banks was probably that they would create sufficient pressure on the HFF to bring about political changes in the residential mortgage market. Generally the mortgage market provides attractive risk-adjusted returns on capital allocated, and therefore mortgages make a strong component in banks' loan portfolios. This is not the case in Iceland, since the banks entered the market without really being able to make money from it under the current circumstances. They justify this with cross-selling and customer loyalty.

In a country where home ownership and incomes are among the highest in the world, it is hard to see a large role for an entity such as the HFF. Being a sovereign entity, and backed by the state guarantee, HFF enjoys excellent access to cheap wholesale funding and can therefore offer very advantageous rates to mortgage customers. This creates a severe bias in the mortgage market and makes it very hard for the banks to compete. The exit of the HFF from the market would relieve these competitive pressures and allow the banks to move their mortgage business onto a more profitable basis.[8]

Regarding the quality of the mortgage loan portfolios, household debt service has not increased as a proportion of disposable income since 2004; instead, it has gone down slightly (Figure 10.5). Lower interest

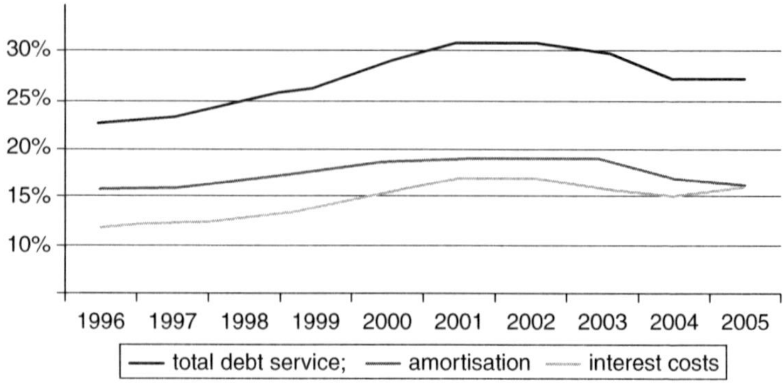


*Figure 10.5* Household debt service

rates and longer maturities are the main reasons for this. Nonetheless, households that increased their debt the most are quite vulnerable to shocks, such as higher unemployment and declining real wages, if the economy contracts. If this were to coincide with a fall in house prices financial companies might need to step up their mortgage write-offs.

Another reason for concern is the increasing level of foreign currency denominated mortgages. During 2007 this proportion rose from approximately 7 to 14 per cent of all mortgage loans provided. Considering the fact that domestic households usually do not earn much of their income in foreign currency, it could be questionable for them to assume debt in other currencies than the ISK.

#### *10.2.3.2 Equity market*

Since shares are frequently pledged as collateral for loans, a bank's exposure to equity is not only direct but also through the loan portfolio. Lending by the largest commercial bank groups against share collateral amounted to ISK 674 billion at the end of 2006, or 12 per cent of their total lending to customers. The bulk of leveraging (59 per cent) involves equities listed on OMX Nordic Exchange in Iceland. According to margining data from the Central Bank the banks have considerable leeway for meeting a drop in equity prices.[9] This is probably the main reason why the sharp fall of the domestic stock market in February 2006 did not have more dramatic effects on delinquency. This does not change the fact that equity investments on OMX in Iceland are being leveraged on a sizeable scale, which could be questionable in the long term if share prices fall substantially.

#### *10.2.3.3 Customer exchange-rate exposure*

The outstanding stock of foreign currency denominated loans by commercial banks on a (parent-company basis) at the end of 2006 stood at approximately ISK 1800 billion. Some 57 per cent of foreign currency denominated lending was to Icelandic residents. The overwhelming majority of foreign currency denominated lending to residents is made to businesses, accounting for 92 per cent, while 6 per cent went to households.

The bulk of foreign currency denominated lending is to borrowers with sizeable incomes in foreign currency. Thus 39 per cent of foreign currency denominated lending at the end of 2006 was to non-residents, 25 per cent to residents with more than 2/3 of their total revenues in foreign currency and 15 per cent to residents with between one-third and two-thirds of their total revenues in foreign currency. These groups therefore have a natural hedge to the exchange rate risk involved. This leaves 21 per cent[10] of lending to residents who earned less than one-third of their total revenues in foreign currency. However, included in this group are several businesses which have a strong enough market position to be able to pass on to prices the extra cost resulting from a depreciation of the krona.

#### *10.2.3.4 Decline in ratio of large exposures*

According to FSA data, total large exposures of the largest commercial banks amounted to ISK 547 billion at end-2006, the equivalent of 59 per cent of their combined own funds. Between them, the banks had 17 large exposures at the end of 2006. By comparison, total large exposures at the end of 2005 numbered 16 and their value was ISK 377 billion or 76 per cent of own funds. It should be remembered that the expansion of commercial banks' capital in 2006 has naturally reduced their number of large exposures. Since the total amount of large exposures has grown by ISK 170 billion year on year, and their number has increased by one, it can be inferred that the largest exposures have been augmented year on year. However, the reduction in the ratio of large exposures to capital between the years is an important consideration from the perspective of financial stability.[11]

### 10.2.4 Market risk

The risk from equity varies between banks, with Kaupthing having market risk of approximately ISK 162 billion (4 per cent of total assets) at year end 2006, Landsbanki ISK 52 billion (2.3 per cent of total assets) and Glitnir ISK 21 billion (0.9 per cent of total assets).

Equity exposure is relatively high for the Icelandic banks, especially Kaupthing. The risk is magnified to a certain extent by the fact that Icelandic banks have all acted as middle-market investment banks investing alongside their clients in leveraged transactions. By doing so, the banks definitely place more than one egg in the same basket. The advantage of this strategy is that it should lead to stronger monitoring of the respective companies.

As previously mentioned, the banks have already gone through a demanding test of their ability to withstand serious simultaneous shocks in the domestic market. This does not, however, necessarily mean that their strength would be the same today. The FSA periodically calculates the effects of simultaneous shocks on capital ratios of the largest Icelandic banks. The shocks imply that a financial undertaking must be in a position to take on certain setbacks that simultaneously may lead to changes in the value of shares, market bonds, non-performing/impaired loans and appropriated assets and the Icelandic krona without having its capital adequacy ratio drop below 8 per cent. These shocks involve a simultaneous 20 per cent fall in the value of non-performing/impaired loans and appropriate assets, a 25 per cent fall in value of foreign shares at own risk of the bank, a 35 per cent fall in value of domestic shares at own risk of the bank, a 7 per cent fall in value of bonds owned by the bank (bonds with less than one year maturity excluded) and a 20 per cent weakening of the krona. The last stress test was performed at the end of June 2007. The results (see Table 10.6) imply that all three banks remain well above the regulatory capital ratio despite a simultaneous shock of this kind. This indicates that the high market risk of Icelandic banks, relative to their peers, is more than offset by higher capital adequacy (CAD) and Tier 1 ratios.

### 10.2.5 Foreign exchange rate risk on regulatory capital

It is important to consider how a depreciation of the krona would affect the banks. All three banks have the majority of their assets in foreign

*Table 10.6* FSA stress test (end of June 2007) (%)

| | *Glitnir* | *Kaupthing* | *Landsbanki* |
|---|---|---|---|
| Capital ratio (CR) | 13.2 | 13.4 | 12.5 |
| Thereof Tier 1 | 9.4 | 10.3 | 11.1 |
| Capital ratio (CR) after stress test | 12.5 | 12.3 | 10.0 |
| Stress test effect | 0.7 | 1.1 | 2.5 |

*Source*: Financial Supervisory Authority, 21 August 2007.

currencies, varying from 67 per cent (Landsbanki) to 81 per cent (Kaupthing) in mid-2007. The liabilities are in similar proportions mostly in foreign currency. The equity of the banks is denominated in ISK, however, and therefore depreciation of the krona could lead to a proportional deterioration of the capital ratios if the banks do not have adequate hedges.

The effect of depreciation is counteracted by two factors. First, the banks have all issued foreign currency denominated subordinate debt, which mitigates exchange rate volatility of Tier 1 capital. Secondly, the banks all have positive foreign currency balances. Sensitivity analysis of the capital adequacy ratio for the banks at mid-year 2007 shows that the banks can resist a significant depreciation of the ISK without a serious deterioration of the ratios (Table 10.7). Kaupthing is basically neutral to fluctuations in the ISK,[12] Glitnir's ratio falls approximately 0.3 per cent against a 10 per cent depreciation and Landsbanki's ratio falls approximately 0.5 per cent when such a depreciation occurs. During the third quarter, however, Glitnir increased their balance 14 per cent and Landsbanki more than tripled its balance, making both banks more or less neutral to changes in the ISK.

Considering the relatively high CAD ratios of the banks, it is evident that all three banks are well equipped to face a severe depreciation of the ISK without the risk of going below the regulatory capital ratios.

### 10.2.6 Earnings quality

During recent years, capital gains have played an important role in the unusually high returns of the Icelandic banks. Return on equity has been very high, and equity positions doubtlessly play a role there. Considering the volatility of financial income, it is likely that the banks' earnings will not be sustainable at these past levels. We therefore calculate the return on equity for the Icelandic banks without the financial income, i.e. we assume 0 per cent returns on equity holdings (see Table 10.8).

*Table 10.7* Effects of the ISK on regulatory capital (as of June 07) (%)

| *Depreciation* | *Glitnir* | | *Kaupthing* | | *Landsbanki* | |
|---|---|---|---|---|---|---|
| | *CAD ratio* | *Change* | *CAD ratio* | *Change* | *CAD ratio* | *Change* |
| 0 | 13.20 | – | 13.4 | – | 12.50 | – |
| 10 | 12.90 | –0.3 | 13.3 | –0.1 | 12 | –0.5 |
| 20 | 12.50 | –0.6 | 13.3 | –0.1 | 11.50 | –1.0 |
| 30 | 12.20 | –1.0 | 13.2 | –0.2 | 11.10 | –1.4 |

*Source*: Annual reports and authors' calculations.

*Table 10.8* Return on equity, excluding financial income

| *P&L (first 9 months of 2007)* | *Glitnir* | *Kaupthing* | *Landsbanki* |
|---|---|---|---|
| Net interest income | 27219 | 56374 | 38825 |
| Net fees and commission income | 27050 | 40898 | 29708 |
| Net financial income | 11479 | 32698 | 16672 |
| Other income | 1 | 5126 | 0 |
| Total income | 65749 | 135096 | 85205 |
| | | | |
| Total cost | (32503)* | (56072) | (40900) |
| Risk provisions | (3150) | (4146) | (4670) |
| Profit before tax | 30096 | 74803 | 39635 |
| Profit after tax | 25164 | 61544 | 35028 |
| | | | |
| Cost/income ratio (%) | 49.4 | 41.5 | 48.0 |
| **ROE before tax (%)** | **29.0** | **31.7** | **37.6** |
| ROE after tax (%) | 24.1 | 27.5 | 33.1 |
| | | | |
| **Corrections** | | | |
| Net financial income | (11479) | (32698) | (16672) |
| | | | |
| **Core income** | | | |
| Net interest income | 27219 | 56374 | 38825 |
| Net fees and commission income | 27050 | 40898 | 29708 |
| Other income | 1 | 5126 | 0 |
| Total income | 54270 | 102398 | 68533 |
| | | | |
| Total cost | (32503) | (56072) | (40900) |
| Risk provisions | (3150) | (4146) | (4670) |
| **Profit before tax** | **18617** | **42180** | **22963** |
| | | | |
| **Cost/income ratio – core income (%)** | **59.9** | **54.8** | **59.7** |
| **ROE before tax – core income (%)** | **17.7** | **18.6** | **21.4** |

* Parentheses indicate negative values.
*Source*: Annual reports and authors' calculations.

The returns on equity fall substantially in this exercise showing that the banks have made substantial excess profits from their equity positions. Returns on equity are still acceptable, however, which indicates that the banks' income is indeed well diversified. It should be considered that the business model of the Icelandic banks is unusual, placing them somewhere between regular commercial banks and investment banks. Considering that all three banks have relatively high capital ratios to compensate for this different nature of their business model, the returns are even more acceptable. In addition, a high proportion of salaries in Icelandic banks are based on performance, indicating that the cost ratios would be much lower with simpler and less profitable operations. Taking that into consideration, the effect of the re-estimation on returns with no return on equities is rather modest.

The extra returns made from equity positions by the banks seem therefore to be a complement to their operations rather than a basic element of their success. The additional market risk from the equity positions is more than offset by the high level of capital, as stress tests indicate.

### 10.2.7 Cross-ownership

One negative factor in external evaluations was apparently extensive cross-ownership and associated lack of transparency. These gave rise to concerns about corporate governance, contagion risk (across financial institutions), and possible related party lending. Considering the fact that the firms themselves cannot control where their shareholders choose to invest their money and that Iceland is a small, fast-growing economy, it is easy to see how such circumstances could arise. Nevertheless, there were certain cases where this cross-ownership was well above appropriate limits, mainly in the case of Kaupthing and Landsbanki. For historical reasons, Kaupthing was a large shareholder in Exista (the largest investment company in Iceland) and vice versa. Also, Landsbanki owned a substantial share in Straumur, which raised concerns about related party lending since ownership was similar for both.

Much of this has been unwound: Kaupthing distributed its shares in Exista as a dividend to its shareholders, changing the relationship to a one-way connection. Landsbanki sold its stake in Straumur so there is no cross-ownership between the banks today.

One of the main transparency problems during the turbulence in February 2006 was due to large holdings of equity by the banks in order to hedge themselves from forward contracts, made by their clients. The market risk of the banks was very opaque, since it was not clear to what extent the equity belonged to the banks compared to what was being held as a hedge. Since the banks were registered owners of the respective shares, and since substantial portions of several listed companies were held through forward contracts, this also indicated severe cross-ownership in certain cases even if this were no longer the case once the forward contracts had been taken into account. As an example, in the spring of 2006 FL Group – the second largest investment company in Iceland – owned a substantial share in Landsbanki which it has now sold. At the same time, 29.9 per cent of all shares in FL Group were held by Landsbanki. Of those shares, only 1 per cent of the 29.9 per cent was being held directly by Landsbanki, while the rest was being held as a hedge against forward contracts. In order to make it clearer to what extent the equity held by the banks is at own risk and under their control, the banks have now separated ownership of shares that are held for customers from the banks.[13]

### 10.2.8 Exposure to sub-prime

One of the strengths of the banks is their low exposure to sub-prime loans. Both Glitnir and Landsbanki have declared that they have no exposure to sub-prime. Kaupthing's sub-prime exposure is limited. The bank is exposed to collateralized debt obligations (CDOs) and asset-backed securities (ABSs) through its asset management company, New Bond Street Asset Management.

In the nine-month interim, the amount of CDO and ABS exposures of the bank and the effect on profit and loss statement in the third quarter of 2007 are explained. The bank's position in corporate synthetic CDOs amounts to ISK 30 billion and the bank's holdings in ABSs total ISK 24.7 billion. Losses due to these instruments, as well as floating rate notes, amounted to ISK 6.9 billion during the third quarter. Supposing that the total exposure of Kaupthing, ISK 54.7 billion, became worthless, the bank would still maintain a capital level above the regulated standards. Since CDOs and ABSs include a pretty broad range of instruments, this scenario is more for theoretical purposes. Calculations show that this would deteriorate the Tier 1 ratio by roughly 1.4 per cent. The calculations are based on unchanged risk-weighted asset base, which should actually fall if this scenario were to happen. Therefore this is rather an overestimated effect than underestimated.

In relation to the recent acquisition of NIBC Bank, it is important to point out that the bank's troublesome sub-prime book will not be sold to Kaupthing along with the bank. As part of the terms of the transaction, the US sub-prime portfolio is to be transferred to a company controlled by the sellers, which are a consortium of shareholders led by J.C. Flowers & Co.

### 10.2.9 Are all the Icelandic banks the same?

The Icelandic financial market tends to be referred to as a single entity, instead of a group of different companies. This is understandable, considering that the main players all share certain characteristics. These include very strong growth, increased presence in foreign markets, low hierarchy and short decision-making channels, relatively young and dynamic executives and unconventional policy.

Comparing the strategy and basic structure of the three major banks, however, reveals that they are much more diverse than they seem at first sight. The growth strategies of the banks have been very different. Kaupthing was the first to expand their operations abroad, when they started Kaupthing Luxembourg SA, a securities firm. In the following decade all three banks have expanded their operations abroad, both through acquisitions and organic growth. Kaupthing has been by far the most aggressive in relation to acquisitions. The total value of companies it has acquired during past decade has been approximately EUR 5 billion. The largest ones have been the recent acquisition of NIBC (approx. EUR 3 billion); Singer & Friedlander, which was acquired in March 2005 (approx. EUR 0.8 billion); and finally the Danish FIH bank, which was acquired in June 2004 (approx. EUR 1 billion). In comparison total acquisitions made by Glitnir (the largest acquisitions include FIM Group and BN Bank) during the same period were close to EUR 1 billion. Landsbanki (largest acquisitions include Teather & Greenwood, Kepler Equities, Merrion Capital and Bridgewell) has acquired foreign companies for a cost of less than EUR 0.5 billion. Therefore, the organic growth has proportionally been the highest at Landsbanki, despite strong organic growth by both Glitnir and Kaupthing.

In terms of geographical focus, the banks vary to some extent. They all focus mainly on Nordic markets, but the concentrations of their operations differ. Kaupthing has the most diverse market, defining northern Europe as their operating market. The recent acquisition of NIBC expands their operations to continental Europe, and they are launching their operations in the Middle East. Kaupthing's primary markets are Denmark, Iceland and the UK. Glitnir has defined Iceland and Norway as its domestic markets. Their recent acquisition of Finnish FIM Group should increase the weight of Finland in their operations. In addition, Glitnir has opened branches which are intended to service companies in industries which are described as key industries in the bank's operations. Those branches are, for example, in New York, London and Shanghai. Landsbanki has placed much emphasis on the UK and Ireland. In addition, Landsbanki operates in continental Europe and Scandinavia and has recently entered the Canadian market. As previously mentioned, the acquisitions of Landsbanki have not been large, but the operations of the companies acquired have been relatively dispersed, especially Kepler Equities, allowing the bank to enter many new markets.

The business model of the banks is in many ways similar. They do, however, operate in different segments, and their strengths lie in different areas. Glitnir focuses on certain niches in terms of corporate customer base, mainly fishery and fish processing, sustainable energy (emphasizing geothermal energy), and financing of offshore service vessels. Kaupthing's main focus is on small and medium companies, institutional investors and wealthy individuals, and the bank provides universal service for these customers. Landsbanki has used the broad European network of branches that it has built up through acquisitions to grow organically, placing main emphasis on providing comprehensive financial services to small and medium-sized European companies.

### 10.2.10 Peer comparison

Although the Icelandic banks differ in many ways, their business model does have strong similarities. They all have a higher than average risk profile, which is compensated by unusually high capital ratios. Their strategy has proven highly successful in recent years, delivering very high returns on equity. Finding appropriate peers for comparison is not easy, since their model is unique. Nevertheless, it is useful to compare Icelandic banks to their Nordic peers, especially on the factors specifically criticized during the spring of 2006. Here we look at the Norwegian bank DnB Nor and the Swedish banks Swedbank and Swenska Handelsbanken (SHB). The market capitalization of these banks is relatively close to Kaupthing, the largest Icelandic bank.

#### *10.2.10.1 Market funding and deposit ratios*

The two main factors criticized in relation to financing of Icelandic banks were heavy reliance on market funding in relation to deposits and the concentrated front-load of debt maturities.

Comparison of deposit ratios shows that Kaupthing and Glitnir have reached the stage where they are more or less in line with their Nordic peers. Landsbanki, on the other hand, has by far the highest deposit ratio of the sample (Table 10.9).

Secondly, we consider the debt maturity distribution of the banks. The distribution in Figures 10.6–10.11 shows the proportion of outstanding market borrowing in each relative year. As an indication of the absolute values involved, the ratio of market funding divided by outstanding loans to customers has been calculated for each bank. The higher the ratio, the more reliant the bank is on market funding.[14]

These graphs show that compared to their peers, Icelandic banks are far from being front-loaded. In fact, the distribution seems to be somewhat more favourable than for the other Nordic banks. However, both Glitnir and Kaupthing have a relatively high ratio of market funding. Landsbanki and DnB Nor have a low market-funding ratio, and SHB and Swedbank are in-between.

*Table 10.9* Deposits/loans of major Nordic banks (%)

| | *Glitnir* | *Kaupthing* | *Landsbanki* | *DnB Nor* | *SHB* | *Swedbank* |
|---|---|---|---|---|---|---|
| End of first 9m 2007 | 37.6 | 42.7 | 75.5 | 58.6 | 39.8 | 40.7 |
| End of 2006 | 24.9 | 29.6 | 47.5 | 57.3 | 48.5 | 42.3 |
| End of 2005 | 25.9 | 31.5 | 33.9 | 58.9 | 41.4 | 41.2 |

*Source*: Annual Reports and authors' calculations.

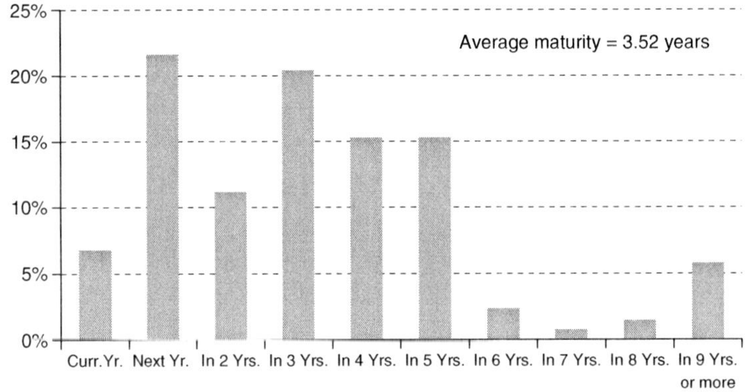


*Figure 10.6* Glitnir (borrowings/loans = 0.77)

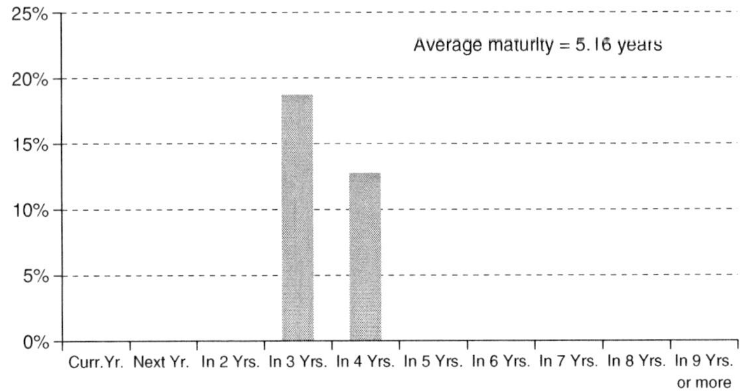


*Figure 10.7* Kaupthing (borrowings/loans = 0.81)

### *10.2.10.2 Earnings and ROE*

Comparing the banks' return on equity shows that Icelandic banks have been much more profitable during the past few years, with average return on equity close to 35 per cent. Their Nordic peers have earned on average roughly 20 per cent return on equity over the respective

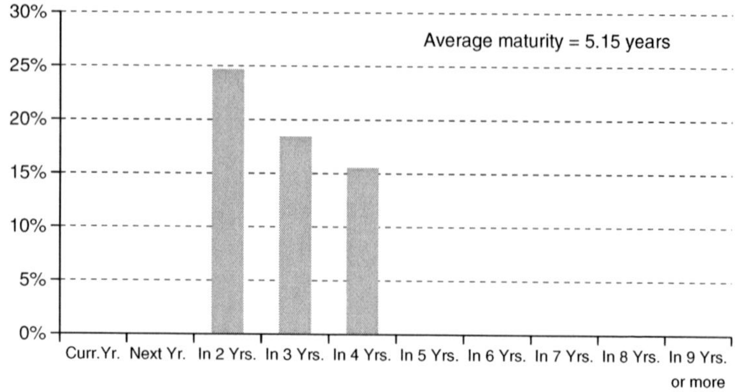


*Figure 10.8* Landsbanki (borrowings/loans = 0.41)

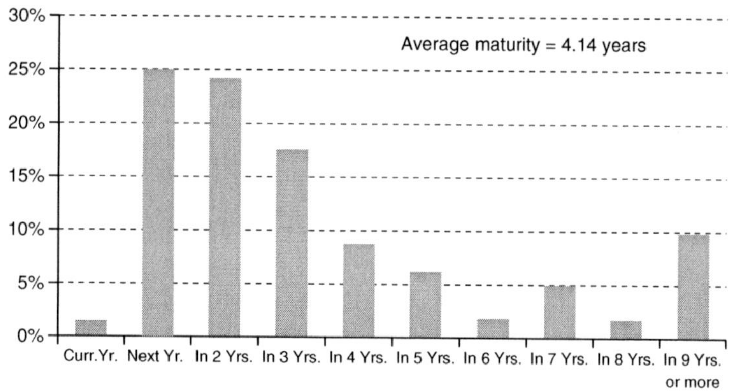


*Figure 10.9* DnB NOR (borrowings/loans = 0.35)

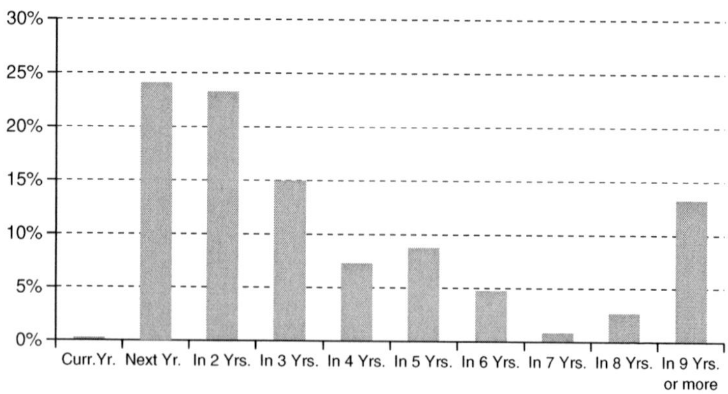


*Figure 10.10* SHB (borrowings/loans = 0.53)

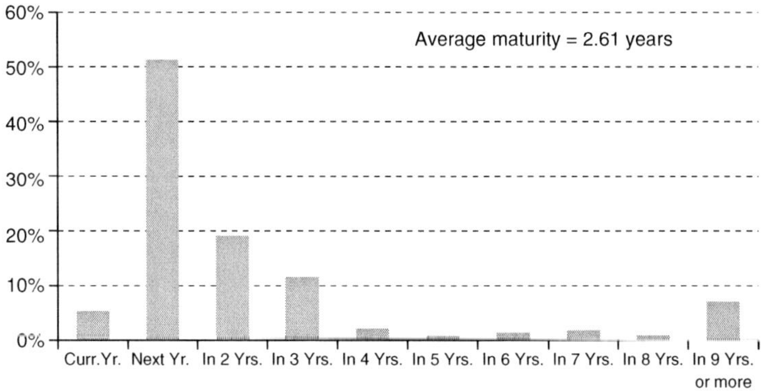


*Figure 10.11* Swedbank (borrowings/loans = 0.6)
*Source*: Bloomberg and authors' calculations.

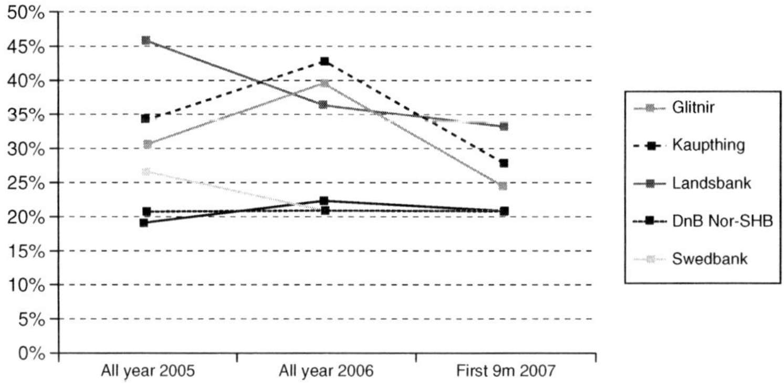


*Figure 10.12* Return on equity, 2005–7

period (see Figure 10.12). Considering the higher financial income of the Icelandic banks, a comparison of core income is appropriate in order to analyse the nature of these high returns. This is done by excluding financial income and making the respective corrections to net interest income. Since the banks could earn interest on the capital invested in equity, net interest income is scaled up accordingly, using short-term REIBOR to calculate interest for Icelandic equities and short-term EURIBOR for foreign equities. The core return is calculated for the year 2006.

As Table 10.10 shows, the core income of the Icelandic banks was the same or higher compared to their Nordic peers in 2006. This indicates that despite high returns on equity positions, the other segments of their operations are highly profitable as well. Considering the relatively

*Table 10.10* Core returns (EUR mil.)

| | *Glitnir* | *Kaupthing* | *Landsbanki* | *DnB Nor* | *SHB* | *Swedbank* |
|---|---|---|---|---|---|---|
| **P&L*** | | | | | | |
| Net interest income | 440 | 615 | 487 | 1 983 | 1 942 | 2 011 |
| Net fees and commission income | 317 | 438 | 333 | 870 | 1 197 | 1 150 |
| Net financial income | 160 | 792 | 230 | 538 | 591 | 417 |
| Other income | 10 | 119 | 0 | 352 | 103 | 209 |
| Total income | 927 | 1 963 | 1 050 | 3 743 | 3 834 | 3 787 |
| Total cost | (328) | (704) | (453) | (1 871) | (1 615) | (1 964) |
| Risk provisions | (56) | (72) | (72) | 34 | 7 | 27 |
| Profit before tax | 543 | 1 186 | 525 | 1 905 | 2 226 | 1 850 |
| Cost/income ratio (%) | 35.4 | 35.9 | 43.2 | 50.0 | 42.1 | 51.9 |
| **ROE before tax (%)** | **46.1** | **50.2** | **40.3** | **26.8** | **29.2** | **27.9** |
| **Corrections** | | | | | | |
| Net interest income | 17 | 106 | 43 | 175 | 203 | 24 |
| Net financial income | (160) | (807) | (230) | (538) | (591) | (417) |
| **Core income** | | | | | | |
| Net interest income | 456 | 721 | 530 | 2 158 | 1 942 | 2 035 |
| Net fees and commission income | 317 | 438 | 333 | 870 | 1 197 | 1 150 |
| Other income | 10 | 119 | 0 | 352 | 103 | 209 |
| Total income | 783 | 1 277 | 863 | 3 380 | 3 243 | 3 394 |
| Total cost | (328) | (704) | (453) | (1 871) | (1 615) | (1 964) |
| Risk provisions | (56) | (72) | (72) | 34 | 7 | 27 |
| **Profit before tax** | **399** | **501** | **338** | **1 542** | **1 635** | **1 458** |
| **Cost/income ratio – core income (%)** | **41.9** | **55.1** | **52.5** | **55.4** | **49.8** | **57.8** |
| **ROE before tax – core income (%)** | **33.9** | **21.2** | **25.9** | **21.7** | **21.5** | **22.0** |

EUR/SEK = 9.20 and EUR/NOK = 7.71.
*Source*: Annual reports and authors' calculations.

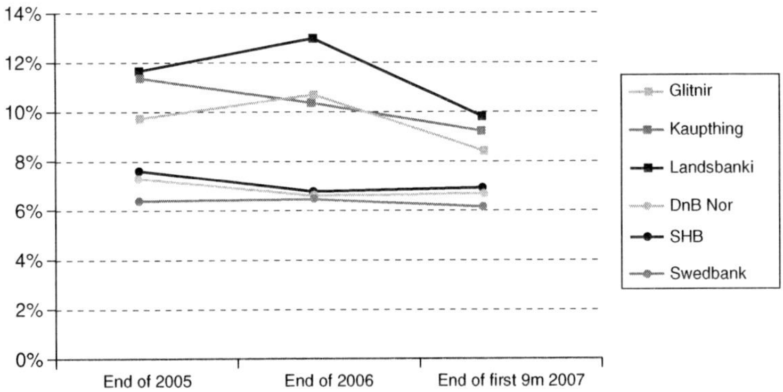


*Figure 10.13* Tier 1 ratios
*Source*: Central Bank of Iceland.

high capital ratios of the Icelandic banks and a large proportion of performance-based salary, the high ROE is even more impressive. It should be noted that the cost of capital has been relatively higher in Iceland over the period and therefore some of the excess return, but by no means all, is due to this.

#### *10.2.10.3 Tier 1 and CAD ratios*

Icelandic banks have compensated for their high risk exposure by retaining high levels of capital. All three banks have implemented the policy of keeping Tier 1 and capital adequacy ratios well above the regulated standards. This becomes apparent when the ratios are compared with their peers. As Figure 10.13 shows, the Tier 1 ratios of the Icelandic banks are on average approximately 3–4 per cent higher than for the other banks. Comparing CAD ratios will lead to a similar result.

### 10.2.11 Does coming from Iceland affect the banks?

The Icelandic banks are a special case in many ways. Not only has their growth been extraordinary in recent years, but their business model is also exceptional. They are relatively aggressive commercial banks with certain features of investment banks. The model is relatively simple, but at the same time unfamiliar. Certainly the roots of this model can be traced to the fact that the banks have followed Icelandic firms into new foreign markets, in order for both parties to take the next step in their advance. This has meant that the banks have engaged in these ventures on more levels than traditional banks would have. As the banks have established a foothold in new markets

*Table 10.11* Ratings

| | *Glitnir* | *Kaupthing* | *Landsbanki* | *DnB Nor* | *SHB* | *Swedbank* |
|---|---|---|---|---|---|---|
| **Moody's** | | | | | | |
| Long term | Aa3 | Aa3 | Aa3 | Aa1 | Aa1 | Aa1 |
| Short term | P1 | P1 | P1 | P1 | P1 | P1 |
| Individual | C | C | C | B– | B | B |
| **S & P** | | | | | | |
| Long term | A– | n/a | n/a | A+ | AA– | A+ |
| Short term | A–2 | n/a | n/a | A–1 | A–1 | A–1 |
| **Fitch** | | | | | | |
| Long term | A | A | A | n/a | A+ | A+ |
| Short term | F1 | F1 | F1 | n/a | F1 | F1 |

*Source*: Annual reports.

in other countries, this same model has been adapted to firms in those markets.

The higher risk of this strategy seems to be more than offset with relatively high capital ratios, diverse markets and customer base, and strong risk management. This has been reflected in reasonably good ratings, relative to the size of the banks. Yet their ratings are uniformly lower than those of Nordic banks, which seem unjustified based on the comparison above (see Table 10.11).

*10.2.11.1 Why have analysts and ratings firms not responded to the changes made and the apparent robustness of the banks?*

Some analysts have a reputational stake in the views they took in spring 2006 – for example, Danske Bank has consistently taken a highly pessimistic view of Iceland, having forecast in March 2006 a 5–10 per cent drop in Icelandic GDP over the following two years. Danske Bank has since been consistently negative on the ISK, as well – investing on its forecasts would have led to significant losses.[15]

S&P on 20 February 2007 expressed concern that the very rapid expansion of the banks might raise execution risk and also lead the banks to misprice risk. Our view, which appears to be shared by the regulatory authorities (the FSA and the CBI), is that these are in fact very well-run banks. Their management is indeed entrepreneurial, but they are wary of becoming involved in anything they do not understand, and they are very focused on risk management. As for the potential mispricing of risk, experience since July 2007 and the information which the banks have provided to the markets suggest they had relatively little involvement with the excesses that underlie the current turmoil.

### *10.2.11.2 Country risk premium*

Comparing CDS paths of the Icelandic banks with those of other Nordic banks and the German Commerzbank is interesting (see Figure 10.14).[16] As could be expected, the Icelandic banks experienced a hike in their CDSs during the turbulence in 2006. Afterwards the trend was downward until autumn 2007, when it has risen substantially, reaching a peak which is much higher than in 2006. This is surprising, considering that the main risk factor during the current turmoil is on one hand exposure to sub-prime markets and illiquid structured finance and on the other hand unfavourable funding structure. The Icelandic banks have almost no exposure to the sub-prime market, and their funding structure has improved enormously during the past year. Even banks heavily affected by the sub-prime problems, like Commerzbank, do not seem to be experiencing anything similar to the Icelandic banks in regard to CDS spreads. It thus appears that the banks are paying a high premium for their Icelandic origin.

It should be noted that Kaupthing's CDS has diverged recently. The main reasons for this are uncertainties regarding the NIBC acquisition and a higher exposure to CDOs and ABSs relative to the other two banks.[17] The acquisition will be partially funded by a pre-emptive rights issue of 40 million shares (estimated to deliver EUR 1.6 billion in cash) in December 2007. There may be some concerns that these shares need to be priced at a discount in the current situation.

*Figure 10.14* CDSs for Icelandic banks, Nordic banks, Commerzbank, Jan. 2006–Oct. 2007

The turmoil in February 2006 seems to have marked the reputation of the Icelandic banks, making them much more sensitive to risk adversity. This is despite their successful efforts to improve the factors that were criticized at the time. Coming from Iceland seems to put a premium on both share price and, especially, on funding terms. Considering the imbalances in the Icelandic economy, this would be natural if the banks had a high exposure to their domestic economy. But for these banks, that is not the case. Therefore, it seems that they are paying a premium for their origin rather than actual risk exposure.

#### *10.2.11.3 Strong domestic market*

There are certain benefits that the banks gain from being Icelandic. The Icelandic economy has been among the fastest-growing developed countries in the world, creating a very favourable environment for the banks in many respects. The smallness of the market also comes with benefits, since foreign competition is nearly non-existent. Therefore, the incomes from their domestic operations have been both stable and strong. Iceland offers a very favourable tax regime, both in terms of corporate tax, as well as the capital income tax. The low corporate income tax has increased profitability substantially, and the low capital income tax encourages equity investments in the domestic market. This has been complemented by the strong pension funds, creating vast sources of liquidity in relation to equity funding.

In addition, the volatility in the Icelandic economy has actually benefited the banks in many ways. All three banks have a positive indexation balance, meaning that inflation actually enhances their income. The volatility has also boosted the turnover in equity, bond and foreign exchange markets, with a resulting increase in commission fees for the banks.

Comparing these costs and benefits is not easy. During stable periods in world markets, the benefits definitely outweigh the cost. But during periods of turbulence in the global financial markets, the cost of the risk premium paid for their origin can be very high.

Considering this, it is extremely important for the banks to retain a steady and transparent information flow on their operations in order to limit the effects from this country premium. The banks are well equipped to face disruptions in capital markets and contraction in the Icelandic economy, but the premium will obviously affect their profitability. The long-term prospects of the banks should, however, not be threatened, considering their strong funding structure, high capital ratios and diversity regarding income and market exposure.

### 10.2.12 Fast growth in the financial sector and investments abroad

Iceland's financial services sector has grown enormously in recent years, catalysed by deregulation in the 1990s and, in particular, by the privatization of two commercial banks, completed in 2003. International acquisitions and internal growth have increased the banks' combined balance sheets tenfold from 2000 to 2006. This development has puzzled many, especially since it was not until quite recently that outsiders took an active interest in the affairs of this small country.

#### *10.2.12.1 Why have the banks grown so fast?*

It is natural to ask why the banks have grown so fast and expanded so much abroad. We discuss some of the key elements below.

*Financial liberalization.* As was previously mentioned, Iceland has undergone comprehensive financial liberalization in the past three decades, before which the strict regulatory environment specifically discouraged growth in the banking sector. The reforms carried out since 1979 involved the standard approaches to liberalizing financial markets: reforms at the CBI, the development of securities markets, privatization of the state banks (discussed in detail below), the diminished role of public investment credit funds, and the liberalization of both short- and long-term international capital movements.

*Consolidation and privatization of the banks.* The main stimulus for strong growth in the financial system was privatization, undertaken in earnest over the past decade. The two state-owned commercial banks, Landsbanki and Búnaðarbanki (which later merged with Kaupthing bank), were privatized in stages between 1999 and 2003; FBA (an investment credit fund that later merged with Glitnir Bank) was privatized over the period 1998–99. Today, the government's participation in financial markets is limited to mortgage lending institutions, such as the Housing Financing Fund, and a few other much smaller credit funds (see Figure 10.15).

In the preceding decade, the banking sector was consolidated through mergers of both investment credit funds and commercial banks.

The process of consolidation and privatization improved efficiency within the financial sector and equipped the largest players with the tools necessary for further development with relatively favourable credit ratings and vast opportunities for improvements. This restructuring has been complemented by strongly favourable market conditions, both domestically and internationally.

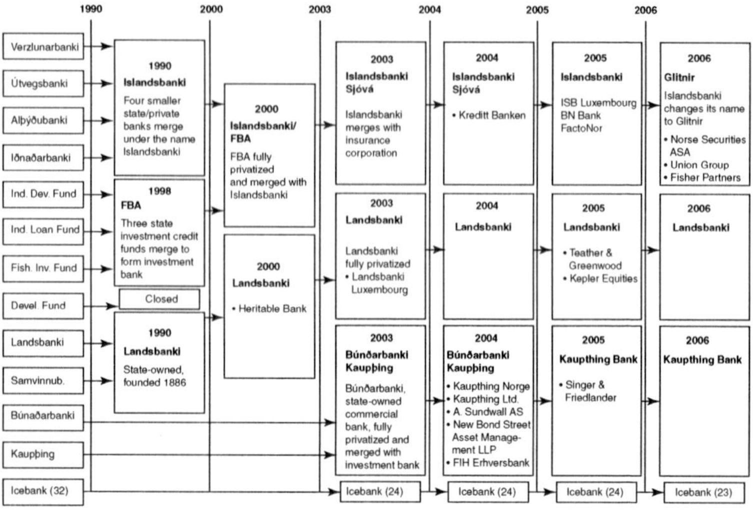


*Figure 10.15* Bank consolidation
*Source*: Central Bank of Iceland.

*Exhausted market opportunities and diversification.* A domestic economy of 300,000 people does not offer the market opportunities that investors and executives in the Icelandic financial sector consider promising for future growth. With the opportunities of further consolidation and streamlining domestically exhausted, the banks have naturally sought to expand their operations abroad to ensure a profitable future. Icelandic banks and firms in general have successfully adopted a strategy of aiming high in their acquisitions, creating extensive growth opportunities.

Another factor that is likely to have motivated Icelandic firms to expand their operations abroad is to diversify risk. Icelandic banks have combined acquisitions abroad and organic growth to diversify their income streams, using a variety of approaches.

*Increased access to funds.* Profound structural changes, combined with promising macroeconomic conditions, have resulted in a breakthrough in Icelandic business life. Since 2000, real GDP has grown substantially, and along with it, both real disposable income and productivity. Asset growth has been strong in all markets, particularly in equity and real estate, creating high liquidity in domestic markets. Historically low global interest rates and reduced credit spreads generated ideal conditions for the rapid expansion of the financial sector. Although Icelandic banks have exploited these globally relaxed liquidity conditions, the continuing solvency of the Icelandic banking sector faced with stricter liquidity conditions has proven its resilience to changing conditions.

#### *10.2.12.2 Foreign advance of Icelandic businesses*

The foreign advance of Icelandic businesses has not just been in banking, but also has been taking place across the retail, pharmaceutical, food production, high-tech manufacturing, airline services and real estate sectors. The main factors leading to foreign expansion within these sectors are generally the same as those driving the banks' expansion: going beyond exhausted market opportunities in Iceland, decreasing risk through income diversification and capitalizing on favourable economic conditions. These firms and the banks have complemented each other in their advance into new markets.

Icelandic firms' focus on foreign markets encouraged banks to capitalize on the trend by expanding their businesses abroad further. The banks, with well-established reputations and relationships in the main foreign markets, have in turn been very helpful for Icelandic firms pursuing business ventures abroad. In addition to providing resources to fund projects, the banks' support and business relations have facilitated these ventures. In this context, the international rating of Icelandic banks is a valuable asset, allowing them to give credible reference for Icelandic companies to accelerate transactions and to underwrite credit facilities when necessary.

The banks have gained substantially from this evolution as well. Projects supporting foreign ventures have provided opportunities for them to prove themselves in new markets and to show that they are quite capable in the field of investment banking and financial consulting. The expansion of Icelandic banks shows that they have predominantly moved to markets where they can serve their Icelandic customers, while at the same time gaining a new customer base. Of course, these projects have also been very profitable in their own right, generating substantial royalties and service fees.

#### *10.2.12.3 Where does the money come from?*

Icelandic investment in other countries averaged 33 per cent of its own GDP in each of the years 2004–7. It is often asked how this 'Icelandic advance' has been financed. The simple answer is that to a large extent, international investments have been financed by borrowed funds; Icelandic entrepreneurs seized the opportunity provided by ample international liquidity and low interest rates. An investor must, however, always put up a share of equity in order to secure funding. The question is therefore where the equity needed for these large investments has come from. The answer is that it has been built up by a number of factors. There are, however, a few important items on the balance sheet that are worth mentioning. The first is new equity created in fisheries, through the establishment of the individual transferable quota system, estimated at 350 billion ISK, or 36 per cent of GDP, at year-end 2005. The second is the equity created by privatization, especially in the banking sector, estimated at 370 billion ISK, or 38 per cent of GDP, in 2005. Finally, a few very successful ventures had already netted a profit of some 40 billion ISK at the end of 2005, adding another 4 per cent of GDP.[18] These numbers add up to a total of 670 billion ISK, or 78 per cent of GDP, in 2005.

It is obvious that Iceland's small domestic economy did not and could not provide sufficient opportunities to put this new capital to work. International investments were not just an exciting prospect – they were a necessity if adequate return was to be made on this equity. The favourable circumstances in international financial markets in recent years created the opportunity for this expansion to happen. With 78 per cent of GDP in new equity in the domestic market, it does not require excessive leveraging to fund the foreign investments of Icelandic firms in the last few years. This is where the money comes from.

### 10.2.13 The lender of last resort

The law on the CBI gives it the role of promoting financial stability, including acting as a lender of last resort (LLR). The Bank also sets prudential regulations on the liquidity and foreign exchange balance of credit institutions.

The LLR provision states that when the CBI thinks it necessary in order to protect the safety of the domestic financial system, the Bank may issue guarantees or grant loans to credit institutions that are in liquidity difficulties against other collateral than is customary or against other conditions laid down by the Bank. The law follows the Bagehot doctrine – although it does not mention 'very high rates' on the CBI's loans as suggested by Bagehot (1873) – in allowing the Bank to provide such help only to solvent banks having liquidity problems: the CBI will not provide assistance 'to boost the capital position of institutions which run into difficulties'.[19] As noted by the Bank, however, '[it] can prove difficult to distinguish between a liquidity problem and wide-reaching ones when an institution experiences difficulties'.[20]

It is important that the FSA, as prudential supervisor, and the CBI work closely together in a crisis. The institutions hold contingency exercises to prepare for meeting problems in financial markets should they arise.

Icelandic banks now all operate in several countries and are classified as cross-border banks. The same applies to most large Nordic banks. The Nordic central banks and the FSAs cooperate on financial stability. They too hold regular contingency exercises and have signed memoranda of understanding on cooperation in managing crises.

Failure of any of the three large Icelandic banks would inevitably have repercussions for the others and be extremely disruptive, financially and economically, for Iceland. In this sense these banks are each individually 'too big to fail'. This is recognized by market participants; for example, Moody's counts 'Strong likelihood of state support in the event of systemic shock' as one of the main strengths of the Icelandic banking system.[21]

But the international character of the banks and their size relative to the economy limits the capacity of the CBI to come to their rescue. The banks' combined assets are now eightfold GDP, and most of their lending is in foreign currency. For example, 78 per cent of Kaupthing's lending is now outside Iceland, and with the acquisition of NIBC this share is set to grow. The most likely scenario where a lender of last resort would be needed is probably that of a drying up of market funding in international markets.

The question therefore arises whether the banks are not just too big to fail, but also too big to rescue. Can the CBI draw on its currency reserves or borrow enough to bail a bank out in dire times? An indication of the size of the amount that the CBI would have to inject, say over the span of three months, is given by the amount of foreign currency market funding maturing in a typical quarter. With the current funding structure of the banks this could be in the range ISK 50–100 billion for any single bank. Current reserves are now ISK 155 billion so it would be feasible for the CBI to provide these funds, but it could come close to exhausting currency reserves by doing so. Were all three banks to need funding of such magnitude the CBI would clearly have to resort to borrowing abroad – or guaranteeing the banks' borrowing. Given the sound financial situation of the government of Iceland, this would probably also be feasible, although borrowing what would amount to almost a year's worth of tax revenues for the central government would stretch its credit lines.

Another way of looking at this issue is considering what the banks themselves can withstand. In October their net foreign currency position was ISK 446 billion. The banks now maintain a currency surplus (to hedge their equity) and could draw on these funds to meet a temporary closure of markets for their bonds.

## 10.3 The financial sector in the global economy

### 10.3.1 External finance

#### *10.3.1.1 Sustainability*

A current account deficit (CAD) is typically not a 'primary factor promoting financial instability' (Mishkin and Herbertsson, 2006). There may nevertheless be reasons for concern about a high current account deficit.

If the external position and its dynamics are unsustainable in the long run, investors may in due course perceive this and exit, even if there is ample time for a correction – indeed, even if the correction has already begun.

If expectations about sustainability change suddenly, then there may be an abrupt exit. This 'sudden stop' or reversal of capital flows is a familiar phenomenon in emerging market countries (Calvo, 2006), but it can also occur in an advanced economy like Iceland or even the United States (see Krugman, 2007). It may bring the economy to a 'hard landing': a sharp depreciation of the exchange rate, generating inflationary pressures, particularly strong in a highly open economy; a rise in interest rates to prevent 'overshooting' and contain the inflationary threat; a fall in consumption and investment (if the interest rate effect outweighs the rise in profitability of investment in tradeables); a fall in output and rise in unemployment; a deterioration of household finances that will hit some non-tradeables, like housing. These developments can in turn pose problems for the financial system, even if banks' balance sheets do not show currency mismatch. They may be exacerbated if the private sector has taken on liabilities to the domestic banking system denominated in foreign currency (domestic liability dollarization [euroization]).

Monetary policy may be responding in part to the external position, even in an inflation-targeting regime, because of the influence of the exchange rate on domestic inflation – again, this will be more pronounced in a small open economy. Conversely, monetary policy will directly affect the external position – a particular example (discussed below) is the 'carry trade'.

We therefore consider here the relationships among capital flows, the exchange rate, interest rates, the current account, macroeconomic stability and the financial system – all this in the context of the Icelandic economy. We do not find that the dynamics of the external position are unsustainable, nor that a 'sudden stop' and 'hard landing' are likely. We do conclude that there are difficulties in running monetary policy in Iceland, some of which are self-imposed and could be corrected. The carry trade is costly to the economy but is unlikely to subside until policy rates are brought down substantially.

One issue that is unresolved is the future of the currency itself. A shift towards use of the euro could gather momentum. That might be a cause of monetary instability, but it is likely that the financial sector would be able to cope with the consequences.

#### *10.3.1.2 Capital inflows problems*

The 'classical' capital inflows problem (see Portes and Vines, 1997) often starts with a rise in the return to investment or financial liberalization, or both. In Iceland, recent developments are closely related to the exploitation of aluminium and hydroelectric resources as well as the culmination of financial liberalization with the privatization of the big banks at the beginning of the century. Investment increases strongly, but domestic saving lags behind, partly because of consumption smoothing: households expect substantial increases in per capita income when the investments come on stream, and they take some of the expected future consumption in the present. Thus aggregate demand exceeds aggregate supply, and financial reforms facilitate capital inflow that meets the gap and finances a current account deficit. A standard example of this phenomenon in an advanced economy is the case of Norway in the 1970s, where the current account deficit rose to 15 per cent during the development of the oil fields.

The authorities may find the macroeconomic disequilibrium excessive and may try to reduce it with a tightening of monetary policy. But the boom is too strong to subside easily, and the rise in interest rates just brings in more capital flows. The nominal exchange rate appreciates. Pressure on the labour market generates inflationary impulses. On both counts, the real exchange rate appreciates. Competitiveness deteriorates. Investment in effect 'crowds out' net exports. And in a small open economy, the exchange rate appreciation, by lowering import prices, will stimulate consumption further, thereby adding to aggregate demand.

The authorities then face the unappealing choice between allowing inflation (inadmissible for an inflation-targeting central bank), allowing nominal appreciation, or trying to prevent both with fiscal tightening. They are likely to see cutting interest rates as too dangerous on the inflation front, even if they recognize that the exchange rate effect might both dampen consumption and stop the capital inflows that are based only on the 'search for yield'. Meanwhile, the current account deficit continues or even rises, and the external debt burden grows.

A common response is the so-called 'Lawson doctrine' (referring to the UK finance minister of the late 1980s, who presided over a boom and an associated current account deficit): *Why do anything? Where is the market failure?* Unless the excess demand is in good part due to fiscal excess, it is private decision-making that has generated the macro outcome. We can reasonably suppose that investors expect to be rewarded amply for their decisions, that households are far-sighted in their consumption smoothing, and that the external debt – again, the result of private decisions to borrow – will be repayable from the future savings of firms and households.[22]

There are several reasons, however, to believe that there may indeed be market failures. First, there can be asymmetries of information, in particular for foreign investors. These can lead to bandwagon or herding effects that initially exaggerate the capital inflows, then exacerbate the 'sudden stop' if investors react to 'news' by reversing the flows. Informational problems can also lead to self-fulfilling speculative attacks on the currency. And deposit insurance or the expectation of lender-of-last-resort bailouts if the banks misjudge their lending can create a moral hazard in the banking system, hence overborrowing and the accumulation of excessive private debt – that is, private decisions are not in fact optimal. Down the road awaits currency crisis, debt crisis, or both.

#### *10.3.1.3 Putting the current account deficit into perspective*

It is not unreasonable to see the Icelandic CAD and large negative net international investment position (NIIP) as sustainable, especially if the economy is on a path that will bring the current account deficit down substantially from its peak at 25.5 per cent of GDP in 2006. As we shall see, it has indeed fallen sharply in 2007. There are also important issues of measurement that suggest a nuanced interpretation of the official data (see the discussion below). Even if the current account as measured in official statistics follows international conventions, there are unusual features for Iceland that lead us to believe that the 'true', or the underlying, or at least the relevant current account data would show a significantly smaller deficit and that the NIIP is indeed less negative than it appears to be. An alternative view is that some external income may be unrecognized or deferred and will appear in the accounts over the next few years. Moreover, the special characteristics of the Icelandic economy suggest that conventional comparative statistics for the current account and NIIP are misleading.

The common standard of reference for the current account and NIIP is GDP – that is, the numbers are often expressed as percentages of GDP. This does measure appropriately the 'resource burden' of the debt and its long-run sustainability or the degree of macroeconomic adjustment that would be required to 'correct' the deficit. But such figures have little to do with the ability to finance the deficit (or increasing debt) in the short to medium term. Nor do they represent well the situation of a very small, very open economy that does an enormous amount of financial intermediation – like Iceland, but also like Luxembourg, or in a different way, New Zealand.

Indeed, one way of seeing the Icelandic external position is to view the country as a very large venture capital firm. It has been borrowing short and medium term to finance very substantial foreign investments in portfolio equity, acquisitions, and organic foreign expansion of its financial institutions, as well as the growth of its non-financial corporations. One reflection of this is that the stock exchange, though 'small' (only 25 firms listed), has a market capitalization of 260 per cent of GDP (69 per cent for Denmark, 40 per cent for New Zealand, 139 per cent for Australia, all end-2006).

A better standard of reference than GDP might be national wealth. But full national wealth accounts, though highly desirable for this and other purposes (Buiter, 1985), are not available for most countries. An alternative might be household wealth, but a measure of household wealth that takes account of funded pension assets. Iceland does have very large fully funded pension funds, and these are clearly part of household financial assets. Housing wealth is also part of the picture. The capacity to finance current account deficits and service external debt is better measured by the stock of household wealth than by the flow of GDP.

At the end of 2006, the net international investment position of Iceland was in deficit, in the amount of 121.5 per cent of GDP. This is very high by international standards. But household wealth was 287 per cent of GDP, including housing and pension wealth. Thus the (negative) NIIP was 42 per cent of total household wealth. For comparison, New Zealand at end-2005 had a negative NIIP of 22 per cent of household wealth, Australia 13 per cent.

But the data for Iceland significantly underestimate household equity wealth. Market capitalization on the stock exchange at end-2006 was BISK 2596. The international investment position data show foreign holdings of domestic equity at 6 per cent of total foreign liabilities of ISK 5916 billion, i.e. ISK 354 billion (this is probably an overestimate, since it ignores shares owned by holding companies in low-tax jurisdictions, of which Icelanders own a substantial part). The pension funds owned ISK 250 billion in shares at end-2006. That leaves at least ISK 1992 billion for Icelandic households. The CBI figures show only ISK 248 billion, but these are the shares owned directly by households. Most wealthy individuals hold their shares in private corporations, which may themselves be registered in tax shelters. The difference is ISK 1744 billion (138 per cent of GDP!). If we add that ISK 1744 billion to total household wealth, we find that the NIIP is negative 27 per cent of adjusted total household wealth.

*10.3.1.4 Data*

*The financial account.* The net international investment position of Iceland, as conventionally measured,[23] was substantially negative but fairly stable for the two decades prior to the end of the 1990s. It then went much more deeply into negative territory (see Figure 10.16).

There were substantial capital outflows as well as inflows, and consequently the country appears highly leveraged, in the sense that external assets exceed 400 per cent of GDP and external liabilities exceed 500 per cent of GDP. As a result, the factor income flows in the current account are very large and highly sensitive to the rates of return on Iceland's external assets and liabilities. The composition shows significantly more Icelandic foreign direct investment than foreign

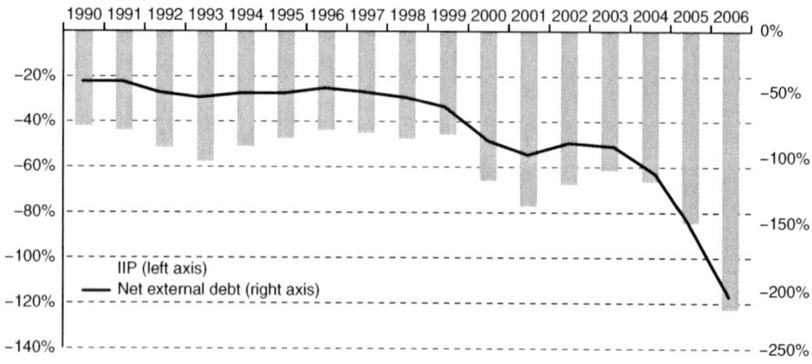


*Figure 10.16* External debt position, 1990–2006 (at end of year and latest quarter)

investment in Iceland (see Figure 10.17). The most notable feature, however, is the explosion of portfolio liabilities from 2003 onwards, in particular 2005–6. Much of this, we may conjecture, is carry trade.

Carry trades relate to cross-border investments in high interest rate currencies funded in low interest rate currencies. The interest rate difference is the 'carry'. There are two distinct types of carry trade in Iceland. A standard retail transaction would be the purchase by individual foreign investors of medium- to longer-term international bonds denominated in ISK – the 'glacier bonds' issued since 2005. There are also transactions in which institutional investors or hedge funds outside Iceland seek ISK exposure and put highly leveraged transactions through foreign banks, which place the funds in Icelandic banks. The two banks swap out their exposure, and the Icelandic bank is left with ISK deposits which it then uses for domestic funding.[24] The main reason why Icelandic banks have sought these funds is to finance their domestic mortgage lending, and some argue that this demand for funding has been just as important in generating carry trade as foreign investors' search for yield.

The carry trade is highly sensitive to changes in the level and volatility of exchange rates. If carry trades unwind in an abrupt fashion, the very large exposures involved could destabilize financial markets and institutions (Ferguson et al., 2007).

Since carry trades are risky, traders will pursue them only if they generate an expected return sufficient to compensate for the risk. The carry-to-risk ratio (a form of Sharpe ratio) is the interest differential divided by the expected volatility of the exchange rate.[25] Carry trades can unwind if the interest rate differential tightens, if the high-yielding currency depreciates or if exchange rate volatility increases.

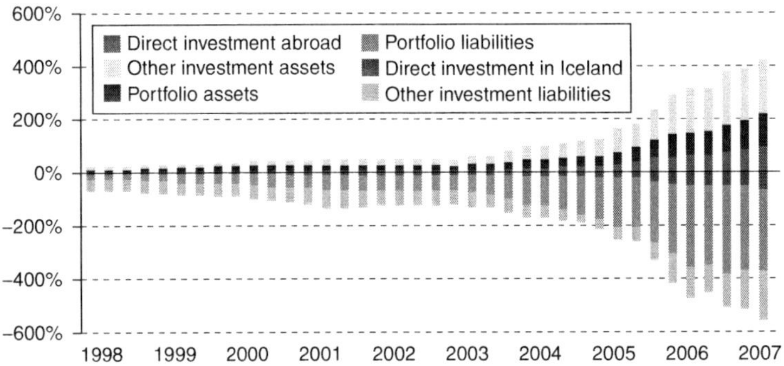


*Figure 10.17* External debt and assets, Q1/1988, Q2/2007 (at current prices)
*Source*: Central Bank of Iceland.

Plantin and Shin (2006) find that carry trades can generate large, persistent deviations of exchange rates from fundamentals as well as the failure of uncovered interest parity. And they show that the exchange rate dynamics for the high-yield currency exhibit a pattern of slow appreciation punctuated by sharp depreciation, known in the markets as 'going up by the stairs, coming down in the elevator'.

In Iceland, the carry-to-risk ratio has apparently been closely related to the exchange rate. A rise in the attractiveness of the carry trade appears to bring a capital inflow and exchange rate appreciation (Figure 10.18).

Foreign bond issuance in the Icelandic krona (glacier bonds), directed at the carry trade, has been substantial since 2005. A large segment matured in September, without any market disturbance. The nominal value of the outstanding glacier bond stock now stands at ISK 373 billion. There appears to be some correlation of issuance with the exchange rate, but the causation could go either way, and both are directly influenced by interest rates (see Figure 10.19).

A considerable portion of foreign debt for both non-financial and financial firms is naturally hedged by foreign revenues (Mishkin and Herbertsson say that 78 per cent of total OMX I15 revenues were in foreign currency, and this has not changed much overall). On the other hand, this is not the case for households, 7–8 per cent of whose debt is foreign currency denominated. It would be unwise and a potential source of instability for household borrowing in foreign currency to continue to rise, unless firms move to paying wages in foreign currency (see below). Monetary policy may contribute to household foreign currency borrowing, insofar as households may expect CBI policy to

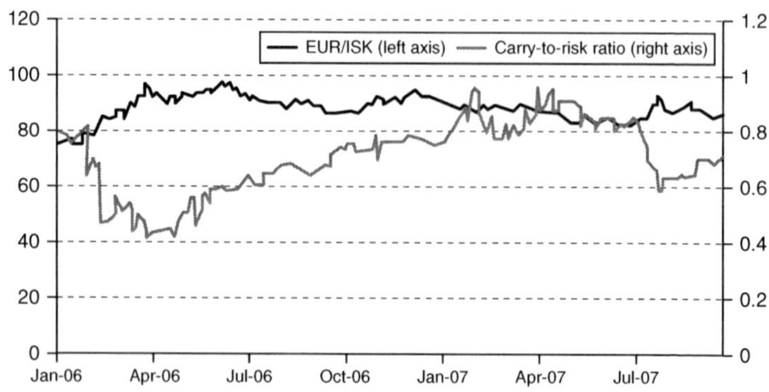


*Figure 10.18* Carry-to-risk ratio vs EUR/ISK exchange rate
*Source*: Central Bank of Iceland.

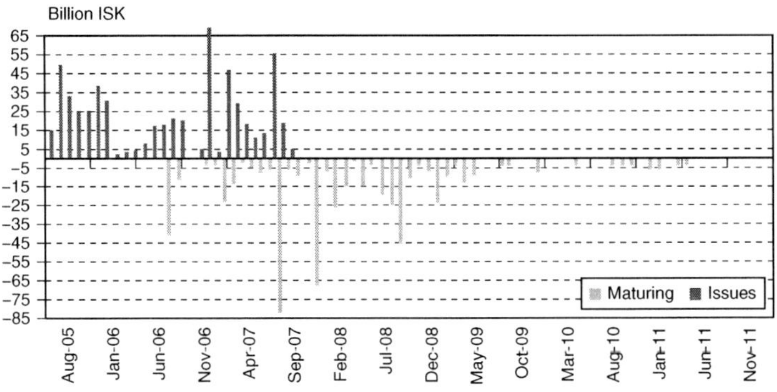


*Figure 10.19* Glacier bonds
*Source*: Kaupthing Bank *Monthly Market Focus*, 5 November 2007.

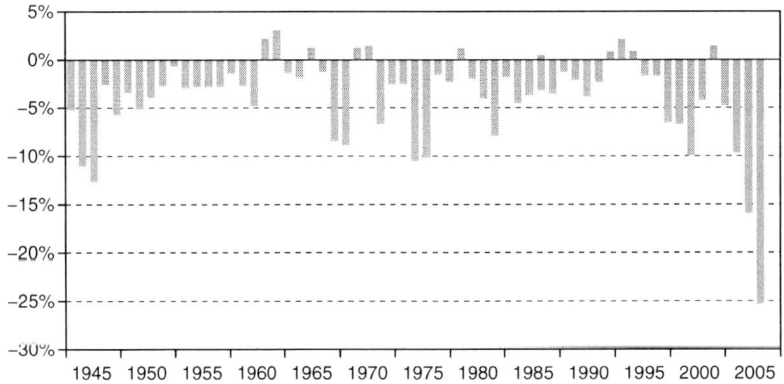


*Figure 10.20* Current account balance, 1945–2007

support the ISK or at least to limit any medium-term depreciation of the exchange rate (this reinforces the interest rate advantage of non-ISK borrowing). The recent rise in the policy rate after the ISK depreciation of the summer may reinforce such perceptions (see below).

*The current account.*

*Official data.* Iceland's current account has been in deficit for all but a handful of years in the past half-century. There have been several years when deficits exceeded 10 per cent of GDP, but these were usually quickly corrected (Figure 10.20).

Yet it is clear that the deficits for 2005–6, according to the official statistics, were exceptionally high, and after the 25.5 per cent of GDP deficit of 2006, the CBI projections show 17 per cent for 2007, 14 per cent for 2008, and still 10 per cent at the end of the decade.[26] A private forecast is more optimistic, showing 15 per cent for 2007, 11–12 per cent for 2009–10, with the trade deficit falling from 13.5 per cent in 2006 to 8 per cent in 2007 and 4–5 per cent thereafter.[27]

In addition to the fall in the trade deficit, there has been a significant improvement of the officially measured income balance so far in 2007. Revenues were up strongly, so that although expenditures rose as well, the balance for the first six months was ISK −14.7 billion, as compared with ISK −25.0 billion in the first half of 2006 (the total deficit on income in 2006 was ISK 90.1 billion). The components of the current account may be seen in Figure 10.21.

Among the macroeconomic factors behind these large current account deficits, we need not pay much attention to the government fiscal balance, which has been in significant surplus (although this is now falling). On the other hand, gross saving, which was running at 20 per cent of GDP in 2002, fell to less than 10 per cent of GDP in 2006.[28] This appears to have been temporary, but it coincided with a peak of investment at 32 per cent of GDP. This was directed primarily at a very large aluminium smelter and hydroelectricity development. The recent cut in the cod fishing quota can also be viewed as an investment, with the same effect on the current account – namely, we can expect significant increases in aluminium exports in the medium term

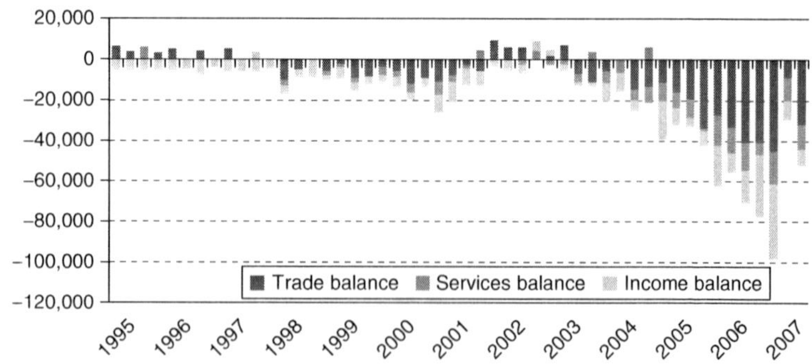


*Figure 10.21* Components of current account, quarterly data in ISK (net current transfer is included in factor income)
*Source*: CBI Economic Indicators, October 2007.

and fish exports in the longer term. Judging by consumer confidence surveys, the exchange rate affects the current account also through its effect on consumption: ISK appreciation makes households feel richer, so that consumption rises and imports with it. And there has been a trend appreciation over the past several years (see below). But real estate prices have trended upwards strongly too during this period, and it is hard to disentangle the two effects.

*Controversies.* There is considerable controversy surrounding the data on Iceland's current account and NIIP. Because the economy is so highly leveraged, factor incomes and expenditures are very large. In the official statistics, interest income and dividends are reported as 13.7 per cent of GDP in 2006, while expenditure was 22.5 per cent of GDP. But these figures are hotly debated.

One set of issues is dealt with by the CBI (Svavarsson and Sigurdsson, 2007). There we find calculations of the balance on factor income that mark portfolio equity holdings to market, but not FDI (which is therefore still undoubtedly undervalued, with a corresponding undervaluation of the NIIP[29]). This leads to revising the factor income deficit for 2006 downwards by ISK 49 billion, which takes the current account deficit down by approximately 5 per cent of GDP.

That is of course still very high, even relative to New Zealand (−9 per cent in 2006, previous peak −13.6 per cent), though it begins to look closer to the mid-1970s Norwegian data. But there are two further points that the CBI article excludes. First, some expenditure is part of the profit of firms owned by holding companies registered outside Iceland but controlled by Icelandic residents (there are capital gains tax incentives for such transfers of domicile). One estimate puts this at ISK 100 billion.[30] Adding this to the adjustment above would bring the factor income account into a surplus of ISK 50 billion in 2006, so that the current account deficit would be 13.5 per cent of GDP – roughly half the official estimate. Second, the banks have made considerable debt-financed acquisitions abroad – the debt service begins immediately, the income accrues with a lag. There are no estimates of this effect. But Egilsson (2007) applies various adjustments (including an estimate of net capital gains) that bring net factor income in 2006 (excluding employee compensation) into the range ISK +10 to +170 billion, so ISK 110–270 billion greater than the official data.

There is evidently very high uncertainty attached to estimates of returns on Iceland's foreign assets. This matters enormously, because of the exceptionally high leverage of the Icelandic economy: net debt was 210 per cent of GDP at end-2004, the highest for any country in the Lane–Milesi–Ferretti (2006) data set; but net equity investment abroad was 88 per cent of GDP, higher than all countries except the United Arab Emirates (whose sovereign wealth fund is now estimated to be approximately USD 800 billion[31]).[32] Our own efforts to estimate the returns on various categories of foreign assets and liabilities (based on the official NIIP and balance of payments data) yield results that are surprising – in particular, for all types of investments, Iceland appears to earn lower rates of return on its foreign investments than foreigners earn on their investments in Iceland. The difference is particularly marked for direct investment. This simply does not correspond to the outstanding profitability and growth of the Icelandic banks and large companies over the past five years.

The NIIP has deteriorated much more since 2000 than the cumulative current account deficit for 2000–6 would indicate. The difference is ISK 200 billion. This is partly because the official statistics value FDI at book value even when it has just been purchased for considerably more – it is in effect immediately written down.

A recent Fitch report on Iceland[33] speaks of a 'widening current account deficit'. Fitch downgraded Iceland's sovereign rating in December 2006 and has not revised it since. In fact, however, the deficit is not widening but falling in 2007, and the official data for 2006 undoubtedly overstated both the deficit and the deterioration of the NIIP. Forecasts differ, but the IMF base case (for example) has the current account deficit falling to 6 per cent of GDP in 2010 – well in the range that Australia and New Zealand have sustained for many years. The IMF project that the 'official' returns on Iceland's FDI and foreign equity investment will rise significantly. The medium-term depreciation of the ISK assumed in all forecasts will have a negative 'valuation effect', because Iceland has large net foreign currency denominated liabilities. But this will have much less effect on the NIIP than on the net external debt.[34]

We conclude that analysis should focus less on the current account deficit and NIIP numbers, more on the resiliency of the financial system and the flexibility of the economy, which will determine whether an adverse shock could lead to a bad equilibrium.[35] We return to this below when considering the shocks of early 2006 and mid-2007. Here we simply note that Iceland's past ability to turn around large current account deficits suggests that the flexibility is there. The current account was −10.2 per cent of GDP in 2000 and two years later had improved by 12 per cent of GDP to +1.5 per cent.

### 10.3.2 The exchange rate and the ISK

#### *10.3.2.1 The nominal exchange rate*

The ISK is the currency of a very small country, doubtless the smallest with a floating exchange rate and an inflation-targeting monetary policy regime. Because Iceland is so small, it is also highly open to trade and capital flows, as we have seen. That does not necessarily imply instability, in the sense of high volatility: in fact, across countries one finds openness to trade has been negatively correlated with exchange rate volatility. One reason is that relatively closed economies are less affected by exchange rate movements and hence less prone to seek to stabilize the exchange rate. As inflation targeting has spread, however, we may find that empirical regularity is disrupted, because central banks will not be willing to sacrifice their inflation performance for exchange rate stability. On the other hand, the CBI is very conscious of the effect of exchange rate movements on inflation itself (see Section 10.3.4). This warrants a closer look at both the level and the volatility of the ISK.

From the end of 2001 to early November 2005, the ISK appreciated steadily against the euro, with a total appreciation of 35 per cent (and substantially more against the dollar and most other currencies). Then there was a sharp decline, hitting bottom on 19 April 2006, when the exchange rate with the euro had returned almost exactly to the end-2001 level. This is indeed the 'up the stairs, down the elevator' pattern of a carry trade currency, mentioned above. Yet the annualized daily volatilities have not been exceptionally high (see Figure 10.22).

There is a high (and recently rising) degree of comovement between the ISK and the NZD and other carry trade target currencies (and negative comovement with JPY and CHF). Figure 10.23 is quite striking.

This is *prima facie* strong evidence that the carry trade has a substantial influence on the exchange rate. That does not mean that the determinants of the exchange rate of the ISK are entirely 'external' – the domestic interest rate is a major determinant of the carry-to-risk ratio. It is also striking, however, that domestic 'news' has recently had little impact on the exchange rate, which responded very little to the recent sovereign rating downgrade and the announcement of a delay in the coming on stream of the major aluminium investment.

The volatility of the ISK has fluctuated within a surprisingly narrow range, with two major recent 'spikes' precisely where one would expect to see them (see Figure 10.24). It is interesting to note that the volatility in the 'mini-crisis' of February–March 2006 was greater, and the period

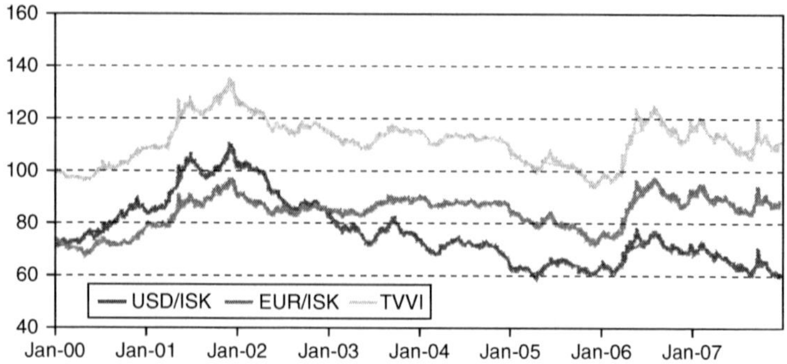


*Figure 10.22* ISK/EUR, ISK/USD, TWI
*Source*: Central Bank of Iceland.

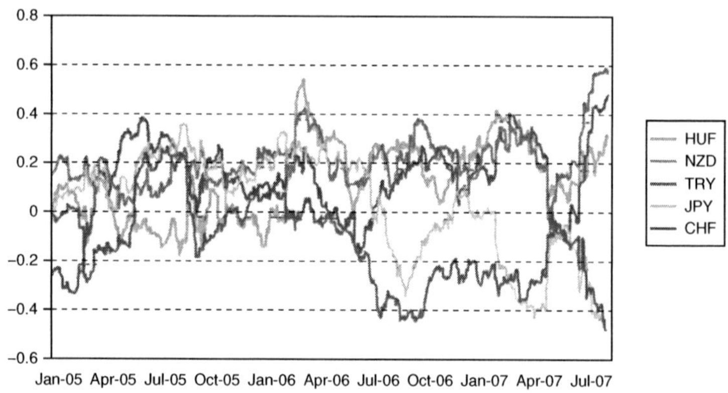


*Figure 10.23* Correlation of various currencies with the ISK, daily changes (3m moving correlation)
*Source*: Reuters. From 'The Icelandic Economy 2007–2011', Glitnir Research, September 2007.

of high volatility more extended, than in the period of international turmoil in summer/autumn 2007. The volatilities of the NZD, SEK and AUS (exchange rate with USD) are normally in a very similar range – that of the ISK is not exceptionally high. So this is not a particular source of instability for domestic firms and households, relative to other countries.[36]

Moreover, whereas the exchange rate dropped precipitously in early 2006, it has been much more stable in the recent turmoil. ISK/EUR depreciated by 12 per cent from 24 July to 17 August; in the following

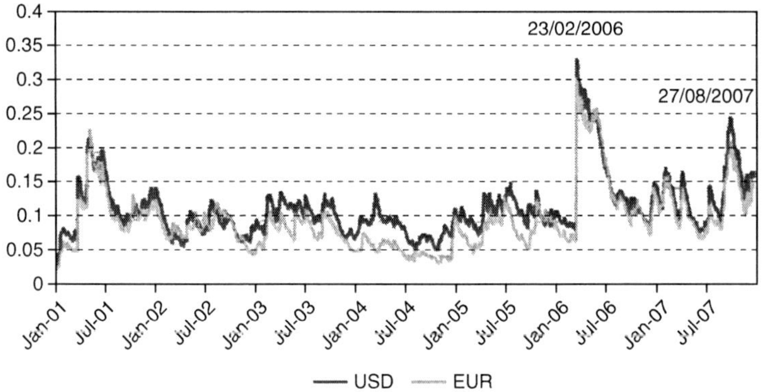


*Figure 10.24* Exchange rate volatilities
*Source*: Central Bank of Iceland and authors' calculations.

week it recovered half that and has since been fairly flat. Again, this is a strong sign of Icelandic financial resilience in the face of market shocks.

### *10.3.2.2 The real effective exchange rate*

The real effective exchange rate (REER) shows a clear upward (appreciating) trend over the past seven years (see Figure 10.25). This is to be expected for a fast-growing economy. The REER appreciation came mainly from nominal ER appreciation during 2002–5, but mainly from differential inflation in 2006–7 (until July).

According to the IMF, CPI-linked measures of the REER suggest overvaluation by 7–16 per cent, unit labour cost (ULC) measures by 18–25 per cent (the latter do not fully take account of productivity increases). These estimates were based on 2006 data, when the average level of the index was at 104.2; but at the end of August 2007 it was 106.4. So the required adjustment to reach 'equilibrium' was in the range 9–27 per cent. But the IMF methodology is debatable, as it uses three different methods, one of which gives an overvaluation of only 6–9 per cent on the basis of 2006 data. Moreover, the required adjustment (or degree of overvaluation) assumes that all the correction to the current account deficit must come through the trade balance. An improvement in the income balance deficit (which has indeed occurred in 2007) would reduce the estimated overvaluation.

So the degree of REER overvaluation lies in a wide interval that might indeed include zero. If real depreciation is necessary, the ideal adjustment path is clear: a gradual fall in interest rates, a gradual fall in the

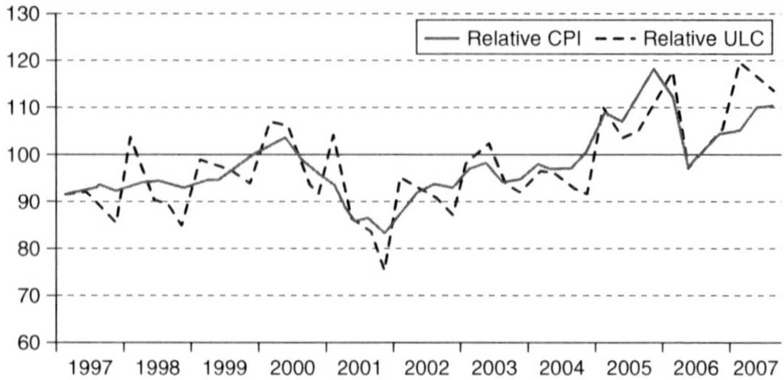


*Figure 10.25* Real effective exchange rate (2000 = 100)

carry trade, and a gradual nominal depreciation, with the inflation differential disappearing as inflation goes to its target level. But that would not be easy to manage.[37]

*10.3.2.3 Correlation between the ISK and domestic share prices*

Iceland having its own currency does not seem to entail significant funding constraints for the banks. Foreign currency bond issuance, glacier bonds, and the carry trade[38] have provided market funding. But there are equity funding barriers, i.e. foreign investors are generally unwilling to take on both equity risk and currency risk, as long as bank equity is denominated in ISK. Normally, one would also find country limits on foreign institutional investors that are in part constrained by the size of the currency area.

The ISK exchange rate is strongly positively correlated with the OMXI15 index. Thus a currency depreciation is associated with a fall in equity valuations. In fact, we have a stronger result: excess returns (on the OMXI15 relative to either DJ EuroSTOXX or the S&P 500) are positively correlated with the exchange rate (ISK/EUR and ISK/USD, respectively).[39] It is also evident that the volatility of the ICEX index is greater in euros than in ISK (see Figure 10.26).

This is a further strong disincentive to foreign investors who combine equity risk and FX risk. That is, an investor choosing between Icelandic and US or euro-area equities would avoid Icelandic ones, unless he or she were highly risk-loving. According to most participants in the Icelandic financial markets, this is in fact a major reason why it is difficult to attract foreign portfolio equity investment to Iceland. And the data bear this out: at end-2006, Iceland's holdings of foreign equity were valued at ISK 904 billion, while foreign residents (some of whom are

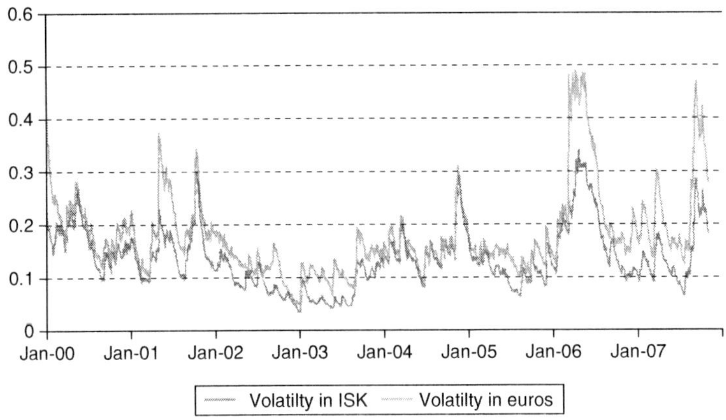


*Figure 10.26* OMX15 index volatility in ISK vs EUR
*Source*: OMX Iceland and authors' calculations.

Icelanders living abroad) held only ISK 354 billion of Icelandic equity, just 16 per cent of the total Icelandic market capitalization.

### 10.3.3 Euroization

We have just seen one reason why the Icelandic financial markets and institutions have increased their use of the euro in various contexts. Some indeed support official adoption of the euro, either as an effect of accession to the European Union, or in explicit euroization of the economy.

Bank lending in foreign currency is already 63 per cent of total domestic bank lending to businesses (end-August 2007). It is natural for firms that derive a substantial part of their income from exports to finance themselves in foreign currency – the loans are then naturally hedged. But many firms that do not have substantial foreign currency income also borrow in foreign currency, because of the large interest rate differential between Iceland and its trading partners. This does not appear risky to them since the real exchange rate has appreciated over the past several years.

Firms listed on the stock exchange – all of which have a substantial share of foreign income – increasingly keep their accounts in foreign currency in order to avoid the adverse effects of volatility of the ISK.[40] Kaupthing Bank announced on 26 October 2007 that it intends to adopt the euro as its 'functional currency' (in accordance with IFRS) from 1 January 2008. The board of the bank will propose to shareholders that the bank's shares be redenominated in euros.

A new phase in this development is that firms are moving to list their shares on OMX ICE in foreign currency: Straumur Investment Bank has already asked to be listed in euros, Kaupthing Bank has announced that it would list its shares in euros as soon as possible. Other firms such as Bakkavor Group – whose income is wholly in foreign currency – intend to follow suit.[41] This may have little substantive implication for adoption of the euro economy-wide, because these firms are already largely foreign companies; but there will be a psychological impact.

An important reason behind this development is the positive short-term correlation between prices on OMX ICE and the exchange rate, which leads to volatile share prices in foreign currency terms. Not only does this make shares of listed companies less attractive as an investment, but also employee stock options on krona-denominated shares become relatively unattractive.

Icelandic households have traditionally borrowed in ISK. They have increasingly begun to borrow in foreign currency as well, however, in particular to finance their homes and cars. The share of banks' foreign currency linked loans to households is still low, at 14 per cent, but 42 per cent of the increase in loans to households over the year to 31 August 2007 were foreign currency linked. The main driving force behind this development is the high domestic interest rate. Foreign borrowing creates a risk for most households, since generally their income is in ISK. The natural response is for households to hedge that risk by taking some of their wages in foreign currency. Some firms with a substantial foreign currency income already offer this as an option for their employees, and it is likely that labour market partners will discuss such contracts in the coming round of wage negotiations.

There has been a discussion in Iceland for some time about the costs and benefits of adopting the euro as its currency, either through membership of the EU and subsequently EMU or unilaterally. But regardless of policy, the euro is evidently becoming more important in Iceland.

#### *10.3.3.1 Unilateral euro adoption*

Policy-makers in Iceland will have to consider explicitly the option of formally adopting the euro. Euroization,[42] using a stable currency issued by a monetary authority outside the country whose domestic supply is limited to that earned through balance-of-payments surpluses, would be feasible for Iceland. At the end of October 2007, foreign exchange reserves were ISK 157.6 billion, much more than enough to cover base money of ISK 91 billion. Euroization would have potential advantages relative to a currency board or a pegged exchange rate regime, neither of which would be appropriate for Iceland (indeed, the latter was only recently abandoned). In the euroized economy, speculative attacks are no longer possible, so there is no currency risk, and domestic interest rates no longer incorporate that premium. There are typically lower transaction costs and greater transparency in policy. Using a stable foreign currency may itself implant or reinforce a 'stability culture' in monetary affairs and in private expectations.

There are clear costs as well: the loss of seigniorage revenues, which for Iceland come to between 0.5 and 0.8 per cent of GDP,[43] the absence of a lender of last resort; and the definitive renunciation of an exchange-rate 'escape clause' from overvaluation (an exit option). Moreover, in the short term, a move from the current policy rate of 13.75 per cent to the euro area rate of 4 per cent would be highly destabilizing – the Icelandic policy rate would have to converge substantially beforehand.[44]

The European Central Bank and the European Commission oppose euroization, at least for countries that are members of or might accede to the EU (and thus to EMU, in due course). The Council (Ecofin) opinion of 7 November 2000 asserts that before finally adopting the euro, candidates must fulfil the Maastricht criteria: 'any unilateral adoption of the single currency by means of "euroisation" would run counter to the underlying economic reasoning of EMU in the Treaty. [It would] be a way to circumvent the stages foreseen by the Treaty for the adoption of the euro.' The DG ECFIN paper for Ecofin, 'Exchange Rate Strategies for EU Candidate Countries' (22 August 2000) went further, claiming that the 'sequencing entrenched in the Treaty for the adoption of the euro' would be altered, the 'principle of equal treatment between present and future as among future member states would be violated' and that negotiating euroization would alter the *acquis communautaire*.

It is true that once a country enters the EU, its exchange rate policies become legally a matter of common concern – but not before. And using the euro in no way prejudices or impinges on the accession process or the subsequent process of entering into monetary union. It cannot run counter to any legal provision of the treaties. Using the euro is not equivalent to participating in the European Monetary Union (EMU), nor 'unfairly' getting a 'head start', nor does it implicate the European Central Bank in any significant way, except insofar as the euroizing country is providing seigniorage to the ECB. Unilateral euroization cannot affect the credibility of the euro, since the euroizing country cannot participate in the economic institutions of EMU.

Iceland is in the position, along with Norway and Liechtenstein, of being a member of the EEA but not yet, at least, a candidate for EU membership. Thus it should not encounter the EU–ECB opposition suggested above, and indeed there are countries that use the euro and are not (yet) EU members or 'accession countries' (Kosovo, Montenegro). This, however, is perhaps not a 'club' to which Iceland would wish to belong.

The CBI sees relatively little cause for concern regarding informal euroization, except insofar as it might lead to withdrawal of the banks from the ISK money markets and FX market.

There is an untidy alternative: international companies (and their employees) could shift to using the euro, while the rest of the economy stays on the ISK. This degree of domestic liability dollarization would be an emerging-market response, not appropriate for Iceland. Moreover, the dynamics of partial euroization could be unstable: if exchange rate adjustment is needed, a diminishing local currency base would have to support the required change, which could make people switch even more aggressively out of the currency. And if it were believed that this was a prelude to adoption of the euro, that could provoke major, destabilizing capital inflows.

That listed firms have adopted the euro or the dollar as their unit of account or chosen to list in euros does not create a significant problem for monetary policy. Indeed, in some ways it can support the CBI's actions. Currently, the positive correlation between ISK-denominated shares and the ISK discussed above implies that a rise of interest rates leading to an inflow of foreign currency and a rise in the exchange rate may actually be expansionary to some degree, rather than restrictive as intended. A weakening of this correlation may therefore make monetary policy more effective. The correlation, as long as it continues, must be a factor of financial instability: for example, exchange rate depreciation would be accompanied by falls in share prices, both of which have negative wealth effects, and the two could be self-reinforcing in a downward spiral.

### 10.3.4 Monetary policy in this external environment

Before the ISK was set afloat in March 2001 its exchange rate was an 'intermediate target' of monetary policy: the exchange rate was seen as one of the primary channels by which policy was transmitted from interest rates to prices, and the Bank expressly set an interval within which it allowed the ISK to float.

After floating the krona, the CBI's own description of its monetary policy and instruments does not express any policy regarding the exchange rate of the ISK – there is no official exchange rate policy. It is quite clear from various statements the Bank has made recently, however, that it still sees the exchange rate as an extremely important part of the monetary transmission mechanism. It has stressed that a sharp fall in the exchange rate would raise inflation and inflation expectations and that this poses a serious risk to the inflation outlook. The Bank has also repeatedly indicated that it would respond to such a fall.[45]

The Bank has lived up to its promise: as Icelandic banks came under pressure in early 2006 and the krona fell sharply the CBI – predicting near-term inflation in double digits – raised interest rates aggressively. The policy rate rose by 0.75 percentage points in March, May and July of 2006 and subsequently by 0.5 percentage points in August and September. To underpin its credibility the CBI, as of *Monetary Bulletin* 2007: 1, publishes not only a predicted policy-rate path, but also a predicted exchange rate path which it sees as consistent with its inflation forecast. The predicted path of July 2007 saw a near-term strengthening of the krona – predicting more or less exactly the current exchange rate – and then a subsequent gradual weakening of about 5.5 per cent per year through 2010. The most recently predicted path (Nov. 1) is consistent with this forecast.

By its statements the CBI may be regarded as having adopted a policy regarding the exchange rate, viz. that of 'responding firmly' should the krona fall, in order to restore it to a level the bank sees as consistent with its inflation target. Given the published most likely path for the exchange rate and the absence of statements regarding what the Bank would see as an overly strong krona, this amounts to ensuring that with a reasonable degree of certainty, the krona may be sold at a certain value throughout the forecast interval. With some risk of oversimplifying, the CBI may be seen as having issued a free put option on the krona.

One result is the carry trade, which has added to the difficulties of the CBI in taming inflation. Issuance of so-called glacier bonds began relatively late, in August 2005, but has increased rapidly and the total amount of such bonds now stands at one-third of GDP. Since issuers always hedge against currency risk, the glacier bonds end up – in one way or another – as demand for Icelandic paper. This puts a downward pressure on interest rates, especially in the medium-term range of the spectrum. This may explain why the yield differential Icelandic 5-year T-notes with trading partners' bonds has increased by only 1–1.5 per cent since the CBI began raising its policy rate in 2004, while the policy rate differential has increased by 4.5–5.5 per cent over the same period (see Figure 10.27).

The glacier bonds are part of a larger picture: there has been substantial position-taking in the krona through other channels. The banks' net position in foreign currency denominated forwards and options, now at

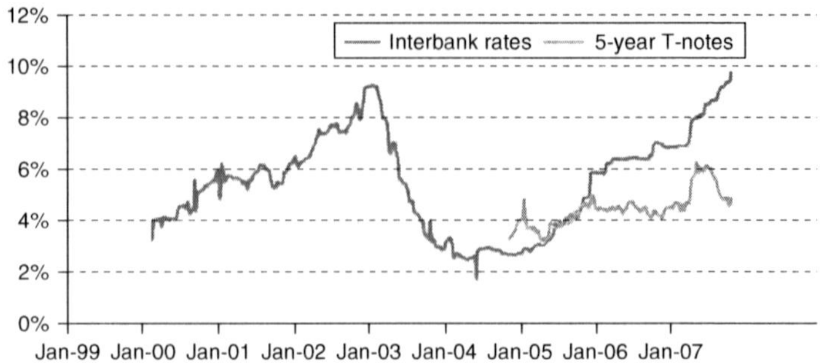


*Figure 10.27* Interest rate differential with weekly data

*Figure 10.28* Net position of banks in currency forward and options contracts

69 per cent of GDP, provides an indication of the overall level of position-taking in the krona (see Figure 10.28). Interestingly, the rapid rise of this measure began at the same time as the differentials on short- and medium-term interest rates parted ways, at the end of 2004,[46] and it also seems related to the carry-to-risk ratio (see Figure 10.18). This rapid inflow of foreign currency has limited the effectiveness of monetary policy by halting the progression of the policy rate throughout the spectrum of (non-indexed) interest rates, as well as through the wealth effect of exchange rate appreciation.

The well-intended forthrightness of the CBI regarding the exchange rate has probably undermined its fight against inflation. A rational response of market participants to the implied krona put is of course to utilize the differential between domestic and foreign interest rates. Carry-traders have responded strongly, which has weakened transmission of the policy rate. Furthermore, Icelandic households and firms now borrow increasingly in foreign currency.

### 10.3.5 Effectiveness of monetary policy

All aggregate indicators of economic activity in Iceland over the last few years show buoyant growth; average annual demand growth 2004–6 was 11 per cent, and GDP grew by 5.8 per cent annually over the same period (see Table 10.12). Aggregate credit measures tell a similar story: annual average credit system lending growth was 21 per cent over these years. Despite a substantial inflow of immigrant labour, since mid-2005 the labour market has been extremely stretched, with registered unemployment below 2 per cent; the measure of the balance between production capacity and output – a key indicator used by the CBI – shows a similar picture.

The task of the CBI is to keep inflation in check; more precisely, it has the mandate to aim for an annual rate of inflation of 2.5 per cent as measured by a 12-month increase in the CPI. This has clearly not been an easy task (see Figure 10.29). Inflation, as measured by the CPI, has been high since early 2004 and in excess of the set 4 per cent upper tolerance limit since mid-2006.[47] By far the most important single driver of CPI-inflation has been a sustained rise in housing prices. Annualized inflation less the housing component has been 2.7 per cent since May 2004 when the CBI began the process of raising its policy rate,[48] whereas the overall measure for the same period is 5.3 per cent. In particular,

*Table 10.12* Macroeconomic indicators (volume changes on previous year unless otherwise stated)

| *GDP and its main components* | *2004* | *2005* | *2006* | *2007e* |
|---|---|---|---|---|
| Private consumption | 6.9 | 13 | 4.4 | 3.6 |
| Public consumption | 2.2 | 3.5 | 3.9 | 3.2 |
| Gross fixed capital formation | 28.5 | 33.9 | 19.8 | −19.5 |
| National expenditure | 9.9 | 15.4 | 9.2 | −3.4 |
| Exports | 8.4 | 7.2 | −5.1 | 4.2 |
| Imports | 14.4 | 29.4 | 10.1 | −8.6 |
| Gross domestic product | 7.7 | 7.1 | 4.2 | 0.9 |
| *Other key aggregates* | | | | |
| Current account balance, % of GDP | −9.8 | −16 | −25.5 | −18 |
| Fiscal balance, % of GDP | 0.2 | 5.2 | 7 | 4.8 |
| Unemployment, % of labour force | 3.1 | 2.1 | 1.3 | 1.1 |
| Inflation, 12-month % change in CPI | 4 | 4.4 | 6.9 | 4.8 |

*Source*: Central Bank of Iceland.

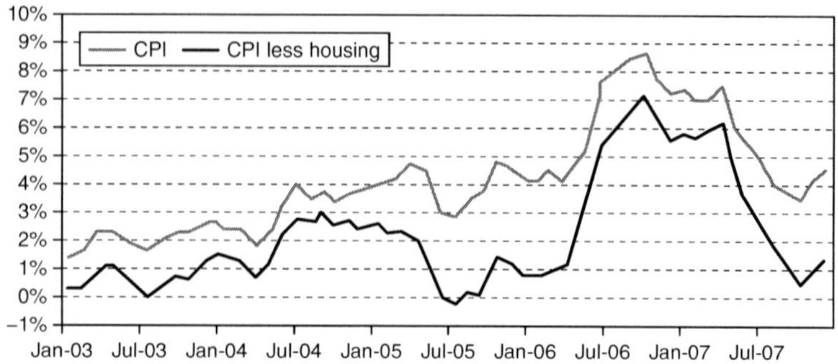


*Figure 10.29* 12-Month change in Consumer Price Index
*Source: Statistics Iceland.*

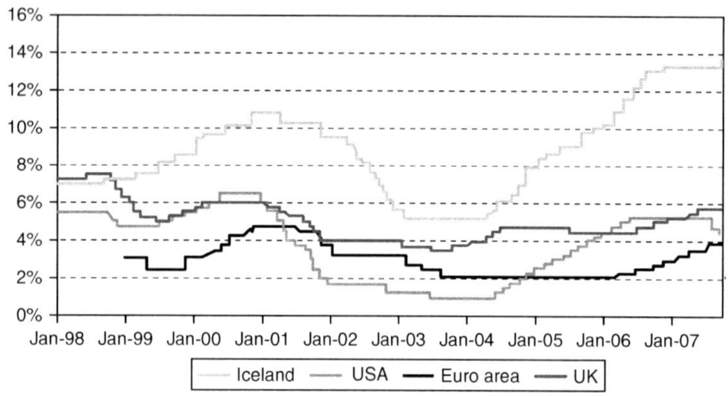


*Figure 10.30* CBI policy rate
*Source*: Bloomberg.

since May 2007 CPI-inflation less housing has been at or below the target of 2.5 per cent (see Figure 10.29).

In an effort to combat inflation, the CBI has raised its policy rate, in steps, by a total of 9.4 per cent since May 2004. The current nominal interest rate is now 13.75 per cent (see Figure 10.30).[49] This steep rise has brought short-term interest rates to rather extraordinary heights when compared with Iceland's main trading partners and short-term real rates are at approximately 10 per cent, a very high level which is bound to entail substantial costs in terms of output and jobs if sustained over a longer term. Yet, the inflation measure the CBI focuses on has remained rather stubbornly at around or over 4 per cent.

The CBI has had a difficult task. Fixed business investment grew by an average of 25 per cent per annum in 2004–6. While fiscal policy cannot be said to have been slack – the average annual public sector surplus was 3.6 per cent of GDP in these years – it has been procyclical: the government has used part of its surplus to lower personal income taxes, boosting private consumption which increased by 8 per cent on average over 2004–6. Furthermore, a more or less sustained rise in important asset markets – housing, land and stocks – has supported and fuelled growth in private consumption. This year, however, overall demand is set to fall and GDP is predicted to grow by only 0.9 per cent. This should help the CBI in its endeavour.

The CBI has been fighting an uphill battle and has not been helped much by fiscal policy. Yet, even under these circumstances, monetary policy seems to have been rather ineffective; the current policy with real short-term interest rates at 10 per cent would seem to be likely to lead to an abrupt halt of economic growth in most developed economies.

It is important to consider the underlying reasons for this ineffectiveness. One important sector to look at in this regard is the housing market. Prices of residential housing have grown at 20 per cent p.a. on average since August 2004, when the commercial banks entered a market until then dominated by the Housing Financing Fund (HFF) and started competing with the state-owned fund.[50] The rise in the price of housing has slowed down considerably, to 5–10 per cent this year from its peak of 40 per cent around mid-2005, but housing is still the most important component of inflation.[51] Apparently, monetary policy has had very limited effect on this important component of prices and the underlying demand for housing which drives the price developments. The reason for this anomaly is that the policy rate has, at least until very recently, had little impact on the financing of residential housing. Most existing residential housing loans are indexed with fixed indexed interest rates. Also, the HFF, still the single most important lender in the residential housing market with approximately the same market share as all the banks combined, has raised its indexed rate to a very limited degree – it is now lower than it was before the entry of the banks into the housing market.[52] The banks have, however, recently upped rates on their krona indexed loans. Households have responded by borrowing increasingly in foreign currency to complement HFF loans. Households have therefore been able to circumvent interest rates influenced by the CBI to finance their investments in housing.

Demand for housing has continued to rise, driving prices steadily upwards. Supply has also been on the rise, and if residential housing price inflation should slow down or even be reversed in the coming months it is caused as much by increased supply as by reduced demand due to restrictive monetary policy. It is obvious that the HFF – financing about one-half of all housing investments – is a serious obstacle for the effective transmission of monetary policy to this important market. It is also clear that foreign borrowing of households also limits the CBI's ability to influence, not only the housing market, but also households' overall demand. Of the increase in households' debt to banks over the last year (August 2006–August 2007) 42 per cent of the increase was due to a rise in foreign-denominated loans, whereas 63 per cent of the increase was in indexed loans; noting that these two percentages sum up to more than 100 per cent it is clear that non-indexed ISK-denominated debt of households decreased over this period.

The widespread practice of indexation – very much related to the problem regarding the HFF – also limits the effectiveness of monetary policy in fighting inflation. Indexation was initially introduced in Iceland to neutralize the adverse effects of inflation on financial assets; now it tends to neutralize the intended effect of monetary policy. It has proven to be hard for the CBI to influence indexed interest rates, although an effect has been seen recently, especially on the shorter end of the spectrum. The underlying reason is that non-indexed rates such as the policy rate of the CBI only influence indexed rates indirectly. As explained in the following section, managing inflation expectations is crucial in affecting indexed rates. Since the longer end of the non-indexed spectrum has also been relatively unaffected by the policy rate it is even more difficult to manage indexed rates.

#### *10.3.5.1 Indexation of financial contracts in Iceland*

Indexation of deposits and loans has a long history in Iceland. It began as a response to the hyperinflation of the late 1970s and early 1980s. Bank deposits at regulated interest rates had been rapidly eroded by inflation, and savings were falling along with confidence in the krona as a store of value. An important purpose of indexation was to re-establish that confidence. Even if hyperinflation is a thing of the past, indexation is still very important in domestic credit in Iceland, especially on long-term contracts. For example, at commercial banks, indexed loans account for almost 60 per cent of domestic krona lending.[53]

Indexed loans and deposits carry an indexed – often referred to as real – interest rate which comes on top of inflation adjustments to nominal values. To take a simple example, suppose a loan of 1 million kronur is to be repaid with 4 per cent indexed interest after one year. The CPI is 100 when the loan is issued and there is 5 per cent inflation, so it stands at 105 when then loan is repaid. At repayment date the inflation-adjusted principal amounts to ISK 1.05 million (the initial 1 million plus 5 per cent, or ISK 50,000) and the interest payment is ISK 42,000 (4 per cent of 1 million = ISK 40,000, adjusted for 5 per cent inflation). Therefore, the total payment is ISK 1.092 million. Alternatively, the total nominal payment with 4 per cent interest would be ISK 1.04 million, which, adjusted for 5 per cent inflation, becomes ISK 1.092 million.

There should of course be a relationship between indexed and non-indexed rates on corresponding contracts: the indexed rate plus inflation expectations plus a compensation for inflation risk should equal the non-indexed rate. For example, if a five-year indexed bond has a 4 per cent indexed rate and inflation expectations over the five-year term are 2.5 per cent then a corresponding non-indexed five-year bond must have at least a 6.6 per cent nominal rate to be competitive with the indexed bond with no premium for risk. The more volatile and uncertain is inflation, the larger the additional risk term will be. Given a certain non-indexed interest rate, high-inflation expectations and/or a volatile inflation outlook (the two usually go hand in hand) will tend to push the indexed rate down. Conversely, in order for a rise in non-indexed rates to be translated into a rise in indexed rates the former must rise by more than the combined change in inflation expectations and risk premium. It is obvious that for monetary policy to work in a highly indexed system it must be able to influence inflation expectations – no easy task.

## 10.4 Conclusions and recommendations

### 10.4.1 The banks: successful and resilient

The internationalization of the Icelandic financial sector proceeded from market liberalization, European integration, and privatization, on the base of a strong, funded pension system and an exceptionally healthy institutional framework. The banks have been highly entrepreneurial without taking unsupportable risks; good supervision and regulation have contributed to that, using EU legislation. And they have grown spectacularly fast. Nevertheless, the rapid financial sector expansion and growing cross-border activities, together with macroeconomic tensions, led to market suspicion and the mini-crisis of early 2006.

After the initial shock, the Icelandic financial sector responded quickly and decisively:

- deposit ratios are higher
- market funding has longer and more dispersed maturities

- cross-holdings have been mainly eliminated
- there is much greater transparency and information dissemination about the banks' structure and activities.

On the same criteria, Icelandic banks come out well in a comparison with Nordic peers – and their overall and core profitability is higher. That is despite the high CAD and Tier 1 ratios with which they counterbalance their equity exposure. They are well hedged against volatility in the krona. Stress tests by the FSA indicate that the banks can withstand quite extreme movements in market variables specific to Iceland. The banks have negligible exposure to the US sub-prime market, structured finance products, and related financial vehicles that have hit many financial institutions hard recently. Most fundamental, the banks exploit strong competitive advantage, arising from their entrepreneurial management, flat management structures, and unusual business models.

Yet in spite of their strong performance, Icelandic banks have lower ratings than their Nordic peers, and a much higher risk premium is being placed on their debt during the present turmoil. We see no justification for this in their risk exposure. This suggests that either the markets are not fully aware of their situation or markets place a *country premium* on the banks.

### 10.4.2 Macroeconomic imbalances and the country premium

A large current account deficit and negative net international investment position are no doubt important reasons for the country premium. One might say the economy is running at an excessive pressure of demand, but the fiscal balance is positive and the government has very little net debt. The external imbalances are therefore due to decisions of firms and households, and it is often maintained that private decisions are optimal and should not be a cause of concern, whatever their aggregate effect.

In principle, however, there are legitimate reasons for concern. Asymmetries of information can lead to herding effects that initially exaggerate capital inflows, then exacerbate the 'sudden stop' if investors react to news by reversing the flows. Informational problems can also lead to self-fulfilling speculative attacks on the currency. And deposit insurance or the expectation of lender-of-last-resort bailouts can create moral hazard in the banking system, hence overborrowing and the accumulation of *excessive private debt* – that is, the private decisions are not in fact optimal. Down the road could be a currency crisis, a debt crisis, or both.

Our analysis concludes, however, that it is *reasonable to see the Icelandic current account deficit and negative net international investment position (NIIP) as sustainable,* assuming appropriate policies are followed. There are also important issues of measurement that lead us (like other observers) to regard the official data as overestimates of these deficits.

There is very high uncertainty attached to estimates of returns on Iceland's foreign assets. This matters enormously, because of the exceptionally high leverage of the Icelandic economy. Our own efforts to estimate the returns on various categories of foreign assets and liabilities yield implausible results. For *all* types of investments, Iceland *appears* to earn lower rates of return on its foreign investments than foreigners earn on their investments in Iceland. The difference is particularly marked for direct investment. This simply does not correspond to the outstanding profitability and growth of the Icelandic banks and large companies over the past five years.

One example of misleading aggregate data is that the NIIP has deteriorated much more since 2000 than the cumulative current account deficit for 2000–6 would indicate. The difference is ISK 200 billion. This is partly because the official statistics value FDI at book value even when it has just been purchased for considerably more – it is in effect immediately written down to book value. Again, we find it implausible that the Icelandic investors are systematically overpaying.

### 10.4.3 Resilience and stability

We conclude that analysis should focus less on the current account deficit and NIIP numbers and more on the *resilience* of the financial system – which has proven to be excellent – and the flexibility of the economy, where Iceland has a proven track record over many decades. The resilience, demonstrated both in early 2006 and since the summer of this year, is based on a strong institutional structure, flexibility, the quality of supervision and regulation, the quality of assets, and a good funding structure.

In an economy so small and so highly leveraged in international financial markets, one might expect high volatility of financial variables – the exchange rate, equity prices and bond yields. We do not find especially high volatilities. We focus in particular on the Icelandic krona, which many see as an important risk factor for Iceland and the Icelandic banks. In fact, the krona is not much more volatile against major currencies than the currencies of New Zealand, Sweden and Australia. So this is not a particular source of instability for domestic firms and households, relative to other countries. The banks are now hedged more or less perfectly against currency volatility, so their exchange rate risk is primarily associated with loan quality. Icelandic firms have a long history of borrowing in foreign currency. For many this provides a natural hedge, others are in a strong market position and can pass exchange rate effects into prices. Households have increasingly been borrowing in foreign currency, but it is still only a minor share (7–8 per cent) of overall lending, so the overall risk is rather small.

The krona does represent a disadvantage for listed firms because it tends to fluctuate with equity prices. Exchange rate volatility is therefore added to stock market volatility. This makes shares in firms listed in ISK less attractive for foreign investors, so equity financing is more costly for firms. These firms are now moving to adopt the euro as their listing currency and to use the euro rather than the krona in other ways as well.

### 10.4.4 Recommendations

There has been a discussion in Iceland for some time about the costs and benefits of using the euro as its currency, and the euro is evidently becoming more important in Iceland. Iceland is not a member of the EU, so at present the option of joining the EMU is not open to Iceland. The possibility remains, however, of unilateral adoption of the euro as legal tender – 'euroization'. Euroization would have potential advantages. In the 'euroized' economy, speculative attacks are no longer possible, so there is no currency risk, and domestic interest rates no longer incorporate that premium. There are typically lower transaction costs and greater transparency in policy. Using a stable foreign currency may itself implant or reinforce a 'stability culture'.

There are clear costs as well: the loss of seigniorage revenues, which for Iceland come to 0.5–0.8 per cent of GDP; the absence of a lender of last resort; and the definitive renunciation of an exchange rate 'escape clause' from overvaluation. Moreover, in the short term, a move from the current policy rate of 13.75 per cent to the euro area rate of 4 per cent would be highly destabilizing – the Icelandic policy rate would have to converge substantially to the euro rate beforehand.

We do not recommend for or against unilateral euroization. This is an issue that requires extensive political as well as economic debate. We do, however, caution against the *possible destabilizing consequences of a gradual shift to using the euro.*

The CBI is on an inflation target of 2.5 per cent. Inflation driven by housing prices has however remained above the target for some time.[54] The CBI has not had an easy task given the strong demand growth in

Iceland in the last few years. And fiscal policy has not been supportive of monetary policy. Yet the policy rate of the CBI is very high compared with trading partners of Iceland, and monetary policy appears to be ineffective. There are several underlying reasons. First, the Housing Financing Fund is a major obstacle to the transmission of monetary policy. We agree with many other commentators, including the IMF, that *the HFF's role should be changed so that it no longer competes with banks in mortgage markets*. Second, price indexation of financial contracts is widespread and tends to weaken monetary policy. Third, the CBI has undermined its own policy by linking its decisions to exchange rate developments. The high policy rate leads to distortions in the financial system, such as the large carry trade. If only for that reason, *we urge the CBI to reconsider its strategy*.

We strongly recommend efforts to improve the collection of data to *account better for the balance of international income and the international investment position*. Some of the problem may be due to international standards that are inappropriate for countries with the financial structure of Iceland. In that case, the authorities should seek a reconsideration of those standards. The CBI should also publish parallel accounts for items such as equities where the most glaring inconsistencies arise.

## Notes

1. For a more extensive general overview of Iceland's economy, see *Economy of Iceland*, Central Bank of Iceland (2007).
2. The Icelandic Securities Depository is also owned by OMX, and acts as a registry, depository and clearing house for securities in dematerialized (electronic) form. Settlement of bonds takes place on a T + 1 basis but equities on a T + 3 basis.
3. CBI *Monetary Bulletin*, November 2007, p. 81.
4. Fitch Ratings (2006).
5. Merrill Lynch (2006).
6. It is notable that Fitch did not actually downgrade Iceland until 10 months later on 22 December 2006. At that point, the exchange rate depreciated again, but quickly recovered between Christmas and the New Year. Then, however, it depreciated again on rumours that Kaupthing would adopt euro-denominated accounting, but that too was short-lived, and an extended appreciation began. Note that when Kaupthing did confirm the rumours, that had no effect on the ISK – appreciation continued.
7. Data from Bloomberg. The current debt distribution was extracted on 23 October 2007.
8. It seems that under the EU/EEA competition policy regime, the HFF could be judged to be in receipt of illegal state aid, in the light of the recent moves against the German regional banks on these grounds.

9. CBI, *Financial Stability* 2007, p. 51.
10. CBI, *Financial Stability* 2007, p. 50.
11. CBI, *Financial Stability* 2007, p. 53.
12. Kaupthing did not publish its foreign currency balance in the consolidated interim for Q2. The balance was calculated as the sum of the bank's total foreign currency balance, reported by the Central Bank, minus the foreign currency balance of Glitnir and Landsbanki.
13. Voting rights belong to the clients. However, prior to shareholders' meetings, they need confirmation from the banks of their ownership.
14. The ratios are calculated according to the Q3 2007 interim. The debt distribution is from Bloomberg, 23 October 2007.
15. Ólafsson (2007).
16. Since CDS data were not available to the authors on Swedbank and SHB and average of DnB Nor, Danske Bank, and SEB CDSs was taken instead.
17. Morgan Stanley (2007).
18. Kristinsson (2007).
19. CBI *Financial Stability Report*, April 2005, p. 58.
20. There is a continuing debate on the need for a lender of last resort (see e.g. the papers in Goodhart and Illing, 2002). Indeed, one way of interpreting the Icelandic mini-crisis of 2006 is as an example of banks' saving themselves rather than falling back on an LLR. Bagehot's doctrine has, however, been placed on a sounder footing in recent years; see e.g. Rochet and Vives (2004) and Freixas et al. (2004).
21. Moody's Investor Service (2006).
22. The 'Lawson doctrine' is supported by Belkar et al. (2007), discussing the long-running current account deficit of Australia. Note that the Lawson boom had an unhappy ending, in a recession and exchange rate tensions.
23. That is, according to official statistics and expressed as a ratio to GDP. We suggest that on both counts, there are mitigating factors.
24. See 'Iceland: Selected Issues', IMF Country Report 07/296, August 2007, Appendix I.
25. See Bank for International Settlements *Quarterly Review*, September 2007.
26. CBI *Monetary Bulletin* 2007, p. 3.
27. Kaupthing Bank, *Quarterly Economic Outlook*, 26 October 2007.
28. As noted below, the current account deficit may be overestimated, and gross savings are correspondingly underestimated.
29. The IMF acknowledges this in para. 22 of the 2007 Article IV Consultation Staff Report. In Appendix I they conjecture that the net equity investment abroad might be undervalued by as much as one-third, which would bring the NIIP below 100 per cent of GDP.
30. Landsbanki, 'Macroeconomic Insight', 5 June 2007.
31. See Portes (2007).
32. The data are cited in Svavarsson and Sigurdsson (2007).
33. A presentation by Paul Rawkins in Stockholm on 7 June 2007, IMF.
34. Article IV Consultation Staff Report, Appendix I.
35. See Mishkin and Herbertsson (2006) and Ferguson et al. (2007) on multiple equilibria in the context of financial stability.
36. On the other hand, we note that unlike the ISK and the OMXI15 index, the volatilities of Icelandic five-year bond yields are about double those of the

5–10 year bonds in the same countries. This suggests that there is actually considerable underlying stability in the nominal exchange rate. That may be due to monetary policy: see below.

37. In this context, there are attractions of Goldstein's (2002) proposal for 'managed floating plus' – a regime that combines inflation targeting with some exchange rate management. And as we suggest below, the CBI seems to have some inclinations in this direction, but its actual policy is open to question.
38. E.g. Glitnir in September 2007.
39. The coefficients are significant at the 5 per cent and 1 per cent levels, respectively. This result is the opposite of that observed for 17 countries (individually and pooled) relative to the United States for the period 1995–2001 in Hau and Rey (2006). This is a further example of the highly distinctive features of the Icelandic financial markets.
40. The IMF points out that 'a bank which prepares its accounts in krona may find it difficult to attain the corresponding ratio of foreign items in its Own Funds and RWA without building a positive net currency position' and cites the FSA as saying that to attain the required balance, the three big banks would have had to increase their net foreign currency position by around USD 3.2 billion (IMF, 'Iceland: Selected Issues', Country Report 07/296, August 2007). In fact, however, this increase has already taken place. The FSA calculated that the banks would have to increase their currency holdings by ISK 230 billion over the end-2006 position of ISK 188 billion. They have already raised them by ISK 258 billion.
41. The CBI has delayed these moves on the ground that it cannot clear euro-denominated securities trades because it is not a member of the European System of Central Banks (ESCB). Therefore OMX (the securities registry) has asked the Bank of Finland to take on this role in cooperation with the CBI, but the Bank of Finland cannot provide this service until May 2008. There is also a degree of legal uncertainty regarding whether institutions other than the CBI can do the clearing. It is likely that a provisional solution is reached until the legal basis is clarified.
42. The extensive literature on this issue normally speaks of 'dollarization', but in the Icelandic context it would clearly mean a move to the euro rather than the dollar. The weight of the euro in the 2006 'narrow' trade-weighted effective exchange rate basket was 44.8 per cent, with the pound sterling at 12.8 per cent and the US dollar at 9.8 per cent (http://www.sedlabanki.is). A recent, comprehensive paper on dollarization is Levy Yeyati (2006).
43. Jonsson (2007).
44. A recent IMF conference saw 'little support for Iceland adopting the euro'. In particular, participants stressed that 'the Icelandic economy is not well synchronized with continental Europe and instead faces large idiosyncratic shocks'. On the other hand, 'the high degree of labour market flexibility in Iceland reduced the need for independent monetary policy' ('Iceland: Selected Issues', IMF Country Report 07/296, para. 79). And one might add that an active fiscal policy might be easier to operate in a small country like Iceland than in most others. Buiter (2000) claimed that 'the economic arguments favour membership in the EMU, but not the unilateral adoption of the euro ... The lack of institutions for ensuring the political accountability

of the ECB in Iceland means that euroisation of Iceland is unlikely to happen, except as part of Icelandic membership in the EU.' Much has happened since then – not least, floating the ISK and internationalization of the Icelandic financial sector.

45. See several recent monetary policy statements in the CBI *Monetary Bulletin*.
46. The total position-taking on the krona at end-December 2004 was ISK 111 billion, and by September 2007 it had risen to ISK 823 billion. This measure is thought by market participants to be closely related to the carry trade, for which there are no agreed estimates (see Bank for International Settlements, *Quarterly Review*, September 2007).
47. If inflation deviates by more than 1.5 per cent from the 2.5 per cent target, the Central Bank is obliged to submit a report to the government of Iceland where it explains the reason for the deviation, how it intends to respond and when it expects the inflation target to be reached again. The report is made public.
48. CBI *Monetary Bulletin* 2007, p. 3 (CBI forecast).
49. As of July 2007 the Bank announces its policy rate in terms of nominal interest rate rather than yield.
50. The housing component of the CPI has not risen this fast. The reason is that it takes real rates on HFF loans into account when rent on owner-occupied housing is imputed.
51. It is of course debatable whether the price of housing and other assets should be included in the reference measure of inflation. Most European countries use the Harmonized Index of Consumer Prices, which does not include housing inflation.
52. The current rate on HFF indexed loans is 4.85 per cent. The fund actually lowered interest rates in April 2007. The HFF is able to do this by selling indexed bonds with very long maturities – mostly 40 years.
53. Krona lending is approximately 50 per cent of total domestic lending of the commercial banks.
54. Mishkin and Herbertsson (2006) recommended targeting the HICP (as in the euro area and the UK), which excludes house prices.

## References

Bagehot, W. (1873) *Lombard Street: a Description of the Money Market*, London, H S King.

Bank for International Settlements (2007) *Triennial Central Bank Survey of Foreign Exchange and Derivatives Market Activity in April 2007*, September.

Bank for International Settlements (2007) *Quarterly Review*, September.

Belkar, R., L. Cockerell and C. Kent (2007) 'Current Account Deficits: the Australian Debate', RBA Research Discussion Papers rdp2007-02, Reserve Bank of Australia, available at http://www. rba.gov.au/rdp/RDP2007-02.pdf.

Buiter, W. (1985) 'A Guide to Public Sector Debt and Deficits', *Economic Policy*, 1(1), November 1985, 13–79.

Buiter, W. (2000) 'Is Iceland an Optimal Currency Area?', Central Bank of Iceland Working Paper 10, available at http://www.sedlabanki.is/uploads/files/WP_10.pdf

Calvo, G.A. (2006) 'Monetary Policy Challenges in Emerging Markets: Sudden Stop, Liability Dollarization, and Lender of Last Resort', NBER Working Papers 12788, National Bureau of Economic Research, Inc.

Central Bank of Iceland (2005) *Financial Stability,* available at http://www.sedlabanki.is

Central Bank of Iceland (2006) *Financial Stability,* available at http://www.sedlabanki.is

Central Bank of Iceland (2007a) *Economy of Iceland,* available at http://www.sedlabanki.is

Central Bank of Iceland (2007b) *Financial Stability,* available at http://www.sedlabanki.is

Central Bank of Iceland (2007c) *Monetary Bulletin* 2007:1, March, available at http://www.sedlabanki.is

Central Bank of Iceland (2007d) *Monetary Bulletin,* 2007:2, July, available at http://www.sedlabanki.is

Central Bank of Iceland (2007e) *Monetary Bulletin,* 2007:3, November, available at http://www.sedlabanki.is

Egilsson, V. (2007) 'Rich or Bankrupt? Is the Current Account Deficit in Iceland Overstated?', speech at conference at Central Bank of Iceland, May.

Ferguson, Jr., R.W., P. Hartmann, F. Panetta and R. Portes (2007) *International Financial Stability,* Geneva Reports on the World Economy 9, International Center for Monetary and Banking Studies (ICMB) and Centre for Economic Policy Research (CEPR).

Goodhart, C. and G. Illing (2002) *Financial Crises, Contagion, and the Lender of Last Resort, a Reader,* Oxford University Press.

Fitch Ratings (2006) 'Fitch Revises Iceland's Outlook to Negative on Widening Macro Imbalances', 21 February.

Freixas, X., B. Parigi and J.-C. Rochet (2004) 'The Lender of Last Resort: a 21st Century Approach', *Journal of the European Economic Association,* 2(6), 1085–115.

Glitnir Research (2007) 'The Icelandic Economy 2007–2011', September.

Goldstein, M. (2002), *Managed Floating Plus* Institute for International Economics, Policy Analyses in International Economics, 66, Washington, DC.

Hau, H. and H. Rey (2006) 'Exchange Rates, Equity Prices and Capital Flows', *Review of Financial Studies,* 19(1), 273–317.

IMF (2007) *Country Report 07/296,* August.

Jonsson, A. (2007) 'Einhliða upptaka evrunnar', presentation, Kaupthing, October.

Kaupthing Bank (2007a) *Monthly Market Focus,* 5 November.

Kaupthing Bank (2007b) *Quarterly Economic Outlook,* 26 October.

Kristinsson, Y.O. (2007) 'Var kommer pengarna från: Globaliseringen af den islandske ökonomi', presentation, Landsbankinn, 29 September.

Krugman, P. (2007), 'Will there be a Dollar Crisis', *Economic Policy,* 51, 436–67.

Landsbanki (2007) *Macroeconomic Insight,* 5 June.

Lane, P. and G. Milesi-Ferretti (2006) 'The External Wealth of Nations Mark II: Revised and Extended Estimates of Foreign Assets and Liabilities, 1970–2004', CEPR Discussion Paper, No. 5644, April.

Levy Yeyati, E. (2006) 'Financial Dollarisation', *Economic Policy,* 45, 61–118.

Merrill Lynch (2006) 'Icelandic Banks: Not what You are Thinking', 7 March.

Mishkin, F.S. and T.T. Herbertsson (2006) *Financial Stability in Iceland,* Iceland Chamber of Commerce.
Moody's Investors Service (2006) 'Banking System Outlook: Iceland', December.
Morgan Stanley (2007) 'Nordic Banks: Switching out of Kaupthing into DnB', 7 November.
Ólafsson, F. (2007) 'Skidegodt Carsten!', *Vísbending,* 25 (40), 3–4.
Papaioannou, E. and R. Portes (2007) 'The Euro as an International Currency vis-à-vis the Dollar', paper for Euro50 Group meeting, Rome, 3 July.
Plantin, G. and H. S. Shin (2006) 'Carry Trades and Speculative Dynamics', available at http:// faculty.london.edu/gplantin/Research.htm
Portes, R. (2007) 'Sovereign Wealth Funds', available at http://www.voxeu.org/index.php?q=node/636
Portes, R. and D. Vines (1997) *Coping with Capital Inflows,* Commonwealth Secretariat, Economic Paper No. 30, April.
Rawkins, P. (2007) 'Iceland: Macro Imbalances Challenge Sovereign Fundamentals', presentation, Fitch Ratings' Sovereign Hotspots Seminar, Stockholm, 7 June.
Rochet, J.-C. and X. Vives (2004) 'Coordination Failures and the Lender of Last Resort: was Bagehot right after all?', *Journal of the European Economic Association* 2(6), 1116–47.
Standard & Poor's (2007) 'Bank Industry Risk Analysis: Icelandic Banks' New Model Faces First Real Resilience Test', 20 February.
Svavarsson, D. and P.O. Sigurdsson (2007) 'Iceland's International Investment Position and Balance on Income', Central Bank of Iceland *Monetary Bulletin* 2007/2, pp. 53–73.

# 11

# The Icelandic Banking Crisis and What to Do about it: the Lender of Last Resort Theory of Optimal Currency Areas

*Willem H. Buiter*
*London School of Economics and Political Economy, NBER and CEPR*

*and*

*Anne C. Sibert*
*Birkbeck, University of London and CEPR*

## Summary

Iceland has, in a very short period of time, created an internationally active banking sector that is vast relative to the size of its very small economy. Iceland also has its own currency. This chapter argues that this 'business model' for Iceland is not viable. With most of the banking system's assets and liabilities denominated in foreign currency, and with a large amount of short-maturity foreign currency liabilities, Iceland needs a foreign currency lender of last resort and market maker of last resort to prevent funding illiquidity or market illiquidity from bringing down the banking system.

Iceland therefore has two options. First, it can join the EU and the EMU, making the Eurosystem the lender of last resort and market maker of last resort. In this case it can keep its international banking activities domiciled in Iceland. Second, it keeps its own currency. In that case it should relocate its foreign currency banking activities to the euro area.

## 11.1 Introduction and overview

Despite the high quality of its economic institutions, governance and policy making, the sustainability of its public finances, the flexibility of its markets and the quality of its labour force, Iceland is facing a potential, and possibly unnecessary, financial and economic crisis. The ratings agencies have downgraded its sovereign debt or put it on negative watch. The cost of the private banks' credit default swaps – a rough measure of the likelihood of default – are among the highest in the world. The underlying reason for this is that Iceland possesses both its own currency and a banking sector with vast assets and liabilities and with short-term foreign currency liabilities that dwarf its foreign currency assets and credit lines. Given the country's tiny size, it is not surprising that most of its banks' business is done in foreign currency, rather than in Icelandic krónur.

The assets of the Icelandic banking sector, although generally believed to be of good quality, are – as is usual for banks – of relatively long maturity compared with its liabilities and they are illiquid. Thus, Icelandic banks face the possibility of a run on their liabilities and, if there were to be a run on their foreign currency denominated liabilities, there is no effective lender of last resort. In the current financial crisis, even fundamentally sound banks are threatened with illiquidity. In the United States, a solvent but illiquid bank can count on its Central Bank to make it a loan against its fundamentally sound, but illiquid or temporarily impaired assets; the same is true in the euro area or the United Kingdom. But an Icelandic bank has no such safety net: the readily available foreign exchange resources of the Icelandic authorities (the Central Bank and Treasury) are too small compared to the short-term foreign currency exposure of its domestic banks. The market realizes this, increasing further the likelihood of a crisis for Icelandic banks and thus, the Icelandic economy.

The appropriate policy response to the current situation is straightforward, if not politically or technically easy. First, the government must immediately secure contingent emergency funding for its banks and the banks themselves should explore all available sources of liquid foreign exchange. Icelandic banks have subsidiaries in the euro area, the United Kingdom and elsewhere. The extent to which these subsidiaries are entitled to borrow from the host countries' central banks should be clarified. Foreign branches and subsidiaries of the Icelandic banks should try to raise foreign currency deposits. The Central Bank of Iceland should explore setting up swap arrangements – along the lines of the arrangements concluded on 16 May 2008 with the central banks of Sweden, Norway and Denmark – with other central banks, such as the ECB, the Federal Reserve and the Bank of England.[1] The Icelandic government could approach the IMF for a (revived) contingent credit line. As a last resort, the government should try to borrow foreign exchange in the global capital markets by offering its natural resource wealth, mainly hydro and geothermal energy, as collateral.

The Icelandic government must also decide the extent to which it is willing to risk its taxpayers' money in what might be an unsuccessful and expensive rescue attempt. A rescue attempt could be unsuccessful for two reasons. First, the authorities could fail to raise enough foreign exchange to deter runs on the Icelandic banks and to convince the markets to refinance the banks' assets until maturity. Second, the quality of the banks' assets could turn out to be of lower quality than is generally believed at present. If, however, the authorities think that the Icelandic banks are fundamentally sound, and most knowledgeable economists, including the authors of two recent reports on Iceland's economy and financial system (Miskin and Herbertsson, 2006 and Portes et al., 2007), believe this to be true, then it is likely to be worth the risk to attempt to avert a crisis that could result in the insolvency of one or more of the banks.

Assuming the immediate crisis can be resolved, Iceland is faced with a choice between two alternatives. The first, favoured by us, is for Iceland to become, as soon as possible, a member of the EU and then a full member of the EMU. This would both ensure that Icelandic banks have a credible foreign currency lender of last resort and, we believe, offer a preferable monetary regime from the perspective of macroeconomic stability: low and stable inflation and no unnecessary real exchange rate volatility. The EU/EMU route is the only one that allows Iceland to have an internationally active banking sector domiciled in Iceland. The only alternative is to encourage the banking system to move the bulk of its foreign currency denominated activities and portfolio overseas, most likely into the euro area. This would leave a much smaller banking system, with a mainly domestic currency denominated balance sheet, domiciled in Iceland. The quickest way to do this is to move foreign currency assets and liabilities into the existing subsidiaries in the euro area and, if necessary, to turn euro area branches into subsidiaries or create new subsidiaries in the euro area. Unlike branches, subsidiaries can have access to the Eurosystem's discount window and can be eligible counterparties in Eurosystem repos.

In Section 11.2 we discuss how the current liquidity crisis and the potential for a bank run arose in Iceland. We discuss the conventional policy steps that a central bank can try to take to solve a banking crisis independently. In Section 11.3 we evaluate the Icelandic government's ability to solve this crisis by acting as a lender of last resort and we conclude that Iceland is too small to provide the necessary foreign currency liquidity without extraordinary measures. In Section 11.4 we discuss how Iceland might acquire additional external funding. In

Section 11.5 we discuss the costs and benefits of Iceland retaining its own currency and conclude that, from an economic viewpoint, Iceland would be better off as a member of the euro area. Section 11.6 is the conclusion.

## 11.2 The Icelandic banking crisis

In this section we discuss the possibility of a run on Icelandic banks and how the current international liquidity shortage has contributed to the likelihood of such a crisis. We describe the conventional policy tools for dealing with this crisis.

### 11.2.1 All banks are vulnerable to runs

There is no such thing as a safe deposit-taking bank on its own, even if its assets are of good quality and it has enough liquid assets to cope with normal variations in the net flow of deposits and other short-term liabilities. The events since August 2007, and in particular the demise of Northern Rock in the United Kingdom and Bear Stearns in the United States, have made it clear that any highly leveraged institution with assets that are mostly long term and illiquid and liabilities that are mostly short term can be subject to a catastrophic liquidity shortage.

In the case of deposit-taking institutions, the canonical liquidity crisis is a bank run. Deposits can be withdrawn on demand and those who wish to withdraw are paid on a first-come, first-served basis. A bank run can occur if it is believed – rightly or wrongly – that a bank is balance-sheet-insolvent (with assets worth less than liabilities). But, as assets are illiquid, a bank run that cripples the bank is always possible, even if the bank is not believed to be balance-sheet-insolvent: if each depositor believes that all other depositors are going to withdraw their assets then each depositor's rational response is to withdraw his own. The outcome – a bank run – validates the depositors' beliefs: it is individually rational, but socially disastrous. The risk of cash-flow insolvency – inability to meet one's obligations including the obligation to redeem deposits on demand for cash – is always present when assets are illiquid.

For highly leveraged institutions that fund themselves mainly in the wholesale capital markets, including the asset-backed securities and asset-backed commercial paper markets, an analogous event is possible: in the belief that other creditors will be unwilling to roll over their loans to a borrower whose obligations are maturing or to purchase the new debt instruments the borrower is issuing, each creditor finds it optimal to refuse to roll over his own loans or to purchase the new debt instruments the borrower is trying to issue, let alone to extend new credit. As with a classic bank run, this scenario can occur even when the assets of the bank are believed to be sound, if only they could be held to maturity.

### 11.2.2 The current international liquidity crisis and Iceland

In the current international economic environment, the difficulty in valuing many repackaged collateralized debt obligations and the difficulty in determining the exposure of individual banks has increased counterparty risk and raised the global price of liquidity. This has had three implications for Icelandic and other banks. First, banks' funding costs have increased, raising the likelihood that any bank will become insolvent. Second, by coordinating market beliefs about Icelandic and other banks it has made bank runs that are based solely on self-fulfilling expectations, rather than fundamentals, more likely. Third, it has made it more difficult for banks to insure themselves against runs. Any attempt by Icelandic banks to lower their risk of a bank run by selling their longer term assets before their scheduled maturity dates would, at best, result in a severe discount relative to the value of the asset held to maturity. At worst, an attempted fire sale in an illiquid market could realize next to nothing.

As a deposit run or a run on a bank's other short-term liabilities cannot be prevented or overcome by any individual financial institution faced with it, third-party support is necessary. Sometimes the banking sector collectively can effectively support an individual institution among their number faced with a run by providing the threatened bank with lines of credit and cash. But, when enough banks in the system are threatened, such private solutions are ineffective. In Iceland, there are only three internationally active banks, Landsbanki, Glitnir and Kaupthing, and all of them have been affected by the international liquidity crisis since last September: no private solution is feasible.

### 11.2.3 The banking system and the crisis

Figure 11.1 shows the size of the three main Icelandic banks. Total assets of the three banks (including their foreign subsidiaries) at the end of the first quarter of 2008 amounted to 14,069,370 million krónur. This is almost 11 times the Ministry of Finance's estimate of 2007 GDP of 1,319,200 million krónur and equals about $176 billion at an exchange rate of 80 kr./$. Total liabilities of the three banks amount to 13,265,311 million krónur, or roughly $166 billion.

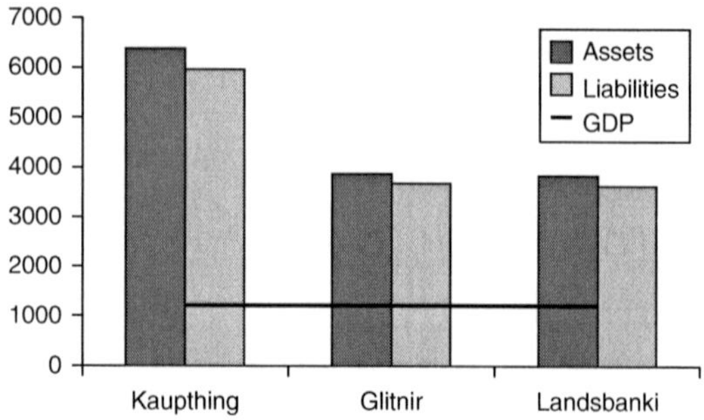


*Figure 11.1* Assets and liabilities of the three main banks compared to GDP (m.kr.)
*Source*: Ministry of Finance, interim financial statements.

The spectacular internationalization of the three internationally active banks is shown in Figures 11.2 and 11.3. Figure 11.2 depicts the geographical distribution of Icelandic banks' assets. Roughly half of Landsbanki's assets and two-thirds of the assets of Glitnir and Kaupthing are located outside of Iceland. Total bank assets located inside Iceland, however, still amount to a massive 5,160,475 million krónur, almost four times GDP.

Figure 11.3 shows the currency composition of the assets and liabilities of the three large internationally active banks for 2008Q1. About 21 per cent of all assets and 15 per cent of all liabilities are in krónur. Thus, most of the Icelandic banks' business is done in foreign currency and there is a mismatch: the share of assets denominated in foreign currency is significantly smaller than the share of liabilities denominated in foreign currency.

The Icelandic banks get about a third of their total funding from deposits. The remaining two-thirds come mainly from the international wholesale markets.[2] The proximate cause of the Icelandic banking crisis was not, however, a deposit run, but rather an extreme international wholesale liquidity shortage – a liquidity crunch. Icelandic banks were unable to borrow in the international financial wholesale markets despite having, by the usual metrics, more than adequate capital ratios, liquidity provisions and profitability of their operations.

Evidence of the effect of the current financial crisis on Iceland is seen in Figure 11.4, which shows the path of the default risk spreads on Icelandic banks' debt in the credit default swap markets between May 2006 and mid July. For comparison, the European benchmark for

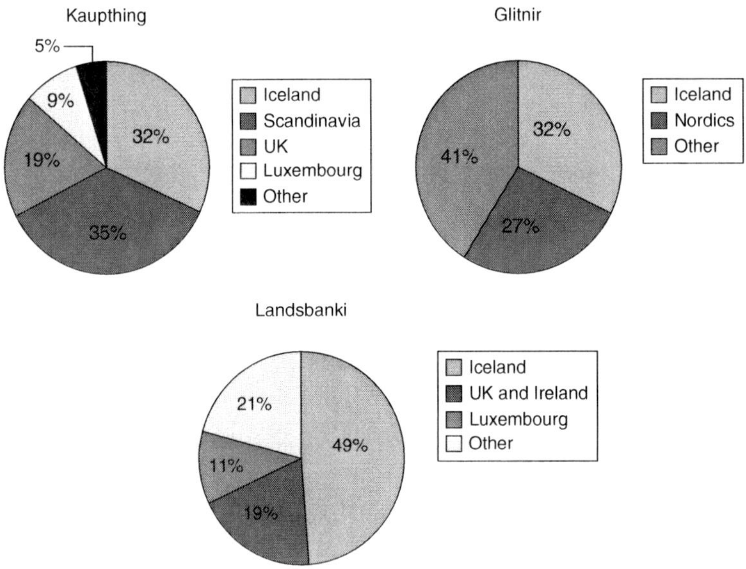


*Figure 11.2* Geographical breakdown of Icelandic bank assets, 2008Q1
*Source*: Interim financial statements.

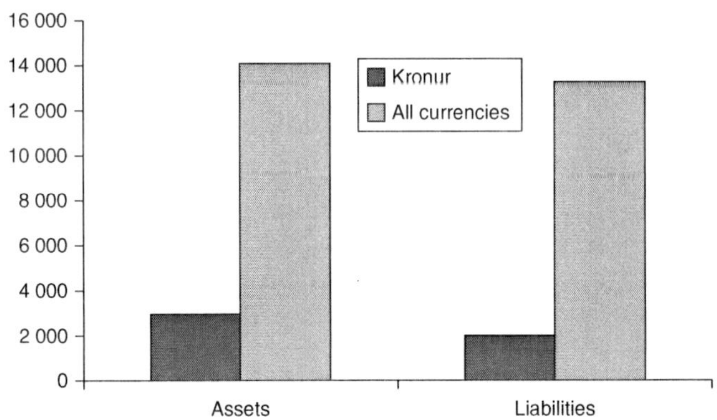


*Figure 11.3* Assets and liabilities of the three main banks (b. kr.)
*Source*: Consolidated interim financial statements

credit risk in the financial sector, the iTraxx Financial Europe index, is also shown.

A credit default swap (CDS) is a derivative where one party makes periodic payments to another party in return for that other party

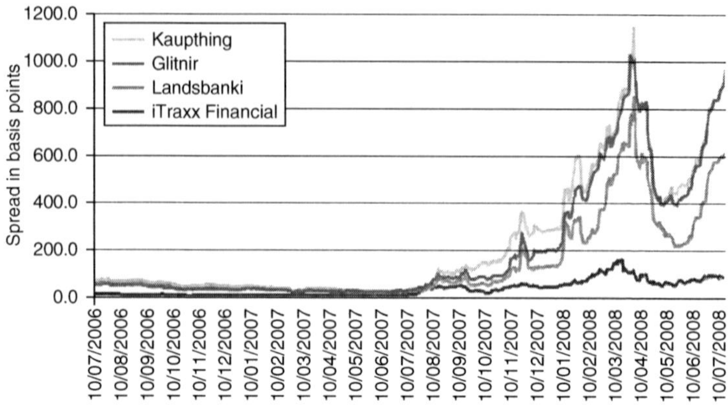


*Figure 11.4* CDS spreads for three Icelandic banks and iTraxx Financial Europe, 10/07/2006–10/07/2008
*Source*: Central Bank of Iceland.

making a payment if some specified third party defaults. If the CDS for a business trades at, say, 100 bps, then the annual cost of insuring 10 million euros of its debt is 100,000 euros, or 1 per cent. Thus, credit default swaps are a rough measure of a bank's likelihood of default.

From Figure 11.4, it can be seen that at the beginning of 2007 credit default swap rates for Landsbanki, Kaupthing and Glitnir were a fairly unremarkable 18, 27 and 24, respectively. However, they began rising after that, fairly slowly at first but accelerating in 2008. They peaked at 850 (Landsbanki), 1140 (Kaupthing) and 1026 (Glitnir) in late March/ early April. The rates declined in May, but were back at 613 (Landsbanki), 961 (Kaupthing) and 960 (Glitnir) on 17 July 2008. Illiquidity – driven by fear and uncertainty – is no doubt distorting the CDS markets, and not just for Icelandic banks, just as it has distorted interbank markets and asset-backed securities markets around the world. It is also clear that the CDS spreads during the current phase of the crisis have ceased to reflect the marginal funding costs of the Icelandic banks.[3] Nevertheless, these are some of the highest CDS rates in the world and compare with a 270 bps CDS spread for the Icelandic sovereign (on 17 July 2008).

On 17 April 2008, Standard & Poor's lowered the long-term foreign currency rating on the Republic of Iceland to 'A' from 'A+' and its long-term local-currency rating to 'AA–' from 'AA'. Moody's still maintains an 'Aaa' rating for the Icelandic Sovereign, but put it on a negative outlook on 5 March, as did Fitch on 1 April.[4] The three main internationally active Icelandic banks were put on negative watch.[5]

Displaying unusual (and commendable) candour for a central bank, in its latest *Financial Stability* report, the Central Bank of Iceland says, 'Critics have asserted that the Icelandic banks have grown too large. This might be true if a major financial crisis was imminent and the Icelandic Government was forced to resolve a critical situation affecting banking operations both in Iceland and abroad' (May 2008, p. 7). Unfortunately, it is this inability of the government to control a financial crisis that is likely to cause one.

In a bank run on a solvent bank, each depositor (or other lender) withdraws his money in the belief that all other depositors will withdraw their money and the bank will fail. A bank run is a classical coordination failure. But it is not a usual outcome. Why would depositors all simultaneously choose to believe that other depositors are going to run if they believe that the bank is solvent? In normal times, bank runs are rare.

For a run on a solvent bank to occur, something must coordinate depositors' beliefs. A failure of a similar bank might do this. The typical depositor has little idea about the health of his own bank. A failure of a similar bank increases his perception of the riskiness of his own bank and tells him something about what other depositors will do. In addition to providing information, a run on one bank can coordinate depositors at another bank on a bank run outcome. The obvious fact that Iceland has no foreign currency lender of last resort could coordinate lenders. This fact both increases beliefs about the riskiness of Icelandic banks and provides information about what other depositors will do.

Perhaps more worrying, the government's announced inability to deal with a crisis of significantly large magnitude might tempt a few large investors to coordinate deliberately – to collude to launch a speculative attack. This could be done through a range of markets, including short selling the banks' equity, selling aggressively in the banks' OTC credit default swaps markets or shorting the currency. The absence of an effective foreign currency lender of last resort may make Iceland an attractive potential prey for hedge funds and other highly leveraged institutions able and willing to speculate against the Icelandic currency and banks. Even just a few of them acting in consort – and some acting individually – can achieve enough critical mass to move prices significantly in markets where the Icelandic banks are exposed.

Earlier this year, the stock of HBOS, a large UK clearing bank and mortgage lender, fell precipitously on rumours that it had requested assistance from the Bank of England. The FSA launched a formal enquiry into the source of these unfounded rumours. There is a danger that such unprincipled activity may be more damaging in the future. Unscrupulous traders using 'trash and trade' strategies, are already said to have shorted the krona or the stock or bonds of one or more of the Icelandic banks, while spreading rumours unfavourable to the currency or the bank's prospects, and benefiting from the subsequent price movements.

### 11.2.4 Conventional solutions to financial crises

Third-party support in the case of a bank run on deposits can take the form of a central bank or government loan to the bank or deposit insurance backed by a sovereign guarantee. For this to be effective against a worst-case scenario, the government must have access to a sufficient amount of liquid assets to meet any conceivable redemption demand from depositors or to recapitalize banks that are insolvent as well as illiquid. As long as the domestic banks' deposits and short-term liabilities *are denominated in domestic currency*, this is always the case. The central bank has a potentially unlimited supply of domestic currency liquidity through its ability to issue legal tender at will.

If the government is credible in its commitment that it will insure a bank's deposits or make available loans against illiquid assets, then this in itself may be sufficient to avert a bank run or solve a liquidity crisis. If not and the crisis recedes quickly enough, then fundamentally solvent banks will eventually cover their liabilities; the central bank will be repaid. If the loan was at a penalty rate, the central bank makes a profit. In this case crisis aversion requires neither inflation nor a change in fiscal policy.

However, if the deposit insurance does not convince the private sector that a bank is solvent or a bank turns out to be insolvent as well as illiquid, the bank may eventually fail and the central bank may not be repaid in full. As long as the central bank is not repaid in full, the issuance of the base money to provide the insurance or loan will be inflationary. The government can prevent the ensuing inflation by undertaking offsetting open-market operations, selling some of its holdings of securities for the domestic currency. If the securities sold are government debt, then the government must repay the principal and interest to the private sector; it the securities are private securities, the government loses the principal and interest it would otherwise have received. Either way, the government must raise current or future taxes or, for given taxes, lower its current or future public expenditure. Ultimately, the taxpayers or the beneficiaries from future public spending provide the funds for an unsuccessful rescue if inflation is to be avoided (see Buiter, 2007, 2008).

If domestic banks have deposits and other short-term liabilities denominated in *foreign* currencies, a solution may not be possible, even if deposit insurance or a loan would be sufficient to avert a crisis. If a government wants to guarantee foreign currency deposits or make a foreign currency loan, it must possess or be able to acquire the needed amount of foreign currency. If, say, the United States wanted to provide a foreign currency loan to a US bank it could do this by issuing home money, selling the home money for foreign money and then lending the foreign money to the bank.

The ability of a central bank to provide foreign currency loans, however, is limited by the foreign exchange market's willingness to exchange foreign currency for the central bank's domestic currency. This willingness is finite: as the central bank issues more base money, the value of a unit of base money in terms of foreign currency declines and, although this is an empirical matter, it appears likely that at some point issuing further home money lowers the value of the home money stock in terms of foreign currency. That is, there is a Laffer curve in the foreign currency value of seigniorage. Unfortunately, the size of the foreign currency liabilities of the Icelandic banking sector is sufficiently large that it is unlikely that the Icelandic government could provide full foreign currency deposit insurance or sufficient foreign currency liquidity to replace maturing non-deposit short-term foreign currency liabilities to ward off a liquidity crisis simply by printing its own money.

## 11.3 Can Iceland act as a lender of last resort?

In this section we attempt to draw some conclusions about whether the government of Iceland has the necessary resources to act as a lender of last resort in the current crisis.

### 11.3.1 How much foreign currency does Iceland need?

We will argue later on in the section that Iceland would not need to bail out the foreign subsidiaries of its domestic banks. Thus, in the event of a liquidity crisis affecting all three large private Icelandic banks, Iceland might need as much foreign currency as the required short-term foreign currency needs of the parent banks and any foreign branches, less the liquid assets of these parent banks and any foreign branches. Unfortunately, precise data are not available to us, but we can make a very rough estimate.

As seen in Figure 11.2, the shares of assets located in Iceland are 51 per cent for Landsbanki and 68 per cent for both Glitnir and Kaupthing.

We assume that all of the assets located abroad are subsidiaries and not branches; to the extent that this is not true (and it is indeed not true) our estimate may be too low. We also assume that liability shares are the same as asset shares. The shares of total assets held in krónur are 25, 30 and 13 per cent for Landsbanki, Glitnir and Kaupthing, respectively. The shares of total liabilities held in krónur are 19, 20 and 9 per cent for Landsbanki, Glitnir and Kaupthing, respectively.

We assume that all krona assets and all krona liabilities are held in Iceland. Thus, we estimate that foreign currency assets in Iceland as a percentage of total assets are 24, 2 and 19 per cent for Landsbanki, Glitnir and Kaupthing, respectively. We also estimate that foreign currency liabilities in Iceland as a percentage of total liabilities are 30, 12 and 23 per cent for Landsbanki, Glitnir and Kaupthing, respectively. We assume that these shares are constant across maturities.

As an imperfect measure of the difference between short-term liquidity needs and available liquid assets we use the difference between short-term liabilities and short-term assets. In particular we look at assets and liabilities with maturities up to three months and assets and liabilities with maturities up to a year. Using the percentage shares that we calculated in the previous paragraph and data on assets and liabilities of different maturities found in the three large banks' 2008Q1 interim financial statements, we find that the difference between short-term liabilities and short-term assets denominated in foreign currency and located in Iceland is 481,336 million kr. or $6.0 billion if short run is defined as three months and 534,056 million kr. or $6.7 billion if short run is defined as a year.[6]

Unfortunately, subtracting assets of a particular maturity from liabilities of the same maturity may yield an underestimate of the net liquidity deficit. Landsbanki publishes a table showing the cash flow payable by its group, classified by remaining contractual maturities. This yields a number that is about one and a half times as high as simply looking at assets and liabilities classified by maturities. If similar figures resulted for the two banks that do not publish these numbers, then it may be that the Central Bank requires foreign reserves of $10 billion or about 800 million kr. if the short run is defined as a year.

### 11.3.2 Does Iceland have adequate foreign exchange reserves to act as a foreign currency lender of last resort?

The government of Iceland's foreign assets are mainly the official foreign reserves of the Central Bank of Iceland. A typical central bank's official foreign reserves are mainly foreign exchange, typically acquired through foreign exchange intervention, but they also include gold, SDRs and the country's reserve position in the IMF.

The Central Bank of Iceland has pursued a programme of regular foreign exchange purchases and on 11 July 2008, Iceland held foreign exchange reserves equal to $2567.56 million, or about 205 billion krónur. Almost all of it (over 96 per cent) is in foreign currency reserves. To get an idea of the size of these official foreign reserves, we expressed them as a share of GDP and compared Iceland's position with that of the other Nordic central banks and the central banks of three other small open economies. As can be seen in Figure 11.5, with foreign assets equal to about 13 per cent of GDP, the Icelandic Central Bank holds a relatively large amount of foreign reserves for a country of its size. No Nordic country's central bank holds more, nor do the central banks of Australia or Canada. Only the Central Bank of Australia, with reserves of just under 14 per cent of GDP, holds slightly more.

In addition to its official reserves, Iceland entered into bilateral currency swap arrangements with Sweden, Norway and Denmark on 16 May 2008. Each arrangement provides access to 500 million euros in exchange for krónur. Thus, at an exchange rate of 124 kr/euro there is access to about 186,000 million krónur worth of foreign currency. Thus, the Central Bank of Iceland has already acquired access to a total of 391 billion kr. or $4.9 billion. Unfortunately, our estimates in the previous subsection suggest that this might be less than half of what it needs.

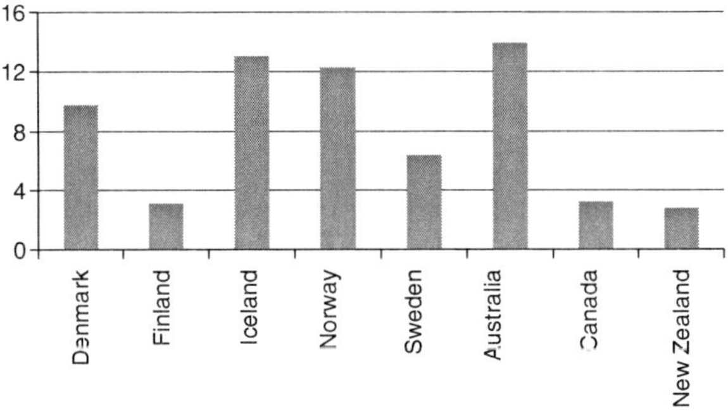


*Figure 11.5* Official foreign reserves of the Central Bank as a percentage of GDP
*Source*: International Monetary Fund. Reserve data are from end June/early July and the GDP is projected GDP for 2008.
*Note*: The Norwegian data exclude investments for the government pension fund.

### 11.3.3 Could Iceland acquire enough additional reserves by issuing base money?

As mentioned in the introduction, a central bank might attempt to raise foreign currency revenue by engaging in foreign exchange intervention, selling the domestic currency for foreign currency. As we mentioned in the previous subsection, Iceland has been pursuing this strategy. The amount of revenue that can be raised this way is not clear.

Our calculations, however, assume that the foreign exchange market is functioning normally and does not become illiquid. Unfortunately, this is no longer the case. The Central Bank of Iceland abandoned its attempt to raise additional reserves this way at the end of March 2008 because market conditions no longer permitted it (*Financial Stability*, May 2008, p. 70).

### 11.3.4 Iceland must seek assistance from abroad

In addition to being ineffective, any attempt by Iceland to assist its banks on its own may be counterproductive. The reason for bailing out a bank, when one would not bail out a manufacturing company, is the fear of contagion that could spark bank runs on solvent banks.

As previously mentioned, a run on a solvent bank is an unusual event. It requires something that coordinates the beliefs of individual investors. An example is the visible failure of a similar bank. The typical depositor may have little idea about the balance sheet of the bank in which he holds his money. A publicly observed failure of a similar bank both increases each depositor's perception of the riskiness of his own bank and tells the depositor something about what other depositors will do. Thus, in addition to providing information, a run on one bank can coordinate depositors at another bank on a bank run outcome.

Other things can coordinate depositors as well. One that we previously mentioned is the obvious fact that Iceland has no foreign currency lender of last resort although its banks have large short-term foreign currency liabilities. This publicly observed fact both increases an individual's assessment of the riskiness associated with his deposit and provides information about what other depositors will do, increasing the likelihood of a bank run. Another way to coordinate depositors – or to alert hedge funds of potential prey – is for the government to make a frantic attempt to secure foreign exchange that is both observable and believed likely to be ineffective.

Iceland has limited foreign exchange reserves and limited means to obtain more through normal, unilateral foreign exchange operations. Currently, it has limited access to other foreign exchange resources, such as swaps and credit lines. Its massive mismatch between the currency of the lender of last resort and the foreign currencies of operation of the banking sector is unique, as far as we know.[7] The Central Bank of Iceland cannot act as an effective lender of last resort for a domestic banking system whose lending, borrowing and investment activities are mainly in foreign currencies and whose balance sheet is largely foreign currency denominated. The scenario is an invitation to a bank run or a market strike. The government should move to secure foreign funding and, as soon as possible, an alternative lender of last resort.

## 11.4 Obtaining external funding

Only full participation in the EMU of the EU provides a long-term solution that will permit Iceland to maintain an Iceland-domiciled banking sector of its current size relative to the rest of the Icelandic economy. This requires EU membership. Even under the most favourable conditions, EU membership for Iceland, let alone full EMU participation, is several years away. The only immediate solution is for the banks, directly or indirectly, through the government, to gain access to foreign exchange on a sufficient scale. In this section we make some suggestions about how this can be done.

### 11.4.1 What the banks can do: using their subsidiaries abroad

Foreign branches of Icelandic banks do not have access to the discount window of the central bank in their host country, nor are they eligible parties in open market operations by their host-country central bank. Subsidiaries, however, can have both privileges. This is why we excluded them when we calculated the amount of foreign exchange that the central bank might need. The three Icelandic banks should use the discount windows accessible to their foreign subsidiaries to the maximum extent possible, and should also engage in collateralized open market transactions with their host country central banks to the maximum amount possible.

A Kaupthing subsidiary in the UK, Kaupthing Singer & Friedlander Limited (KSF), is a participant in the Bank of England's Reserve Scheme and in its Standing Facilities. This means that KSF is an eligible counterparty in the Bank of England's open market operations and that it can borrow overnight, on demand against appropriate collateral, at the standing lending facility, the Bank of England's discount window, at a penalty over bank rate of 100 basis points. Kaupthing subsidiaries are also on the MFI (monetary financial institutions) list in Sweden, Finland

and Luxembourg. In the last two countries they are subject to the Eurosystem's minimum reserves and are, therefore, eligible counterparties at the marginal lending facility and for open market operations.

A Landsbanki subsidiary is on the MFI list in the UK, although it is not on the Bank of England's list of eligible counterparties at its Standing Facilities or for its open market operations. A Landsbanki subsidiary is an eligible counterparty at the Marginal Lending Facility and for open market operations with the Eurosystem in Luxembourg. A Glitnir subsidiary is an eligible counterparty for the Eurosystem in Luxembourg. We have not been able to verify the eligibility for discount window access or the open market operation counterparty eligibility of Glitnir's Norwegian and US subsidiaries. Icelandic banks should, where possible, turn their euro area and UK branches into subsidiaries with access to Eurosystem, respectively Bank of England, liquidity.

Euro area and US subsidiaries of UK banks have borrowed since August 2007 from the ECB and the Federal Reserve System, respectively, both through the discount window and through open market operations. It is not clear, however, that the ECB, the Fed or the Bank of England would be happy to see Icelandic parent banks borrow on a large scale from them, using their euro area, US or UK subsidiaries as intermediaries or vehicles. Because of possible contagion effects, these central banks would not like to see the Icelandic parent banks fail. But it is possible that the governments in the euro area, the United States and the UK would believe that it is politically costly to bail out foreign banks and that funding foreign parent banks through subsidiaries is a violation of the spirit of the law.

### 11.4.2 Government borrowing from other central banks and the market

It is clear that the Central Bank of Iceland must borrow additional foreign exchange. The most attractive option is probably to attempt to establish additional contingent foreign currency credit lines or overdraft facilities besides the ones that they have established with three Nordic central banks. Swaps are a common arrangement among central banks. In December 2007 the Fed and the ECB agreed to a $20 billion swap facility and the Fed and the SNB (Swiss National Bank) agreed to a $4 billion swap facility. Unfortunately, Iceland is at a disadvantage for swaps, because few foreign central banks would naturally wish to take a significant long position in the Icelandic krona. However, the threat of the global contagion fallout from an Icelandic bank failure is likely to be quite persuasive and the ECB, the Bank of England and the Fed may be willing counterparties.

The government of Iceland could also borrow from the markets. It no longer has a triple A credit rating, and on 1 April 2008, Fitch Ratings revised the outlooks for the Republic of Iceland's long-term foreign currency and local currency issuer default ratings to negative from stable. The long-term foreign currency and local currency issuer default ratings are 'A+' and 'AA+' respectively. Iceland also possesses some excellent collateral, even if using it might prove politically unpalatable.

We believe that neither the country's recent large current account deficits, nor its (misreported and overstated) negative net external investment position should be an obstacle to the Icelandic authorities borrowing abroad. In a nutshell, the end of the aluminium investment boom will dramatically lower the country's cyclically corrected current account deficit. The cyclical downturn will further reduce the external deficit. The market-to-market net international investment position of the country is much less negative than the commonly reported book or historic cost measure of the net international investment position (see Svavarsson, 2008).

One option is for the government to use the assets of the publicly owned Housing Financing Fund as collateral for loans from the market, or indeed for loans from other central banks. The HFF has roughly ISK 500 billion of assets on its books, or about $6.6 billion at current exchange rates. There are two problems with this. First, these assets are mortgages or residential-mortgage-backed securities, and the global popularity of such assets is at an all-time low. Standard & Poor's on 17 April 2008 lowered the long-term foreign currency rating on HFF, alongside that of the Sovereign, to 'A' from 'A+', and its local currency ratings to 'A+/A-1' from 'AA-/A-1+'. HFF's short-term foreign currency rating of 'A-1' was affirmed. These assets are 'Aaa'-rated by Moody's, but were placed on a negative outlook on 5 March 2008. The second problem is that the HFF is already being enlisted to lend the commercial banks up to 30 billion krónur ($380 million) to allow them to refinance mortgages.

The assets of the privately owned (by the social partners) pension funds of Iceland could also be mobilized by the government to lower the financial pressures on the country and the banks. At the end of January 2008, the assets of the pension funds stood at ISK 1622 billion, or approximately $21.6 billion worth. Of that, about ISK 442 billion were foreign securities – about $5.9 billion worth. The pension funds could be encouraged to use their liquid foreign assets, or foreign exchange obtained by borrowing against their illiquid foreign assets, to buy back some of their long-term debt to the Icelandic banks, write credit default swap (CDS) insurance for the banks or engage in a range of other measures that either provide the banks with liquid foreign assets or discourage speculative attacks against them in the CDS, stock and bond markets. If the banks are indeed solvent provided they can hold their assets to maturity, and if the market 'strike' is indeed mainly a liquidity phenomenon, it ought to be possible to offer terms to the pension funds that compensate them fully for their increased risk exposure yet at the same time help take the pressure off the banks. Nevertheless, using pension funds to back banks that have expanded as aggressively as the Icelandic banks might be a political hard sell.

From the perspective of the international financial community, the most promising form of collateral for official borrowing from abroad is Iceland's natural resources. Iceland is rich in hydro and geothermal energy resources that are currently only exploited for exports indirectly, by being embodied in the exports of aluminium smelted and refined in Iceland. Before too long, however, there may be a power cable linking Iceland to Scotland and possibly to other countries as well. This valuable resource could be used today by borrowing against it. In particular, exploration rights and exploitations options could be auctioned off to foreign enterprises. Future foreign currency energy revenues of the Icelandic Treasury could be securitized today, with bonds that will only start paying a coupon in the future, when the exports and taxes are actually flowing. While also possibly politically unappealing, tens of billions of dollars could be mobilized through this channel.

### 11.4.3 The International Monetary Fund

Iceland, with its strong fiscal position and sound economic policies, is not the usual candidate for IMF funds. However, a look at the IMF's lending position, shown in Table 11.1, suggests that Iceland and the IMF may be an excellent match: the IMF is desperate to lend to worthy and credit-worthy borrowers.

*Table 11.1* IMF lending, 2008

| | |
|---|---|
| Loanable funds | \$209.5 billion |
| Loans outstanding | \$16.1 billion |

*Source*: IMF.

Iceland currently has access to IMF resources in the IMF's General Resources Account (GRA). The two IMF facilities that would be available to the Icelandic authorities are the Stand-By Arrangements (SBA) and the Supplemental Reserve Facility (SRF). The SBA is designed to help countries with short-term balance of payments difficulties. The length of an SBA is typically one to two years and repayment is normally expected in two and a quarter to four years. There are surcharges for high access levels.

The SRF provides sizable loans on a short-term basis. This facility was introduced in 1997 after the crises in emerging markets during the 1990s. Emerging market economies suffered massive capital outflows after sudden losses in market confidence and their governments required much larger loans than they had previously been able to get from the IMF. The Fund expects SRF loans to be repaid in a year to a year and a half and they carry a substantial surcharge of 3–5 percentage points.

The maximum amount that a country can borrow varies and is different for different types of loans. It typically depends on a country's IMF quota, but in exceptional circumstances some loans may exceed the usual limits. Access is typically limited to an annual amount equal to the country's quota and a cumulative amount equal to three times the country's quota. The IMF's willingness to extend exceptional loans depends on a country's balance-of-payments needs, its ability to repay, its current indebtedness to the Fund and its track record. Iceland's current IMF quota is about $193 million. Iceland already has access to $25 million of this, it is part of Iceland's official reserve assets; none of the rest has been drawn on.

Unfortunately, the most obvious IMF loan facility for Iceland, the Contingent Credit Line (CCL), no longer exists. The CCL was introduced in 1999 as part of the IMF's response to the Asian crisis of 1997–98. It was intended to provide a precautionary line of defence for countries with sound policies that were at risk of a capital account crisis because of contagion effects from other countries. A country had to meet four criteria to access this facility. First, it must not otherwise have needed IMF lending; second, its policies must have been progressing towards internationally accepted standards; third, it must have had constructive relations with its private creditors and been making progress towards limiting its external vulnerability; fourth, it must have had a satisfactory macroeconomic and financial programme and a commitment to adjustment. Funds were available for up to a year on a stand-by basis. There was no formal limit on the amount available, but it was generally expected that commitments would be about three to five times a country's quota. Repayment was expected in a year to 18 months and there was a surcharge of 1.5–3.5 percentage points.

The CCL was never used and it was allowed to expire in 2003. However, the Directors of the IMF emphasized during the debate on the CCL's expiration in 2003, that the IMF stands ready to respond quickly and flexibly to approve the use of Fund resources. It seems reasonable to believe that Iceland would have been allowed to borrow five times its quota under this facility – almost 1 billion dollars – and that it might still be able to arrange similar IMF financing. One billion dollars may not seem like a lot, but even before the current systemic crisis started in August 2007, there was at least one occasion in 2006 where one of the Icelandic banks found itself in considerable difficulty having to come up with just over 600 million dollars at short notice, when faced with a short-lived market liquidity shortage. A billion dollars of additional liquidity would come in handy when total foreign exchange reserves are around 2.8 billion dollars.

Borrowing from the IMF or resurrecting its contingent credit facility may be hard to swallow for a country that is not an emerging market or a developing country. It is also possible that there is so much 'stigma' attached to a country requesting even a contingent credit line with the Fund, that it could end up harming the country's access to funding from the markets. The rating agencies, for instance, may take an (unjustified) dim view of a country seeking even contingent assistance from the IMF, and the markets might react negatively. But if, as we believe, at least $1bn could be made available through this channel, and quite possibly a lot more, it is a line of defence that ought to be given serious consideration.

### 11.4.4 Can Iceland raise what it needs in the short run?

We have argued that a ballpark figure of what Iceland might need in the short run is $10 billion of foreign currency. It already has almost $5 billion. It should be possible for the Icelandic authorities to raise, at short notice, say, $1 billion from the IMF and perhaps $2.5 billion from other central banks. The private banks might be able to raise the remaining $1.5 billion through their foreign subsidiaries. Any shortcoming could be made up by the Central Bank borrowing from the markets using the assets of the pension funds, the assets of the HFF, or claims against its natural resources as collateral. With a bit of luck, the banks and the rest of the financial system ought to be able to survive the current crisis.

However, in the longer run, if Icelandic banks were to be taxed for the costs of the foreign exchange liquidity insurance mechanisms that reduce the likelihood of a future liquidity crunch to an acceptable level, this would put Icelandic banks at a competitive disadvantage relative to banks domiciled in jurisdictions whose currency is a serious global reserve currency.

The concerns we express about the competitiveness and even the viability of an internationally active banking sector domiciled in Iceland with the Icelandic krona continuing as the country's currency, therefore apply not only to Iceland but, albeit to a lesser degree, to other countries with internationally active banking sectors that are large relative to the rest of the economy, but without a domestic currency that is also a serious global reserve currency.

There are now only two serious global reserve currencies, the US dollar and the euro. The list of countries with internationally active banking sectors that are potentially vulnerable to funding- or market-liquidity crises due to the absence of a foreign currency lender of last resort and market maker of last resort includes Switzerland and the UK, but not Luxembourg, which is part of the euro area.

The Switzerland-domiciled part of the Swiss banking system owes its continued profitability to a significant extent to its banking secrecy and its associated status as a tax haven. Those subsidiaries of the internationally active Swiss banks that are located in the euro area or in the US are eligible for liquidity support from the Eurosystem and the Fed, respectively. As we noted, the subsidiaries of the Icelandic banks domiciled in the euro area (mainly Luxembourg at the moment) are eligible for access to the Eurosystem's marginal lending facility and are eligible counterparties in Eurosystem repos. The UK has, in sterling, a second-class global reserve currency. While this represents a competitive disadvantage compared to eurozone and US-domiciled banks, it is better than nothing, which is the condition Iceland finds itself in.

## 11.5 Should Iceland join the euro area?

As we have argued, if Iceland wishes to maintain an internationally active banking sector domiciled in Iceland that is as large as the current one, relative to the Icelandic economy, it is only sensible for it to join the euro area. This is the only way to guarantee a permanent foreign currency lender of last resort. In this section we argue that joining the euro area would also result in a more sensible monetary regime – a precondition for macroeconomic stability.

### 11.5.1 Making monetary policy in Iceland is too difficult

One reason for Iceland to contemplate abandoning its national currency is the difficulty it has had in making monetary policy. To illustrate the problems, we consider Iceland's recent aluminium investment boom.

In 2004 and 2005 Iceland had an externally financed investment boom in aluminium projects; this is seen in the spike in real gross fixed investment in Figure 11.6. In 2004 gross fixed investment increased by 28 per cent; it rose by nearly 35 per cent in 2005. The prospect of favourable future growth, coupled with lower income taxes, led to a sizeable, if less impressive, growth in domestic consumption: almost 7 per cent in 2004 and nearly 3 per cent in 2005.

An obvious lesson from the boom is that a shock affecting a single industry can have a large effect on an economy as tiny as Iceland's. As seen in Figure 11.7, aluminium already makes up about a quarter of Icelandic exports, a number expected to grow much larger in years to come, as additional capacity comes on stream. There are only two other export industries of significant size: marine products and services, each accounting for about a third of Iceland's exports. Given Iceland's size, we conjecture that three large export industries is a sensible amount of economic or real diversification. But, on its own it is not enough to adequately insure Iceland against sector-specific shocks having a substantial impact on the economy as a whole.

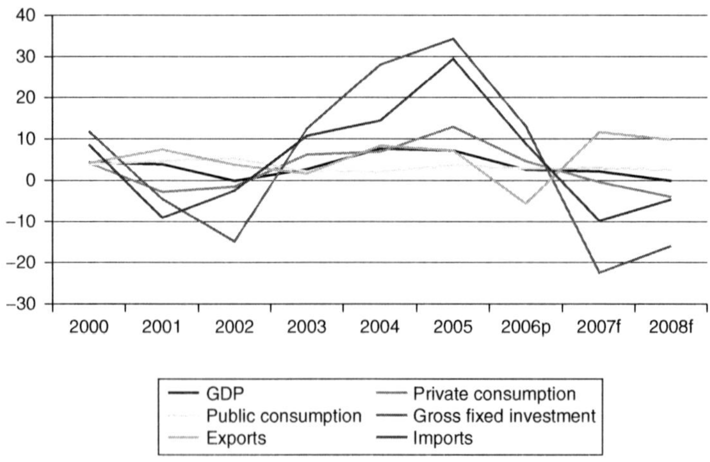


*Figure 11.6* Icelandic national accounts at constant prices (percentage change)
*Source*: IMF.

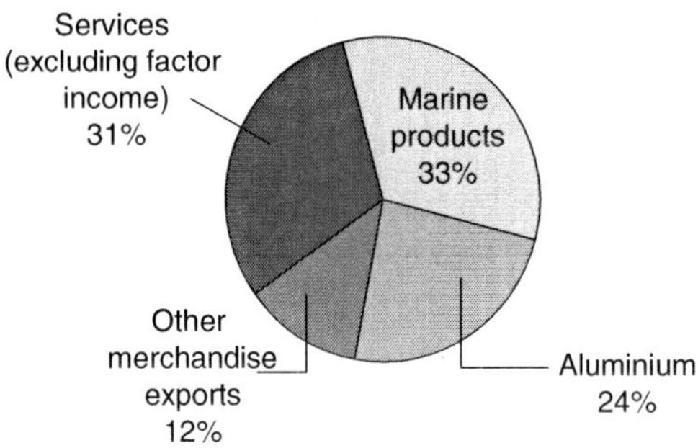


*Figure 11.7* Export composition (excluding income), 2007
*Source*: Finance Ministry, Iceland.

The aluminium boom was associated with large swings in domestic investment demand and domestic consumption demand and, as a result, there were significant changes in capacity utilization. Two measures of this are unemployment (an inverse measure) and the output gap, defined as the difference between actual output and estimated potential output as a percentage of estimated potential output. These measures are shown in Figure 11.8. The output gap swung from –2.6 per cent in 2003 to 5.2 per cent in 2005 and then fell to 1.3 per cent in 2007. Unemployment fell from 3.4 per cent in 2003 to 1.3 per cent in 2006, before rising to 2.0 per cent in 2007.

The boom was also associated with extreme swings in investor sentiment, as shown in Figure 11.9. Residential housing prices, which had increased at an average rate of about 6.5 per cent per year in 2001, 2002 and 2003, rose by over 23 per cent in 2004 and by 31 per cent in 2005. Share prices fell by nearly 20 per cent in 2000 and rose an average of 60 per cent per year in 2003, 2004 and 2005. Clearly, these swings in capacity utilization and mood resulted in nominal and real volatility and made monetary policy challenging.

Further problems for monetary policy have resulted from another startling feature of the Icelandic economy: roughly three-quarters of the total domestic currency lending of the credit system is index-linked to the CPI. About a quarter of the domestic currency loans of the Icelandic deposi tary monetary banks (DMBs) are index-linked, as shown in Figure 11.10. Roughly 50 per cent of non-exchange-rate linked loans are indexed, to the CPI. Mortgages from the state HFF are all indexed, as is most pension fund lending to residents. This means that the overwhelming majority of bank lending is either foreign currency denominated or index-linked

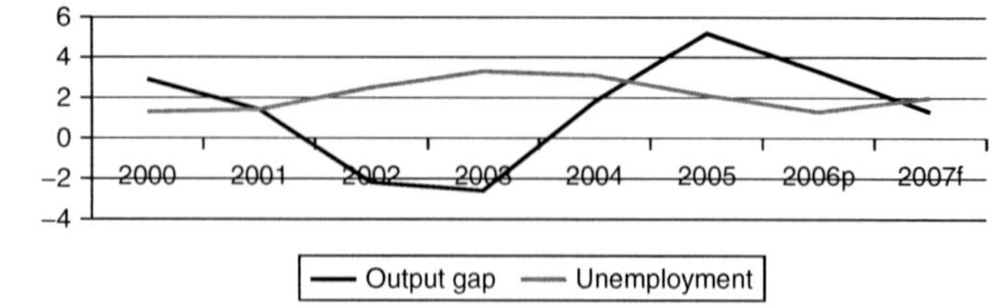


*Figure 11.8* Measures of capacity utilization (%)
*Source*: IMF.

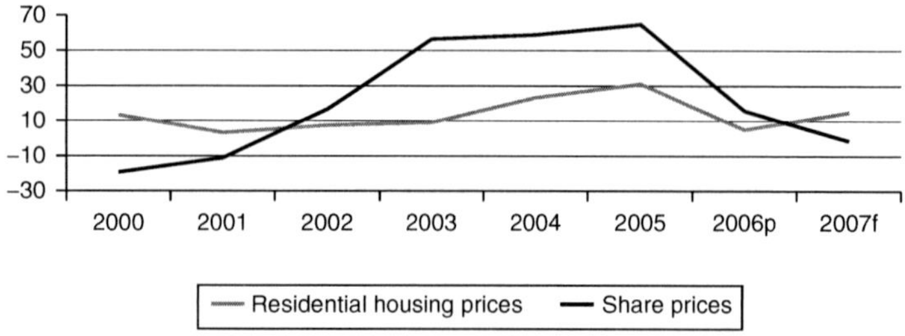


*Figure 11.9* Asset prices (annual percentage change)
*Source*: Central Bank, Iceland.

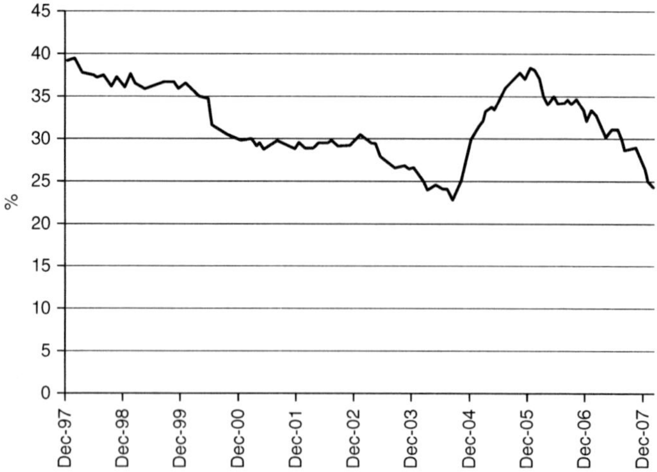


*Figure 11.10* Indexed loans of DMBs to residents, % of total loans to residents
*Source*: Landsbanki.

to the domestic CPI. Therefore, the interest rate channel for monetary policy, which works through changes in short-term domestic nominal interest rates, is effectively emasculated. Monetary policy therefore works almost exclusively through the exchange rate. The extreme swings in the nominal and real exchange rate of the Icelandic krona are consistent with this.

The CPI and nominal exchange rate are seen in Figure 11.11. The overriding goal of the Icelandic Central Bank is to keep the rate of inflation on average as close to its target of 2.5 per cent as possible. However, inflation was volatile and well above target during the period 2000–7. The Central Bank last attained a year-over-year percentage change in inflation below target in 1998 when inflation was 1.7 per cent.[8] In March 2008, inflation edged towards 9 per cent – despite a policy rate of 15.5 per cent!

Figure 11.12 shows the behaviour of short-term domestic nominal interest rates up to the end of 2007. It does not include the most recent rate increases, which brought the official policy rate to 15.5 per cent. These extremely high rates (motivated during the past year also by the need to defend the currency and the rest of the financial system against speculative attacks) were not enough to stop inflation rising steadily, reaching 8.7 per cent year-on-year in March 2008.

The volatility of the nominal exchange rate and, as shown in Figure 11.13, of the real exchange rate, and the persistent failure of the Central Bank to come close to meeting its inflation target, suggest that Iceland may be just too small and too internationally exposed to gain from having its own currency.

The fact, noted earlier, that most of the lending of Icelandic financial institutions to the domestic economy and most borrowing by the Icelandic non-financial private sector from any source is either denominated in foreign currency or index-linked (an extreme version

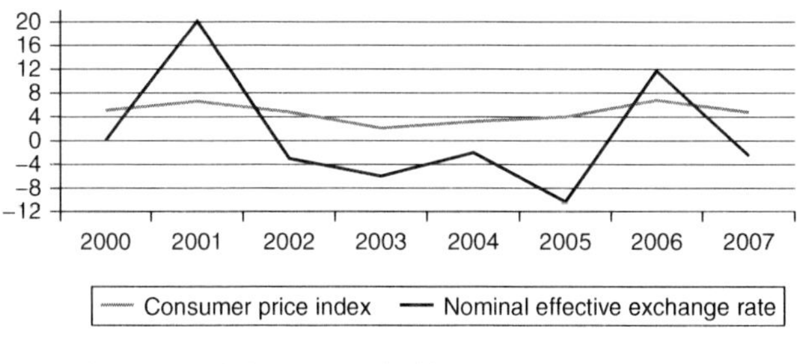


*Figure 11.11* The CPI and the nominal effective exchange rate
*Source*: Central Bank of Iceland.

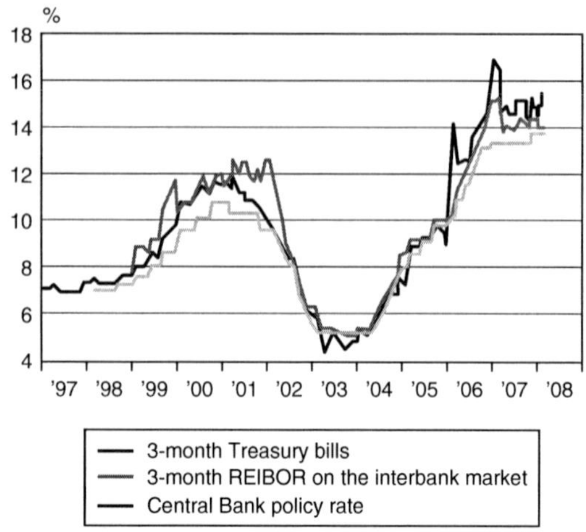


*Figure 11.12* Short–term interest rates, January 1997–February 2008 (at end of month)
*Source*: Central Bank of Iceland.

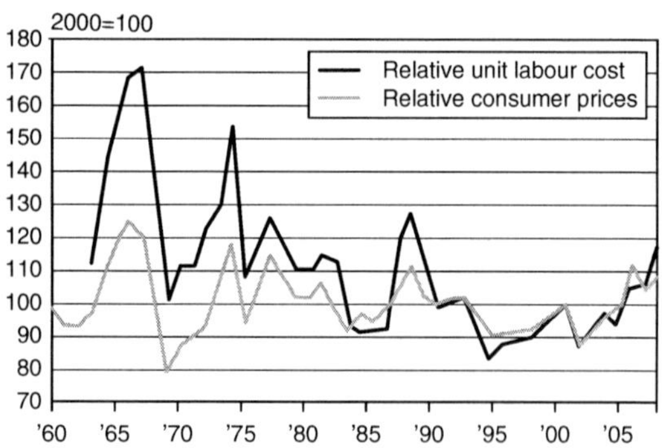


*Figure 11.13* Real effective exchange rate of the Icelandic krona, 1960–2007 (Preliminary 2007)
*Source*: Central Bank of Iceland.

of 'original sin'), means that the Central Bank of Iceland's interest rate 'hammer' has but a tiny anvil to hit.

Despite its pride in having a national currency that goes back over 200 years, it is probably time for Iceland to consider the costs and benefits of alternative arrangements. These costs and benefits are the subject of the next subsection of this report.

### 11.5.2 New optimal currency area criteria

The study of the costs and benefits of common currency areas goes back to the seminal work of Mundell (1961). Conventionally, the major cost of joining a common currency area is the loss of one's own monetary policy – the ability to set the short, risk-free nominal interest rate or the nominal spot exchange rate. This loss is harmful for two reasons. First, if there are asymmetric shocks in different member countries of a common currency area, then the common central bank cannot smooth output and employment in individual countries, even if there are persistent nominal price and/or cost rigidities. Second, if countries have different consumption baskets and if relative prices are changing, then even with a single monetary policy there will be different inflation rates in different countries. If, say, 2.5 per cent inflation per year is optimal then a central bank may be able to attain something close to this for the currency area as a whole, but not for individual countries.

The old literature on optimal currency areas looked at how various attributes of a country affected these costs. For example, if countries have flexible labour markets or there is labour mobility across countries, then this tends to offset not having a country-specific monetary policy to counteract the effect of idiosyncratic shocks affecting labour demand. If there are no material nominal wage or price rigidities, then monetary policy is ineffective in offsetting asymmetric shocks. If countries consumed similar consumption baskets, then even a one-size-fits-all monetary policy would produce similar rates of inflation across countries.

We argue, however, that these old optimal currency area criteria are not particularly relevant to the case of Iceland. It is true that cultural differences, language barriers and geography ensure that labour is unlikely to be especially mobile between Iceland and continental Europe. Although there have in recent years been quite sizeable labour flows between Iceland and both the Nordic countries and the Baltics, and although Iceland's internal labour market is flexible compared with much of continental Europe, it is not as flexible as those in the United States and New Zealand. The Icelandic consumption basket is unlikely to be similar to the Italian one. However, Icelandic monetary policy is certainly not delivering optimal inflation for Iceland and even if the Central Bank had a policy of offsetting shocks to the real economy in their own right (that is, as distinct from what shocks to the real economy imply for inflation), it clearly has not been effective and it is hard to believe that it would be effective in the future.

For these reasons, Buiter (2000) concluded that even on the conventional macroeconomic stabilization criteria for optimal currency area arguments, it made sense for Iceland to adopt the euro. With the spontaneous euroization of much of the economy that has taken place since then, the ability to conduct an independent monetary policy – even the best-practice form of inflation targeting with a flexible exchange rate – has been further impaired. National monetary independence makes no sense for Iceland today, even apart from the financial stability considerations we have emphasized in this chapter.

A conventional benefit of a common currency area is the reduction in transactions costs. While transactions costs in the financial wholesale markets are miniscule per transaction, volume is high. The European Commission (1990) estimated that these costs were 0.25–0.40 per cent of the total European Community GDP.

The krona, as measured by variations in the nominal and real effective exchange rates, is volatile relative to that of other advanced economies.[9] Moreover, the openness and small size of the Icelandic economy make its inhabitants particularly vulnerable to foreign exchange volatility. Every business and household in Iceland is in the position of having to be a foreign exchange speculator.

There is evidence to support the view that not all households have been wise speculators. Around 80 per cent of the foreign currency loans to households, for instance, were denominated in the two currencies with the lowest interest rates; the Japanese yen and the Swiss franc (see Figure 11.14). Iceland's households have therefore been enthusiastic proponents of the 'carry trade', borrowing where the interest rates are lowest, and forgetting about currency risk.

The real resource cost of this must be substantial and it leads to redistributions of income and wealth that are typically regarded as unfair: the wealthy and the educated gain at the expense of the poor and the unsophisticated.[10]

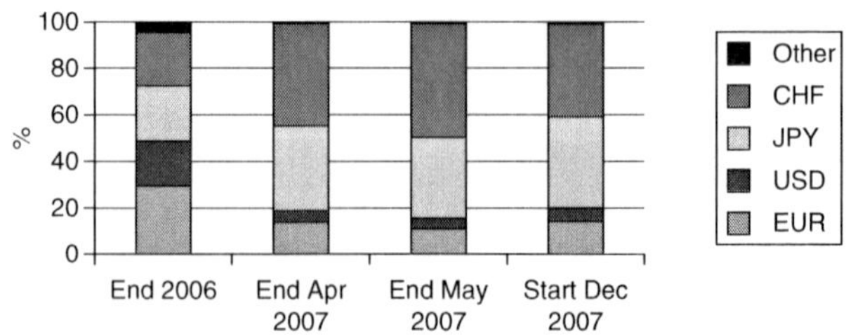


*Figure 11.14* Currency composition of household foreign currency borrowing from banks
*Source*: Central Bank of Iceland, borrowing from Kaupthing, Landsbanki and Glitnir.

### 11.5.3 Is there a third way? Temporary suspensions of capital account convertibility or a sovereign wealth fund for Iceland

#### *11.5.3.1 Temporary suspensions of capital account convertibility*

Other small countries with supposedly open capital accounts, including Latvia, have discouraged speculation against their currencies by not authorizing large transactions involving domestic currency borrowing, if these large amounts were not justified, in the opinion of the private banks and the Bank of Latvia (the Central Bank), by the needs of trade and normal financial transactions, but were instead part of an attempt to short the lats and cause the currency peg with the euro to collapse. Effectively, therefore, the Latvian commercial banks and the Bank of Latvia restricted the capital account convertibility of the lats. This clearly is against the letter of the *acquis communautaire*, but appears nevertheless to have been common practice during recent speculative attacks on the lats. We have off-the-record confirmation of this from sources in the Bank of Latvia, private Latvian banks and would-be lats borrowers who were sent away empty-handed.

This course of action – the de facto temporary and selective suspension of capital account convertibility – is not open to Iceland, if it wishes to retain its international banking business. In Latvia, about 80 per cent of the banking system is foreign-owned, mainly through subsidiaries of Swedish and other Nordic banks. These subsidiaries do not themselves engage in significant foreign banking business, other than funding themselves through the parents.

#### *11.5.3.1 A sovereign wealth fund for Iceland?*

Recently there have been proposals that Iceland should establish a sovereign wealth fund to bolster its volatile economy's defences against outside threats. An example is the proposal reported in the *Financial Times* of Thursday April 24 2008, by Björgólfur Gudmundsson, owner and chairman of Landsbanki. These proposals are quite distinct from our recommendation that the Icelandic authorities (and banks) acquire as many liquid foreign currency resources and establish as many foreign currency credit lines as possible. We view this as a short-term, emergency measure. When order is restored, the country will, in our view, have to choose between an internationally active banking sector and its national currency. The 'sovereign wealth fund proposals' are presented as a way for Iceland to retain both its internationally active banking presence and its national currency. It is meant to be a long-term solution.

We believe that the sovereign wealth fund terminology and the references to Norway's oil fund are rather misleading. We can distinguish three kinds of funds: sovereign wealth funds, stabilization funds and reserve funds, corresponding to investments made, respectively, for the long, the medium and the short run.

Sovereign wealth funds save, invest and disburse to smooth income and consumption across generations. Since they invest for the ages, they often invest in illiquid assets with long maturities. They are relevant especially for countries with exhaustible resources such as oil and natural gas. Norway is a country with large non-renewable resources. Intergenerational equity requires a sovereign wealth fund or some other public sector institutions for transferring resources among generations if private intergenerational concerns are not sufficiently strong.

Iceland does not have non-renewable resources that require a sovereign wealth fund to manage intergenerational equity. Its hydroelectric and geothermal energy resources are, for all practical purposes, renewable.

Stabilization funds aim to smooth cyclical fluctuations in real income and consumption, due to changes in the external terms of trade. They tend to be used by producers of renewable commodities for which the relative price in terms of the domestic consumption basket can swing wildly for reasons beyond the control of the country. Agricultural commodity producers are an example. Stabilization funds tend to be invested in rather liquid assets, as the timing of commodity price cycles is unpredictable. Iceland fits this category quite well, and will do so even more in the future when it may engage in direct exports of power via a cable to Scotland.

Reserve funds aim to provide liquidity for everyday transactions needs in the markets for internationally traded goods and services and for financial instruments. They also provide emergency liquidity to defend the currency, the stock market or the banks against speculative attacks or against the consequences of liquidity crises that are not due to reasonable concerns about the long-term solvency of the banks or other institutions of the country. Reserve funds have to invest in highly liquid foreign assets, as a crisis may strike at any time, and the availability of liquidity exactly when it is needed is key.

Given enough time, Iceland could build up a stock of liquid foreign exchange reserves large enough to compensate for any conceivable interruption in the supply of external credit to its banks and for any illiquidity in the markets for the banks' foreign currency assets. Building up a stock of reserves large enough to discourage speculative attacks on its stock market or on its currency would be more difficult, if the authorities maintain a truly open set of international financial markets. As long as it is possible for a would-be speculator to borrow from the Icelandic banks any amount of kronur and to invest these kronur in foreign currencies, it is not possible to build up a stock of reserves so large it cannot be exhausted in a speculative attack. Of course, domestic interest rates can be raised to make this expensive, but even a small depreciation of the exchange rate over a short time interval swamps the cost of high interest rates over that time interval.

So building up a stock of liquid foreign assets large enough to prevent large swings in exchange rates and in the stock market driven by speculative attacks is not a realistic possibility. It is, however, possible to build up a stock of liquid foreign assets large enough to ensure the survival of the banking system when this is faced with a liquidity crunch that prevents it from borrowing abroad and from selling its foreign currency assets at acceptable prices. There are two problems with this 'third way', however.

First, it would take time to build up a sufficient stock of liquid official foreign assets. Iceland may not have enough time to get to the point that it can self-insure against interruptions of international funding liquidity and of international market liquidity. Second, even if there were to be, following the current crisis, a period of tranquillity long enough to permit the necessary stock of foreign assets to be accumulated, it is likely that the venture would be unprofitable. The fund would be quite unlike a sovereign wealth fund. It would have to be held in the most liquid possible form, to ensure its immediate availability in case of a crisis. By effectively undoing the maturity and liquidity transformation of the banking sector, this large investment in liquid assets could destroy the social profitability of Iceland's international banking activities. It is questionable whether these international banking activities would be privately profitable, if the authorities were to charge the banks the full opportunity cost of the liquidity insurance services provided by the authorities through their liquid foreign asset holdings.

## 11.6 Conclusion

Iceland's economy is highly vulnerable to financial shocks. Iceland's banks have recently been exposed both to interruptions of funding liquidity and to interruptions of market liquidity in key markets for their assets. As regards shocks to funding liquidity, although Iceland's banks have not experienced classical bank runs (a sudden withdrawal of deposits), they have been subject to its credit market counterpart – the refusal by the bank's creditors to roll over maturing credit, secured or unsecured. As regards shocks to market liquidity, there have been wholesale financial market 'strikes' – liquidity shortages in the wholesale financial markets in which banks and other highly leveraged financial institutions fund themselves to a growing extent. Exchange rate volatility and instability, the huge spreads in the Icelandic banks' CDS markets and the de facto exclusion of these banks from the international wholesale financial markets, are but the most visible manifestations of the financial difficulty Iceland finds itself in.

In the years leading up to the crisis, there were indeed speculative inflows of capital, followed by sudden reversals, and these have been associated with large swings in the nominal and real exchange rates. There is also a quite familiar story of structural reform and financial liberalization leading to a massive investment boom (first in aluminium smelting and then in residential and commercial construction) which resulted in an overheating economy, a very large current account deficit and a growing negative net international investment position.

But these fundamental distortions are not capable of explaining the magnitude of the financial disturbances that have been part of Iceland's economic landscape for the past few years. The massive financial dislocation can only be explained by considering Iceland's spectacular growth as a financial intermediary, with gross foreign assets and liabilities rising eight- and ninefold as a share of GDP in less than a decade. Iceland has indeed become a highly leveraged financial institution with massive asset–liability mismatch – a 'hedge fund' in tabloid language. The North Atlantic financial crisis hit the country, not because its investments had been of poor quality – its sub-prime exposure is quite limited – but because the liquidity crunch and disorderly financial markets in North America and Europe are making it difficult if not impossible for the internationally active Icelandic banks to refinance their maturing obligations.

While there has not been a deposit run on any of the Icelandic banks, the seizing up of the interbank markets, the ABS markets, ABCP markets and other sources of wholesale funding have created a crisis. The Icelandic banks need a foreign currency lender of last resort. Unfortunately, the Central Bank of Iceland cannot print foreign currency, so its undoubted competence and good intentions are not enough to cope with the crisis. The short-term solution is to seek funding abroad: from other central banks, the market and the IMF. The best medium-term solution is for Iceland to join the EU and to adopt the euro as soon as possible.

The only alternative is to move its foreign currency banking activities to the euro area.

The reason Iceland is no longer a viable currency area has nothing to do with the familiar trade and normal capital flows-based OCA arguments – although these arguments also suggest that Iceland would be better off in the euro area. Unilateral euroization would deliver macroeconomic stability benefits, but would not provide Iceland with a lender of last resort and market maker of last resort capable of creating euros at will. It would therefore do nothing to enhance Iceland's financial stability. Iceland's business model, operating internationally in the financial markets with high leverage, is not compatible with its currency regime.

A convincing case for Iceland becoming a full member of the euro area as soon as possible can be based solely on financial stability arguments: only the ECB and the Eurosystem can act as a viable lender of last resort and market maker of last resort for Iceland.

## Notes

1. The arrangements with the central banks of Sweden, Norway and Denmark were for euro/Icelandic krona bilateral swap facilities. In an earlier version of this chapter, circulated in April 2008, we recommended the pursuit of swap arrangements with the three Scandinavian central banks, all three of which are outside the euro area.
2. Glitnir and Kaupthing each get about a quarter of their funding from deposits, the same fraction as Northern Rock. Landsbanki raised its share of total funding coming from deposits to around 40 per cent in July 2008 from 25 per cent before the crisis started.
3. See e.g. Glitnir Bank (2008a).
4. Fitch affirmed the long-term foreign currency and local currency issuer default ratings at 'A+' and 'AA+', respectively.
5. On 1 April, Fitch placed Glitnir Banki hf.'s, Kaupthing Bank hf.'s and Landsbanki Islands' long-term and short-term issuer default ratings, senior and subordinated debt ratings and individual ratings on rating watch negative. The long-term issuer default ratings and the senior debt ratings of all three banks were affirmed at 'A'.
6. See Glitnir (2008b), Kaupthing (2008) and Landsbanki (2008).
7. The Switzerland-domiciled part of the Swiss banking system (this excludes the foreign subsidiaries of Swiss banks) derives an unknown but probably substantial part of its revenues and profits from the rents Switzerland creates and appropriates through its bank secrecy laws and its resulting position as a tax haven. We do not recommend that Iceland actively pursue tax haven status, both for practical and for ethical reasons.
8. There are some obvious things that Iceland could do to make monetary policy easier. The first is for the government to change the way it subsidizes

housing and to exit the home lending market. Currently, the HHF competes with private banks in the mortgage market. It funds its lending by issuing government-guaranteed long-term index bonds, making its costs insensitive to monetary policy. Firms in the oligopolistic private banking sector have an incentive to squeeze their profit margins, rather than raise their rates when the policy rate increases. Another thing that Iceland could do is to rethink the way that house prices are included in the price index, so that what is measured is the user cost of house prices and so that the price index is not distorted by house price volatility.

9. See Kallestrup (2008) for a recent study.
10. It should also be noted that having an independent monetary policy is not costless. The Central Bank employs 115 persons and the payroll and other operating costs in 2007 were 1,334,290,000 kr. With a population of only 312,872 and at an exchange rate of 74 kr/dollar, this amounts to a cost of almost $57 per person per year.

## References

Buiter, Willem H. (2000) 'Is Iceland an Optimal Currency Area?' in Mar Gudmundsson, Tryggvi Thor Herbertsson and Gylfi Zoega (eds), *Macroeconomic Policy; Iceland in an Era of Global Integration*, University of Iceland Press, Reykjavik, pp. 33–55.

Buiter, Willem H. (2007) *'Seigniorage'*, *economics* – The Open-Access, Open-Assessment E-Journal, 2007–10. http://www.economics-ejournal.org/economics/journalarticles/2007-10.

Buiter, Willem H. (2008) 'Can Central Banks go Broke', CEPR Policy Insight 24, May 17, http://www.cepr.org/Pubs/PolicyInsights/CEPR_Policy_Insight_024.asp.

Central Bank of Iceland (2007) *Financial Stability* 2007.

Central Bank of Iceland (2008a) *Financial Stability* 2008.

Central Bank of Iceland (2008b) *Monetary Bulletin*, July 2008 and earlier issues.

Commission of the European Communities (1990) 'One Market, One Money'. In *European Economy*, special issue, European Commission, Brussels.

Glitnir Bank (2008a) Glitnir Research News, 17/07/2008, http://www.glitnir.is/english/markets/research/?BirtaGrein=621887

Glitnir Bank (2008b) *Condensed Consolidated Interim Financial Statements*, 31 March 2008.

IMF (2007) Article IV Consultation, Staff Report.

Kallestrup, René (2008) 'The Volatility of the Icelandic Krona', *Monetary Bulletin* 10, Central Bank of Iceland, 101–112.

Kaupthing Bank (2008) Condensed Consolidated Interim Financial Statements, 1 January–31 March 2008.

Landsbanki (2008) Condensed Consolidated Interim Financial Statements, 1 January–31 March 2008.

Miskin, Frederic S. and Tryggvi Thor Herbertsson (2006) Financial Stability in Iceland, Iceland Chamber of Commerce, Reykjavik, Iceland; http://www.verslunarrad.is/files/555877819Financial%20Stability%20in%20Iceland%20Screen%20Version.pdf

Mundell, Robert, 2861 'A Theory of Optimum Currency Areas'. *American Economic Review*, 51, 657–1965.

Portes, Richard, Fridrik Már Baldursson and Frosti Ólafsson (2007) *The Internationalisation of Iceland's Financial Sector*, Iceland Chamber of Commerce, Reykjavik, Iceland.

Svavarsson, Daniel (2008) 'International Investment Position: Market Valuation and the Effects of External Changes', *Central Bank of Iceland, Monetary Bulletin*, 2008/1.

# 12

# Iceland on the Brink? Options for a Small, Financially Active Economy in the Current Financial Crisis Environment

*Daniel Gros*

## Summary

Iceland has developed an oversized banking system – with assets valued at eight times its GDP which has effectively transformed the country into a hedge fund. Domestic banks have borrowed heavily abroad to buy foreign banking assets, leveraging their capital base several times over. As a bust is following the global boom in the banking sector, the country is highly exposed to the current crisis. The lender of last resort in Iceland would not be able to save even one of the large domestic banks should write downs in the value of foreign assets bring any one of them into difficulties. Other European countries with financial centres have either avoided becoming lender of last resort for their banks (Luxembourg) or accumulated large foreign assets as a cushion (Switzerland). By contrast, Iceland's extremely high net foreign debt ratio adds to the vulnerability of the country, which thus resembles a hedge fund with negative capital.

Moreover, Iceland has experienced a construction/housing boom even more extreme than in the US or the one now ending in Spain.

This exposes the country to the classical combination of an exchange rate cum banking crisis coupled with a long real estate bust.

Exchange rate devaluation can provide only limited compensation for the housing construction bust that seems unavoidable because Iceland is a rather closed economy, with manufacturing exports accounting for less than 10 per cent of GDP.

## Introduction

For small financially active countries the exchange rate assumes particular importance, not only as a shock absorber, but potentially also as a source of shocks during financial market crises. This is very much in evidence today in the case of Iceland which is being hit hard by the recent turbulence in financial markets.

In March of 2008, the Icelandic Central Bank was forced to increase interest rates to unprecedented levels in an effort to stem a rapid depreciation of the currency. This raises the question of whether the authorities in the special case of Iceland would have eliminated one source of shock to the economy and thus helped to stabilize the currency if it had abandoned the national currency.

Euro area members, including Luxembourg, which is also home to large internationally active banks, have so far been spared the worst effects of the ongoing 'sub-prime' crisis. But this positive experience of member countries of the euro area might not be relevant for Iceland since its economy differs in some key aspects from that of the 'average' euro area member – and even that of Luxembourg, as will be documented below.

The prime example of a country adopting the euro outside the euro area is Montenegro. The euro in Montenegro has been a success so far. Even the European institutions (especially the ECB), which were very hostile at the start, have now come to the conclusion that Montenegro should keep this arrangement for the time being. Montenegro is also a very small state (with a population of ±600,000) but it offers few lessons (except that unilateral euroization is technically feasible) for Iceland because it practically did not have any banking system and was not integrated in the global financial system.

Iceland has two features that distinguish it from most euro area members (apart from size): its limited degree of trade integration and the extraordinary degree of financial integration. Both features are relevant for the choice of an exchange rate regime. On both counts joining the euro should be advantageous for Iceland.

In short the argument would be that adopting the euro should stimulate trade. Moreover, adopting the euro could avoid large shocks that arise from the mixture of very large onshore and offshore banking activities in domestic banks, which have become 'too big to be saved'. However, it is also clear that the choice of the currency cannot affect the fundamental problem of Iceland, namely that the country as such is highly exposed to the international banking market. Whatever the choice of the currency, living standards in Iceland will have to adjust to the real value of the banking assets bought in recent years.

The remainder of this chapter elaborates on these two points, keeping in mind that the most useful comparator countries for Iceland are Luxembourg, Switzerland and Cyprus, all of which have very large financial systems and share a high degree of financial integration. So far it seems that Luxembourg, which is a member of the eurozone, is the most successful.

## 12.1 Real openness

The main economic argument for euro area membership has always been that it facilitates commerce. Recent research indicates that this has indeed been the case, but the effects are only now slowly building up.

For Iceland the limited degree of trade integration suggests that the static gain from eliminating transaction costs on trade might be limited, but the potential dynamic gain from an increase in trade integration might be very large. Despite its small size Iceland has a smaller trade/GDP ratio than Germany or many other EU member countries. It is possible that euro area membership might lead to a quantum change in the degree of trade integration, as predicted by a large body of research, but progress in terms of trade integration within the eurozone itself has in reality been gradual.

Table 12.1(a) shows that both in terms of the importance of trade (for both imports and exports) and the composition of trade, Iceland is relatively closed relative to its size. Exports of manufacturing goods in particular seem to be very small relative to its comparators.

An often commented feature of the Icelandic economy is its large trade deficit, which is mainly due to the surge of capital goods imports in 2006. However, most of this is destined for the construction of an aluminium smelter, which will export most of its production. Hence, the 2000 data give a better idea of the degree of import penetration of Iceland, which for its size was rather low in 2000, at around 27 per cent of GDP. Table 12.1(b) provides a comparison with Germany, which shows that despite the huge differences in size, Germany is, on most measures, more open to imports than Iceland.

The fiscally weaker member countries had an additional reason to join EMU, namely to forestall potential speculative attacks and participate

*Table 12.1(a)* Iceland's import boom (% of GDP)

| | *1995* | *2000* | *2006* |
|---|---|---|---|
| Imports of consumption goods | 8.8 | 8.6 | 9.8 |
| Imports of capital and consumption goods | 13.4 | 15.4 | 20.3 |
| Imports of capital goods | 4.6 | 6.8 | 10.5 |
| Imports of intermediate goods | 11.5 | 11.9 | 16.4 |
| Imports | 24.9 | 27.3 | 36.7 |

*Source*: UN trade database.

*Table 12.1(b)* Germany and Iceland: comparing degrees of openness (% of GDP)

| | *Imports of intermediate goods* | | *Total imports* | |
|---|---|---|---|---|
| | *1995* | *2006* | *1995* | *2006* |
| Germany | 20.0 | 18.5 | 30.4 | 30.8 |
| Iceland | 11.5 | 16.4 | 24.9 | 36.7 |

*Source*: Ameco.

*Table 12.1(c)* How important are exports? (% of GDP)

| | *Goods* | | *Goods and services* | |
|---|---|---|---|---|
| | *1995* | *2007* | *1995* | *2007* |
| Iceland | 26.0 | 20.4 | 35.5 | 35.6 |
| Germany | 8.5 | 14.4 | 24.0 | 46.6 |
| Cyprus | 1.8 | 2.1 | 50.0 | 46.8 |
| Luxembourg | 4.8 | 5.6 | 106.4 | 172.0 |
| Switzerland | 25.7 | 38.1 | 35.9 | 54.7 |

*Source*: AMECO.

in the credibility of the new institution (itself based initially on that of the Bundesbank). Given its very strong fiscal position (essentially zero public debt) and the high quality of its strong institutions in general, Iceland would also not need to import the credibility of the ECB.

More importantly, Iceland stands out even more in its extraordinarily low level of exports. The export-to-GDP ratio is much below the average euro area member country, and only a fraction of the smaller euro area countries, or that of Switzerland (also financially active) or even that of Germany, as shown in Table 12.1(c).

Table 12.1(d) shows that especially in terms of exports of manufacturing goods, Iceland (which amount to less than 9 per cent of GDP) is a rather closed economy. The distinction between manufacturing goods and other, resource-based goods, is important because the supply of the latter is really not influenced by domestic wage and cost elements. An adjustment in the real exchange rate can stimulate the economy mainly by making domestically manufactured goods more competitive on the world market. However, this mechanism seems to be less important in Iceland than one would expect given the small size of the economy. For Germany, Luxembourg and Switzerland, exports of manufacturing

*Table 12.1(d)* The importance of manufacturing exports (% of GDP)

| | *1995* | *2006* |
|---|---|---|
| Iceland | 5.7 | 8.6 |
| Germany | 19.0 | 33.5 |
| Cyprus | 5.9 | 4.2 |
| Luxembourg | | 29.0 |
| Switzerland | 24.6 | 34.0 |

*Source*: UN trade database.

goods are more than three times as important. Only Cyprus has an even lower export ratio for manufacturing goods, but Cyprus exports mainly services (tourism) to an extent that could never be replicated in Iceland.

## 12.2 Financial integration

The most remarkable feature of Iceland's economy in recent years has been the explosion of financial openness. In a very short period of time Iceland seems to have reached the level of Switzerland (on a per capita basis) as shown in Table 12.2. For Luxembourg, the gross foreign investment positions would be an order of magnitude larger, but this would be a misleading comparison given the special 'offshore' nature of its banking system.

The key difference between Switzerland and Iceland is that, on a per capita basis, Switzerland has accumulated a surplus position that is equivalent in size (close to one full year of GDP) to Iceland's net debtor position. Moreover, Icelandic banks have issued a total of over $40 billion in debt securities in the last few years of which 'only' $14 billion were needed to finance the cumulative current account surpluses since 2000, with the remaining funds (around $28 billion) used to finance foreign equity acquisitions (about $11 billion) and $17 billion in banking assets abroad.

One concern about large gross foreign asset and liabilities positions is that the reported returns might be variable and thus distort the measured current account. However, this does not seem to be the case for Iceland since the reported rates of return (calculated as investment income divided by the gross position) all seem reasonable. On average, Iceland pays an interest rate of about 7 per cent on its net foreign debt (Table 12.3).

*Table 12.2* Net foreign investment positions ($ billion)

| | *Iceland* | | | *Switzerland* | |
|---|---|---|---|---|---|
| | *2000* | *2006* | *Change* | *2006* | *Scaled to size of ISL* |
| Net FDI | 0.2 | 5.7 | 5.5 | 314.1 | 9.5 |
| Net PI | −1.9 | −37.8 | −35.9 | 119.1 | 3.6 |
| Net PI EQ | 2.1 | 7.9 | 5.8 | 262.5 | −8.0 |
| Net PI debt | −4.0 | −45.7 | −41.7 | 381.6 | 11.6 |
| Net banks | −2.0 | 14.6 | 16.6 | −55.1 | −1.7 |
| Net other | −1.3 | −4.0 | −2.7 | | |
| Net IIP | −5.3 | −19.5 | −14.1 | 459.2 | 13.9 |

PI = private investment; IIP = international investment position; EQ = equity.
*Source*: IMF, IFS.

*Table 12.3* Rates of return on foreign assets and liabilities of Iceland (%)

| | *2006* |
|---|---|
| Assets | 3.8 |
| Liabilities | −4.7 |
| NIIP (net/net) | 7.4 |

NIIP = net international investment position.
*Source*: IMF, IFS.

## 12.3 Consequences of financial openness

### 12.3.1 Shift in sources of foreign exchange earnings–outlays

One implication of the foreign financial activities of Icelandic firms is that the importance of 'normal' exports of goods and services as key sources of foreign exchange income (and outlays) has diminished rapidly in recent years. Since investment income does not respond to the exchange rate, this implies that movements of the exchange rate have a relatively smaller influence on the current account, and that larger movements might be required to adjust to shocks (whether to investment income or just to the availability of foreign capital).

Tables 12.4(a)–(c) show this for Iceland and provide a comparison with three European economies that are also engaged in global financial activism. It is apparent that the financial sector is even more important in Luxembourg, but Iceland seems to have surpassed Cyprus and reached the level of Switzerland.

*Table 12.4(a)* Evolution in the structure of foreign exchange sources in Iceland

| | *Foreign exchange earnings* | | *Foreign exchange outlays* | |
|---|---|---|---|---|
| | *1999* | *2006* | *1999* | *2006* |
| Goods | 65.5 | 45 | 64 | 47 |
| Services | 30.3 | 24 | 28 | 21 |
| Investment income | 4.2 | 31 | 8 | 32 |

*Table 12.4(b)* Distribution of foreign exchange earnings, 2006: a comparison

| | *ISL* | *CH* | *LUX* | *CY* |
|---|---|---|---|---|
| Goods | 45 | 51 | 10 | 14 |
| Services | 24 | 16 | 31 | 77 |
| Investment income | 31 | 33 | 59 | 8 |

*Table 12.4(c)* Percentage distribution of foreign exchange outlays, 2006

| | *ISL* | *CH* | *LUX* | *CY* |
|---|---|---|---|---|
| Goods | 47 | 63 | 13 | 57 |
| Services | 21 | 11 | 19 | 29 |
| Investment income | 32 | 26 | 68 | 14 |

*Source*: IMF, IFS.

### 12.3.2 Lender of last resort responsibility for the banking sector

One key aspect of the stability of a banking system is the credibility of the lender of last resort (LOLR). Under normal circumstances, this is not an issue because the public institutions that provide this function (either central banks or national treasuries) have deep pockets compared to the size of any individual bank. In an economy that functions as a global financial centre, however, this might no longer be the case. For example, the Swiss National Bank is increasingly concerned that the cost of support for the large global Swiss banks might be beyond its capacity.

In Luxembourg, where the banking sector is even larger (compared to the local economy), the problem does not arise because the Luxembourg authorities have always insisted that the subsidiaries of foreign banks

*Table 12.5* Loan–deposit ratios

| | *ISL* | *CH* | *LUX* |
|---|---|---|---|
| 2007/11 | 3.42 | 2.22 | 0.52 |
| 2003/11 | 1.93 | 1.04 | 0.48 |

*Source*: IMF banking statistics.

have a clear owner that is also a bank so that the home country remains the LOLR.

Liechtenstein has retained responsibility for lending of last resort, but has a special arrangement with the Swiss National Bank in order to be able to dispose of Swiss francs, its national currency.

In Cyprus the main foreign financial activity is not via banks, but investment via Cyprus-domiciled enterprises that take advantage of existing favourable double-taxation treaties to recycle savings from Russia and other Eastern European countries.

How large is the risk for the lender of last resort? One indicator of the risk is the loan–deposit ratio because it indicates to what extent banks depend on sources other than (usually very stable) deposits to finance their business. Given the large size of the Icelandic banking system it might not be useful to compare it to other large OECD countries, but Iceland constitutes an outlier even among financial centres such as Switzerland or Luxembourg (Table 12.5).

Given that banks everywhere are facing problems at present in raising funds on the capital markets, this extreme dependency of Icelandic banks on the capital market constitutes a potentially very serious problem. There might not be a short problem à la Northern Rock, since Icelandic banks have secured sufficient long-term financing and stand-by facilities for the coming year, but in the longer term the risk remains.

## 12.4 Has financial integration paid off? The growth record so far

The special feature of the Icelandic economy that dominates all other aspects is the (recent) explosion of global financial activity. This is why one has to compare Iceland to the other European countries with large financial sectors: Luxembourg and Switzerland. Cyprus can also provide a useful comparison since it also has a population only twice that of Iceland, but as a recent member country and an even more recent member of the euro area, it is difficult to draw any conclusions yet.

Since Switzerland is not in the eurozone, it is also difficult to draw direct lessons from its experience, but a triangular comparison (ISL, LUX, CH) might be useful. In short it seems that Luxembourg has in the medium term benefited strongly from euro area membership, performing much better than Switzerland since the euro's launch.

Financial centres or economies with a very large globally active financial sector face the problem of how to insulate the domestic economy, which depends on regular flows of production of goods and services, from the large shocks that might come from shifts in the values of the stock of assets and liabilities in the financial sector. In Luxembourg this problem has been resolved by joining the eurozone and making the banking system offshore (Cyprus has recently made the decision regarding the currency). In Switzerland the domestic economy has so far been large enough to absorb the shocks in the financial sphere, and the national currency has been managed, de facto, very tightly. Moreover, the country has consistently run large current account deficits, providing an extra cushion.

How have these three economies performed over the last decade? In terms of GDP per capita (at purchasing power parity) Luxembourg has grown far more strongly than either Iceland or Switzerland, both of which seem to be in relative decline (Figures 12.1 and 12.2).

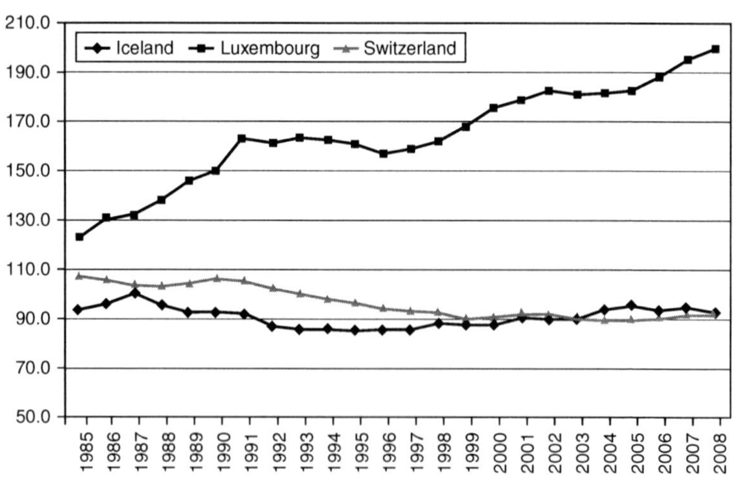


*Figure 12.1* GDP as % of US GDP (PPP per capita)
*Source*: Ameco.

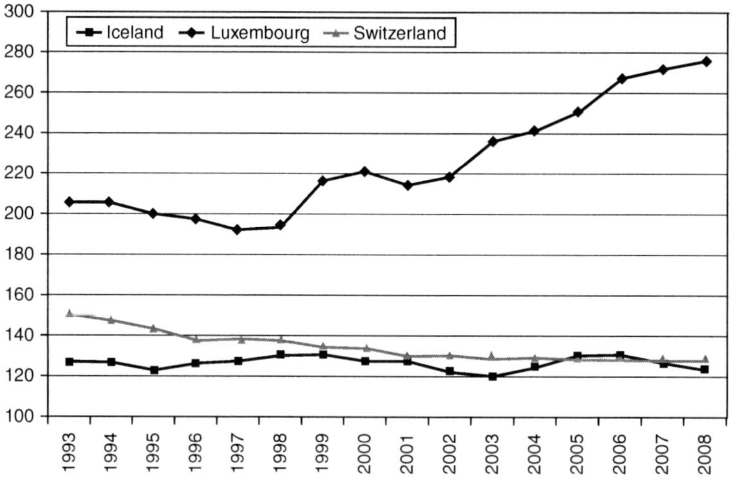


*Figure 12.2* GDP (PPS per capita)
*Source*: European Commission.

## 12.5 Housing/construction boom

Iceland has recently experienced a housing boom, which does not seem to have an equivalent anywhere else among OECD countries. Two figures provide a graphic description of the phenomenon.

Figure 12.3 shows that the overall construction investment has now reached 20 per cent of GDP, which is almost twice the value of the US and higher even than the value reached by Spain (18 per cent of GDP).

It might be argued that part of the construction activity in Iceland will create productive capacity for the export sector (hydroelectricity capacity coupled with aluminium smelters). Hence one might want to look at investment in housing alone to measure the extent of the real estate boom. However, even on this metric, the boom in Iceland beats all records. Investment in dwellings is still close to 11 per cent of GDP, which is almost twice the US value and much higher than the Spanish value (which is the highest among the euro area countries) (see Figure 12.4). Since investment in housing has been above the norm required for an essentially stable population for some time, it follows that a substantial housing overhang is likely to have been built up. The coming housing slump thus promises to be long and deep – as in the case of Germany whose values are also shown for purposes of comparison.

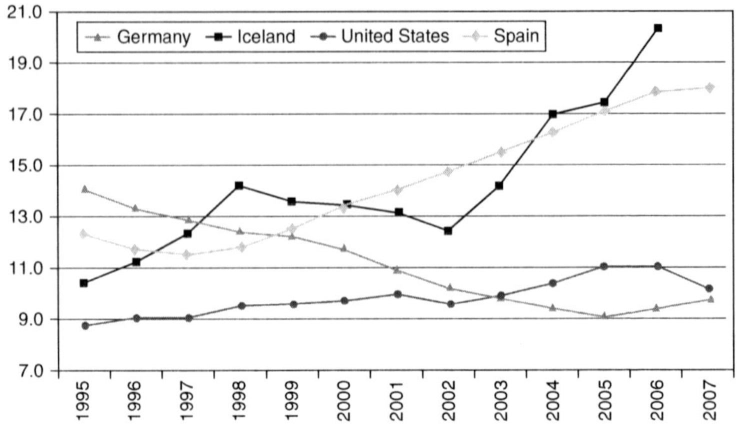


*Figure 12.3* Investment in construction (% of GDP)
*Source*: Ameco.

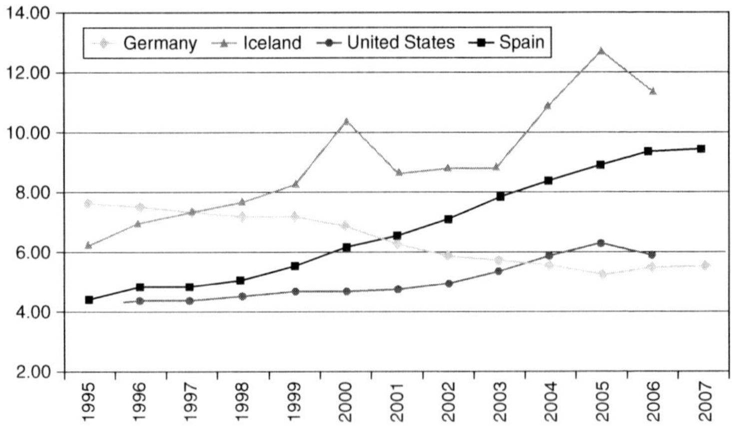


*Figure 12.4* Investment in dwellings (% of GDP)
*Source*: Ameco.

The loss of domestic demand from the construction sector alone could easily amount to 10 per cent of GDP over the next few years. This will be difficult to compensate for with exports, given that manufacturing exports amount only to less than 10 per cent of GDP, as documented in Table 12.1(d). These exports (the only ones that respond to the exchange rate) would have to double if the adjustment to the unavoidable retrenchment in the construction sector is not to lead to a large drop in demand and GDP.

Sweden during the 1990s constitutes a similar case: housing investment had also been increasing in that country until the early 1990s. However, when the crisis broke, the currency had to be devalued massively and interest rates rose to extremely high levels and the banking system was under intensive stress. As a result housing investment fell from over 6% of GDP (still far below the current value for Iceland) to less than 2% of GDP. See Figures 12.5 and 12.6.[1]

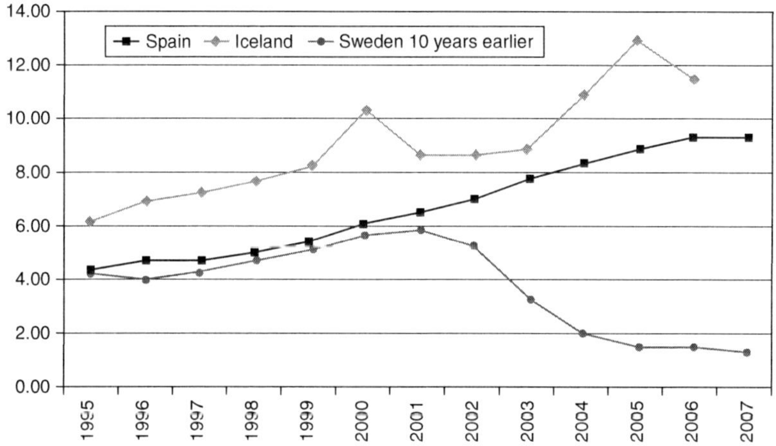


*Figure 12.5* Investment in dwellings

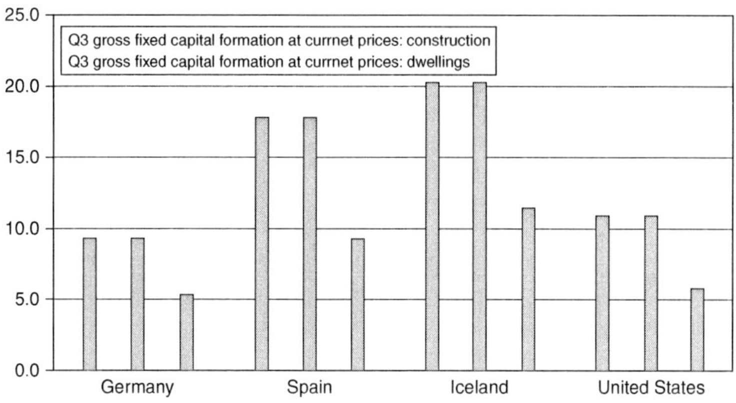


*Figure 12.6* Investment in constructions and dwellings, 2006

## 12.6 Concluding remarks

This chapter has argued that a priori the most useful comparators for Iceland should be other small economies with large and sophisticated financial sectors. Hence, Luxembourg (founding member of the eurozone), Switzerland (outside) and possibly Cyprus (recent eurozone member). However, Iceland differs even from these comparators because of its lower degree of trade integration, the concentration of its foreign financial activity in the banking sector (here Switzerland is most similar) and its very large foreign debt (unique).

What do the special features of the Icelandic economy imply for the choice of the exchange rate system?

The low degree of trade integration of Iceland might be related to the small size of the national currency area. Joining the EMU might bring large dynamic benefits, but experience so far suggests that these benefits will take time to materialize.

The high degree of financial integration in Iceland could be problematic and here the details matter. If the onshore and offshore parts of the banking system were neatly separated, fluctuations in the exchange rate might not be a cause for concern. However, the mixture of both elements, moreover concentrated in just three very large banks, creates a potential for serious problems. A particular reason for concern is that the correlation between the stock market (i.e. the market value of domestic banks) and the exchange rate is close to unity. The foreign activities of the banks now provide a large proportion of their profits. In principle, the euro value of these foreign profits should be independent of the exchange rate of the krona against the euro. Hence the correlation between the stock market and the exchange rate should in principle be negative (this is why some banks would like to list their shares in euro). However, the strong positive correlation between the stock market and the external value of the krona suggests that in reality the market expects that a depreciation has a negative impact on bank profits. This could happen only through the one channel that always renders domestic lending in foreign currency problematic: when the exchange rate devalues, domestic enterprises have difficulty servicing their foreign exchange debt.

The financial markets themselves thus suggest that exchange rate fluctuations might be an important source of shocks (rather than a shock absorber). This suggests that Iceland might want to follow the example of Luxembourg and Cyprus in opting for the euro, or it would have to clearly separate the onshore and offshore parts of its banking system.

In going for the euro, Iceland would face the additional difficulty that it is particularly difficult at present to determine the appropriate exchange rate. The ongoing boom in the real estate sector is likely to have boosted domestic demand above the level sustainable in the long term. This suggests that a very large adjustment of the real exchange rate will be needed once the housing market turns. Germany experienced a much smaller construction boom after unification and, despite being a much more open economy than Iceland, it took ten years to digest the bust that followed that boom.

While adopting the euro might be an optimal long-term approach for Iceland, it is also clear that the country faces a fundamental problem that is independent of the choice of the exchange rate regime: over the last few years, its banks have leveraged a relatively small capital base to buy up banking assets worth several times the country's GDP. These assets were bought close to the height of the global credit and banking boom. Now that the boom has turned to a bust and banking assets have to be revalued everywhere, the key risk for the country is that these foreign banking assets will turn out to be worth much less than what Icelandic banks paid for them. If this scenario materializes, the country would incur an even larger foreign debt and the authorities might be called upon to save Icelandic banks from insolvency. As this would clearly overstretch the financial capacity of both the Central Bank and the Ministry of Finance, the best solution to this looming problem would be arrange for the sale of these banks, which are 'too large to be rescued' to foreign bank groups. The currency question could then be solved rather easily.

## Note

1. The busts in Scandinavia (not only in Sweden as discussed, but also in Finland and Denmark) during the 1990s were sharper, but also shorter than the real estate-induced slowdowns in Germany (post-1995) and Japan (since 1990). For more details, see Daniel Gros (2008), *Bubbles in Real Estate? A Longer-Term Comparative Analysis of Housing Prices in Europe and the US*, CEPS WD No. 276, CEPS, Brussels.

# 13

# Events in Iceland: Skating on Thin Ice?

*Thorvaldur Gylfason*

## Summary

Recent events have commentators discussing whether Iceland is in danger of an economic meltdown. This chapter examines the situation in detail, explaining the sources of today's financial woes and why, despite serious need for reform, Iceland's fundamentals are strong.

Is Iceland in danger of financial collapse? The *Wall Street Journal* recently commented that 'Iceland looks like an ideal bearish bet'. But many economists disagree. A bit of political history may help illuminate recent developments.

For decades, beginning in 1927 when a farmers' party gained a majority in parliament with the support of just a third of the electorate, the Icelandic economy was more heavily regulated than most in Western Europe, with the possible exception of Ireland. Interference and planning were the norm; enterprise and markets were viewed with scepticism if not hostility. Without much exaggeration, the state tried to restrain almost anything that moved. The state owned the largest commercial banks and used them to allocate scarce funds to favoured industries and firms; undervalued foreign exchange was rationed the same way. Domestic saving dried up, which necessitated external borrowing on a large scale because, for nationalistic reasons, foreign investment was kept at bay (and banned from the fishing industry, a ban still in force).

A radical liberalization of the policy regime in the 1960s helped modernize the nation by reducing subsidies to the fishing industry and devaluing the krona. Even so, the liberalization was incomplete; for one thing, it left the banks in the hands of the state. Besides, the tight, almost suffocating, embrace of producers and the government remained intact, an embrace that helps explain why, to this day, the Confederation of Icelandic Employers remains unwilling to advocate EU membership and thus go against the wishes of the senior coalition party in government, the sole mainstream centre-right party in Europe so disinclined.

## Iceland became Russia

The first wave of liberalization in the early 1960s was not accompanied by a necessary depoliticization of economic life, nor was the second wave that started in the late 1980s. The second wave involved deregulation of domestic interest rates and foreign capital flows, indexation of financial obligations to prices, entry into the European Economic Area in 1994, and privatization of commercial banks and investment funds during 1998–2003 when two of the largest state banks were sold. They were, however, sold both at once at a price deemed modest by the National Audit Office. Moreover, the banks were sold not to foreign banks like in Eastern Europe – Estonia, for example – but to individuals closely linked to the political parties in power. One beneficiary of the banks' privatization – a politician whose private-sector experience consisted of running two small knitwear factories in the 1970s, a few months each – became an instant billionaire. Another flew in Elton John for a birthday celebration. I could go on, but you get my drift: Iceland became Russia. A former prime minister 1991–2004, demoted after an election loss to foreign minister 2004–5, unilaterally announced his retirement from politics as well as his appointment, with immediate effect, as governor of the Central Bank in 2005; his salary was quickly lifted above that of the President of the Republic. The banks and the borrowing public got the message: the sky is the limit.

## Escalating debts

Free at last from state control, the banks kicked up their heels like cows in spring and went on an unprecedented borrowing and lending spree that increased the amount of domestic credit from the banking system from 100 per cent of GDP in 2000 to 450 per cent in 2007. The banks' business model was in essence imported from abroad: with few questions asked, loan officers were rewarded according to the volume of loans they made and other transactions. The banks appeared to believe, as did at least one international rating agency, that the state guarantees behind them while in public ownership were still in force, and the government did little to counter this impression. The banks borrowed short at low interest in foreign markets to finance long-term loans, including 25–40 year mortgages, thereby creating maturity mismatches in their books. Many customers who signed mortgages with variable interest rates – that is, 4 per cent real rates subject to renegotiation after a five-year grace period – were unaware that their mortgages were being financed by short-term loans. Household debt reached 240 per cent of their disposable incomes in 2007, up from 40 per cent in 1983 and 80 per cent in 1990. The boom in the housing market has now come to an abrupt halt.

Public debt, on the other hand, was cut in half from 55 per cent of GDP in 1994 to 28 per cent in 2007 as the government repaid earlier loans with receipts from privatization and other revenue, including substantial tax payments by the banks. More importantly, individual income tax receipts increased from 10 per cent of GDP in 1995 to 14 per cent in 2006 as the tax burden on low- and middle-income earners rose. Government revenue from taxes and other sources, including privatization, increased from 38 per cent of GDP in 1990 to 49 per cent in 2005 – that is, from five points below the OECD average in 1990 to four points above average in 2005. Yet, despite heavier taxation of all except the rich, in 2006 the government borrowed from abroad the equivalent of nearly 10 per cent of GDP to more than double the Central Bank's gross foreign reserves and restore them to the equivalent of three to four months' import coverage; this loan was recorded separately, and is, therefore, not included in the official public debt figures cited above. During 2004–7, the current account deficit averaged 18 per cent of GDP as imports and interest payments surged; exports, however, continued to hover around a third of GDP as they have done since 1870 (this is not a misprint), a clear sign of systemic overvaluation of the krona. External debt rose to 550 per cent of GDP in 2007, including short-term liabilities equivalent to 200 per cent of GDP. Net foreign debt in 2007 amounted to almost 250 per cent of GDP, up from 50 per cent in 1997. Further, the net investment position, including FDI and portfolio equities, deteriorated from −47 per cent of GDP in 1997 to −125 per cent in 2007.

These numbers raise two related concerns. First, the worth of some of the assets that were purchased with borrowed funds is intrinsically difficult to assess. Second, the quality of the investments that were financed with borrowed funds is a crucial determinant of the sustainability of the long-term debts that Iceland has piled up. The profitability of the new and, for Iceland, huge hydroelectric project to feed an associated aluminium smelting operation under construction is a matter of some controversy because the government is unwilling to disclose the price at which the energy will be sold to the smelter. Besides, some of the borrowed money was used to finance consumption.

## Further signs of overvaluation

Three further factors point to a systemic overvaluation of the krona. First, Iceland remains a high-inflation country (at present, the annual inflation rate is 9 per cent and rising); high-inflation countries tend to have overvalued currencies. Second, the government's unwavering support for agriculture through severe import restrictions and for the fisheries through gratis allocation of valuable catch quotas (although, by law, fish in Icelandic waters is a common property resource) exerts a further upward pressure on the exchange rate. The mechanism is straightforward: by restricting food imports, the government reduces the demand for foreign exchange and thereby also its price. Likewise, by indirectly subsidizing the fisheries, the government reduces the price of foreign exchange that is consistent with adequate profitability of the fishing industry to the detriment of other export industries. Third, as Figure 13.1 shows, Iceland's per capita GDP measured in dollars bypassed the US level in 2002, and, in 2007, surpassed it by a half, flying off the chart. In this light, the depreciation of the krona in 2008 must be viewed as a welcome correction. Will it fall further? How far? How rapidly? That

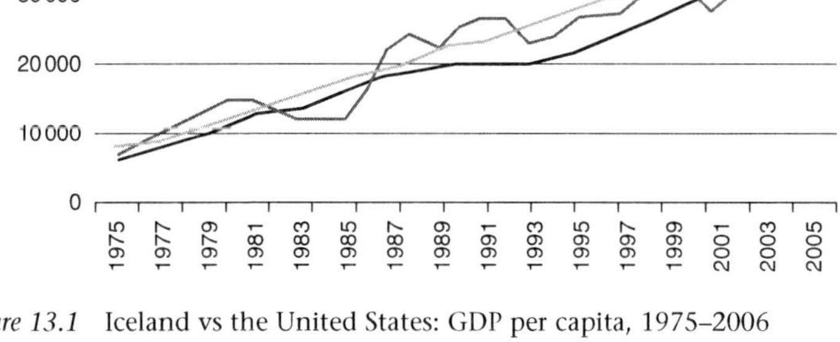


*Figure 13.1* Iceland vs the United States: GDP per capita, 1975–2006

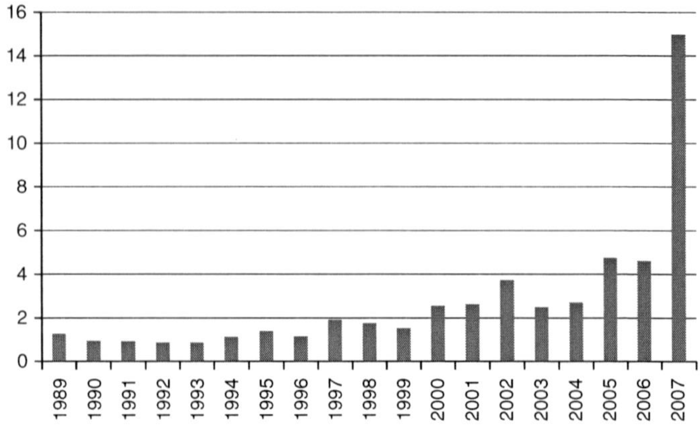


*Figure 13.2* Ratio of foreign short-term bank liabilities to Central Bank foreign reserves, 1989–2006

is, as always, impossible to know, except overshooting seems likely. Rather than try to reverse the recent depreciation, the authorities need to address the underlying sources of the krona's chronic overvaluation over the years.

Figure 13.2 shows that the foreign short-term liabilities of the banking system are now 15 times larger than the Central Bank's foreign reserves. In view of the lessons learned from the Asian crisis of 1997–98, this should not have been allowed to happen. This is not hindsight. The government and the Central Bank were warned, publicly and unambiguously, every step of the way. Their line was that Iceland is not Thailand. Now, as in 2006, they are looking for ways to bolster the Central Bank's reserves – again, through foreign borrowing.

## The banks need more competition

The sudden depreciation of the krona in 2008 and the current liquidity problems of the banks, evidenced by their recent sky-high credit default swap ratings, need to be viewed as two different issues even if the banks' reckless accumulation of short-term liabilities seems to have triggered the recent fall of the krona. The need for depreciation is not new, even if it recently became acute. It was only a question of time. Therefore, unfounded rumours seem unlikely to have undermined the krona. The problems of the banks, by contrast, are new. The turbulence in world markets following the sub-prime loan crisis triggered the Icelandic event, but it would have occurred anyway. There is no other way to read Figure 13.2. Several factors contributed to the current situation, including weak financial supervision that seemed caught by surprise when foreign confidence in the banks began to falter, policy mistakes made by a politically run Central Bank without sufficient credibility and power of persuasion, poor advice from international rating agencies, lax fiscal policies ill-suited to an inflationary environment, and the failure of the authorities to react in time to rapidly escalating debts. They heard the warnings but chose not to heed them.

How the banks and their creditors will fare is impossible to know, but their debtors and depositors will almost surely suffer as the spread between lending and deposit rates rises in a domestic market that remains insulated from foreign competition. This is how a bank crisis was concealed once before, without any official acknowledgement, at the time of the Nordic bank crisis in the early 1990s. At that time, the Icelandic state banks wrote off bad loans on a scale that was comparable with Iceland's crisis-stricken Nordic neighbours – that is, relative to GDP. And this is one of the many reasons why EU membership, including protection under the EU's competition policy, is important for Iceland. Icelandic banks need competition at home as well as abroad, where they offer their customers significantly better terms than they do in Iceland.

## Will Iceland go under? No!

Do not get me wrong: Iceland's fundamentals are strong. Since achieving Home Rule in 1904, Iceland's per capita GDP has increased by a factor of 15. Today, Iceland's per capita GDP is roughly on a par with Denmark, the old ruler, compared with a gap of about 50 per cent in Denmark's favour in 1900. True, Iceland's transformation was attained at the cost of high inflation over extended periods, the pile-up of foreign debts, and rundown of fish stocks in Icelandic waters. On the other hand, the education and culture of the population improved markedly over the years. Hard work also helps explain Iceland's rapid growth. Icelanders, like Americans, still must work much longer hours than most other OECD nations to maintain a high standard of life despite various homegrown inefficiencies in the structure and organization of economic life. EU membership would help reduce these inefficiencies.

# 14
# A Spending Spree

*Gylfi Zoega*

## Summary

Iceland's economic turbulence sounds like a familiar macroeconomic story – a credit expansion fuelled excessive borrowing and spending. But there are unfamiliar details – an unusually large banking sector and a central bank unable to serve as a credible lender of last resort – that raise concerns. Nevertheless, Iceland should be able to weather the current turmoil.

The recent economic turbulence in Iceland is in some ways familiar, while in others it is unique. The macroeconomics of current account deficits, inflation and asset price bubbles is the familiar part; the creation of a large banking sector in a country with no tradition of modern banking is the unique part. Both developments were driven by borrowing in the international credit market – the global savings glut has been the mover and the shaker of the Icelandic economy in recent years. While foreign borrowing to finance a domestic credit expansion explains a large part of the macroeconomic development, external borrowing to finance a credit expansion at home as well as abroad explains the expansion of the banking sector. And just as the two are joined in their cause, they are also joined in the distress caused by the current credit market turmoil. In a way, Iceland is testing the limits of small open economy macroeconomics by building a banking industry that by nature is dependent on foreign leverage while still maintaining an independent currency and a central bank whose possibilities to serve as lender of last resort are quite limited.

## A familiar credit cycle

A credit expansion at home fuelled the national economy. Domestic households and enterprises took advantage of the abundance of low-interest capital in international capital markets to finance domestic investment and consumption as well as the acquisition of foreign companies.[1] The inflow of credit after 2003 had a predictable effect on asset prices, the stock market and the current account. The same applies to the construction boom, wage pressures and influx of workers from abroad. The sub-prime-related credit crunch in world markets has had the expected effects on the national economy, i.e. asset prices, the real exchange rate and real wages have fallen. There is nothing remarkable about this response; relative prices are adjusting so as to create the trade surplus necessary to finance interest payments on foreign debt.

What sets Iceland apart from most other countries is the magnitude of the current account deficit (10 per cent of GDP in 2004, 16 per cent in 2005, 25 per cent in 2006 and about 17 per cent in 2007).[2,3] This reflects a fall in national savings (from over 20 per cent in 2000 to below 10 per cent in 2006) and a simultaneous increase in private investment. Household debt has risen from 160 per cent of disposable income in 2000 to 240 per cent of disposable income in 2006, and net foreign debt went from 90 per cent of GDP in 2000 to 240 per cent at the end of 2006. Numbers on the accumulation of net foreign debt do not give full credit to the extent of external borrowing, which has caused gross foreign debt to increase from a level of about one year's GDP in year 2000 to almost six times GDP in 2006. This was matched by a very significant accumulation of assets abroad, which by 2006 had taken foreign assets from a very low level to one quarter of GDP. A lot of borrowing and spending indeed!

There are several possible reasons why the Icelanders have borrowed (and spent!) more than other countries in this period. One reason is of course the impact of the asset price inflation on consumption and investment. Another is the recent liberalization of the banking system. Clearly there were many unexploited investment opportunities and business ideas that could not have been carried out during the reign of state-owned banks. There is also a visible appetite for risk taking in the level of borrowing by households and firms as well as in the role played by the banking system in the expansion of credit. For example, businesses borrowed over 60 per cent more from the banking sector in the first quarter of 2006 than in the first quarter of 2005 and households borrowed 30 per cent more, even though in 2005 the credit expansion was growing at rates similar to the peak of the previous expansion in 1997–2002.

The inflationary pressures created by the credit boom – mostly through high asset prices raising investment and consumption in the traditional way – have put great strains on the newly independent Central Bank. The Central Bank – having adopted an inflation-targeting interest-rate setting scheme in 2001 – has repeatedly raised interest rates, bringing the policy rate up to its current level of 15 per cent, an increase of more than 10 per cent since 2004. These interest rate changes have not been very effective at curbing inflationary pressures through lower domestic demand. There has, however, been an effect going through higher exchange rates and lower import prices on the one hand and lower profits in exporting industries on the other, but the effect on demand has been limited.

There are several reasons for the ineffectiveness of monetary policy. First, the bulk of domestic debt is CPI-indexed while some is in foreign currencies. The Central Bank interest rates have a very limited effect on interest rates on long-term CPI indexed debt and of course no effect on debt in foreign currencies. There is also the familiar result that it is the supply of credit that fuels investment more than the rate of interest. This leaves the transmission channel that goes through exchange rates and this is where most of the action has taken place. The high policy rates have provided profit opportunities for the carry trade, which has magnified the rate of credit expansion, the stock market bubble and the housing boom. Monetary policy has in this way contributed to financial instability. Unfortunately, due to the small size of the economy there has not been much expenditure switching due to the high real exchange rates. Painting with a broad brush, the country exports mainly fish and aluminium while consumers spend their money on imported goods, which leaves little room for switching from domestic products to imports.

We can conclude this section by saying that the macroeconomic story is familiar in most respects apart from the intensity of the credit cycle as well as the apparent ineffectiveness of monetary policy.

## A remarkable banking development

A credit expansion abroad has expanded the banking sector's balance sheets. Icelandic banks, operating in a country with a population similar to that of the city of Coventry (306,000), have become significant players in international capital markets. Iceland has the appearance of a country turned hedge fund![4] In total, the asset side of the bank's balance sheets was tenfold the country's annual GDP at the end of 2007. Their expansion was driven by borrowing in international capital markets, which has put them in a precarious position in the current international environment.

The Central Bank is weak – its reserves of foreign exchange (official reserve assets)[5] are currently around 200 billion krona (2.8 billion dollars) in an economy with GDP around 1200 billion krona. Foreign investors hence face a prisoner's dilemma vis-à-vis the Icelandic banks due to the lack of a credible lender of last resort. The asset side of their balance sheets is apparently fairly robust because it contains almost no sub-prime-related products and because – in the case of the big three banks – they are more or less immune to a housing bust in Iceland due to the significance of their foreign operations. But they are not immune to foreign banks refusing to renew loans or hedge funds using credit default swaps (CDS) to speculate on changes in credit spreads and betting on the banks' demise. If everyone 'cheats' the banking system may collapse, while if they cooperate and provide credit the banks will survive.

The essence of the remarkable banking story is hence the emergence of big banks – through foreign borrowing and the creation of credit at home and abroad – which are very large in comparison to the national economy and the size of the Central Bank. This is the main source of the current turbulence. It has not been a story of hidden losses, collateralized debt obligations and exposure to sub-prime lending. It is a story of banks using foreign savings instead of domestic deposits to fund an expansion that lacks a credible lender of last resort.

## More than a hedge fund

The spending spree of the past few years has generated a macroeconomic boom and an expansion of the banking sector that is out of proportion to the size of the local economy. Both are apparently coming to an end, and this has created turbulence in the real economy at home and some tensions in international capital markets.

However, it should not be forgotten that Iceland is more than a hedge fund. The contribution of the banking sector to GDP should not be exaggerated. Iceland has three resources that weigh much more in both GDP and exports that are becoming ever more valuable. First, the nation of 300,000 controls large segments of the North Atlantic with fertile fishing grounds. The price of fish products has been rising and can be expected to rise further in the future with growing demand and the depletion of fish stocks worldwide. The foreign currency price of local fish products has risen by 20 per cent since 2000. Second, the country is rich in energy resources, both hydro and thermal, which are used to turn bauxite into aluminium, and the world market price of aluminium has increased by about 25 per cent since 2000. Third, there is significant human capital in the country. A rapidly rising proportion of the population have a university degree and a large number of them go on to do postgraduate studies abroad. This has helped create the foundations for a range of solid and profitable firms that benefited from the availability of credit, such as the generic drug producer Actavis with a market value close to that of the big banks, as well as banks and investment funds.

In addition there are some obvious strengths. One is a fully funded pension system with assets around 130 per cent of GDP in 2007 and a state that has paid down its debt to around 7 per cent of GDP. The institutional framework is also broadly conducive to good business. The economy is not stifled by regulations, the labour market is very flexible, and the country does well on indices measuring economic freedom.[6] For example it ranks fifth in the world in the Heritage Foundation's ranking of economic freedom.

In sum, we can say that the Icelandic economy is resource-rich, the population is well educated and there are institutional advantages, but it has undergone a massive spending spree which is the cause of the current turmoil.

## An afterthought

In the future, when the crisis is over, the froth has been washed away, and the bubbles have burst, Icelanders may do well to heed the advice given in their old poem Havamal:

Once he has won wealth enough,
A man should not crave for more:
What he saves for friends, foes may take;
Hopes are often liars.

## Notes

1. During the initial stages of the credit expansion, in 2003 and 2004, the credit expansion was driven primarily by the lowering of reserve requirements by

the Central Bank and changes in banking regulations that let commercial banks into the domestic mortgage market. Since 2004 an influx of capital from abroad, such as the carry trade, has propelled the credit expansion.

2. These and other numbers in this chapter are taken from the Central Bank's *Monetary Bulletin* (see http://www.sedlabanki.is/?PageID=771 for the November 2007 issue).
3. There is some suspicion that the current account deficit has been overestimated (perhaps by 5 per cent of GDP!) by the underestimation of returns on portfolio investments in the balance of payments accounts.
4. Kaupthing Bank, the largest one with over 3000 employees, has operations in 13 countries. At the end of 2007 its assets were 58.3 billion British pounds when the GDP of Iceland was just over 10 billion pounds (using an exchange rate (31/12/07) of 125 kronur to one pound). Kaupthing ranked number 177 in 2006 among the world's largest banks (see *The Banker*, 2007) and both Glitnir and Landsbankinn were among the top 300 in the world.
5. See http://www.imf.org/external/np/sta/ir/isl/eng/curisl.htm.
6. See http://www.heritage.org/research/features/index/searchresults.cfm?factor=Regulation.

# 15
# Monetary Turbulence and the Icelandic Economy

*Robert Z. Aliber*

> One of my favorite sentences of the last five years – that is, the one that I have rewritten most often – is that 'The last thirty five years has been the must tumultuous in monetary history.' 'The Age of Turbulence' is the title of Chairman Greenspan's memoir.

The financial turbulence centres on three sets of events, including several waves of financial crises; the credit crunch now under way in the United States and Britain and Iceland and Ireland is one of these waves. The term 'crisis' means that the decline in the market value of certain classes of assets – in this case both residential and commercial real estate – is so large and so extensive that lenders are sceptical of the solvency of a large number of banks and other lenders. The term 'wave' means that similar market phenomena are observed in several different countries at about the same time. Countrywide Financial, the largest US mortgage lender, was on its way to insolvency in August 2007 before being rescued by the Bank of America. Northern Rock, the largest British mortgage lender, would have closed if credits had not been available from the Bank of England; Northern Rock has been nationalized. Both Countrywide and Northern Rock experienced runs on their IOUs in the commercial paper market. Bear Stearns, the fourth largest US investment bank, failed in March 2008 because the counterparties in the wholesale financial markets would no longer accept its commitments; Bear was subject to a run on its shares as well as a run on its IOUs. Bear would have failed if the Federal Reserve had not agreed to buy up to $29 billion of its dodgy assets so that JPMorgan Chase would acquire Bear. Several German banks have collapsed because of losses on their holdings of mortgage-backed securities. The accumulated losses of the commercial banks and the investment banks and insurance companies are now estimated at nearly $400 billion.

The second set of turbulent events centres on several credit bubbles, which usually have involved four or five or more countries in a wave. The term 'bubble' means a non-sustainable increase in the prices of certain currencies and classes of assets. The most recent wave involved increases in real estate prices in the Anglo-Saxon countries (except Canada) as well as in Ireland and in Spain; the surge in real estate prices and stock prices in Iceland between 2002 and 2006 is part of this wave.

The first wave of credit bubbles involved the rapid increase in loans from the major international banks headquartered in New York, London, Toronto and Tokyo to governments and government-owned firms in Mexico and other developing countries in the 1970s. The surge in real estate prices and stock prices in three of the Nordic countries – Finland, Norway and Sweden – in the second half of the 1980s comprised the second wave; about the same time there was a surge in the real estate and stock prices in Japan. Mexico, Thailand, South Korea, Brazil and Russia were among the countries in the third wave in the mid-1990s. (A brief note on terminology: a bubble is a non-sustainable pattern of financial flows from lenders to borrowers; when the flow of new money to the borrowers declines, a crisis follows because the borrowers prove unwilling or unable to adhere to the terms of the loan agreements. A credit bubble involves a rapid increase in bank loans to a specific group of borrowers; an asset bubble involves a rapid increase in the price of stocks or of real estate. Most asset bubbles follow from a rapid increase in bank loans, however the US stock price bubble in the late 1990s was not based on a rapid increase in credit.)

The third feature of turbulence has been the large changes in the values of national currencies relative to those projected from national differences in inflation rates. The US dollar price of the euro has increased by nearly 75 per cent between 2001 and 2008, even though the differences between the inflation rates in the United States and Europe generally averaged less than 2 per cent a year. An increase in the flow of money to a country usually led to an increase in the value of its currency; the country's imports increased significantly relative to its exports. Once the inflow of money slowed, the value of the currency declined, in some cases rapidly. There was a significant real appreciation of the Mexican peso between 1990 and 1994, and then the peso depreciated sharply at the end of 1994. The rapid depreciation of the Thai baht and the South Korean won in the second half of 1997 resulted in massive revaluation losses by the borrowers resident in these countries that had IOUs denominated in the US dollar or some other foreign currency.

The large changes in the values in national currencies, the bubbles in real estate prices and stock prices, and the subsequent financial crises are systematically related. An increase in the flow of money to a country leads to an appreciation of its currency and induces increases in the prices of stocks and real estate in response to purchases by those that have moved money to the country. The economy booms as investment spending and household consumption spending surge. Because the inflow almost always is at a rate that is too high to be sustained for more than three or four years, the inevitable and subsequent decline in the inflow leads to a depreciation of the country's currency.

Iceland experienced a rapid increase in the foreign demand for krona securities and extremely rapid increase in stock prices between the end of 2002 and the end of 2006. The motivation for this chapter was that the impacts of an autonomous increase in the foreign demand for securities denominated in the Icelandic krona on asset prices would be directly evident in a small open economy, more so than in a Mexico or a Britain. The next section of this essay reviews a model that relates the increases in the prices of securities in a country to an autonomous increase in the foreign demand for these securities. This model is inspired by Keynes' view of the transfer problem at the end of the First World War; he concluded that the reparations that the French wanted to impose on the Germans were too large relative to the ability of the Germans to depress domestic consumption relative to production, and the willingness of the French to increase consumption relative to production. Then the increases in prices of stocks and of real estate in Iceland that began about 2002 are reviewed in terms of this model; the surge in money inflows to Iceland triggered a rapid increase in real estate prices, and an extremely rapid increase in stock prices and in bank capital. Subsequently three financial anomalies or imbalances in Iceland are identified: the first is the ratio of Iceland's current account deficit to its GDP; the second is the ratio of asset prices in Iceland to its GDP, and the third is the ratio of the assets of the Icelandic banks to the country's GDP. Several statements that 'Iceland is an international financial centre' are evaluated. The sixth and concluding section deals with the two policy issues; one involves the structure of the financial system and the range of activities of the deposit money banks and the other involves the value of the Icelandic krona.

## 15.1 The transfer problem process when currencies are floating

France imposed large reparations payments on Germany at the end of the First World War. Keynes' classic analysis of the transfer problem highlighted the distinction between the production of goods and services in a country and the absorption of resources within that country. The counterpart of the flow of money from Germany to France would have been the flow of real resources of comparable value; Germany would have to develop a trade or current account surplus while France would have to have the counterpart current account deficit. If real resources were to flow from Germany to France, then consumption spending or absorption (which would include spending by households, business and governments) in Germany would have to decline relative to production by an amount that corresponded to the annual reparations payment. If France were to absorb the real resources from Germany, then consumption or absorption in France would have to increase and exceed French production by the amount of the intended payment. The Germans would have to increase taxes sharply to increase the wedge between production and consumption, while the French would have to reduce taxes to encourage the demand for the resources that would be made available by the Germans.

The formal description of the transfer problem involves two countries, one that is obliged to make the payments and the other that is scheduled to receive the payments. The model can be readily extended to more countries; the essential requirement is that the payor generate a current account surplus and the payee a comparable current account deficit.

The transfer problem model can be used to analyse the adjustments within a country to a shock in the form of an autonomous increase in the foreign demand for its assets. These adjustments are necessary so the country absorbs the real resources – the goods and services – that are the counterpart of the inflow of money; in terms of the balance-of-payments accounting framework, if currencies are not pegged, the country must develop a larger current account deficit that is the counterpart of the increase in its capital account surplus.

Two adjustments facilitate absorption by the country that experiences an inflow of money. One is that as the country's currency appreciates, its imports increase relative to its exports due to the change in relative prices. The real appreciation is sometimes characterized as 'overshooting'. By itself this adjustment would lead to a decline in the country's GDP because of the increase in spending on foreign goods and the counterpart reduction in spending on domestic goods. The second adjustment is the increase in the prices of assets and of securities within the country, and the resulting growth in household wealth leads to an increase in spending on both domestic goods and on imports.

The increase in the prices of assets and of securities reflects that those who sell their assets to the foreigners use most of their receipts to buy other assets from other domestic residents, and at ever higher prices. The foreign money becomes like the proverbial 'hot potato', and asset prices continue to increase until the decline in the country's savings more or less corresponds to the increase in the inflow of money from abroad. The combination of the decline in the price of imports and the increase in the country's GDP leads to the increase in absorption.

The increase in absorption may involve some combination of an increase in the government's fiscal deficit, an increase in business investment, and an increase in household consumption (its dual is a reduction in household saving). The stylized fact is that the only time that the inflow of money has been associated with an increase in the fiscal deficit has been when the inflow is a response to an autonomous increase in government borrowing, as in Mexico and other developing countries in the 1970s. In the other country experiences, the fiscal deficit declines because the boom that follows from the increase in the inflow of money leads to a surge in government revenues. Much of the counterpart to the inflow of money is that household consumption increases in response to the increase in household wealth. Indeed, asset prices increase until the decline in household saving corresponds with the increase in the inflow of money.

The increase in the indebtedness of the country often is at a rate which is several times higher than the rate of growth of the country's GDP, and two or three times higher than the prevailing interest rate. As long as the rate of increase in indebtedness is significantly higher than the interest rate on the indebtedness, the borrowers incur no real debt servicing burden, since the cash from new loans is much larger than the money that is needed to pay the interest on the outstanding loans. At some stage, the lenders are likely to become concerned that the borrowers' indebtedness is increasing at too rapid a rate relative to its GDP, and the rate of growth of new loans will slow. As long the rate of growth of indebtedness is higher than the interest rate, the borrowers do not incur an interest rate burden. However, as the excess of the rate of growth of the indebtedness over the interest rate declines, the borrower's currency depreciates; at some stage, the decline in the value of the currency will induce a sharp decline in the willingness of the lenders to extend more credit.

The decline in the value of the Mexican peso in 1994 resulted from the decline in the foreign demand for Mexican securities, which was inevitable and hence predictable since Mexico's external indebtedness was increasing three or four times as rapidly as its GDP. The sudden depreciation of the peso had an inflationary impact since the supply of resources available to the country declined, while the cost of imported goods increased. Moreover interest rates increased sharply, so there was a deflationary impact on the economy.

## 15.2 The transfer problem and asset prices in Iceland

The increase in the foreign demand for Icelandic securities that began in 2001 induced an appreciation of the Icelandic krona and contributed to dramatic increases in the price of residential real estate and in the price of Icelandic stocks. While most of the time series summarized in this chapter begin in 2000 and conclude in 2007, the discussion is centred on the changes in values during the five years from the end of 2001 to the end of 2006 when the increase in asset prices was most rapid. (Correspondingly, the changes in flow variables like GDP and the current balance are from the 2002 values to the 2006 values.) The Icelandic krona appreciated by nearly 30 per cent relative to the US dollar from the end of 2001 to the end of 2006 and by nearly 35 per cent to the end of 2007; Iceland's current account deficit increased from 4 per cent of its GDP in 2001 to 27 per cent in 2006.

Two measurement problems are encountered when using the data on the changes in the ratio of Iceland's current account deficit to its GDP to measure the impact of money inflows on the value of the krona. The first involves the lack of dimensional equivalency because Iceland's trade balance is measured in the US dollar and its GDP is measured in krona. The krona GDP is converted to a US dollar GDP at the prevailing value for krona in the currency market, usually the average value for the year. Iceland's GDP in US dollar terms increased relative to its GDP in krona terms as the krona appreciated. The larger the appreciation of the krona induced by the money inflows, the larger the increase in the US dollar equivalent of Iceland's GDP, and the lower the ratio of Iceland's current account balance to its GDP – as measured in the US dollar or in the euro. (If the ratio of Iceland's current account deficit to its GDP had not increased, then the US dollar value of Iceland's GDP would have increased at the same rate as the krona value of its GDP, and the ratio of Iceland's current account deficit to its krona GDP would have been 30–40 per cent larger.)

The scope of the distortion about the ratio of Iceland's current account balance to its GDP depends on the elasticity of the krona in response to changes in the inflow of money. The lower the elasticity, the larger the increase in the value of the krona for a given increase in money inflows. Because of the skewed nature of Iceland's exports of goods and services – 50 per cent are fish-related – and the small size of the domestic manufacturing sector, the (conservative) assumption is that each increase of money inflows of 1 per cent of Iceland's exports led to an increase in the value of the krona of 1.2 per cent.

The second measurement problem has resulted from the impacts of the investment in the extremely capital-intensive hydropower smelter project on the value of the krona. The total cost of this investment is estimated at $2.5 billion, 15 per cent of Iceland's GDP in 2006. Most of the resources or 'machine tools' used in construction – such as the turbines – were imported. Much of the labour necessary to build the dams, install the generators, construct the electrical transmission lines from the power plants to the smelters, and build the smelters and the ports also was imported. To the extent that the machine tools and the labour were imported, the flow of money to Iceland summarized in its balance of payments accounts is imputed and did not affect the market value of the krona. In contrast to the extent the foreign investors made money payments to Icelandic firms and individuals, the krona appreciated. The first assumption is that one-third of the total capital costs of $2.5 billion led to payments to firms and individuals in Iceland and the second is that the amounts of these payments were similar in 2005, 2006 and 2007.

This first measurement problem leads to an understatement about the impacts of money inflows on the Icelandic economy. In contrast, the second problem leads to an overstatement of this impact.

Several different measures of Iceland's GDP and several values for its international accounts are shown in Table 15.1. The increase in the value of the krona and the increase in Iceland's current account deficit were especially rapid from 2003 to 2005. The money flows associated with the aluminium smelting complex increased the current account deficit as reported in the balance of payments accounts by 4–5 per cent of Iceland's GDP in each of three years 2005, 2006 and 2007, but the flows that led to a direct impact on the value of the krona were less than 2 per cent of its GDP.

The increase in Iceland's current account deficit was associated with a sharp increase in household consumption (Table 15.2). Between 2002 and 2006 Iceland's GDP increased by 330 ISKbn (from 812 ISKbn in 2002 to 1142 ISKbn in 2006) and its current account balance changed by

*Table 15.1* Icelandic macro parameters

| | 2000 | 2001 | 2002 | 2003 | 2004 | 2005 | 2006 | 2007 |
|---|---|---|---|---|---|---|---|---|
| *Variables* | | | | | | | | |
| GDP, ISKbn | 682 | 770 | 812 | 840 | 926 | 1022 | 1142 | 1279 |
| GDP 2000 prices | 682 | 709 | 708 | 728 | 783 | 839 | 861 | 914 |
| GDP growth, % | 4.5 | 3.9 | 0.2 | 2.5 | 7.6 | 7.4 | 4.2 | 3.1 |
| GDP, US$bn | 8.7 | 7.9 | 8.9 | 10.9 | 13.2 | 16.2 | 16.3 | 15.9 |
| ISK/USD | 78.6 | 97.4 | 91.7 | 76.7 | 70.2 | 62.9 | 70.2 | 64.1 |
| ISK/EUR | 72.6 | 87.4 | 86.2 | 86.7 | 87.1 | 78.2 | 87.9 | 87.7 |
| Exchange rate index | 100 | 87.5 | 93.0 | 98.9 | 101.6 | 114.6 | 106.7 | 112.8 |
| Current account balance, US$m. | –847 | –336 | 145 | –534 | –631 | –2632 | –4457 | –3190 |
| Current account balance/GDP | –10 | –4 | 2 | –5 | –5 | –16 | –27 | –20 |
| Current account balance, ISKbn | –68 | –31 | 16 | –42 | –46 | –164 | –308 | –204 |

*Sources*: Statistics Iceland, Bank for International Settlements, International Financial Statistics 'Landsbanki', Daniel Gros, 'Iceland on the Brink?' CEPS Policy Brief no. 157.

*Table 15.2* Sectoral absorption parameters (ISK, billions)

| | 2000 | 2001 | 2002 | 2003 | 2004 | 2005 | 2006 | 2007 |
|---|---|---|---|---|---|---|---|---|
| GDP | 682 | 769 | 812 | 840 | 926 | 1022 | 1141 | 1214 |
| Private investment | 159 | 180 | 205 | 217 | 231 | 251 | 281 | 314 |
| Fiscal balance | –9 | 26 | –4 | –13 | –9 | –52 | 69 | 106 |
| Current account balance | 50 | 8 | 13 | 26 | 52 | 127 | 204 | 136 |
| Household consumption | 582 | 571 | 598 | 584 | 746 | 950 | 995 | 930 |

*Source*: International Financial Statistics.

324 ISKbn (from a surplus of 16 ISKbn in 2002 to a deficit of 308 ISKbn in 2006). The supply of goods and services available to households, business firms and government increased by 654 ISKbn – the sum of the increase in domestic GDP and the increase in the current account deficit. Iceland had a small fiscal deficit in 2002 and a large fiscal surplus in 2006; this increase in government receipts relative to payments of 73 ISKbn meant that the supply of goods available for private investment and household consumption together increased by 727 ISKbn. Private investment in 2006 was 76 ISKbn larger than in 2002, while household consumption spending was larger by 651 ISKbn.

The implication of the model is that the dramatic increase in household consumption spending both absolutely and as a share of GDP resulted from the increase in household wealth. Stock prices and real estate prices are shown in Table 15.3. The surge in these prices began in 2003.

Icelanders spend a higher proportion of their incomes on housing than Americans, in part because construction costs are higher and in part because of the long winters. The market value of US residential real estate was 110 per cent of US GDP in 2000; the assumption is that Icelanders spend one-third more of their income on housing than Americans, which would mean that the comparable ratio of Iceland is about 150. The increase in the market value of real estate for subsequent years is the product of this assumption for the base year and the index for the changes in the price of real estate.

Two time series are available for stock prices, one is from International Financial Statistics and one from the Icelandic Stock Exchange. The data from the Icelandic Stock Exchange indicate that stock prices in Iceland at the end of 2006 were more than eight times higher than at the end of 2002; the IFS data indicate that stock prices at the end of 2006 were almost five times higher.

The estimates of household wealth shown in Table 15.3 are based on the assumption that households own 'three assets' – fixed price assets

*Table 15.3* Real estate prices, stock prices and household wealth

| | *2000* | *2001* | *2002* | *2003* | *2004* | *2005* | *2006* | *2007* |
|---|---|---|---|---|---|---|---|---|
| GDP, ISKB | 682 | 770 | 812 | 840 | 926 | 1022 | 1142 | 1279 |
| *Asset prices* | | | | | | | | |
| Real estate prices (100 = 2000) | 100 | 111 | 116 | 129 | 143 | 184 | 215 | 235 |
| Real estate values | 998 | 1108 | 1158 | 1287 | 1427 | 1836 | 2146 | 2345 |
| OMX ICE equities, ISKbn | 369 | 362 | 317 | 589 | 1019 | 1815 | 2596 | 2543 |
| OMX ICE equities (100 = 2000) | 100 | 98 | 86 | 159 | 276 | 492 | 704 | 689 |
| IFS stock prices (100 = 2005) | NA | NA | 24.9 | 39.1 | 63.5 | 100 | 120.2 | 120.4 |
| Market value stocks/GDP | 54 | 47 | 39 | 70 | 110 | 178 | 227 | 212 |
| GDP (100 = 2000) | 100 | 113 | 119 | 122 | 135 | 149 | 167 | 188 |
| Real estate prices/GDP | 100 | 98 | 97 | 106 | 104 | 124 | 129 | 125 |
| Stock prices/GDP | 100 | 87 | 72 | 139 | 204 | 330 | 422 | 367 |
| Household wealth/ISKbn | 2049 | 2240 | 2287 | 2716 | 3372 | 4673 | 5884 | 6138 |
| Household wealth/GDP | 300 | 291 | 282 | 323 | 364 | 457 | 515 | 491 |

*Sources*: Statistics Iceland, Iceland Stock Exchange, International Financial Statistics.

like demand deposits and savings deposits and bonds whose market value is equal to GDP, and variable price assets including real estate and stocks. Because of increases in the prices of stocks and of real estate, the absolute value of household wealth at the end of 2006 was nearly three times the absolute value at the end of 2001, and the ratio of household wealth to GDP at the end of 2006 was 180 per cent of the value of the same ratio at the end of 2002.

Rapid increases in real estate prices almost always result from a rapid increase in bank credit, since a significant part of most purchases is financed with borrowed money. Nearly every country that has experienced a significant increase in real estate prices has had a comparable increase in bank credit.

The values of major assets and liabilities and capital for the deposit money banks summarized in Table 15.4 are reproduced from International Financial Statistics. Some line entries with low values in the IFS presentation are not reproduced in Table 15.4, and the totals for assets and liabilities shown in the table are not shown in IFS. The capital account entry in the table is identical with line 27A in IFS.

The assets of the Icelandic banks at the end of 2006 were six times larger than at the end 2002. At the end of 2002 the assets of the banks

*Table 15.4* Financial parameters for Icelandic banks (billions of krona, end of period)

| | *2000* | *2001* | *2002* | *2003* | *2004* | *2005* | *2006* | *2007* |
|---|---|---|---|---|---|---|---|---|
| *Assets* | | | | | | | | |
| Reserves | 26 | 21 | 26 | 13 | 29 | 37 | 47 | 101 |
| Foreign assets | 21 | 29 | 46 | 113 | 174 | 538 | 1332 | 1025 |
| Claims on private sector | 664 | 773 | 859 | 1097 | 1531 | 2543 | 3733 | 5205 |
| Assets – total | 717 | 838 | 939 | 1240 | 1740 | 3126 | 5121 | 6337 |
| *Liabilities* | | | | | | | | |
| Demand deposits | 65 | 63 | 80 | 106 | 133 | 164 | 191 | 398 |
| Savings deposits | 226 | 272 | 306 | 367 | 406 | 534 | 931 | 1615 |
| Bonds | 169 | 196 | 274 | 564 | 999 | 1992 | 3075 | 3003 |
| Foreign liabilities | 224 | 258 | 226 | 216 | 223 | 337 | 681 | 756 |
| Due to monetary authorities | 39 | 54 | 69 | 24 | 33 | 79 | 120 | 281 |
| *Liabilities – total* | 685 | 790 | 887 | 1254 | 1761 | 3527 | 4878 | 6053 |
| Capital accounts | 66 | 96 | 117 | 157 | 336 | 587 | 967 | 1378 |
| Other | –73 | –101 | –134 | –194 | –391 | –566 | –849 | –1779 |

*Source*: International Financial Statistics.

were slightly more than twice as large as the sum of their demand and savings deposits; at the end of 2006, the assets of the banks were five times larger than the sum of their demand and savings deposits.

Because banks are subject to capital–asset regulatory ratios, in the long run bank assets cannot increase significantly more rapidly than bank capital. In most countries bank capital is in the range of 10–12 per cent of bank assets. The capital of the Icelandic banks at the end of 2006 was nearly eight times larger than at the end of 2002.

Banks can increase their capital from external sources by selling common stock and preferred stock; banks also can increase their capital from internal sources – from income on interest rate spreads, fees, and profits from owning and trading securities. A cliché is that banks earn 1 per cent on their assets and 10 per cent on their capital; the implication is that surge in bank capital cannot be explained by current earnings. The third row in Table 15.5 shows the annual increase in bank capital from one year to the next, and the fourth row shows the percentage increase in bank capital during the year relative to value of bank capital at the end of the year. The more rapid the increase in bank capital, the greater the likelihood that the increase in bank capital resulted from the increase in the prices of stocks and other variable price assets owned by the banks.

The thrust of Table 15.6 is to bring together the data on the stock price indexes in Table 15.3 and the entry for the capital accounts of the deposit banks in Table 15.4. The third row sets the value for the capital at 100 in the year 2000 to facilitate the comparison between the increase in stock prices and the increase in bank capital; the capital of the banks increased twice as rapidly as stock prices. The annual

*Table 15.5* Return on bank capital

| | *2000* | *2001* | *2002* | *2003* | *2004* | *2005* | *2006* | *2007* |
|---|---|---|---|---|---|---|---|---|
| *Assets* | | | | | | | | |
| Assets – total | 717 | 838 | 939 | 1240 | 1740 | 3126 | 5121 | 6337 |
| Capital | 66 | 96 | 117 | 157 | 336 | 587 | 967 | 1378 |
| Increase in capital | | 30 | 21 | 40 | 179 | 251 | 360 | 411 |
| Return on capital, % | | 46 | 22 | 34 | 118 | 75 | 61 | 43 |
| Capital/total assets | | 9.2 | 11.7 | 12.4 | 12.7 | 19.4 | 18.8 | 18.9 |
| Equities | 26 | 36 | 29 | 89 | 165 | 396 | 422 | 545 |
| Equities/assets | 3.6 | 4.3 | 3.1 | 7.2 | 9.5 | 12.7 | 8.2 | 8.6 |

*Source*: International Financial Statistics.

*Table 15.6* Increases in stock prices and bank capital

| | 2000 | 2001 | 2002 | 2003 | 2004 | 2005 | 2006 | 2007 |
|---|---|---|---|---|---|---|---|---|
| Stock price index, | 100 | 98 | 86 | 159 | 276 | 492 | 704 | 689 |
| % change | | –2 | –12 | 85 | 74 | 78 | 43 | –2 |
| Capital accounts | 66 | 96 | 117 | 157 | 336 | 587 | 967 | 1378 |
| (100 = 2000), | 100 | 145 | 177 | 238 | 509 | 889 | 1465 | 2088 |
| % change | | 45 | 22 | 35 | 113 | 75 | 65 | 42 |

*Table 15.7* Stock market valuations

| | 2000 | 2001 | 2002 | 2003 | 2004 | 2005 | 2006 | 2007 |
|---|---|---|---|---|---|---|---|---|
| Three banks | 80 | 82 | 100 | 210 | 515 | 1001 | 1247 | 1376 |
| Market | 370 | 362 | 317 | 590 | 1019 | 1815 | 2595 | 2543 |
| Three banks/market | 22 | 23 | 32 | 36 | 51 | 55 | 48 | 54 |

*Source*: Previous tables.

percentage changes in stock prices and in the capital accounts of the banks are shown; the years when bank capital increased most rapidly are the years when stock prices increased rapidly.

In 2004 and 2006, the percentage increase in the capital of the banks was significantly larger than the percentage increase in stock prices, in 2003 the percentage increase in stock prices was significantly larger, and in 2005 the percentage increases in the two series were in the same ball-park. The large amount of capital in excess of the regulatory minimum is consistent with the rapid increase in capital that occurred as a result of a 'passive activity' on the part of the banks.

At the end of 2006, the market value of the shares in the index was eight times higher than the market value at the end of 2002 (the increase in the index would have been significantly more rapid if Actavis had not been dropped from the index when the firm was privatized). At the end of 2006, the market value of the shares of the three large banks was 48 per cent of the market value of the shares of all the firms in the index; at the end of 2002, this ratio had been 32 per cent (Table 15.7).

The increase in the share of the market value of the three banks might have resulted from one of several different factors. The price–earnings ratio for the banks may have increased relative to the same ratio for the non-bank firms whose stocks are included in the index. The earnings of the banks may have increased more rapidly than the earnings of the non-banks. The banks may have purchased shares of non-bank firms.

The rapid increase in stock prices led to sharp increases in the net worth of every investor and institution that owned stock. As prices increased, one group increased its holdings of stocks as this group was willing to pay the price necessary to bid the shares away from other investors.

An individual investor can buy the shares of the non-bank Icelandic firms directly, or this investor can buy these shares indirectly by purchasing the shares in one or several of the Icelandic banks; in the second case the investor is buying shares in a financial intermediary that resembles a closed-end mutual fund that owns a diversified portfolio of variable price assets and fixed price assets. This financial intermediary has a window that sells demand deposits and other fixed price liabilities and that manages the payments system with the other two similar firms. The Icelandic banks differ sharply from those in most other countries, in that the variable price assets in their portfolios are more than 40 per cent of their total assets.

Consider two competing explanations for the increase in stock prices. One story is that someone – perhaps Eric the Red – paid a higher price for stocks and so he was willing to pay the price necessary to induce others to sell the stocks. If Eric had been the buyer, stock prices would have increased, and the three banks in effect would have sold some of their stocks to Eric. The ratio of the market value of the shares of the three banks to the market value of all firms would have declined. The competing story is that on the margin the banks were the winning bidders, and they bought shares from the other market participants.

The price–earnings ratio of the banks did not increase relative to the same ratio for the other firms in the index. The rapid increase in the capital of the banks suggests that their 'earnings' were increasing at a rapid rate.

These same statements can be made about an individual investor, again say Eric the Red. If Eric buys more shares, the prices of shares increase, and Eric's net worth increases. The major difference between the purchases of shares by any of the three banks and by Eric the Red is that the increase in the capital of the banks that follows from the increases in the price of shares enables them to increase their lending – and they benefit from ten to one or eight to one leverage – which is much greater than the leverage available to Eric the Red.

By deduction the increase in the market value of the shares of the three banks relative to the non-banks reflected that the banks were buying shares. Their purchases induced increases in the prices of shares of these firms. The market value of the shares of the three banks increased because the banks increasingly were becoming more like mutual funds, and hence the value of the shares of the banks reflected some combination of the earnings from their banking activities and from their management of mutual funds.

The data confirm that the increase in the flow of foreign money to Iceland was associated with a consumption boom that followed from a surge in household wealth. The increase in the flow of foreign money was associated with a rapid increase in stock prices, which contributed to a surge in the capital of the three banks, and in the rapid increase in bank credit.

The increase in stock prices in Iceland in the last few years seems similar to the sixfold increase in stock prices in Japan from the end of the 1970s to the end of the 1980s. The Japanese banks owned large amounts of stock and of real estate. (One difference is that real estate prices in Japan increased at about the same pace as stock prices.) As stock prices and real estate prices increased, the value of the shares and real estate owned by the banks increased. Because the share of these variable-price assets in the total bank assets was larger than the regulatory capital as a share of bank assets, the increase in real estate and stock prices led to an increase in the excess capital of the banks – the amount of capital over and above the regulatory minimums. The Japanese banks then were in a position to grow their loans which led to further increases in the prices of stocks and real estate. The Japanese appeared to have the financial equivalent of a perpetual motion machine.

## 15.3 The ratio of the current account deficit to GDP – the first Icelandic anomaly

A key question for a small open economy like Iceland is the appropriate size of its current account balance relative to its GDP.

One projection is that Iceland's current account deficit will be about 10 per cent of its GDP until 2012. Since the rate of GDP growth might be in the range of 3–4 per cent, Iceland's net international indebtedness will increase significantly relative to its GDP, perhaps by 50 per cent – the ratio of its external indebtedness to its GDP would then be nearly 100 per cent at the prevailing value for the krona, and proportionately higher at lower values for the krona.

The 'facts' about the size of Iceland's current account deficit are somewhat ambiguous, because in part the reported current account balance does not include two 'receipts' of 'investment income' that Icelandic individuals earn on their foreign assets – one is the increase in the wealth of Icelandic individuals when prices of the foreign shares that they own increase, and the second is the increase in the value of their shares in foreign holding companies. One story is that if the reported current account balance were adjusted to include these two 'receipts', then Iceland would have a current account surplus. (One reason for scepticism about this assertion is that it implies that Iceland once had a significant current account surplus, which is at variance with the data – although individuals may have moved money abroad by understating export receipts and overstating import payments.)

A country with a current account deficit is subject to the same limit theorem that affects every economic unit; in the very long run, the country's net external indebtedness cannot increase more rapidly than its GDP. Since the ratio of Iceland's current account deficit to its GDP has been much higher than the rate of growth of its GDP since 2003, Iceland has been violating the limit theorem. A country can violate the limit theorem in the short run and in the intermediate run, as Iceland has since 2003. Moreover a country can violate this theorem for decades as long as the ratio of its net international indebtedness to its GDP is 20 or 30 or 40 per cent – but the country cannot violate this theorem in the long run if the ratio of its net international indebtedness to its GDP is high because financing the current account deficit is likely to become increasingly difficult.

The irony is that Iceland's current account deficit has increased because foreign purchases of securities denominated in the krona are significantly larger than they were four and five years ago; as these purchases decline, the krona will depreciate. These foreign buyers might reduce their annual purchases because they have concluded that the share of krona-denominated securities in their portfolios has attained the appropriate size or because they anticipate that the krona might depreciate – which then would become a self-fulfilling projection.

Iceland is a 'young debtor' country; all of the money to pay the interest on its net international indebtedness is obtained from new foreign loans. That situation is explosive and not sustainable; at some stage Iceland will need a modest trade surplus so that the money from the excess of its export earnings over its import payments can be used to pay some of the interest to its foreign creditors.

The likelihood is low that Iceland will be able to finance a current account deficit that is two to three times as large as the projected rate of growth of its GDP given the high ratio of its net international indebtedness to its GDP. At some stage Iceland must develop a trade surplus – more precisely a current account surplus exclusive of net investment income payments abroad – to obtain some of the dollars and the euros that can be used to pay some of the interest to the foreign creditors.

The adjustment to a sustainable value for the current account balance might occur at the current value for the krona if there were a surge in the export earnings from the current and planned aluminium smelters. Otherwise the move to a sustainable value for Iceland's current account balance will involve a depreciation of the krona.

The adjustment to a sustainable external financial position for Iceland might occur smoothly, which would involve a decline in the ratio of the current account deficit to Iceland's GDP by one to two percentage points a year perhaps for six or eight years until the ratio reaches a sustainable value. Alternatively, the adjustment to a sustainable value might involve a sudden sharp depreciation because foreigners would become sellers of krona securities; interest rates on krona securities would surge because of the sharp reduction in the credit supply.

The experience of most other countries suggests that there must be a significant depreciation of the krona to position Iceland so it can earn some of the foreign currencies necessary for the payment of interest on its net international indebtedness.

A reduction in the ratio of Iceland's current account deficit to its GDP of five or six percentage points or more is very large, especially since most of the change would involve a decline in imports. The decline in the value of the krona could be 10 or 20 per cent or more – a reversal of the real appreciation that began in 2002.

## 15.4 Icelandic income and wealth – the second anomaly

Iceland has one of the highest GDP per capita in the world; the 2007 edition of the Economist's *Pocket World in Figures* places Iceland in the number 8 position with a per capita income of $41,910. The United States is in the number 9 position with a per capita income of $39,430.

Icelandic households are 'wealthy' compared with those in traditional industrial countries, with a higher ratio of assets to income. Most families own their homes. The country's pension system is 'fully funded'. There probably is a lot of business proprietorship wealth that is unrecorded – fishing boats, shops, small service establishments. Moreover, Icelanders own significantly more foreign stocks than foreigners own of Icelandic stock.

One of the stylized facts from financial history is that when there is a sharp increase in the price of stocks or of real estate in a country,

*Table 15.8* Private sector wealth (ISKbn)

| | *2000* | *2001* | *2002* | *2003* | *2004* | *2005* | *2006* | *2007* |
|---|---|---|---|---|---|---|---|---|
| Stocks | 370 | 362 | 317 | 590 | 1019 | 1815 | 2595 | 2543 |
| Homes | 682 | 757 | 949 | 1084 | 1324 | 1881 | 2455 | 2853 |
| Demand savings | 291 | 335 | 386 | 474 | 538 | 697 | 1122 | 900 |
| Sum | 1353 | 1454 | 1652 | 2058 | 2881 | 4393 | 6172 | 6296 |
| GDP | 682 | 770 | 812 | 840 | 926 | 1022 | 1142 | 1214 |
| Ratio | 198 | 189 | 203 | 245 | 311 | 430 | 540 | 519 |
| Stocks/GDP | 54 | 47 | 39 | 70 | 110 | 178 | 227 | 209 |

*Source*: International Financial Statistics.

household balance sheets 'explode' – the value of household assets increases very rapidly, both absolutely and relative to household income. Household liabilities also increase, but since these are fixed price liabilities while the most of the assets acquired with the borrowed money were variable price assets, household net worth surges.

At the end of 2002, the value of household wealth shown in Table 15.8 was about twice GDP; at the end of 2006, wealth was nearly five times GDP. (The figure for 2002 seems much too low, the intuition is that this ratio should be in the range of three to four. The striking increase in this ratio is much more significant than the absolute value of the ratio.)

The scheduled interest payments of the households increase at a rate commensurate with the increase in their indebtedness. Some households may have a cash flow problem, in that their scheduled interest payments may have increased more rapidly than their rental income if they have purchased properties and their dividend income if they have purchased stocks. As long as asset prices and their net worth are increasing, these households can borrow to obtain the money for these payments; increasing the amounts borrowed should not be a problem.

At some stage it is inevitable that the rate of increase in the prices of stocks and real estate will decline below the interest rate. Household net worth will increase at a less rapid rate or more likely decline. Some households will decide that their most attractive financial option is to shrink their balance sheets; they will sell some of their variable price assets and use the proceeds to reduce the amounts owed lenders.

Inevitably the sale of assets by these households will depress their prices. More households will come to the same conclusion. Their sales of variable price assets will depress their prices further. An increasing number of households will observe that the market value of their variable price assets is less than the amounts borrowed to finance their purchase of these assets.

The value of bank claims on the private sector was in the same ballpark as GDP from 2000 to 2003, and then the value of bank claims began to surge at about the same time as stock prices began to increase sharply. The coincidence of the changes in these two time series probably is not an accident; some of the money that borrowers obtained from bank loans was used to buy stocks. The sellers of the stocks increased their holdings of bank deposits.

The tentative assumption is that the real rate of return on Icelandic krona bonds is modestly higher than on US dollar bonds. The implication of this assumption is that the price of Icelandic equities should be below the price of US equities. The implication of the assumption that the US corporate sector is more vibrant than the corporate sector in Iceland is that the price–earnings ratio for Icelandic stocks should be below the comparable ratio for US stocks.

There is then a sharp conflict between the current level of stock prices in Iceland and the level that seems consistent with the interest rates and the rate of growth of profits. Stock prices in Iceland are now much above their equilibrium level, much as in the United States in the late 1990s, with the difference that interest rates in Iceland now are more than twice as high as they were in the United States in the late 1990s.

A large number of investors that purchased Icelandic stocks with borrowed money have a 'negative carry' – their interest payments are several times or many times larger than their investment income. Some of these investors will become distress sellers of stocks.

The invisible hand will lead to a reduction in the ratio of the market value of household wealth to GDP. The reduction could involve a decline in prices of residential real estate, either rapidly or slowly, and to a more rapid reduction in stock prices.

## 15.5 Bank assets and GDP – the third anomaly

The value of the assets of the three Icelandic banks at the end of 2002 was 110 per cent of Iceland's GDP in 2002; the value of their assets at the end of 2006 was 450 per cent of Iceland's GDP in 2006. The foreign assets of the banks at the end of 2006 were 30 times larger than at the end of 2002, while the domestic assets were more than four times larger – and more than three times as large as Iceland's GDP.

That the total assets of the Icelandic banks are so much larger than the country's GDP has led to several different clichés – one is that 'Iceland is an international financial centre', and another that 'Iceland is a hedge fund.'

Virtually every international centre promises political stability; without the promise of stability, a centre will not attract foreign money. Stability is the necessary condition, but not the sufficient condition.

Financial centres develop because they have a cost advantage or a regulatory advantage relative to the domestic markets of those who demand or buy their services. Usually a financial centre attracts investors or business from abroad because it offers an advantage; the firms in the centre may have developed cost savings that enable them to pay higher interest rates than foreign centres. London is an offshore banking centre, especially for those who want to buy deposits denominated in the US dollar; the reserve requirements applied to US dollar demand deposits in the United States are not applied to US dollar deposits in London. These reserve requirements are like a tax on deposits; to the extent that the tax can be avoided, the centre can pay higher interest rates. Similarly the deposit insurance premium is not applied to US dollar deposits in London. Banks headquartered in many different countries have established branches in London to compete with British banks for deposits denominated in the US dollar and in other foreign currencies.

Some of these centres specialize in providing tax avoidance services; they are low-tax jurisdictions for 'parking income' that had been earned in high – or at least higher— tax jurisdictions. Some Swiss cantons sell tax avoidance services; they have especially low taxes on the income of wealthy non-Swiss. Some centres provide privacy from the tax collectors of nearby countries.

Some financial centres provide money laundering services or a place to park money of uncertain or disreputable origins. Chinese money is placed with banks in Singapore. Luxembourg developed as an offshore banking centre because it offered tax advantages to Germans.

The 'advantages' of Iceland as an international financial centre do not adhere to 'Icelandic regulatory space'; if they did, one or several foreign banks would have established branches or subsidiaries in Reykjavik to secure these advantages.

The hypothesis is that the rapid increase in the capital of the Icelandic banks led them to 'outgrow' Iceland; the opportunities for domestic expansion were limited because their capital had increased so much more rapidly than Iceland's GDP (Table 15.9).

If the advantage of these banks cannot be attributed to regulatory space, then it must be attributed to Icelandic firms. Foreign residents have been attracted to the high anticipated rates of return on the krona liabilities of the Icelandic banks. These non-Icelanders might have

*Table 15.9* The assets of the Icelandic banks and Iceland's GDP (ISKbn)

| | *2000* | *2001* | *2002* | *2003* | *2004* | *2005* | *2006* | *2007* |
|---|---|---|---|---|---|---|---|---|
| GDP | 682 | 770 | 812 | 840 | 926 | 1022 | 1142 | 1214 |
| Bank assets | 717 | 838 | 939 | 1240 | 1740 | 3126 | 5121 | 6337 |

*Source*: International Financial Statistics.

bought similar krona liabilities from these same banks in London or Luxembourg, but the credit standing of these offshore liabilities of these banks is smaller than that of their parents. The advantages associated with Icelandic banks appear to be specific to their passports.

The Icelandic banks have understood that there is a large (especially relative to the size of the Icelandic economy) international market for high interest rate securities. These yield-oriented investors – the somewhat derisory cliché is Belgian and German and Italian dentists – continued to buy Argentinean government bonds denominated in the US dollar in the late 1990s as interest rates increased from 12 to 15 to 18 per cent; their obsession with the yield induced a myopia with respect to where the government in Buenos Aires would get the funds to pay the interest even though the government was borrowing the money.

The buyers of the liabilities of banks can be fickle friends – as shareholders of Bear Stearns have learned to their great cost. The Icelandic banks depend on the willingness of these investors to buy more of these liabilities when the existing liabilities mature. The banks must have back-up credit lines so they can maintain their loans in response to a decline in liabilities.

The Icelandic banks used much of the money received from sale of these securities to foreigners to buy loans from domestic firms and holding companies; the banks on-lent in the currencies in which they had borrowed and hence they did not have a foreign currency exposure. Some of the borrowers were also the owners of the banks.

It is too soon to tell whether the Icelandic banks' purchases of foreign banks and financial institutions will prove profitable for the shareholders of the banks and in the national interest of the country; the two groups are partially overlapping. Most of the shareholders are Icelandic citizens, but only a few Icelandic citizens are shareholders.

The Icelandic banks' purchases were made near or at 'the top of the mark'; the price of stocks of the banks headquartered in different countries has declined with the global credit crunch. One of the stylized facts about international banks is that banks that set up branches and subsidiaries in foreign countries often are at a cost disadvantage relative to their host country competitors since they incur costs of monitoring lending activity at a distance. Moreover the costs of capital of the Icelandic banks probably are higher than the costs of capital of the banks they purchased and of their host competitors. (The Icelandic banks may serve the banking needs of Icelandic firms that have branches and subsidiaries, but it is not obvious that there is a cost advantage.) Icelandic banks need a compensating advantage or else they will be at a disadvantage relative to their host country competitors; they may have a cost advantage if their staff are younger. And the Icelandic banks may have a compensating advantage in the form of the 'Viking spirit', although it is not clear how this plays out in Norway, Denmark and Sweden.

The markets in bank loans and bank deposits in Iceland are probably less competitive than the markets in Britain and in the Scandinavian countries, at least as judged by the numbers of firms that compete for deposits and loans. There is a non-trivial possibility that the profits earned in Iceland would be used to subsidize their foreign activities. If the rate of return that the Icelandic banks earn on their foreign subsidiaries is below the interest costs, then some of the profits earned on their domestic banking operations will be allocated to the interest payments.

The large volume of assets of the Icelandic banks relative to the country's GDP presents several problems. One is that a run on the Icelandic banks would lead to a run on the krona, even though the economic fundamentals of the country might be strong; interest rates on krona securities would be high. Foreign owners of the banks' krona liabilities would decide not to buy any more bonds when their current holdings of bonds mature.

## 15.6 Policy issues – the unwinding of an imported asset bubble

The first of the two proposals advanced in this section focuses on the structure of the financial institutions in Iceland and the advantages of establishing a new set of institutions that would focus on the management of the Iceland's money supply and its payments system. The second highlights the most appropriate value for Iceland's current account balance and hence the most appropriate value for the krona.

The financial environment from 2002 to 2007 was characterized by declines in the price of risk or what is the same thing, increases in leverage, increases in the cross-border flows of funds, and increases in the prices of residential real estate. In contrast the global financial environment from 2008 is likely to be characterized by increases in the price of risk and the reduction in leverage, lower levels of cross-border flows of funds, and in many countries, declines in the price of real estate and in the price of stocks.

The first signs of the global 'credit crunch' that is now under way in the United States, Britain, Ireland and several other countries that experienced sharp increases in real estate prices between 2003 and 2007 centred on the failure of brokerage firms that originated mortgage loans and packaged these loans for sales to the investment banks. Three large firms – Bear Stearns, Countrywide Financial, Northern Rock – have failed. Numerous other firms – Merrill Lynch, UBS, AIG – have reported very large loan losses. Estimates of the capital that banks and other financial institutions must raise to compensate for the losses on mortgages and mortgage-backed securities range from \$400 billion to \$600 billion. The costs of capital to banks and other financial institutions will be significantly higher. Banks and other financial institutions will seek to recover the higher costs of capital through higher interest rates on their loans.

The increase in asset prices and household wealth in Iceland between 2002 and 2007 was larger in percentage terms than the comparable increases in any other country. The likelihood that Iceland is likely to remain immune from the market forces that are leading to declines in the price of real estate and increases in the costs of capital in the United States, Britain and other countries seems low.

Iceland is in a delicate and somewhat precarious financial situation because purchases of Icelandic securities by foreign investors have positioned the value of the krona that cannot be sustained without continued purchases by the foreign investors at the same pace. The additional risk is that the problems of the foreign subsidiaries of the Icelandic banks would complicate the management of the money supply in Iceland.

The first proposal is to change the financial structure in Iceland to insulate the Icelandic money supply from any possible problems that the Icelandic banks might encounter. The proposal is that each of the three banks (hereafter the 'parent firm') establish a new and separate corporation that would operate as a traditional commercial bank (hereafter the 'narrow bank'). The demand and the savings deposits that each of the parent banks now has would be allocated to the narrow bank that each would establish, and the parent bank's claims on the government sector and some of its most liquid and highest quality claims on the private sector would be allocated to the narrow bank. Some of the capital of each of the parent banks would be allocated to each of narrow banks so that once the change is implemented, the ratio of the capital to assets of the parent bank and of the narrow bank would not be significantly different.

Each of the shareholders in the parent bank would receive shares in the narrow bank in proportion to its shareholdings in the parent bank. None of the current shareholders in the existing banks would be adversely affected by the separation of the commercial banks from the investment banks.

Once the change is adopted, the parent bank would be an investment bank, which would continue to own foreign subsidiaries.

On day one the boards of the narrow banks would be identical with those of the parent bank. Good corporate governance procedures suggests that by the end of the first year, at least one-third of the members of the boards of the narrow banks not be members of the boards of the parent banks, and that by the end of the second year, at least two-thirds of the members of the boards of narrow banks not be members of the boards of the parent bank.

The second policy objective is to secure a significant reduction in Iceland's current account deficit or a modest current account surplus – say 1–2 per cent of Iceland's GDP. As long as Iceland has a current account deficit, the value of the krona is dependent on the willingness of foreign investors to continue to add to their holdings of krona securities. The experience of many other countries suggests that these investors are 'fair-weather friends' – they will continue to buy these securities when economic conditions are propitious, and then when there is a shock to the economy – a bad crop, a surge in import prices, a decline in export prices – they become much more sensitive to the risk of their foreign investments, and may sell some of their holdings in anticipation that the currency will depreciate – which then will become self-fulfilling.

The most plausible way to obtain a reduction in the value of the Icelandic krona is for the Central Bank of Iceland to put its inflation target 'on hold' for 12–24 months. The inflation-targeting policy is pointless if the value of the current account deficit at the current value for the krona is too large to be sustainable; only a 'miracle' would enable Iceland to achieve a sustainable value for the current account at the prevailing value for the krona. The likelihood that exports of aluminium could increase by the amount necessary to reduce the current account deficit to a sustainable value at the current value of the krona is trivially low.

Hence at some stage, a depreciation of the krona seems likely, and to a value not very different from the values – after adjustment for differences in inflation rates – that prevailed before the surge in the flows of foreign money to Iceland. The depreciation of the Icelandic krona by 20 per cent might be associated with a one-time increase in the Icelandic price level by 6–8 per cent, on the assumption that imports are about 25 per cent of GDP.

Once the krona has depreciated to the level so that the current account balance is sustainable, then the Central Bank of Iceland could again adopt its inflation target.

## 15.7 Summary and conclusion

The thrust of this chapter is on the impact of an increase in the foreign demand for Icelandic securities on the value of the krona and on asset prices in Iceland between 2002 and 2007. The balance of payments accounting identity is that the capital account balance and the current account balance must be equal and sum to zero. Thus an increase in a country's capital account surplus in response to an increase in the flow of money to the country must induce adjustments so that its trade deficit increases. The increase in the money flows has two immediate impacts that trigger the increase in net imports. One is that the krona appreciated and the other is that asset prices – both real estate prices and stock prices – also increased. Initially the increase in real estate prices was larger than the increase in stock prices; subsequently stock prices increased much more rapidly.

The increase in stock prices in Iceland was extremely rapid, more so than in any other country.

The three Icelandic banks owned modest amounts of stocks. As stock prices increased, the capital of the banks increased because of the increase in the value of their holdings of stocks. The capital of the banks was increasing at annual rates in excess of 50 per cent as a result of these revaluation gains. Because bank capital was increasing at a rapid rate, banks were able to grow their loans at a comparable rate. Some of the borrowers almost certainly used the money to buy stocks because the rates of return on stocks had been so high.

The surge in the value of Icelandic stocks is a dramatic example of a stock price bubble. The foreign money that flowed to Iceland had to go somewhere, and much of the money went into the stock market (there was no other place for the money to go). Because of the small size of the Icelandic economy, the amount of the inflow required to induce a bubble may have been somewhat smaller adjusted for size than in a larger country.

Bubbles by definition implode; an implosion leads to a hard landing. The date – 'the date of no return' – after which a hard landing was inevitable because the sudden decline in the flow of money to Iceland would have led to sharp depreciation of the krona that would in turn have triggered a rapid increase in domestic interest rates probably was in 2004 or 2005. By 2005, the krona had appreciated by 20 per cent since 2002, and the current account deficit was close to 25 per cent of the country's GDP. An initial modest depreciation of the krona would have triggered a sharp decline in the foreign demand for Icelandic securities and the depreciation would have been very large.

## Bibliography

Aliber, Robert Z. (2005), 'The 35 Most Tumultuous Years in Monetary History: Shocks, the Transfer Problem, and Financial Trauma', *IMF Staff Papers*, vol. 52.

Gudmundsson, Bjorn R. and Ludvik Eliasson (2007), 'Economic Challenges Ahead: a Cool Down But No Melt Down', Landsbanki Research – Macroeconomic Forecast, 5 June.

International Monetary Fund, *International Financial Statistics*, Washington, various issues.

International Monetary Fund (2007), *Iceland-2007 Article IV Consultation, Concluding Statement*, Washington, 11 June.

International Monetary Fund, *Iceland: Selected Issues*, October 2005.

*The Icelandic Economy* (2007), Kaupthing Bank, February.

Icelandic–American Chamber of Commerce, Inc. (2008), 'Global Investment Strategies From the Top of the World', 12–13 March.

Keynes, J.M. (1920), *The Economic Consequences of the Peace,* Harcourt Brace and Howe, New York.

Kindleberger, Charles P. and Robert Z. Aliber (2005), *Manias, Panics, and Crashes: a History of Financial Crises*, 5th edn, Palgrave Macmillan.

Mishkin, Frederic B. and Tryggvi Thor Herbertsson (2006), *Financial Stability in Iceland*, Iceland Chamber of Commerce, May.

# Part III
# Lessons for Other Countries

# 16
# Overbanked and Undersized: Lessons from Iceland

*Anne C. Sibert*
*Birkbeck, University of London and CEPR*[1]

In 2007/8, Iceland was the top-scoring country in the world in the United Nations Human Development Index and fifth in the world in terms of per capita income.[2] In the aftermath of the collapse of its banking sector, Iceland has been forced to go to the IMF for a $2.1 billion loan; Icelandic GDP may contract by about 10 per cent in 2009 and private domestic consumption will probably fall by roughly 25 per cent. Icelandic government debt may now be about 150 per cent of GDP, or 200 per cent if the Icesave obligations are included.[3] Based on CDS spreads, the market views Iceland as the world's fifth-riskiest sovereign debtor: riskier than even Kazakhstan and Lithuania.[4] In this chapter I revisit the reasons for this debacle and consider the lessons other countries, as well as Iceland, might draw from it.

## Overbanked

The primary structural problem with Iceland's economy was that it was overbanked in the following sense: the total assets of the three main banks were almost 11 times GDP. If a country's financial institutions were to become insolvent, the government might prevent those financial institutions that are systemically important from failing by making them loans or recapitalizing them. However, given Iceland's severely restricted fiscal capacity, even with quite limited unsoundness, its banks were too big to save. In addition to having a banking sector that was too large relative to its fiscal capacity, Iceland has its own currency and – as discussed in Buiter and Sibert (2008) – this makes it vulnerable to bank runs, even if its banks are sound.

### Iceland was vulnerable to bank runs

Financial markets can exhibit unfortunate outcomes due to coordination failures and the possibility of multiple equilibria. To see this, imagine a bank with uninsured or underinsured depositors. If each such depositor believes that all other such depositors will keep their funds in the bank and that will be sufficient to prevent the bank from failing, then each such depositor finds it optimal to keep his money in the bank and the bank does not fail. However, if each such depositor believes that all other such depositors will withdraw their funds and that this will be sufficient to cause the bank to fail, then each such depositor withdraws his funds and the bank fails. In each case, depositors' expectations are self-fulfilling and rational. Both scenarios can be consistent with the same set of fundamentals. Thus, either outcome is possible: the bank fails or it does not.

In addition to causing old-style bank runs, coordination failures can cause new-style runs: wholesale creditors of a bank may fail to roll over their loans or to extend new loans because they believe that other creditors are going to fail to roll over their loans and that as a consequence the bank will fail and be unable to repay.

Bank runs are not usual outcomes in good times, however, and there are two reasons for this. First, when the fundamentals are strong it is hard to see why a large group of depositors or other creditors would suddenly coordinate their beliefs in the required manner. Second, a good financial architecture can lessen the likelihood of bank runs. Old-style bank runs, where uninsured depositors flee, can be largely prevented by a system of deposit insurance where it is credible that depositors will have immediate access to their funds in the event of a bank failure. The likelihood of runs on banks by wholesale creditors can be greatly reduced if there is a lender of last resort with deep enough pockets and it is sufficiently credible that this lender will make the necessary loans.

As long as its banks' deposits and other short-term liabilities are denominated in domestic currency, a government can always issue enough currency to avert a bank run. If the government is fully credible that it will do this, the run is averted. However, if banks' short-term liabilities are denominated in foreign currency, the country must be able to come up with sufficient foreign exchange. In Iceland, only 21 per cent of the banks' assets and 15 per cent of their liabilities were denominated in Icelandic kronur and this made it questionable that the government would be able or willing to do this. The market's realization that Iceland might not have been willing or able to prevent a banking crisis is exactly the sort of event that can coordinate market participants' beliefs on a bad outcome.

Bank runs can also be precipitated if market participants' do not aggregate information properly. Imagine that a few depositors hear a rumour that a bank might be in trouble and withdraw their funds. Other depositors, seeing this, withdraw their deposits, not because they have heard anything negative about the bank, but because of what they infer the other depositors must have known to have withdrawn their deposits. A cascade of withdrawals may result, based solely upon a small amount of noisy information embodied in the rumours heard by the few initial withdrawers. Anecdotal evidence has it that, knowing that the government might be unable to prevent a financial crisis, traders from a now defunct investment bank met in the bar of a Reykjavik hotel to discuss the profitability of precipitating such a run using 'trash and trade' strategies: shorting the krona or the stock or debt of one of the banks and spreading unfavourable rumours.

**Are there other countries that overbanked?**

Are there other countries that are overbanked, either because the ratio of bank assets to GDP is too high or because the country has its own currency and a large, internationally exposed banking sector? The answer to this question is a rather disconcerting 'yes' and perhaps the scariest example is Switzerland.

As shown in Figure 16.1, Switzerland has a bank-asset-to-GDP ratio of about seven, down from over nine in 2006: it was and is seriously overbanked. Moreover, the Swiss banks were among the most highly leveraged in the world and they had significant exposure to the US sub-prime mortgage market. A relatively prompt reaction by the Swiss authorities and, perhaps, a belief that larger countries would be more

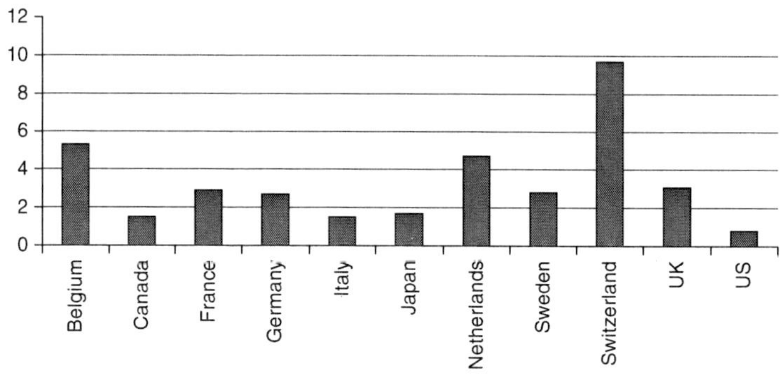


*Figure 16.1* Size of the banking sector (ratio of total bank assets to GDP)
*Source*: Swiss National Bank, *Financial Stability Report*, 2007.

anxious to assist in saving Swiss banks than Icelandic banks have so far saved Switzerland from financial collapse. Elsewhere, the UK's bank-asset-to-GDP ratio of about 3.6 is probably too high and with assets that are twice the size of GDP, Danske Bank is probably too large for Denmark. Belgium and the Netherlands, with bank-asset-to-GDP ratios of almost six and about five, respectively, can turn to the ECB as foreign currency lender of last resort. However, they have limited fiscal capacity to address serious insolvency problems: they too are overbanked.

## How can a country avoid being overbanked?

I have used the term 'overbanked' to refer to a scenario where the ratio of total bank assets to GDP is too large. I had assumed that this was a made-up word and was surprised when my spellchecker raised no objections. It turns out that 'overbanked' is a term that is used to describe a situation where there are too many banks and where no bank is large enough to earn a satisfactory rate of return: a problem in some transition economies, for example. However, as seen in Figure 16.2, in the countries where the total-bank-assets-to-GDP ratio is too large, it is typically because of just a few banks that grew rapidly. Iceland had only three large banks. In Switzerland the increase in the ratio of total assets to GDP from well under 4 in 1992 to 9.2 at the end of 2006 was almost entirely due to the growth of foreign business at its two large banks: UBS and Credit Suisse. The Dutch and Belgian banking sectors are also highly concentrated. This suggests that the solution to the problem of a country having too large bank assets relative to its GDP is to make it difficult for any bank to become too big.

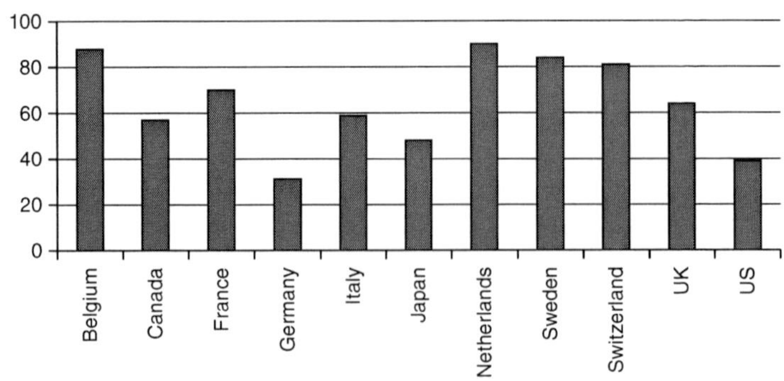


*Figure 16.2* Concentration in the banking sector (assets of the three largest banks as a percentage of total bank assets)
*Source*: Swiss National Bank, *Financial Stability Report*, 2007.

What should be done to protect national real economies from banks and banking systems that are too large? The G30 report on financial reform suggests that larger banks should be restricted from certain activities and be subject to greater supervision and regulation. But regulators and supervisors tend to be captured by the industry that they are supposed to oversee and the disparity in possible rewards tends to cause the bankers to always be a step ahead of their minders.

Other commentators, as well as the Swiss National Bank, have suggested that to protect financial systems from a vulnerability to aggregate shocks, all banks (and all other financial institutions) should have – in additional to any maximum allowable risk-adjusted ratios of capital to assets – a minimum allowable ratio of capital to total assets. The allure of this is that it is simple and automatic; it avoids the problem of sophisticated bankers making their risk models too complicated for the regulators to understand. The floor could, of course, be made time-varying to prevent it from amplifying the effect of crises.

Willem Buiter suggests a modification of this approach: if the problem is that banks are too big, put a tax on size. The tax can be implemented as follows. If a minimum allowable ratio of capital to assets is adopted, this floor should be decreasing in the size of a bank's assets. This tax on bank size would help protect countries from being overbanked or from allowing any single institution to become too big to fail. It is justified because of the social cost of rescuing a threatened financial institution or recapitalizing a failed one.

## Undersized

Iceland's pre-crisis financial system was unsustainable because it was too large relative to the Icelandic banking system. However, Iceland's small population size also played a significant role in the financial crisis.

### Could Greenland be the new Iceland?

Greenland's population of about 60,000 makes it about the same size as Bismarck, North Dakota. It is blessed with natural resources: it has rich deposits of minerals and oil and gas reserves are believed lie below its ice cap. It is protective of both its fishing industry and its long tradition of killing appealing marine fauna. Greenlandic, its Eskimo-Aleut language, is spoken by few outside its borders.

On 1 May 1979, this tiny country began its move toward autonomy when the Danish parliament granted Greenland home rule. Greenland swiftly distanced itself from Europe by exiting the European Union (then the European Economic Community) – the only country ever to do so – in 1985 to avoid fishing regulations and because it was provoked by a ban on sealskin products. The country passed a referendum on greater autonomy on 25 November 2008 and on 21 June 2009 Greenland expanded its sovereignty by assuming authority over its judiciary, policing and natural resources, leaving only finances and foreign affairs in Danish hands. The Danish queen attended a celebration at the parliament in Nuuk and Greenlandic became the country's official language.

### Can a country be too small?

Although it is not (yet) running a global banking system, Greenland's progression toward independent statehood – its desire to maintain its own culture and protect its natural resources at the cost of isolation from the rest of the world and its wish to limit its economic relationship with Europe – is strikingly reminiscent of the experience of Iceland. This raises questions: does the recent experience of Iceland suggest that a country can be *too* small to be a nation state and what are the costs and benefits of being isolated from the rest of the world? The answer to these questions is relevant not only for Iceland and Greenland, but also for other tiny countries that have gained sovereignty in recent decades: since 1990, 33 new countries have been formed and, as seen in Figure 16.3, many are very small.[5]

In this section, I argue that there is little economic justification for preferring small size and that there can be significant costs. I also argue

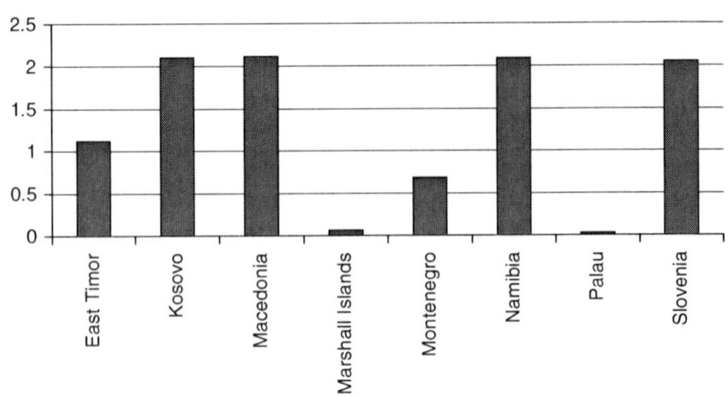


*Figure 16.3* Country size (population in millions)

that Iceland's small size was probably a key factor in Iceland's failure to stop its financial crisis.

### Do smaller countries enact better economic policies and grow faster?

It is usually claimed that the benefit of small size is social homogeneity which leads to cohesion and an ability to build a consensus. This may promote flexibility in the face of changing circumstances and make it easier to enact policies that promote growth. Indeed, some small economies such as New Zealand, and, in many respects, Iceland, are widely viewed as paragons of economic virtue. Formal empirical evidence linking small size to growth-promoting policies appears to be lacking, however. Easterly and Levine (1997) find a strong negative correlation between ethnic diversity and indicators of growth-promoting public goods such as the number of telephones and paved roads and the amount of schooling. However, Easterly and Kraay (1999) assert that a lack of consistent data makes it hard to test whether small size is associated with growth-promoting public goods.

While many small economies have grown rapidly, the existing empirical literature finds that the effect of country size on growth is inconclusive. Easterly and Kraay (1999) find that, after controlling for location, small states are wealthier than large ones, but do not have significantly different growth rates. This may be because country size has an insignificant effect on growth or it may be due to limited data: there is a lack of consistent data sets that include a large number of small countries.[6]

### Smaller countries have more volatile output

The recent experience of Iceland suggests that, while there is no clear evidence that small countries experience *higher* average growth rates, they do have more *volatile* growth rates. As shown in Figure 16.4, Iceland's output growth is less smooth than that of either the UK or the United States. The reason for this seems clear: as a small country, Iceland is far less diversified in endowments and production than the much larger UK or United States. A shock in the aluminium, fishing or banking sector has a major effect on Icelandic output; shocks to different sectors in much larger economies tend to average out.

### Smaller countries have more volatile consumption

Output volatility is not necessarily costly; countries care about smoothing consumption, not about smoothing output. Residents of a country

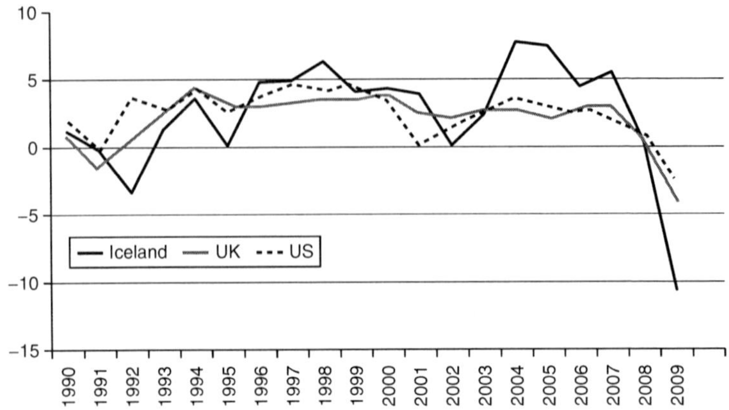


*Figure 16.4* Percentage change in GDP at constant prices

with variable output can smooth their consumption across states of nature by holding a diversified portfolio of home and foreign equity. However, most countries hold relatively small amounts of net foreign assets. In addition, such risk sharing is partial at best if it is not possible to hedge against adverse shocks to the return to human capital.

If shocks to a country's output are purely transitory, a country could also use its current account to smooth its consumption: borrowing in states where output is low and lending in states where it is high. Unfortunately, from the point of view of smoothing consumption, most shocks appear to have a large permanent component. Thus, it seems likely that a country with relatively variable output will have relatively variable consumption as well.

In a study of 56 countries over the period 1950–85, Head (1995) finds that the variances of both output growth and consumption growth are indeed negatively correlated with population size. Moreover, this effect is especially pronounced in high-income countries. Figure 16.5 shows the relationship between population size and (detrended) consumption volatility for 20 relatively high-income countries. It is seen that while some small countries can have very low consumption volatility (Norway, Luxembourg), many have very high volatility (New Zealand, Trinidad and Tobago and Iceland).[7]

### Other problems in small countries

A small population has other costs; I mention three. First, as the provision of many public goods has an important fixed cost component,

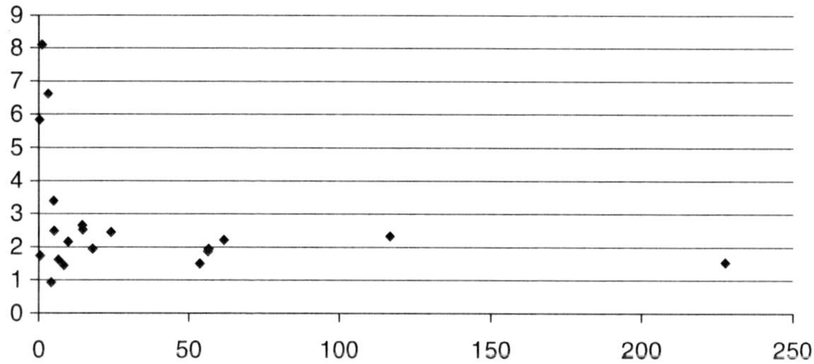


*Figure 16.5* Consumption volatility and country size (in millions). Countries included: United States, Japan, Germany, France, United Kingdom, Italy, Canada, Netherlands, Australia, Belgium, Sweden, Switzerland, Austria, Denmark, Norway, Finland, New Zealand, Trinidad and Tobago, Luxembourg, Iceland; detrended annual data for 1950–85
*Source*: Head (1995).

the per capita cost of public good provision is likely to be decreasing in country size. Second, it is also likely that the per capita administrative cost of income taxes is decreasing in country size. As a result smaller countries tend to rely less on relatively efficient income taxation and more on relatively inefficient taxes, such as customs taxes.[8] Third, a lack of competition in the provision of non-traded goods in small countries can lead to inefficiency.

I have focused on costs associated with small populations, but there is also an important cost associated with small geographical size. Many countries are vulnerable to natural disasters and environmental damage and self-insurance against these sorts of shocks is easier for larger countries. If an American city is damaged by a hurricane, residents can move to another American city. If global warming causes sea levels to rise sufficiently, the consequences for the residents of Tuvalu are likely to be less favourable.

## Problems for civil servants in small economies

In October 2005 David Oddsson was appointed chairman of the board of governors of the Icelandic Central Bank. The multi-talented Oddsson had studied law, been a theatre director, the producer of a comedy radio show, a political commentator, and the co-author of several plays. He had previously been the mayor of Reykjavik, a long-time prime minister and, for a brief period, the foreign minister. Unfortunately, he appears to have had no expertise in economics and banking and was ineffective at either averting the financial crisis or playing a positive role in its aftermath.

In addition to Oddson's apparent acquiescence in the face of looming disaster, neither the prime minister, the finance minister nor the financial regulator seems to have made any serious attempt to stem the growth of the Icelandic banks. This suggests that a significant cost of small size is the burden that it places on senior government officials.

Despite its miniscule size, Iceland has ministries of business affairs, communications, science and culture, environment, finance, fisheries and agriculture, foreign affairs, health, industry and tourism, justice and ecclesiastical affairs, social affairs and social security. This causes two problems: first, it is difficult for such a small country to find enough talented civil servants and second, each civil servant is forced to play more roles than he would in a more populous society. Such multitasking can be demanding and makes it difficult to build up expertise in a particular area.

In an interesting article, Farrugia (1993) suggests that very small countries may also suffer because of their high degree of interpersonal relations. In a tiny nation, everyone knows everyone. This can facilitate things getting done quickly, but it has its costs. Farrugia comments that, 'Many necessary decisions and actions can be modified, adjusted and sometimes totally neutralized by personal interventions and community pressures. In extreme cases, close personal and family connections lead to nepotism and corruption.' In Iceland, it has been alleged that personal animosity may have played a role in the Central Bank denying Glitnir a loan in October 2008 and that the Independence Party played an unseemly role in the privatization of Landsbanki, with agreements made to offer plum executive positions to Independence Party members. Even if such suspicions are untrue, the widely held belief that they might be is damaging to social cohesion and the state's legitimacy.[9]

A sensible policy solution to the problem of filling sufficiently important posts when there is limited local talent or to filling a politically sensitive post where the independence and impartiality that are required cannot be found at home is to hire foreigners. Prime Minister Johanna Sigurdardottir has already adopted this strategy by hiring a Norwegian expert to be the acting Central Bank governor and a Norwegian-born French magistrate to investigate the possibility of criminal activities by Icelandic banks. In the long run, if supervising the banking system requires more expertise than can be acquired locally, Iceland should hire supervisors from abroad: the banks can be taxed to fund them.

### Icelandic officials should get out more

Many very small countries are islands, and thus isolated. It is more difficult for senior officials to travel to a neighbouring country if they live on a remote island than if they live in Luxembourg. This leads to a danger that policy makers in small and far away locations might become insular in their thinking and that they might not have access to advice that their counterparts abroad might offer. It is thus important that senior officials in out-of-the-way locations make an attempt to attend conferences and other professional gatherings abroad.

## Notes

1. The author is an external member of the Monetary Policy Committee of the Central Bank of Iceland.
2. See United Nations (2007/8). The human development index is based on life expectancy, schooling and standard of living; per capita income is computed on a PPP basis.
3. See Danielsson (2009).
4. Based on figures calculated by the credit information specialist firm CMA using five-year CDS spreads.
5. At least Pitcairn Island – with its 48 inhabitants – remains a non-self-governing territory.
6. See Armstrong and Read (2002) for a discussion of this literature.
7. A caveat is that the extreme variances for some small countries in the sample make matters seem somewhat worse than they are as the consumption data include durable goods.
8. See Easterly and Rebelo (1993).
9. Gylfason (2009) comments that 'Iceland is a clan-based society more heavily permeated by politics than any other in Northern or Western Europe'.

## References

Armstrong, Harvey and Robert Read (2002). 'The Phantom of Liberty?: Economic Growth and the Vulnerability of Small States', *Journal of International Development* 14, 435–58.

Buiter, Willem and Anne Sibert (2008). 'The Icelandic Banking Crisis and What to Do about It: the Lender-of-Last-Resort Theory of Optimal Currency Areas', April 11, reprinted as CEPR Policy Insight No. 26, 29 Oct. 2008.

Danielsson, Jon (2009). 'Iceland Applies for EU Membership, the Outcome is Uncertain', VoxEU.org, 21 July.

Easterly, William and Aart Kraay (1999). 'Small States, Small Problems?' Policy Research Paper 2139, The World Bank.

Easterly, William and Ross Levine (1997). 'Africa's Growth Tragedy: Policies and Ethnic Divisions', *Quarterly Journal of Economics* 112, 1203–50.

Easterly, William and Sergio Rebelo (1993). 'Fiscal Policy and Economic Growth: an Empirical Investigation', *Journal of Monetary Economics* 32, 417–57.
Farrugia, Charles (1993). 'The Special Working Environment of Senior Administrators in Small States', *World Development* 21, 221–6.
Gylfason, Thorvaldur (2009). 'Iceland Warms to Europe', VoxEU.org, 21 July.
Head, Allen C. (1995). 'Country Size, Aggregate Fluctuations, and International Risk Sharing', *Canadian Journal of Economics* 28, 1096–119.
United Nations (2007/8). *Human Development Report*, published for the United Nations Human Development Programme, http://hdr.undp.org.

# Appendix: Statistical Tables

| | *Consumer prices*[1] | | *Krona effective exchange rate* | | | | *Interest rates (%)* | | *Money and credit* | | | | | |
|---|---|---|---|---|---|---|---|---|---|---|---|---|---|---|
| | | | | *Real exchange rate*[3] | | | *Banks' secured lending (real yield)* | | *% change over year* | | | | | |
| | *Consumer price index*[1] | *CPI inflation (%)* | *Nominal exchange rate*[2] | *Relative CPI* | *Relative ULC* | *Gov. bonds average yield*[4] | *Non-indexed* | *Indexed* | *M3* | *DMB lending* | *Credit system lending* | *Ratio of gr. reserves to merch. imports*[5] | *Net external debt*[6] | *Growth of real GDP (%)* |
| 2000 | 199.1 | 5.0 | 313.3 | 100.0 | 100.0 | 5.1 | 12.7 | 9.5 | 11.2 | 26.1 | 17.2 | 2.1 | 94.0 | 4.3 |
| 2001 | 212.4 | 6.7 | 376.3 | 87.3 | 86.6 | 5.1 | 9.4 | 10.2 | 14.9 | 12.6 | 19.2 | 2.1 | 102.0 | 3.9 |
| 2002 | 222.5 | 4.8 | 365.2 | 91.7 | 90.2 | 5.2 | 13.7 | 10.1 | 15.3 | 0.9 | 3.2 | 2.5 | 89.8 | 0.1 |
| 2003 | 227.3 | 2.2 | 343.3 | 96.0 | 95.2 | 4.4 | 9.4 | 9.1 | 17.5 | 14.8 | 11.4 | 3.5 | 93.1 | 2.4 |
| 2004 | 234.6 | 3.2 | 336.3 | 98.1 | 92.5 | 3.9 | 8.3 | 8.0 | 15.0 | 39.5 | 19.9 | 3.6 | 113.5 | 7.7 |
| 2005 | 244.1 | 4.0 | 301.8 | 111.4 | 104.1 | 3.7 | 10.7 | 7.2 | 23.2 | 51.5 | 31.1 | 2.9 | 152.0 | 7.5 |
| 2006 | 260.6 | 6.8 | 337.2 | 104.2 | 101.7 | 4.6 | 10.9 | 7.1 | 19.4 | 41.4 | 31.0 | 4.8 | 203.2 | 4.3 |
| 2007 | 273.7 | 5.0 | 328.9 | 108.6 | 111.6 | 6.0 | 14.3 | 8.9 | 56.6 | 30.6 | 22.7 | 4.9 | 228.8 | 5.6 |
| 2008 | 307.7 | 12.4 | 462.6 | 85.5 | 111.0 | 9.4 | 8.1 | 10.0 | 36.3 | | | 7.7 | 462.4 | 1.3 |

1. Annual averages (May 1988=100) and changes between years. 2. Annual averages. Exchange rate of the krona against a trade-weighted average of foreign currencies. 1983=100. 3. 2000=100. ULC=unit labour costs. 4. Annual average yield of indexed Treasury bonds of all maturities. Yields on Iceland Stock Exchange (OMX Iceland) from 1987. Before that, primary market yields. 5. Gross foreign exchange reserves at end of period as a ratio of the average monthly value of merchandise imports in the last 12 months. Calculated at fixed exchange rates. 6. External debt ratio is calculated as a percentage of accumulated GDP for the last four quarters at current exchange rate. Taken from the Central Bank of Iceland *Monetary Bulletin*.

| | *Components of GDP (% change from previous year)* | | | *External trade* | | | | *General government (% of GDP)7* | | | *Labour market (% change from previous year)* | | *Wages (% change from Labour market previous year)* | |
|---|---|---|---|---|---|---|---|---|---|---|---|---|---|---|
| | | | | *Goods and services (volume changes)* | | | | | | | *(% of labour force)* | | | |
| | *Private consumption* | *Gross fixed cap. formation* | *National expenditure* | *Exports* | *Imports* | *Terms of trade* | *Current account balance (% of GDP)* | *Financial balance* | *Revenues* | *Expenditures* | *Unemployment* | *Labour particip.*[8] | *Real wages*[9] | *Real disp. income* |
| 2000 | 4.2 | 11.8 | 5.9 | 4.2 | 8.6 | –2.4 | –10.2 | 1.7 | 43.5 | 41.8 | 1.3 | 83.5 | 1.6 | 7.1 |
| 2001 | –2.8 | –4.3 | –2.1 | 7.4 | –9.1 | 0.3 | –4.3 | –0.7 | 41.8 | 42.5 | 1.4 | 83.6 | 2.0 | –0.3 |
| 2002 | –1.5 | –14.0 | –2.3 | 3.8 | –2.6 | 0.6 | 1.5 | –2.6 | 41.6 | 44.1 | 2.5 | 82.8 | 2.3 | 0.2 |
| 2003 | 6.1 | 11.1 | 5.7 | 1.6 | 10.7 | –4.1 | –4.8 | –2.8 | 42.7 | 45.6 | 3.4 | 82.1 | 3.4 | 5.8 |
| 2004 | 7.0 | 28.1 | 9.9 | 8.4 | 14.5 | –1.3 | –9.8 | 0.0 | 44.1 | 44.0 | 3.1 | 80.7 | 1.4 | 6.5 |
| 2005 | 12.7 | 35.7 | 15.7 | 7.5 | 29.3 | 1.0 | –16.3 | 4.9 | 47.0 | 42.1 | 2.1 | 81.9 | 2.6 | 10.9 |
| 2006 | 3.6 | 21.6 | 9.2 | –4.6 | 10.4 | 3.4 | –25.6 | 6.3 | 47.9 | 41.6 | 1.2 | 83.1 | 2.6 | 10.5 |
| 2007 | 5.6 | –12.2 | –0.4 | 17.7 | –0.7 | 0.1 | –20.1 | 5.4 | 47.9 | 42.5 | 1.0 | 83.3 | 3.8 | 8.8 |
| 2008 | –7.8 | –20.4 | –8.6 | 7.1 | –18.3 | –6.1 | –42.2 | –13.6 | 44.2 | 57.8 | 1.6 | 82.6 | –3.8 | 0.4 |

7. Central and local governments and the social security system. 8. Participation rate as per National Economic Institute definition until 1990, but based on Statistics Iceland labour market survey from 1991. 9. Statistics Iceland wage index. Deflated by consumer prices. Since January 2007, the 12-month percentage change in marine product prices denominated in kronur.

*Sources*: Directorate of Labour, Iceland Stock Exchange (Nasdaq OMX Iceland), Ministry of Finance, Statistics Iceland, Central Bank of Iceland. Taken from the Central Bank of Iceland *Monetary Bulletin*.

# Index